UNIVERSALITY AND TRANSLATION

Universality
and Translation

SITES OF STRUGGLE IN PHILOSOPHY AND POLITICS

Gavin Arnall and Katie Chenoweth, Editors

FORDHAM UNIVERSITY PRESS   NEW YORK 2025

Fordham University Press has no responsibility for the persistence or
accuracy of URLs for external or third-party Internet websites referred
to in this publication and does not guarantee that any content on such
websites is, or will remain, accurate or appropriate.

Fordham University Press also publishes its books in a variety of electronic
formats. Some content that appears in print may not be available in
electronic books.

Visit us online at www.fordhampress.com.

Library of Congress Cataloging-in-Publication Data available online at
https://catalog.loc.gov.

Printed in the United States of America
27 26 25   5 4 3 2 1
First edition

Contents

UNIVERSALITY AND TRANSLATION

Introduction

Gavin Arnall

The project of editing this volume began with a hypothesis that hidden (or not so hidden) within every theory of translation is a theory of universality and, vice versa, that hidden (or not so hidden) within every theory of universality is a theory of translation. Neither translation nor universality can be thought without the other, and to think one is already to think the other. Conceptually, they are coextensive and mutually constitutive, affecting each other from the inside. And yet, the pairing of these terms—translation *and* universality— announces neither a straightforward and static mutualism nor an equally straightforward and static antagonism but rather an ambiguous and dynamic relationship of correspondence, competition, and conflict, a meeting and overlapping of different sites of struggle.

To begin to unpack these opening propositions, I would turn the reader (predictably but no less necessarily) to Walter Benjamin's essay "The Task of the Translator," which introduces his German translation of the "Tableaux parisiens" section of Charles Baudelaire's *Les Fleurs du mal*.[1] In this essay, Benjamin theorizes translation as a form whose purpose cannot be reduced to rendering the sense of the original, to reproducing or transmitting the meaning of the source text. Benjamin thus unsettles conventional notions of freedom and fidelity, license and literalness, insofar as they rely on this reductive con- ception of translation as communication, as the imparting of information from the original. Instead of rejecting these terms outright, however, "The Task of the Translator" performs a conceptual translation of said terms to theorize translation anew. This is where the essay's latent theorization of universality is to be found.

To think the "demand for literalness" beyond "the preservation of meaning," Benjamin evokes the image of a broken vessel.[2] Here I refer the reader to Carol Jacobs's translation of the relevant passage:

> Just as fragments of a vessel, in order to be articulated together, must follow one another in the smallest detail but need not resemble one another, so, instead of making itself similar to the meaning of the original [*Sinn des Originals*], the translation must rather, lovingly and in detail, in its own language, form itself according to the manner of meaning [*Art des Meinens*] of the original, to make both recognizable as the broken part of a greater language, just as fragments are the broken part of a vessel.[3]

Fidelity to the original, Benjamin counterintuitively insists, entails emancipation from conveying the original's meaning or sense (*Sinn*). If *Aufgabe*, a keyword for the essay from the start, can signify both "task" and "abandonment"—as in the abandonment of a plan or duty—then the task of the translator, in this instance, is to abandon the conventional task of translation.[4] Instead of dutifully striving for likeness, for a replica or copy of the source text in the target language, the original and the translation are to relate in an alternative way, with the latter faithfully tracing the contour of the former's manner of meaning (*Art des Meinens*). Earlier in the essay, Benjamin provides the example of *Brot* and *pain*; what is meant is the same, yet each word has a very different manner of meaning.[5] The task of the translator, once their conventional task is abandoned, is to attend to this difference and shape the translation accordingly. The result is not resemblance but recognition that both the original and the translation— in their articulation with each other—are the broken part of a larger whole, dissimilar yet joined fragments of a greater language that Benjamin also calls "the pure language," based on the "kinship [*Verwandtschaft*]" of all languages, "the totality [*Allheit*] of their intentions supplementing one another."[6]

The image of the broken vessel is thus the image of a shattered universality, a universality in fragments, that nevertheless implies a possible (re)construction. The reference to the Lurianic symbols of the *Shevirah* and the *Tikkun*, the breaking of the vessels and their restoration, is unmistakable and may reflect Benjamin's growing correspondence and friendship, at the time of composing "The Task of the Translator," with Gershom Scholem.[7] However, Jacobs's translation allows for a more nuanced understanding of Benjamin's allusions to kabbalistic myth by highlighting what the standardly cited English translation obscures: the articulation of the translation with the original does not so much achieve the complete (re)assembly of a greater language as make it possible to grasp the disarticulation of its parts.[8] Indeed, Benjamin is clear that translation "cannot possibly . . . establish [*herstellen*] this hidden relationship" between languages, yet translation does "represent [*darstellen*] it by realizing [*verwirklicht*] it in embryonic or intensive form."[9] The translation's faithful relationship with the original, in other words, is a concentrated actualization of a universal relationship between languages, a (partial, incipient, *keimhaft*) realization of a universality not yet (fully) realized.[10]

This is where the essay's critical engagement with Weimar Classicism and Jena Romanticism is most palpable. As Antoine Berman argues, these literary and philosophical movements hold that "translation is one of the instruments for the constitution of a universality," be it in the form of *Weltliteratur* or of a "universal progressive poetry."[11] But, as Berman also shows, these projects of universality are ultimately bound up with projects of Germanity. The German language is conceived as uniquely capable of appropriating foreign works for the benefit of Germany's own formation and development (*Bildung*), and so the task of the German translator is to contribute to this universalist project of cultural nationalism and imperialism.[12]

In response to this intellectual tradition, Benjamin cites an extended passage from Rudolf Pannwitz's *Die Krisis der europäischen Kultur*, which I include in abbreviated form below:

> Our translations, even the best ones, proceed from a mistaken prem-
> ise. They want to turn Hindi, Greek, English into German instead of
> turning German into Hindi, Greek, English. Our translators have a far
> greater reverence for the usage of their own language than for the
> spirit of the foreign works. . . . The basic error of the translator is
> that he preserves the state in which his own language happens to be
> instead of allowing his language to be powerfully affected by the
> foreign tongue [*er den zufälligen stand der eignen sprache festhält
> anstatt sie durch die fremde sprache gewaltig bewegen zu lassen*].[13]

The stringent fidelity of German translators to their own language halts or arrests its movement; German transforms into a dead language, which inhibits its continued life and further transformation. Once again, the task of the translator is to abandon what has become, in Germany, the conventional task of translation. The cultural program of Germanizing all other languages—of "devouring" them, as Goethe might say[14]—is to be replaced with another mode of translation that would entail a very different relationship between languages, one of kinship and thus reciprocal supplementation.

This alternative mode of translation, for Benjamin, hinges on an alternative understanding of freedom. Instead of taking license with the source text to faithfully reproduce its meaning, the translator is to take license with their own language, to experiment with it and renew it by means of the language of the original. To freely translate in this way is to set German in motion—to revive it, to bring it back from the dead, to launch its continued life, but also to liberate it from Germany's conventionally faithful translators so that it may enter "the freedom of linguistic flux."[15] And yet, this mode of free translation is to be pursued not so much for the sake of German as for the sake of the pure language. In Benjamin's words, "freedom proves its worth in the interest of the pure language by its effects on its own language. It is the task of the translator to release in his own language that pure language which is exiled among alien tongues, to liberate the language imprisoned in a work in his re-creation of that work. For the sake of the pure language, he breaks through decayed barriers of his own language."[16] When free translation opens its language to the forceful influence of another, the pure language is freed from its confinement in the original. This relationship of freedom between the language of the original and the language of the translation, like the relationship of fidelity between the original text and its translation, realizes—in a nascent, condensed, and incomplete way—the universal "reconciliation and fulfilment" of languages.[17] The task of the translator is thus to release or redeem (*erlösen*) a universality that remains in fragments and still awaits its ultimate, messianic redemption.[18]

By conceptually translating the traditional notions of fidelity and freedom, Benjamin's essay illuminates conflicting modes of translation that correspond to conflicting horizons of universality. On one hand, there is a mode of translation that would seek to capture the meaning of the original and appropriate the foreign work in order to elevate the language and culture of the translator. This kind of translation pursues a universality of imperialist expansion, whereby a particular language becomes universal in its absorption of all other languages. On the other hand, there is a mode of translation that would form its text according to the original's manner of meaning and renew the translator's language through the language of the original in order to perform a relationship of reciprocal supplementation between languages. This kind of translation pursues a universality of harmonious reconciliation, whereby every language shapes and is shaped by all others in a way that attends to and negotiates difference rather than absorbing or eliminating it.

If "The Task of the Translator" is read alongside an earlier text by Benjamin, "On Language as Such and on the Language of Man," it becomes clear that these conflicting modes of translation and their corresponding horizons of universality are to be understood as opposed responses to the "linguistic confusion" that—following biblical myth—plagues the world in the wake of the tower of Babel.[19] Yet, in an uncanny way, the conflict between these different modes of translation also translates the conflict at the heart of the myth itself, the originary conflict that sets translation in motion. As Jacques Derrida posits during a roundtable discussion on translation, the tribe of Shems decided to build the giant tower not only to reach the heavens but also to make a name for themselves, and they intended to do this by imposing "their tongue on the entire universe on the basis of this sublime edification. . . . Had their enterprise succeeded, the universal tongue would have been a particular language imposed by violence, by force, by violent hegemony over the rest of the world."[20] Derrida, like Benjamin and Berman, thus alerts us to a horizon of universality that would entail a particular language becoming universal through a violent process of empire. However, the Shems are not successful in fully actualizing the universal tongue. God interrupts the construction of the tower, violently imposes his name (Babel) on the city where the tower was being constructed, scatters its inhabitants across the earth, and condemns them to the confusion or babel (from the Hebrew בָּלַל, bālal, to mix or confuse) of a multiplicity of tongues. As a result, Derrida maintains, translation becomes at once necessary and impossible, a task that must be done because of the punishment of linguistic confusion and yet is forbidden to succeed because of the punishment of linguistic confusion.

Whereas translators may farcically repeat the tragedy of the Shems and attempt to universalize their particular language, Derrida insists—translating Benjamin—that God's deconstruction of the tower and of the universal tongue occasions a different kind of translation that promises a different kind of universality. As Derrida puts it, "a good translation is one that enacts that performative called a promise with the result that through the translation one sees the coming shape of a possible reconciliation among languages."[21] The "messianic character of [good] translation," in other words, is that it can (only) promise universal reconciliation, that it succeeds not in overcoming linguistic confusion but in performing the promise of such an overcoming.[22] Whether this promise can ever be fulfilled—whether the reconciliatory horizon of universality can ever be fully reached or realized—depends on how Benjamin is read, either as a thinker tied to a certain messianism or as a thinker tied to what Derrida elsewhere describes as the "messianic without messianism."[23]

What I want to emphasize, however, is something that can easily get lost in this discussion of the messianicity of translation, its promise of universal reconciliation—namely, that there is already a certain construction of universality in God's deconstruction of the tower and of the universal tongue.[24] Put another way, the conflict of Babel is not so much a conflict *with* universality, *against* universality, as it is a conflict *within* universality. Indeed, it would be tempting to read God's conflict with the Shems as allegorizing translation's inherently antagonistic relationship with universality, for the biblical myth opposes the task of translating across languages with the task of imposing a universal tongue. But such a reading would obscure how the conflict that determines the necessity and impossibility of translation is more fundamentally a conflict of *incompatible universalities*.[25]

Derrida clarifies this point during one of the many *détours* that mark the twisting and turning trajectory of his essay "Des tours de Babel." Consider the following passage:

> In seeking to "make a name for themselves," to found at the same time a universal tongue and a unique genealogy, the Semites want to make the world see reason [*veulent mettre à la raison le monde*], and this reason can signify simultaneously colonial violence (since they would thus universalize their idiom) *and* peaceful transparency of the human community. Conversely, when God imposes and opposes his name, he ruptures the rational transparency but also interrupts the colonial violence or the linguistic imperialism. He destines them to translation, he subjects them to the law of a translation both necessary and impossible; with a blow of his translatable-untranslatable name, he delivers a universal reason (it will no longer be subject to the rule of a particular nation), but he simultaneously limits its very universality: forbidden transparency, impossible univocity.[26]

In attempting to make a name for themselves, Derrida tells us, the Shems *veulent mettre à la raison le monde*: they want to make the world see reason, to make the world conform to reason, to submit the world to reason by force. This reason would extend to the entire world; it would be as universal as the tongue that the Shems seek to universalize. And yet, the universality of this reason is not univocal but equivocal, signifying both violence and peace, colonial subjugation and human community. For Derrida, God's imposition of his name is also equivocal. It signifies a cessation of violence and a continuation of violence, an interruption of subjugation and a resumption of subjugation.[27] As a result, Derrida states, God delivers a universal reason (*il délivre une raison universelle*).[28] We can read in this statement at least two interrelated forms of delivery. God delivers universal reason from the rule of a particular nation, liberating it by de-particularizing it, so as to *also* differentiate it, to deliver a different kind of reason, the universal reason of the law of translation, which holds—universally—that translation is necessary and impossible. In this way, God limits the universality of the reason that he delivers. He does so by restricting universal reason from transparent and univocal meaning, as such meaning is forbidden, impossible. A universality without univocity, a universality that, like the tower of Babel, remains incomplete or, more precisely, "exhibits an incompletion, the impossibility of finishing, of totalizing," a universality in conflict with the totalizing universality and transparency of the one, universal tongue—this is the universality that corresponds to translation when it is theorized as both necessary and impossible.[29]

Benjamin and Derrida are the most widely cited and discussed theorists in the field of translation studies. In fact, in just about any field within the humanities and social sciences, it has become obligatory to refer to their work when addressing the topic of translation. And yet, their contributions to thinking translation *in tandem with* universality have often been misunderstood, if not totally ignored, and thus have rarely been taken up in subsequent work. This may stem—and here, another hypothesis driving this project—from what has become a rather pervasive phenomenon in recent years, especially among US-based academics, which I would characterize as a near automatic reflex of skepticism, suspicion, and even fear when confronted with any appeal to or demand for universality. This is not, of course, a phenomenon limited to the analysis and study of translation; it is a much broader tendency within contemporary theoretical debates.[30] Yet it plays a particularly important role in the work of some of today's best-known and most frequently referenced theorists of translation.

Consider, along these lines, Lawrence Venuti's essay "Local Contingencies: Translation and National Identities," which appears in his suggestively titled book *Translation Changes Everything: Theory and Practice*.[31] At the start of this essay, Venuti turns to Victor Hugo's preface for his son's French translation of the works of Shakespeare. In the preface, Hugo writes: "When you offer a translation to a nation, that nation will almost always look on the translation as an act of violence against itself. Bourgeois taste tends to resist the universal spirit."[32] Venuti reads in these lines an attempt to construe translation as a practice that can "communicate differences and thereby threaten the assumed integrity of the national language and culture, the essentialist homogeneity of the national identity."[33] From this perspective, translation challenges bourgeois nationalism and—for Hugo—does so based on a notion of universality that posits a common human spirit. Venuti quickly complicates the oppositions at work in Hugo's text, however, pointing to the ways in which translation can contribute to "nationalist agendas" of linguistic and cultural identity formation just as it can threaten to undermine such agendas.[34] Venuti likewise signals how nationalism is not necessarily contrary to universalism but rather can be understood as a kind of universalism. This is the case—and here Venuti cites Derrida—insofar as the nation is assigned "a universalistic, essentialist representation."[35]

This discussion of Hugo's universalism leads Venuti to draw a general conclusion about universalism as such, that universalism (always) entails "suppressing linguistic and cultural differences."[36] To develop this point, Venuti moves
from nineteenth-century France to nineteenth-century Prussia and China and
argues that intellectuals from these very different social and political milieux
share the practice of enlisting translation to pursue their respective nationalist
agendas, to develop an essentialist construction of German or Chinese national
identity that "embodies universalistic traits."[37] Friedrich Schleiermacher is
evoked as someone who envisioned German culture achieving "global domination" through the translation of foreign texts, a project that, in Venuti's words,
"ultimately suppresses the cultural differences of other nations by forcing them
to appreciate the canon of world literature in German."[38] Venuti also highlights
Lin Shu's theory and practice of translation, which, according to Venuti, aimed
to establish "the global validity of Chinese cultural traditions, notably Confu-
cianism," so that "the most diverse British novels" could be read as mere
"exempla of the Confucian reverence for filial piety."[39] While specialists might
contest Venuti's interpretation of these various figures, I am more interested
in what he does with them, how—by reading them together—Venuti points to
a seemingly universal feature of different universalisms, to their different ways
of achieving the same effect—namely, the suppression of linguistic and cultural
differences.

If Venuti exposes translation's complicity with the suppression of difference,
he never goes so far as to suggest that translation always entails this kind of
suppression. He argues instead that translation practices vary depending on
"the social situations in which they are deployed, and their varying approaches
to source texts and cultures may be diametrically opposed, seeking either to
preserve or to erase linguistic and cultural differences."[40] What remains un-
thought and is perhaps unthinkable within the logic of this essay is that different
universalisms can also be diametrically opposed, that their respective notions
of universality can vary in deeply conflictual ways as well, including on the
preservation or suppression of difference. The essay recognizes the ambiguity
and equivocity of translation, in other words, but fails to do so in its treatment
of universality.[41] This has the effect of making illegible the plurality intrinsic
to the relationship between translation and universality, as explored by theorists
like Benjamin and Derrida. Instead of conflicting modes of translation corresponding to conflicting horizons of universality, Venuti reverts to a simple
opposition, one that pits universality against difference, and construes translation as divided between these two poles. The relationship between translation
and universality then becomes either narrowly mutualistic or narrowly

antagonistic; translation is pursued in the name of universality or against universality (in the name of difference).

Venuti's essay is representative of an antiuniversalist strain of thinking running through much of his work. He often associates universalism with essentialism, nationalism, and the suppression of different languages and cultures, as well as with chauvinism, conservatism, elitism, imperialism, utopianism, and the imposition of purportedly timeless truths.[42] Such a one-sidedly negative depiction of any appeal to universality leads Venuti to persistently replicate the analysis of his previously discussed essay; he explores how translation contributes to the aforementioned "isms"—all lumped together with universalism—while arguing that another kind of translation is possible, one that would seem to be blanketly antiuniversalist. The multidimensional relationship between translation and universality is thus repeatedly flattened, with the former understood as either serving or opposing the latter.

The irony of an antiuniversalist stance like this one is that it ineluctably transforms into its opposite and becomes an example of what it denounces. Étienne Balibar is especially attuned to this phenomenon in his book *On Universals: Constructing and Deconstructing Community*. He observes that "as soon as one articulates a critique of universalism—whether religious or secular, political or scientific—in terms meant to defend cultures, idioms, or beliefs and their absolute right to particularity, *the enunciation is immediately expressed in the modality of the universal*—that is, expressed at once in a rigorously interchangeable rhetoric and from the perspective of a totalization and justification of *differences* as such, and thus from the perspective of another universalism."[43] Balibar accordingly points to how an antiuniversalist stance in defense of difference is—at the same time and despite itself—a universalist stance in defense of difference. The aim is to critique universalism for its suppression of different cultures, idioms, and beliefs, and yet this critique falls back on another universalism to advance its claims, a universalism that seeks to preserve and defend rather than suppress differences. As a result, the critique undermines its own depiction of universalism as universally antagonistic toward differences; it gestures toward an alternative at the very moment that it denies the possibility of an alternative. However, on another level, the critique does indeed reveal *itself* to be antagonistic toward differences, at odds with its own propositional content, and thus entangled in a performative contradiction. By universally condemning universalism for its suppression of difference, in other words, the critique suppresses the many universalisms that are different, that maintain a different relationship with difference.

The phenomenon of antiuniversalist universalism appears rather nonsensical at first glance, but analyzing this paradoxical yet popular form of critique can be instructive—especially for a volume like this one—if it is read against the grain. Although it posits a stark opposition between universality and difference, it nevertheless reveals upon further inspection that the conflict is actually internal to universality, that universality is not one side of a struggle but rather a *site of struggle*. This becomes clear once it is recognized that this form of critique is actively participating in said struggle, a struggle between different universalisms that enter into conflict—with each other and in some cases with themselves—over their different and even incompatible notions of universality.[44]

Versions of Venuti's argument concerning universality and difference can be found in the work of other leading voices of translation studies.[45] His approach, in this regard, is not specific to him but rather points to a general tendency among scholars in the field. Nevertheless, within this tendency, there is a slight yet significant variant worth considering, which avoids the totalizing justification of differences as such and instead attends to different kinds of differences. The result is a more complex understanding of universality's relationship with difference that nevertheless perpetuates a reductive understanding of universality's relationship with translation. We can begin to appreciate what this looks like if we turn to Naoki Sakai's essay "The Modern Regime of Translation and its Politics," which summarizes and expands upon the major theses of his canonical work, *Translation and Subjectivity: On "Japan" and Cultural Nationalism*.[46]

Sakai begins his essay in a now familiar way by underscoring the ambiguity and equivocity of translation, maintaining that it is "a deeply ambivalent concept and practice. Put simply, translation always cuts both ways: at once a dynamism of domination and liberation, clarification and obfuscation, commerce and exploitation, concession and refusal to the 'other.'"[47] He also contends that there are "different and even antagonistic 'regimes' of translation" that contribute to the ambiguity and equivocity of the concept and practice.[48] As the title of his essay indicates, Sakai's focus is on what he terms the modern regime of translation, an epistemic and discursive apparatus that historically emerged in seventeenth-century Western Europe and eighteenth-century Northeastern Asia when the hybrid languages of these regions underwent similar processes of individuation such that they were gradually conceived as closed and homogeneous entities and as the shared media of equally closed and homogeneous ethnic or national communities. This historical process sets the stage for what Sakai calls "homolingual address," a procedure of conduct whereby an addresser "adopts a position representative of an allegedly homogeneous language community and then relates to the addressee[, who is deemed] representative of an equally homogenous language community."[49] The modern regime of translation is built upon and reinforces this kind of address. If the addresser and the addressee understand themselves to be members of the same language community, transparent and reciprocal communication is thought to be guaranteed. If, in contrast, the addresser and the addressee understand themselves to be members of different language communities, the modern regime of translation represents the translator as someone who builds a bridge between the purportedly separate and self-enclosed languages of said communities so that communication can occur between them.

The "fundamental weakness" of this regime of translation, according to Sakai, is that it "always determines 'difference' as . . . a sort of gap or *species difference* between two individual—and indivisible—languages. . . . The difference at stake in translation is not reducible to *diaphora* or species difference, difference between two *species*, two particular languages under the *genus* of language in general."[50] For Sakai, in other words, there is a certain incommensurable difference at stake in translation. This is due to the heterogeneity within any linguistic medium of address—the many languages implicated in any language—and the discontinuity between the addresser and the addressee as singular beings. The modern regime of translation converts this incommensurable difference into a difference between particular languages, into a difference that is no longer incommensurable insofar as it concerns two entities that are construed as distinct species of the same genus—two homogeneous national languages under the generality of language as such—and the separation between these species is understood as a gap or crevice, a border that can be crossed or bridged through translation.[51] The modern regime of translation is therefore not so much concerned with the preservation or suppression of difference as it is with the displacement of one kind of difference (associated with incommensurability, heterogeneity, and singularity) for another kind of difference (associated with commensurability, homogeneity, and particularity).

And yet, as Sakai insists, the difference at stake in translation is not reducible to this latter kind of difference. In *Translation and Subjectivity*, Sakai theorizes and performs a conflicting regime of translation that opposes the modern regime and its reductivist approach. This alternative regime of translation is built upon and reinforces what Sakai calls "heterolingual address," which does not take for granted the many assumptions of homolingual address, including the putative existence of homogeneous national language communities that guarantee the transparent and reciprocal communication of its members.[52] To adopt the attitude of heterolingual address, in other words, is to recognize that "every utterance can fail to communicate."[53] From this vantage point, translation is not a matter of facilitating communication between an addresser and an addressee who speak different national languages. Here Sakai follows Benjamin's insistence that the task of the translator should not be confused with the communication of information.[54] Instead, according to Sakai, translation is to be understood as an essential feature of the delivery and the reception of any enunciation. The addresser must always translate an enunciation if it is to be delivered to the addressee, and the addressee, in turn, must always engage in a form of "countertranslation" for the addresser's enunciation to be received.[55] Accordingly, within this alternative regime, translation is not understood as a practice of bridging the species difference between particular languages but rather as a practice of negotiating the incommensurable difference between singular beings. This understanding of translation refuses to reduce the singularity of the encounter between the addresser and the addressee to the particularity of their purportedly self-enclosed and homogeneous language communities.

As the reader perhaps will have anticipated, I want to highlight Sakai's subtle theorization of the relationship between translation and universality at work in his discussion of species difference. Within the modern regime of translation, particular languages are held to be different yet comparable or commensurable, bridgeable through translation, precisely because they are members of the same genus, because they fall under the universal notion of language in general or language as such. In other words, species difference, the kind of difference at the heart of the modern regime of translation, rests on the contradictory unity or complicity between particularity and universality.[56] The regime of translation built upon heterolingual address, in contrast, attends to incommensurable difference and to singularity, to that which escapes or "flees" and therefore cannot be fully subsumed under the logic of the particular and the universal.[57]

The modern regime of translation nevertheless strives to achieve this subsumption. At one point in *Translation and Subjectivity*, Sakai terms such a maneuver the "imperialist inscription" of difference.[58] He then goes on to make a broader claim about imperialism as such, asserting that there is a certain "universality to the working of imperialism . . . , which reduces singularity to particularity."[59] Sakai thus implies a strong affinity between the modern regime of translation and the working of imperialism insofar as they both approach difference in the same way, such that the particular forcibly takes the place of the singular.[60] If the modern regime of translation relies on the interdependent notions of particularity and universality then it would seem that said notions are also in some sense bound up and complicit with the working of imperialism. This is developed just a few pages later when Sakai writes: "Precisely

because both are closed off to the singular, . . . neither universalism nor particularism comes across the other; otherness is always reduced to the Other,
and thus repressed, excluded, and eliminated in them both."[61] Notice how this
passage reiterates some basic themes of Sakai's argument while also subtly
inverting the argument's terms. Sakai transitions from the universalism of
imperialism—how imperialism always or universally reduces singularity to
particularity—to the imperialism of universalism, to universalism's shared
project with particularism, which entails the rejection of singularity and the
repression, exclusion, and elimination of otherness. The critique of an imperialist universalism thus morphs into a critique of universalism as
imperialist.

There are two important points to take away from this discussion of Sakai's
work. The first has to do with the conflict between the modern regime of
translation and its heterolingual alternative. For Sakai, this conflict is internal
to translation. In the terminology of this volume, it marks translation as a *site
of struggle* and explains the deep ambiguity and equivocity of the concept and
practice, the way translation oscillates between imperialism and anti-imperialism
or, in Sakai's words, the way that it is "at once a dynamism of domination and
liberation."[62] And yet—now on to the second point—Sakai construes appeals
to and demands for universality as far less ambiguous and equivocal in nature.
No matter how a given universalism positions itself—*Translation and Subjectivity* refers to capitalist, colonialist, egalitarian, ethnocentric, nationalist, internationalist, and theological iterations—it would seem to always perpetuate
the imperialist inscription of difference.[63] In this way, Sakai's analysis shares
the same antiuniversalist impulse found in Venuti's work, and, as a result, it
ends up construing the relationship between translation and universality in
very similar terms. The relationship is, once again, either narrowly mutualistic
or narrowly antagonistic. Translation is understood as advancing a certain
notion of universality in its commitment to overcoming species difference and
particularity or as opposing said notion of universality in its commitment to
negotiating incommensurable difference and singularity.[64]

Many other theorists of translation who draw upon a shared set of keywords
to promote the same kind of reasoning and argumentation could be listed here.
Briefly, let us recall Dipesh Chakrabarty's discussion of "two models of translation" in *Provincializing Europe: Postcolonial Thought and Historical Difference.*[65] There is, first, the kind of translation modeled on commodity exchange
and Newtonian physics, which takes for granted "a universal, homogenizing
middle term" that mediates between particular instantiations of that term.[66]
Just as abstract labor is the universal middle term that enables the exchange
of particular commodities—whereby very different sorts of things are rendered

equivalent—so too does H_2O, under this model of translation, function as the universal middle term that allows the Hindi word "pani" to be exchanged for "water" as the equivalent word in English.[67] Alternatively, there is the kind of translation modeled on barter and Einsteinian physics, which thinks "in terms of singularities" and therefore "resists [any] attempt to see something as a particular instance of a general idea or category."[68] This model of translation entails performing a strictly local trade between words like "pani" and "water," a trade that does not pass through a universal middle term, "the superior positivity of H_2O," and consequently does not "neutralize and relegate differences to the margins" in the name of a more fundamental equivalence.[69]

Recall, likewise, how Sandro Mezzadra and Brett Neilson, in *Border as Method, or, the Multiplication of Labor*, build upon the work of Chakrabarty and Sakai to develop their own notion of "heterolingual translation" as a social and material practice that has the capacity to "create the common."[70] To develop this idea, they turn to numerous examples of disparate peoples and communities who have been (often violently) congregated together, from enslaved persons enduring the Middle Passage to maritime workers forming motley crews aboard ships to migrant taxi drivers organizing in New York City. Speaking different languages and hailing from different cultures, these heterogeneous groupings—in their respective historical contexts—engage in a "labor of translation," a "mutual process of picking up the words of companions," not to communicate between already existing national languages but rather to forge a "new idiom," a common vocabulary and knowledge rooted in shared experiences of living, working, and struggling together.[71] This labor of translation is contrasted with—and antagonistic toward—the "homolingual translation" pursued by the universalizing drive of capital, which attempts to code all "human activity according to the measure of abstract labor and its insertion within the nexus of exchange value and price," thereby reducing "the qualities of diverse activities, forms of life, and languages to the homogeneous measure of value."[72] Mapping these conflicting modes of translation ultimately leads Mezzadra and Neilson to endorse a rigid distinction between the common and the universal, which associates the common with the singular and with difference, and the universal with a "claim to unity" that suppresses differences and singularities.[73]

These additional examples help us identify a general tendency within translation studies and among theorists adjacent to the field. The core feature of this tendency is its struggles to recognize universality as a site of struggle, even as it readily acknowledges and eloquently conceptualizes how translation functions in this way. Indeed, in recent research, it is difficult to find an uncritical celebration or condemnation of translation as such. Although translation studies has a reputation for being overly affirmative and optimistic toward its object of study, as if translation could serve as a kind of panacea for all social ills and divisions, no serious theorist of translation is so one-sided in their approach. Instead, scholarship in this area documents how translation is inextricably tied to past and present efforts of capitalist accumulation, colonialist domination, imperialist expansion, and other violent processes of subjugation, while also demonstrating how translation can open pathways for conceptualizing and enacting resistance to and liberation from said processes.[74] This body of research shows, in other words, that translation is a deeply ambiguous, contradictory, and equivocal concept and practice; that it is, in Vicente Rafael's words, a phenomenon "at war with itself, generating divergent effects"; that it is—to borrow Gayatri Chakravorty Spivak's opportune phrase—"an active site of conflict" over different futures and different worlds.[75] What is frequently overlooked, however, is that these formulations describing translation also hold mutatis mutandis for universality. By treating universality as a, if not the, favorite target for vilification, many of today's theorists of translation have lost sight of universality's own ambiguity and equivocity, the internal tensions and contradictions that, like translation, put universality in conflict or at war with itself, making it, too, a site of struggle.[76]

There are several notable consequences of this inability or refusal to approach universality as a site of struggle. The first is significant conceptual poverty when it comes to theorizing *both* universality *and* the terms that are meant to name an escape from its purportedly invariable, totalizing logic. As Balibar writes in "Ambiguous Universality," the final essay collected in *Politics and the Other Scene*, "no discussion about universality (and, consequently, no discussion about its contraries or opposites: particularity, difference, singularity) can usefully proceed with a 'univocal' concept of 'the universal.'"[77] Instead, Balibar maintains, such a discussion must account for universality's "insurmountable *equivocity*."[78] This basic premise introduces Balibar's own discussion of universality as ambiguously referring to at least three interrelated yet irreducible instances—universality as reality, as fiction, and as symbol—that each contain within themselves tensions, contradictions, and still more *"conflicting realizations of universality."*[79] For Balibar, then, theorists can only misunderstand universality if they fail to grapple with its internal divisions and oppositions, the ambiguity and equivocity that make universality—in his words—"always-already beyond any simple or 'absolute' unity, and therefore a permanent source of conflict."[80] But, as Balibar also implies, insofar as this misunderstanding of universality forms the basis for the way many theorists discuss singularity and difference, they can only misunderstand these terms as well. We learn nothing about singularity or difference, in other words, if we perpetuate the "nursery tale" of universality, this story of a univocally evil specter that haunts so much of contemporary theory.[81]

A related consequence of this approach to theorizing universality—as I have previously suggested—is a rather limited understanding of universality's relationship with translation. To reiterate, theorists of translation tend to posit a simple opposition between universality on the one hand and difference, heterogeneity, incommensurability, singularity, and/or the common on the other. Translation's disposition toward these latter phenomena, as contributing to their preservation or suppression, then determines if translation is conceived as maintaining either a narrowly mutualistic or a narrowly antagonistic relationship with universality as such. Benjamin and Derrida, in contrast, invite a more complex understanding of the relationship between translation and universality, an understanding of this relationship as necessarily plural and multifaceted insofar as conflicting modes of translation correspond to conflicting horizons of universality. This means that a given mode of translation can promote (certain notions of) universality and oppose (other notions of) universality *at the same time.* It follows that the "and" relating translation *and* universality is also a site of struggle, that the relationship between translation and universality—like each of its elements—is ambiguous, contradictory, equivocal, and therefore yet another source of conflict. The full complexity of this relationship cannot be appreciated, however, if one side of it is treated in one-sidedly negative terms.

Along with these conceptual shortcomings, there are more directly political ramifications as well. In their failure to recognize universality as a site of struggle, theorists surrender this territory to the forces of reaction in advance, without combat.[82] The horizons of universality intrinsic to capitalism, colonialism, imperialism, and other related systems of oppression become the only horizons. This precipitates, in turn, a "missed encounter" between the theorists in question and the activists, social movements, and political organizations that are directly engaged in the battle, that approach universality as *a site of struggle for their struggles* and work to *transform this site*—rather than abandon or flee it—by developing their own universalist ideas and projects.[83] Put another way, in failing to recognize universality as a site of struggle, theorists cannot appreciate the central role that this site plays in efforts to imagine and create new worlds beyond today's world and its interwoven systems of oppression.

There are of course exceptions to this rule, theorists who do not develop a univocal, one-sidedly negative account of universality and therefore do not guarantee a missed encounter with contemporary struggles and the diverse universalities of these struggles. Among other possible references, alongside

Balibar, I have in mind the trailblazing contributions of Judith Butler and Lydia Liu. All three thinkers, in their own way, not only recognize universality as a site of struggle but also attend to the role that translation might play within this site.[84] As a result, they help illuminate yet another dimension of the relationship between translation and universality. Whereas Benjamin and Derrida theorize how different modes of translation correspond to different universalities, Balibar, Butler, and Liu invite reflection on how translation might occur *between* universalities.

Butler's contribution to this conversation speaks most directly to its relevance for analyzing and intervening in contemporary struggles. I have in mind the essay "Competing Universalities," one of three texts Butler penned for the multiauthor volume *Contingency, Hegemony, Universality: Contemporary Dialogues on the Left*. In this essay, Butler engages in an amicably polemical exchange with Ernesto Laclau, another author of the aforementioned volume, and challenges his view—developed with Chantal Mouffe—that there is only one kind of universality, what Laclau describes in his nomenclature as "the universality of an empty signifier: for the only possible universality is the one constructed through an equivalential chain."[85] From this perspective, the struggle for hegemony consists of various groups and movements vying for their particular demand or set of demands to assume the "function of universal representation," to be part of a chain of demands emerging from different sectors of society, demands that are linked equivalentially in their common opposition to a repressive system, yet to simultaneously rise above the chain and stand for the general equivalent, the universal term that is emptied of specific content in order to represent "the chain as a whole."[86]

Butler insists, however, that not all political struggle is reducible to the struggle for hegemony as Laclau theorizes it and that not all social movements, in their particularity, strive to construct the same kind of universality. This is the key passage:

> For if the "particular" is actually studied in its particularity, it may be that a certain competing version of universality is intrinsic to the particular movement itself. It may be that feminism, for instance, maintains a view of universality that implies forms of sexual egalitarianism, which figure women within a new conception of universalization. Or it may be that struggles for racial equality have within them from the start a conception of universal enfranchisement that is inextricable from a strong conception of multicultural community. Or that struggles against sexual and gender discrimination involve promoting new notions of freedom of assembly or freedom of association that are

universal in character even as they, by implication, seek to throw off some of the specific shackles under which sexual minorities live, and could, by extension, question the exclusive lock on legitimacy that conventional family structures maintain. Thus, the question for such movements will not be how to relate a particular claim to one that is universal. . . . It may be, rather, one of establishing *practices of translation* among competing notions of universality which, despite any apparent logical incompatibility, may nevertheless belong to an overlapping set of social and political aims.[87]

Butler accordingly describes a situation in which particular movements advance competing notions of universality and do not rely on establishing a hegemonic relation over or above other movements to do so. Here the task is to engage in practices of translation between the universalities intrinsic to these movements, to rework each notion of universality in light of the others and to negotiate—without attempting to domesticate or eliminate—their differences, so that said movements can pursue an overlapping set of social and political aims. The point of this translative project is not to elevate one particular notion of universality to the empty and therefore "truly" universal position of general equivalent, while confining the other notions of universality to their particularity. The point, rather, is to construct a space of compossibility between multiple universalities so that their respective movements can form an alliance or coalition, a relation without hegemony, and engage from *that* position in collective struggle.[88]

Butler thus illuminates an entire realm of political activity that cannot be appreciated without attending to the issue of translation between universalities. Liu complements Butler's analysis by focusing on how this issue manifests itself in specific historical contexts, like the drafting of the Universal Declaration of Human Rights. Liu's essay, "Shadows of Universalism: The Untold Story of Human Rights around 1948," stands out in this regard.[89] Its aim is to unsettle the "parochial understanding" of the discourse of human rights, a view that reduces the very notion of human rights to an American reinvention of the European rights of man.[90] Liu challenges this narrative by highlighting the contributions of United Nations diplomats from around the world in the "translingual and transcultural" making of the Declaration.[91] She underscores in particular the efforts of Peng-chun Chang, vice-chairman of the UN Commission on Human Rights. "Refashioning human rights into a universal principle," writes Liu, "was Chang's stated goal, and he envisioned the ground of that universalism as existing somewhere between classical Chinese thought and European Enlightenment ideas that—as he never tired of pointing out—had crossed paths in the eighteenth century and should cross-fertilize again. . . . [Chang] fought hard to reopen the meeting ground between those radically different philosophical traditions."[92] Through Chang, Liu emphasizes that the radically different traditions in question are not to be conceived as fully separate and homogeneous entities, like national languages under the modern regime of translation. They had already encountered each other and were therefore already to some extent entangled, and yet Chang called for their renewed encounter and entanglement with the purpose of renewing human rights. The task he set for himself, in other words, was to pursue further translation between these traditions in an effort to universalize human rights, to make human rights "more universal than ever before," to ensure that human rights were not "circumscribed to the standards of a single culture."[93]

This is a pluralist view of universalism that—as Liu states elsewhere—"thrives on difference. It does not reject difference but rather translates and absorbs it."[94] It would seem, from this vantage point, that classical Chinese thought and European Enlightenment ideas represent *particular* philosophical traditions and that the conversion of human rights into a universal principle would entail translating and absorbing all such *particulars*. But Liu suggests, not unlike Butler, that if these particular traditions are actually studied in their particularity, it will become apparent that competing notions of universality are intrinsic to them. The kind of translation that Chang pursued, in other words, did not only negotiate difference understood in terms of cultural particularity. It also and perhaps more fundamentally pursued what Liu describes as "a relentless negotiation of competing universals between Chinese and European traditions. [Chang's] method was a translingual reworking of ideas across these traditions—a constant movement back and forth—to open up the universal ground for human rights."[95] Chang's universalism thus entailed reciprocal translation between a plurality of universals stemming from very different yet entangled philosophical traditions. His intervention in universalizing human rights depended on following this method of translation.

To flesh out what this method looked like in action, Liu analyzes the drafting committee's deliberation over what constitutes "the human" in Article 1 of the Declaration. Chang argued that, in addition to "reason," the committee should recognize "two-man-mindedness" as an essential human attribute.[96] Two-man-mindedness, as Liu explains, was Chang's English rendering of 仁, the logogram for the Confucian notion of *ren*. Although Chang's efforts were obscured in the final English version of the document, which misleadingly substituted the notion of "conscience" for *ren*, Liu is more interested in the "precarious wager" of Chang's translation than in its uncertain outcome.[97] She maintains that Chang's translingual reworking of an element from classical

Chinese philosophy "sought to transform the concept of the human for human rights by regrounding that idea in the originary plurality of humanity rather than in the concept of the individual."[98] Again, Liu is not suggesting that the universal ground of human rights, this new grounding of the concept of the human, is merely the product of translation across cultural differences, a melding of Chinese and European particularity. I read her as making a more radical claim: Chang's method converts the concept of the human into a space of compossibility for the competing universalities of reason and *ren*, a space in which these universalist notions and the traditions of philosophy to which they pertain reinvent each other through a process of reciprocal, back-and-forth translation.[99] Neither reason nor *ren* remains the same because of their encounter in this transformative space, which functions as the ground for articulating an overlapping set of social and political aims in the form of a declaration of human rights.

Relative to Butler and Liu, Balibar is more cautious or hesitant when analyzing the "particularly ambiguous form of politics" that he calls "cosmopolitics," which "consists exclusively in conflicts between universalities without ready-made solutions."[100] His preferred examples of cosmopolitical conflict—a form of conflict so volatile that it often leads to *"wars to the death"*—include struggles between the discourses of liberalism and communism, between secular and religious discourses, and between opposing religious discourses.[101] In each of these cases, Balibar tends to emphasize conflict over competition, the collision of conflicting universalities over the negotiation of competing universalities. Perhaps this is because competition suggests, as we have already seen, an opening for cross-fertilization and the pursuit of overlapping social and political aims, whereas conflict—for Balibar—denotes a more fundamental and even irreducible incompatibility between the elements involved.[102] This is how Balibar addresses the problem in *On Universals*:

> For, the fact is, as soon as a major conflict arises over the claims made by certain "truths" and certain "values" in the name of the universal . . . the difficulty has little to do with the competition between universalisms (such as that between liberalism and communism), which at bottom denotes the existence of some point in common (be it a point of heresy), in other words, an agreement concerning the disagreement itself and the stakes of that disagreement, and has everything to do with a fundamental *heterogeneity*. . . . Quite simply, there is *no common language*. Or, in Jean-François Lyotard's terms, the "phrases" (or phrasings) of the universal are not mutually presentable, not even in the context of open debate; instead, they form a violent juxtaposition

of incompatible meanings and claims, which Lyotard calls a
"differend."[103]

The obvious question that this passage raises, especially when read within the
context of this volume, is the following one: If there is no common language
between conflicting universalities, can translation occur between their respective phrasings or do their incompatibility and heterogeneity bar such translation
from occurring?

Balibar begins to answer this question in his essay "Further Reflections on
Exile: War and Translation."[104] There he argues that, for Lyotard, the phrases
separated by the differend are indeed untranslatable, that translation between
them is—in a certain sense—impossible, and yet "what is impossible cannot
be avoided, or *must be attempted*. In Lyotard's terminology: one must 'link
onto' another phrase, which remains heterogeneous. In particular one must
'translate' heterogeneous phrases *as if* they were translatable: *this* is the wager
of judgement, or the wager of politics."[105] It would seem, accordingly, that this
impossible yet necessary task of translation, the linking of heterogeneous phrases
that are separated by the differend, signals what is to be done—the political
wager of an act that must be attempted—when grappling with conflicts between
universalities.[106] It is admittedly not clear what this would look like or why it
would be desirable in terms of the violent conflict (rather than competition)
between liberal and communist universalities.[107] It is my sense, however, that
Balibar ultimately prefers a different case study when fleshing out the implications of his reading of Lyotard. I have in mind his theorization of religious
conflict as a conflict of universalities, especially in *Secularism and Cosmopolitanism: Critical Hypotheses on Religion and Politics.*

In the aforementioned book, Balibar maintains that religious conflict "cannot be reduced to a system of 'cultural differences,'" to a clash between particular cultures rivaling over their different beliefs and customs, such that the
conflict's resolution would entail "a politics of intercultural translation" meant
to foster "the phenomena of alliance and hybridization, of multiple affiliations,
that [would] form the material basis for encounters and exchanges between
distant cultural universes."[108] Balibar recognizes the importance of pursuing
this kind of work but insists that it is ultimately insufficient when the conflict
in question exceeds the realm of cultural differences and clashing particularities and concerns, instead, politico-religious differends and heterogeneous
universalities.[109] At stake in the latter instance is "a (forced) choice, for the
subjects involved, between irreconcilable representations and prescriptions of
the subdivisions of the human, of what separates the human from the inhuman,
or of what separates the various modalities of the human from one another."[110]

This forced choice between conflicting universalist claims concerning the human, given the strictly incompatible and irreconcilable nature of said claims, creates a situation very different from the one explored by Liu. Instead of the translingual and transcultural reworking of different philosophical traditions, Balibar is concerned with the "mutual untranslatability" of religious discourses.[111] Indeed, Balibar associates the religious as such with the untranslatable, with a certain universal untranslatability.[112] At the same time, he invokes the tradition of Benjamin and Derrida (and therefore also to some extent the tradition of Lyotard) to explain that "the untranslatable is not just a barrier in this case, an external limit on the possibility of the encounter; it is, rather, the problem that must be confronted in common."[113]

To confront this problem, Balibar calls for the collective identification or invention of a supplementary element that would function as the differend's "vanishing mediator," a concept he borrows from Fredric Jameson to name that which would be "charged both with bringing religions together and recognizing the irreducibility of their conflict."[114] Balibar conceives of this supplementary element as a new, (self-)critical secularism and discusses the features that would distinguish it from past and present institutions and conceptions of secularization. For the purposes of this volume, however, the specific characteristics of this new secularism are less important than the role that it plays in attempting to mediate an irreconcilable conflict between universalities, to facilitate an encounter between universalist discourses that nevertheless maintain their incompatibility. Balibar implies that this role entails a certain labor of translation, and, indeed, elsewhere he makes explicit the association between the figure of the vanishing mediator and the figure of the translator.[115] To pursue this labor of translation, the vanishing mediator must relativize religious discourses, must "undermine their certainty that they hold the monopoly on truth and justice, without, however, thwarting their search for truth and justice ('salvation') on their own paths."[116] This creates the conditions for linking religious discourses and their phrasings of the universal, for "bringing their interpretations to converge on certain ethical or social rules," without falling back on an "imaginary reconciliation" of an irreconcilable conflict.[117] A convergence of this kind—a product of translation—would result in the *"pacification"* of the conflict, or more precisely its *"conversion"* or *"sublimation"* into a "civil" form, such that the conflict itself would still remain.[118]

As the reader can now appreciate, Balibar's assessment of what it looks like to translate between universalities is more modest and tentative, less optimistic or triumphant, than what can be found in either Butler or Liu. This difference—more so than disagreement—likely stems from the specificity of their respective case studies, whether the universalities in question are in competition or in conflict with each other and what kind of new relationship could be formed between them as a result, which ultimately would point to distinct tasks of translation (e.g., building political alliances, cross-fertilizing philosophical traditions, negotiating religious antagonisms).[119] And yet, Balibar does allude to how translation might contribute to a genuine *transition*, insofar as the vanishing mediator is to be understood not as a structural feature of society but rather as a force that aims to create the conditions for a new society and therefore also the conditions for its own withering away or vanishing.[120]

In sum, movements tied to feminism, antiracism, and sexual and gender liberation; debates surrounding human rights and the encounter of radically different traditions of thought; conflicts between liberal and communist discourses, secular and religious discourses, and opposing religious discourses—this is an incomplete enumeration of the many urgent contemporary issues that can only be misunderstood, with potentially disastrous consequences, if we fail to recognize universality as a site of struggle and thus ignore the role that translation might play within this site. Balibar, Butler, and Liu pave the way for an alternative path in this regard, a path that moves beyond the existing limitations of much of translation studies and theoretical work adjacent to the field. This volume seeks to follow their example.

The essays compiled in this volume contribute to mapping—while simultaneously participating in—a significant but also subterranean current of thought that grapples in meaningful and complex ways with the problem of the relationship between translation and universality.[121] This current of thought is not to be confused with a monolithic school that shares the same general outlook or subscribes to a shared set of propositions. Rather, it consists of many different voices advancing different and even divergent arguments and claims, voices that are nonetheless in conversation with each other, often unknowingly, through their different explorations of the same problem. Some of the names that could be associated with this current of thought include Benjamin but also Antonio Gramsci and Nadezhda Krupskaya, Derrida but also Édouard Glissant and C. L. R. James. For more contemporary voices, we could add to this necessarily partial and heterogeneous list not only Balibar, Butler, and Liu but also Emily Apter, Jacques Lezra, Mukti Lakhi Mangharam, Ngũgĩ wa Thiong'o, and—of course—the contributors to this volume.[122]

Numerous theoretical tendencies inform the essays included in the present book; however, the reader will find that deconstruction and Marxism are predominant throughout. It is important to draw attention to this because deconstruction and Marxism can be and have been construed as occupying opposing sides of an either-or choice, not only in general philosophical and political terms but also and especially in terms of their distinct approaches to theorizing translation and universality.[123] It is as if, within this popular imaginary of deconstruction and Marxism, each forms a separate camp that raises its banner for a different term—either translation or universality—while subjecting the other camp's term to harsh scrutiny.

It has become commonplace, for instance, to associate deconstruction with a generally sympathetic view of translation and with an attitude of skepticism and even scorn when faced with appeals to universality. This is not simply a distortion; there are indeed theorists working broadly within the tradition of deconstruction who draw from Derrida and others to advocate for (a certain notion of) translation and against (any notion of) universality.[124] To complicate this view, I have presented a different reading of Derrida, one that takes seriously the following observation from Balibar:

> When Derrida deconstructs the universal as metaphysical essence, as the crossing-out of the aleatory or unpredictable, the "possibilization of the impossible," the *propriation* and *appropriation* of thought and life through names and institutions, etc., he is also always already *constructing* a certain universality—even if it is in the mode of *fiction*, of a hyperbolic supersession of particular institutions (as in his notion of "the university without condition"), of an internal negation (as in his famous formula of "the messianic without messianism" and, more generally, in all those propositions of the type "X without X" that he borrows from Blanchot), or of a double rejection ("neither the human nor the nonhuman").[125]

In agreement with Balibar, I argued that Derrida's deconstructive reading of biblical myth elaborates upon a certain universality, a universality without univocity, under the post-Babelian sign of the "impossible," which is ultimately bound up with the messianic universality *à venir* that translation (only) promises. Approaching deconstruction in this way, with attention to its own universalist formulations, challenges the perception—held even among some of deconstruction's proponents, however unconsciously—that it is consistently and straightforwardly antiuniversalist.[126] The essays of the present volume depart from this popular and popularized view. In this way, they invite a rethinking of deconstruction that would delve deeper into its own constructions of universality. This would, in turn, allow future deconstructionist work to provide new accounts of translation that would attend more fully to what Derrida theorized as its multidimensional relationship with universality.[127]

It has likewise become commonplace to characterize Marxism as an unapologetically universalist discourse that is indifferent to translation if not openly hostile toward it, especially when translation is conceived as a practice of negotiating linguistic, cultural, political, and philosophical differences. This is, again, not simply a distortion; it is an outgrowth of certain dogmatic tendencies within Marxism's own history, tendencies that have construed the ideas and concepts of Marx, Lenin, and other major revolutionary figures as universally applicable and therefore in no need of translation (broadly construed) when confronted with situations that differ greatly from the situations out of which these ideas and concepts historically emerged.[128] This approach to Marxism is in tension—and is ultimately incompatible—with the imperative to pursue "a concrete analysis of each specific historical situation," which, according to Lenin, constitutes the very basis of Marxist dialectics as such.[129] The dogmatic approach, in other words, obscures the process of translation at Marxism's core, a process of reworking and concretizing Marxism's own universalist formulations and presuppositions in light of new and changing historical circumstances.[130] This volume, in contrast, joins a growing body of research that recognizes the fundamental role of translation in Marxist theoretical and political practice and consequently opens new lines of inquiry for developing a more nuanced understanding of Marxism's appeals to and demands for universality.[131] As a result, the volume also calls for a renewed consideration of the relationship between deconstruction and Marxism, in general and with respect to their different theorizations of the volume's key terms.

With this broader framing in mind, we can now turn to the individual essays of this book, which I will introduce in the order of their appearance. The idea is not to give a summary of each text but rather to highlight certain key arguments as they pertain to the volume's main themes and problems and to underscore points of convergence and divergence between the different pieces. Each essay could be read on its own, and the reader could choose to explore these essays in a different order; however, in what follows, I will also set aside some space to explain the rationale for the volume's overall structure and organization.

This book begins with three essays that are directly in conversation with one another. They register collaborative work that precedes this volume while no doubt anticipating future collaborations as well. The first piece, written by Barbara Cassin and translated by Katie Chenoweth, invites the reader to consider how translation can "complicate the universal" in ways that carry significant implications for both philosophy and politics. As Cassin defines it, "translation is what relates the different worlds and cultures that different languages are." Translation thus immediately subverts any univocal notion of *the* universal by confronting such a notion, which is necessarily articulated in a language and derived from that language's culture(s) and world(s), with other universals stemming from the cultures and worlds of other languages. At the philosophical level, this leads Cassin to promote a form of relativism between multiple universals and their truth claims, whereas politically it propels her commitment to "diversity" understood as "differentiated plurality," as referring to a relation to others "like me not like me." Indeed, it is from this paradigm of translation that Cassin critiques the hegemony of "Globish," the imposition of English as the one, universal language of communication around the globe, as well as the kind of "ontological nationalism" that recognizes the existence of a multiplicity of languages, cultures, and worlds only to order and categorize them hierarchically based on the purported measure of their value.

Cassin explicitly develops her argument in dialogue with Souleymane Bachir Diagne, whose contribution to this volume opposes what he calls—drawing from Aimé Césaire—"diluted" universalism, the kind of universalism that drowns out any and all difference (like Globish). At the same time, and still drawing from Césaire, Diagne cautions that such an opposition should not fall into the trap of essentializing difference (like ontological nationalism) so that one is left with "a world of fragments and insularities." Instead, Diagne proposes "a truly universal universalism" that would entail a horizontal rather than hierarchical relation between languages and cultures, a universalism that would appeal to and strive toward what Maurice Merleau-Ponty calls a "lateral universal" rather than an "overarching universal." For Diagne, the former kind of universal is deeply imbricated with translation—in fact, he holds them to be synonymous—insofar as translation is understood as "the possibility of a universal and horizontal circulation of enunciations." The task of the translator, it follows, is to contribute to producing a lateral form of universality, for such a horizontal web of entanglement between languages and cultures cannot be posited in advance but instead must be actively created.

Although Cassin and Diagne favorably cite each other and draw from each other's work in their respective texts, I wonder if there may be some underlying tension between their arguments, a potential debate that I would like to signal here. I have in mind Diagne's reference to a truly universal universalism. This formulation resonates with Cassin's political commitment to diversity in its insistence on a nonhierarchical form of relation, yet it arguably diverges from her philosophical relativism and its emphasis on multiple universals, positing instead a single universal that is *truly* universal because of its laterality. Is the positing of a single universal not precisely what translation as a paradigm is meant to complicate?[132] Or are we to understand Diagne's formulation as referring to a space of compossibility not only between particular languages and cultures but also between their respective worlds and therefore between their universalist worldviews? Put another way, does a truly universal universalism imagine a new world, one that would replace the existing world as *the* world, or does it envision a new relation between worlds, those already in existence as well as those yet to come?[133]

For Gary Wilder, our next contributor, these two positions are not actually as opposed as they may appear to be. Wilder's essay explores the question: How can solidarity be constructed without erasing difference and eliding singularity? He draws from a wide array of sources to develop his answer to this question, maintaining that a strong commitment to translation is required to build solidarity insofar as translation is understood not as a practice of making equivalent that which is incommensurate but rather as a practice that produces and performs reciprocity between singularities to forge alliances across differences. In this way, he unsettles the familiar construal of translation as a problem, as a necessary evil tied equally necessarily to loss, and instead encourages his readers—drawing inspiration from Cassin—to see translation as an opportunity to cultivate the kind of political relationships that could open onto nonliberal forms of internationalism and universalism. Working with many of the same thinkers as Diagne (as well as with Diagne's previous work), Wilder rejects what he construes as a false choice between the abstract universalism of bourgeois liberalism, with its deep historical ties to colonial domination and imperial expansion, and the concrete particularism espoused by some of today's theorists, which locks political actors and their universalist claims into separate, provincial lifeworlds. In good dialectical fashion, Wilder seeks to overcome this opposition through the notion of concrete universality; however, perhaps contrary to the expectations of some readers, he does not go on to invoke Hegel's theorization of the process whereby the universal becomes concrete.[134] Instead, he turns to Glissant to consider how multiple concrete universals emerge from translation practices between and within multiple languages. "In this view," Wilder writes, "every place (or language, or text) is or refracts both *a* world and *the* world." It is with this statement that Wilder attempts to resolve the old debate—to some extent staged between Cassin and Diagne—of the one and the many, the singular and the multiple.[135]

The next three essays form a group in part because of the movement that they create when read together, one that passes from Marx to Lenin to Gramsci. However, these essays also can be read as a group insofar as they all nuance and expand the terms of debate set by the volume's previous three essays. To start, we have Ben Baer's contribution, which offers a deep dive into Marx's discussion of primitive accumulation, understood not (or perhaps not only) as a diagnostic category to classify "all manner of baleful and expropriative phenomena" but rather (or also) as the "double name for a circulating ideological schema and a critical epistemology of it."[136] This schema concerns a universalizing story of anthropological difference—of fundamentally different and contrary human types, of natural winners and natural losers, of the diligent elite and the lazy lumpen—that explains and justifies socioeconomic dominance or subordination as a consequence of innately belonging to one or the other group. The schema "is taught formally and informally, translated into languages, statements, and representations, institutionalized as an epistemic horizon," and, as a result, anthropological difference becomes not only "a learned, internalized, affective and effective (subject-forming) classification" but also, for that very reason, a "condition" of capitalism's "indefinite prolongation." Baer thus destabilizes any general and generalizing defense of difference as such by focusing on a specific kind of difference—the anthropological difference of naturalized hierarchy—and its role in diverse translations of the universalizing story of primitive accumulation qua ideological schema. Yet the point of Marx's critical epistemology, Baer repeatedly argues, is not to provide an "endless diagnosis" of ongoing primitive accumulation but rather to "outline a practice of disrupting—or redirecting—the uneven inscription of capitalist subjectivity," a practice that would necessarily challenge primitive accumulation's universalizing story and its translation. As Baer explains, this practice would be "directed toward epistemic and subjective change"—toward the production of socialists—and would, in turn, threaten the seemingly indefinite character of capitalism's prolongation.

If many of the volume's contributors theorize translation as a practice of "putting in touch," of fashioning new relationships and refashioning old ones between languages, cultures, and worlds, Cate Reilly broadens the scope of this idea to consider translation's role in bringing together the spheres of psychoanalysis and politics.[137] This is perhaps clearest when Reilly turns her attention to the little-known history of Russian Freudo-Marxism and its efforts to elaborate upon the political potential of psychoanalytic theory and practice, to explore how psychoanalysis might contribute to what Lenin describes as the historical transition of the proletariat from spontaneity to political consciousness. Reilly shows how this transformation, the attainment of a new state of awareness that would make possible a new kind of State, can be and was theorized as the product of a pedagogical labor of translation. But Reilly also considers other, more implicit scenes of translation that put psychoanalysis and politics in touch with each other, from Freud's correspondence with Albert Einstein in the wake of World War I to Derrida's discussion of this exchange at an international gathering of analysts held in Paris in 2000, a gathering whose name, the États Généraux de la Psychanalyse, evoked the assembly of the 1789 Estates-General. Reilly demonstrates how Freud, drawing upon his work with the Wolf-Man, translates Einstein's notion of universal aggression to theorize the death drive as that which lies beyond the pleasure principle, and how

Derrida subsequently translates Freud by posing the same question—what lies beyond (*au-delà*)?—but asking it of a different principle, of the death drive itself. Here I read Reilly as pointing to yet another way that translation might complicate the universal, insofar as Derrida's Freudian gesture of inquiring into a beyond invites us to think from within psychoanalysis of what exceeds psychoanalysis, particularly in light of certain basic questions "about psychoanalysis and universality operative since Freud's attempts at a psycho-anthropology in works like *Totem and Taboo*, *Civilization and Its Discontents*, and *Moses and Monotheism*."

In the next essay of the volume, Peter Thomas seeks to illuminate the centrality of translation, as concept and practice, for Gramsci's *Prison Notebooks*. Thomas argues that Gramsci's experimentation with translation in his prison cell—where he turned to the works of Marx and Goethe, as well as, and perhaps most intriguingly, the Grimm Brothers' fairy tales—not only informed his concurrent theoretical reflections but also provided opportunities for critical intervention into the very texts that he was translating. While working with these texts, Gramsci would often depart from them in significant ways, by omitting certain passages and completely rewriting others, to transform the texts' aesthetic and political potential. According to Thomas, this same approach can be observed when studying the concept for which Gramsci is best known—namely, hegemony—which was actually a term that the Italian Marxist inherited from key debates taking place within Russian Social Democracy around the events of 1917. Considering the term as an instance neither of pure invention nor of mere imitation, Thomas shows how Gramsci once again experimented with translation to produce "a qualitatively new and expanded concept" of hegemony that significantly altered its historical, formal, and methodological reach. To accompany these experiments, Gramsci developed a complex and multifaceted theorization of translation in the *Prison Notebooks*, from his discussion of the "reciprocal translatability" between French politics and German philosophy to his claim that it is only from within the philosophy of praxis that translation is "organic and profound." This latter point leads Thomas to reflect upon the status of Marxism in Gramsci's thinking, which is sometimes described as a qualitatively distinct, universal discourse capable of integrating and deciphering all other particularistic conceptions of the world, while at other times it is construed—more promisingly for Thomas—as a mode of critical inquiry that begins "by annulling the claim to a qualitative distinction between supposedly universal and purportedly particular discourses" so as to historically situate said discourses (including Marxism itself) as constitutive elements of the sociopolitical realities that they constitute. This is where we might locate yet another debate between some of the contributors to this volume, especially if we are to understand the annulment of any qualitative distinction between the universal and the particular as distinct from the dialectical overcoming of this opposition through the notion—that also plays an important role in Gramsci's *Prison Notebooks*—of concrete universality. Indeed, grappling with how Gramsci takes up this notion to theorize translation might problematize Thomas's depiction of universality as (seemingly always) "abstract," "fictitious," and "formalistic."[138]

To close this volume, we include two essays that are very different in terms of their style and argumentation yet form a kind of grouping insofar as they draw from Derridean and Marxian sources to critique and deconstruct long-standing yet underexamined assumptions surrounding the theorization of translation and universality. Naomi Waltham-Smith opens her essay with the following provocation: Whereas well-meaning academics have historically made an ethico-political appeal to the singular and the untranslatable in an attempt to oppose European-expansionist fantasies of universality, fantasies that violently level all difference based on a notion of general equivalence, it is precisely as singularities and untranslatables that certain cultural artifacts, the spoils of colonialist looting and plunder, enter into the global market of exchange. Waltham-Smith thus refines this volume's discussion of some of its most basic categories in a move not unlike that of Baer's approach to theorizing difference. She reminds her readers that sometimes singularities are commodified *as singularities* and that the quality of being untranslatable, of being *without equivalent,* is in some instances precisely what is sold on the global market for an "equivalent" and often exorbitant sum of money. These opening remarks set up Waltham-Smith's discussion of the "economy of translation," an economy that operates at the level of one-to-one exchange between words, which she contrasts with a notion of translation as "the necessity of linking singularities that resist being put into a series." With help from Derrida, Hélène Cixous, and others, Waltham-Smith also proposes a new way of theorizing the relationship between translation and untranslatability that attends to not one but many different kinds of untranslatability, to how the untranslatable—perhaps, we could add, like the universal—can only be understood as differential.

The final essay of this volume, written by Gavin Walker, is also the most polemical. Walker sets his sights on two targets that correspond to the volume's two key terms. He maintains, first of all, that most theorists of translation—and here he might include some of our contributors—are, unbeknownst to themselves, beholden to the modern regime of translation as Sakai theorizes it, a regime that enforces "a universal fiction of specific difference" or "pre-posited, holistic entities" known as cultures and languages that are putatively put into contact with each other through translation. For Walker, this understanding of translation is as misguided as it is banal. He insists, however, that translation can name something absolutely essential if and when it refers to "the differing of difference—or to put it another way, *incommensurability beyond the regime of specific difference*—within the sphere of the social." At the same time, Walker interrogates contemporary desires on the Left for another universality; he alludes to the "competing universalities" of Butler and Liu and the "insurgent universalities" of Asad Haider and Massimiliano Tomba, but here, too, he would likely add the universalities of some of the contributors to this volume.[139] According to Walker, even as this tendency among contemporary theorists offers an important corrective to a much broader tendency, one that he characterizes as "the refusal of universality," it nonetheless misconstrues the nature of the universal as such, which can only be properly understood as a "productive fiction" or "regulative idea" that never basks in the full realization of its plenitude.[140] Instead of positing some utopian futural alternative to the status quo, moreover, such a fiction or idea "orients our capacity to respond to the concrete circumstances in which we are already embedded." And yet, these formulations cannot but take us back to the beginning of the volume, to its discussion of multiple universals and different notions of universality. To put the problem in the form of a question: What is to be done when there is more than one regulative idea orienting our capacity to intervene in the present?[141] How would reflecting on this issue complement or complicate Walker's argument?[142]

I imagine that the reader of this volume might reach its final pages with more questions than answers. As editors, Chenoweth and I embrace this scenario as the ideal response to our project, for the point of this endeavor was never to resolve every problem that we encountered, nor was it ever our intention to establish a single party line that could be rehearsed ad nauseam at future conferences and in future writing whenever someone invoked either translation or universality. Far from putting an end to contemporary theoretical debates surrounding these key terms and their relationship, this volume, we hope, might provide impetus for further inquiry, reflection, and struggle.

Bibliography

Althusser, Louis. "The Underground Current of the Materialism of the Encounter." In *Philosophy of the Encounter: Later Writings, 1978–1987*, translated by G. M. Goshgarian, 163–207. London: Verso, 2008.

Anderson, Kevin. *Marx at the Margins: On Nationalism, Ethnicity, and Non-Western Societies*. Chicago: University of Chicago Press, 2010.

Apter, Emily. *Against World Literature: On the Politics of Untranslatability*. London: Verso, 2013.

———. "Cosmopolitics." In *Thinking with Balibar: A Lexicon of Conceptual Practice*, edited by Ann Laura Stoler, Stathis Gourgouris, and Jacques Lezra, 94–116. New York: Fordham University Press, 2020.

———. *The Translation Zone: A New Comparative Literature*. Princeton, NJ: Princeton University Press, 2006.

Aricó, José. *Marx and Latin America*. Translated by David Broder. Chicago: Haymarket Books, 2014.

Arnall, Gavin. "Hacia una teoría de la práctica teórica: Mariátegui, marxismo y traducción." *Escrituras Americanas* 2, no. 2 (2017): 43–80.

———. "The Idea(s) of Occupy." *Theory & Event* 15, no. 2 (June 2012). http://muse .jhu.edu/journals/theory_and_event/vo15/15.2.arnall.html.

———. "Latin American Marxisms: Reading José Carlos Mariátegui and José Aricó Today." *Journal of Latin American Cultural Studies* 29, no. 3 (2021): 489–99.

———. "The Many Tasks of the Marxist Translator: Approaching Marxism as/in/ with Translation from Antonio Gramsci to the Zapatistas." *Historical Materialism* 30, no. 1 (2022): 99–132.

———. "The Missed Encounter of *Turupukllay*: Marxism, Indigenous Communities, and Andean Culture in *Yawar Fiesta*." *Radical Americas* 5, no. 1 (2020): 1–16.

———. *Subterranean Fanon: An Underground Theory of Radical Change*. New York: Columbia University Press, 2020.

Badiou, Alain. *The Communist Hypothesis*. Translated by David Macey and Steve Corcoran. London: Verso, 2010.

———. "French." In Cassin, ed., *Dictionary of Untranslatables*, 349–54.

———. *Saint Paul: The Foundation of Universalism*. Translated by Ray Brassier. Stanford, CA: Stanford University Press, 2003.

Baer, Ben Conisbee. "What Is Special about Postcolonial Translation?" In *A Companion to Translation Studies*, edited by Sandra Bermann and Catherine Porter, 233–45. West Sussex, UK: Wiley Blackwell, 2014.

Balibar, Étienne. "Ambiguous Universality." In *Politics and the Other Scene*, translated by Christine Jones, James Swenson, and Chris Turner, 146–75. London: Verso, 2002.

———. "Cosmopolitanism and Secularism: Controversial Legacies and Prospective Interrogations." *Grey Room*, no. 44 (2011): 6–25.

——— "Further Reflections on Exile: War and Translation." In *Conflicting Humanities*, edited by Rosi Braidotti and Paul Gilroy, 211–27. London: Bloomsbury, 2016.

———. *Masses, Classes, Ideas: Studies on Politics and Philosophy before and after Marx*. New York: Routledge, 1994.

———. *On Universals: Constructing and Deconstructing Community*. Translated by Joshua David Jordan. New York: Fordham University Press, 2020.

———. "Politics and Translation: Reflections on Lyotard, Derrida, and Said." Translated by Gavin Walker. In "The End of Area: Biopolitics, Geopolitics, History," edited by Gavin Walker and Naoki Sakai. Special issue, *positions: asia critique* I27, no. 1 (2019): 99–114.

———. *Secularism and Cosmopolitanism: Critical Hypotheses on Religion and Politics*. New York: Columbia University Press, 2018.

———. "*Vergangene Vergangenheit?* (A Past with No Future?)." In *Europe and the World: World War I as Crisis of Universalism*, edited by Kai Evers and David Pan, 251–71. Candor, NY: Telos, 2018.

———. *Violence and Civility: On the Limits of Political Philosophy*. Translated by G. M. Goshgarian. New York: Columbia University Press, 2015.

———. *We, the People of Europe? Reflections on Transnational Citizenship*. Translated by James Swenson. Princeton, NJ: Princeton University Press, 2004.

Bardawil, Fadi A. *Revolution and Disenchantment: Arab Marxism and the Binds of Emancipation*. Durham, NC: Duke University Press, 2020.

Bassnett, Susan. "Still Trapped in the Labyrinth: Further Reflections on Translation and Theatre." In *Constructing Cultures: Essays on Literary Translation*, edited by Susan Bassnett and André Lefevere, 90–108. Clevendon, UK: Multilingual Matters, 1998.

———. "Translating for the Theatre: The Case against Performability." *TTR* 4, no. 1 (1991): 99–111.

Benjamin, Walter. "Die Aufgabe des Übersetzers." In *Gesammelte Schriften IV/I*, 9–21. Frankfurt: Suhrkamp Verlag, 1972.

———. "On Language as Such and on the Language of Man." Translated by Edmund Jephcott. In *Selected Writings*, vol. 1, 1913–1926, edited by Marcus Bullock and Michael W. Jennings, 62–74. Cambridge, MA: Belknap, 2004.

———. "The Task of the Translator." Translated by Harry Zohn. In *Selected Writings*, vol. 1, 1913–1926, edited by Marcus Bullock and Michael W. Jennings, 253–63. Cambridge, MA: Belknap, 2004.

Berman, Antoine. *The Experience of the Foreign: Culture and Translation in Romantic Germany*. Translated by S. Heyvaert. Albany: State University of New York Press, 1992.

Bhabha, Homi. *The Location of Culture*. London: Routledge, 1994.

Blanchot, Maurice. "Translating." In *Friendship*, translated by Elizabeth Rottenberg, 57–61. Stanford, CA: Stanford University Press, 1997.

Bosteels, Bruno. *The Actuality of Communism*. London: Verso, 2011.

———. *Marx and Freud in Latin America: Politics, Psychoanalysis, and Religion in Times of Terror*. London: Verso, 2012.

Butler, Judith. "Competing Universalities." In Judith Butler, Ernesto Laclau, and Slavoj Žižek, *Contingency, Hegemony, Universality: Contemporary Dialogues on the Left*, 136–81. London: Verso, 2000.

———. *Parting Ways: Jewishness and the Critique of Zionism*. New York: Columbia University Press, 2012.

———. "Restaging the Universal: Hegemony and the Limits of Formalism." In Judith Butler, Ernesto Laclau, and Slavoj Žižek, *Contingency, Hegemony, Universality: Contemporary Dialogues on the Left*, 11–43. London: Verso, 2000.

Cadava, Eduardo. *Words of Light: Theses on the Photography of History*. Princeton, NJ: Princeton University Press, 1997.

Casarino, Cesare. "Universalism of the Common." *diacritics* 39, no. 4 (2009): 162–76.

Cassin, Barbara, ed. *Dictionary of Untranslatables: A Philosophical Lexicon.*
Translation edited by Emily Apter, Jacques Lezra, and Michael Wood. Princeton,
NJ: Princeton University Press, 2014.

———. "The Energy of the Untranslatables: Translation as a Paradigm for the
Human Sciences." *Paragraph* 38, no. 2 (2015): 145–58.

———. *Philosopher en langues: Les intraduisibles en traduction.* Paris: Éditions Rue
d'Ulm, 2014.

Chakrabarty, Dipesh. *Provincializing Europe: Postcolonial Thought and Historical
Difference.* Princeton, NJ: Princeton University Press, 2000.

Cheyfitz, Eric. *The Poetics of Imperialism: Translation and Colonization from* The
Tempest *to* Tarzan. Oxford: Oxford University Press, 1990.

Cortés, Martín. *Translating Marx: José Aricó and the New Latin American Marxism.*
Translated by Nicolas Allen. Chicago: Haymarket Books, 2020.

de Ípola, Emilio. *Althusser, The Infinite Farewell.* Translated by Gavin Arnall.
Durham, NC: Duke University Press, 2018.

de Man, Paul. *The Resistance to Theory.* Minneapolis: University of Minnesota
Press, 1986.

Derrida, Jacques. "Des tours de Babel." In *L'art des confins: Mélanges offerts à
Maurice de Gandillac,* edited by Annie Cazenave and Jean-François Lyotard,
209–37. Paris: Presses Universitaires de France, 1985.

———. "Des tours de Babel." Translated by Joseph F. Graham. In *Psyche: Inventions
of the Other,* vol. 1, edited by Peggy Kamuf and Elizabeth Rottenberg, 191–225.
Stanford, CA: Stanford University Press, 2007.

———. *Monolingualism of the Other; or, The Prosthesis of Origin.* Translated by
Patrick Mensah. Stanford, CA: Stanford University Press, 1998.

———. "Roundtable on Translation." Translated by Peggy Kamuf. In *The Ear of the
Other: Otobiography, Transference, Translation,* edited by Christie V. McDonald,
93–162. Lincoln: University of Nebraska Press, 1988.

———. *Specters of Marx: The State of the Debt, the Work of Mourning, and the New
International.* New York: Routledge, 2006.

———. "Two Words for Joyce." Translated by Geoff Bennington. In *Post-structuralist
Joyce,* edited by Derek Attridge and Daniel Ferrer, 145–58. Cambridge: Cambridge
University Press, 1984.

———. "What Is a 'Relevant' Translation?" Translated by Lawrence Venuti. *Critical
Inquiry,* no. 27 (2001): 174–200.

de Vries, Hent. "Anti-Babel: The 'Mystical Postulate' in Benjamin, de Certeau and
Derrida." *MLN* 107, no. 3 (1992): 441–77.

Diagne, Souleymane Bachir. *The Ink of Scholars: Reflections on Philosophy in Africa.*
Dakar: CODESRIA, 2016.

Eiland, Howard, and Michael W. Jennings. *Walter Benjamin: A Critical Life.*
Cambridge, MA: Harvard University Press, 2014.

Ertürk, Nergis, and Özge Serin, eds. *Marxism, Communism, and Translation.* Special issue of *boundary 2: an international journal of literature and culture* 43, no. 3 (2016).

García Linera, Álvaro. "Indianism and Marxism: The Disparity between Two Revolutionary Rationales." In *Plebeian Power: Collective Action and Indigenous, Working-Class and Popular Identities in Bolivia,* 305–21. Chicago: Haymarket Books, 2015.

Gonzalez, Mike. *In the Red Corner: The Marxism of José Carlos Mariátegui.* Chicago: Haymarket Books, 2019.

Gould, Jeffrey. "Ignacio Ellacuría and the Salvadorean Revolution." *Journal of Latin American Studies* 47, no. 2 (2015): 285–315.

Haider, Asad. *Mistaken Identity: Race and Class in the Age of Trump.* London: Verso, 2018.

Hanne, Michael. "Metaphors for the Translator." In *The Translator as Writer,* edited by Susan Bassnett and Peter Bush, 208–24. London: Continuum, 2006.

Hrnjez, Saša. "Translational Universality: The Struggle over the Universal." *Labyrinth* 21, no. 2 (2019): 118–37.

Hutchings, Kimberly. "Universalism in Feminist International Ethics: Gender and the Difficult Labour of Translation." In *Dialogue, Politics and Gender,* edited by Jude Browne, 81–106. Cambridge: Cambridge University Press, 2013.

Jacobs, Carol. *In the Language of Walter Benjamin.* Baltimore: Johns Hopkins University Press, 1999.

Jameson, Fredric. *Valences of the Dialectic.* London: Verso, 2010.

Johnson, David E. *Kant's Dog: On Borges, Philosophy, and the Time of Translation.* Albany: State University of New York Press, 2012.

Kapoor, Ilan, and Zahi Zalloua. *Universal Politics.* Oxford: Oxford University Press, 2022.

Klein, Hilary. *Compañeras: Zapatista Women's Stories.* New York: Seven Stories, 2015.

Laclau, Ernesto. "Constructing Universality." In Judith Butler, Ernesto Laclau, and Slavoj Žižek, *Contingency, Hegemony, Universality: Contemporary Dialogues on the Left,* 281–307. London: Verso, 2000.

———. "Why Do Empty Signifiers Matter to Politics?" In *Emancipation(s),* 36–46. London: Verso, 1996.

Laclau, Ernesto, and Chantal Mouffe. *Hegemony and Socialist Strategy: Towards a Radical Democratic Politics.* London: Verso, 1985.

Lacorte, Rocco. "Translation and Marxism." In *The Routledge Handbook of Translation and Politics,* edited by Jonathan Evans and Fruela Fernández, 17–28. New York: Routledge, 2018.

Léger, Marc James, ed. *Identity Trumps Socialism: The Class and Identity Debate after Neoliberalism.* New York: Routledge, 2023.

Lenin, Vladimir Ilyich. "The Junius Pamphlet." In *Collected Works,* vol. 22. Moscow: Progress, 1964.

————. *The State and Revolution: The Marxist Theory of the State and the Tasks of the Proletariat in the Revolution.* In *Collected Works*, vol. 25. Moscow: Progress, 1964.

Lezra, Jacques. *On the Nature of Marx's Things: Translation as Necrophilology.* New York: Fordham University Press, 2018

Liu, Lydia. *The Clash of Empires: The Invention of China in Modern World Making.* Cambridge, MA: Harvard University Press, 2006.

————. "The Eventfulness of Translation: Temporality, Difference, and Competing Universals." *translation: a transdisciplinary journal*, no. 4 (2014): 147–70.

————. "The Question of Meaning-Value in the Political Economy of the Sign." In *Tokens of Exchange: The Problem of Translation in Global Circulations*, edited by Lydia Liu, 13–41. Durham, NC: Duke University Press, 1999.

————. "Shadows of Universalism: The Untold Story of Human Rights around 1948." *Critical Inquiry*, no. 40 (2014): 385–417.

————, ed. *Tokens of Exchange: The Problem of Translation in Global Circulations.* Durham, NC: Duke University Press, 1999.

————. *Translingual Practice: Literature, National Culture, and Translated Modernity—China, 1900–1937.* Stanford, CA: Stanford University Press, 1995.

Liu, Lydia, and James St. André. "The Battleground of Translation: Making Equal in a Global Structure of Inequality." *Alif*, no. 38 (2018): 368–87.

Löwy, Michael. *Redemption and Utopia: Jewish Libertarian Thought in Central Europe.* New York: Verso, 2017.

Mangharam, Mukti Lakhi. *Literatures of Liberation: Non-European Universalisms and Democratic Progress.* Columbus: Ohio State University Press, 2017.

Marx, Karl, and Frederick Engels. "Manifesto of the Communist Party." In *Collected Works of Karl Marx and Frederick Engels*, vol. 6, *1845–1848*, 477–519. New York: International, 1976.

Menon, Madhavi. *Indifference to Difference: On Queer Universalism.* Minneapolis: University of Minnesota Press, 2015.

Merrill, Christi A. "Collaborations at the University of Michigan: Decolonizing Translation Studies." *PMLA* 138, no. 3 (2023): 824–31.

Mezzadra, Sandro. "Living in Translation: Toward a Heterolingual Theory of the Multitude." In *The Politics of Culture: Around the Work of Naoki Sakai*, edited by Richard Calichman and John Namjun Kim, 121–37. New York: Routledge, 2010.

Mezzadra, Sandro, and Brett Neilson. *Border as Method, or, the Multiplication of Labor.* Durham, NC: Duke University Press, 2013.

Mignolo, Walter. "Reflections on Translation across Colonial Epistemic Differences." In *Translatio/n: Narration, Media and the Staging of Differences*, edited by Federico Italiano and Michael Rössner, 19–34. Bielefeld: transcript, 2012.

Ngũgĩ wa Thiong'o. *The Language of Languages: Reflections on Translation.* London: Seagull Books, 2023.

Niranjana, Tejaswini. *Siting Translation: History, Post-structuralism, and the Colonial Context.* Berkeley: University of California Press, 1992.

Rafael, Vicente. "Linguistic Currencies: The Translative Power of English in
    Southeast Asia and the United States." *The Translator* 25, no. 2 (2019): 142–58.

————. *Motherless Tongues: The Insurgency of Language amid Wars of Translation.*
    Durham, NC: Duke University Press, 2016.

————. "Targeting Translation: Counterinsurgency and the Weaponization of
    Language." *Social Text* 30, no. 4 (113) (2012): 55–80.

Reed, Conor Tomás. *New York Liberation School: Study and Movement for the
    People's University.* Brooklyn, NY: Common Notions, 2023.

Ricoeur, Paul. *On Translation.* London: Routledge, 2006.

Sakai, Naoki. "The Modern Regime of Translation and Its Politics." In *A History of
    Modern Translation Knowledge: Sources, Concepts, Effects,* edited by Lieven
    D'hulst and Yves Gambier, 61–74. Amsterdam: John Benjamins, 2018.

————. "The Regime of Separation and the Performativity of Area." In "The End
    of Area: Biopolitics, Geopolitics, History," edited by Gavin Walker and Naoki
    Sakai. Special issue, *positions: asia critique* 27, no. 1 (2019): 241–79.

————. *Translation and Subjectivity: On "Japan" and Cultural Nationalism.*
    Minneapolis, MN: University of Minnesota Press, 1997.

Sakai, Naoki, and Sandro Mezzadra. Introduction to *translation: a transdisciplinary
    journal,* no. 4 (2014): 9–29.

Sakai, Naoki, and Jon Solomon. "Introduction: Addressing the Multitude of
    Foreigners, Echoing Foucault." In *Translation, Biopolitics, Colonial Difference,*
    vol. 4 of Traces: A Multilingual Series of Cultural Theory and Translation,
    edited by Naoki Sakai and Jon Solomon, 1–35. Hong Kong: Hong Kong
    University Press, 2006.

Scholem, Gershom. "Walter Benjamin and His Angel." In *On Jews and Judaism in
    Crisis: Selected Essays,* edited by Werner J. Dannhauser, 198–236. Philadelphia:
    Paul Dry Books, 2012.

————. *Walter Benjamin: The Story of a Friendship.* Translated by Harry Zohn.
    1981. Reprint, New York: New York Review Books, 2001.

Seidman, Naomi. *Faithful Renderings: Jewish-Christian Difference and the Politics
    of Translation.* Chicago: University of Chicago Press, 2006.

Sekyi-Otu, Ato. *Left Universalism, Africacentric Essays.* New York: Routledge,
    2019.

Spivak, Gayatri Chakravorty. "The Politics of Translation." In *Outside in the
    Teaching Machine,* 200–225. New York: Routledge, 2003.

————. "Translating into English." In *An Aesthetic Education in the Era of
    Globalization,* 256–74. Cambridge, MA: Harvard University Press, 2012.

Sprinker, Michael, ed. *Ghostly Demarcations: A Symposium on Jacques Derrida's
    Specters of Marx.* London: Verso, 2008.

Steiner, George. *After Babel. Aspects of Language and Translation.* 3rd ed. Oxford:
    Oxford University Press, 1998.

Tavmen, Güneş, and Senjuti Chakraborti. "Democracy, Oppression, and Universality:
    An Interview with Étienne Balibar." *Verso Books Blog,* December 7, 2017. https://

www.versobooks.com/blogs/news/3518-democracy-oppression-and-universality-an
-interview-with-etienne-balibar.

Teo, Tze-Yin. *If Babel Had a Form: Translating Equivalence in the Twentieth-Century Transpacific*. New York: Fordham University Press, 2022.

Tomba, Massimiliano. *Insurgent Universality: An Alternative Legacy of Modernity*. Oxford: Oxford University Press, 2019.

Tymozcko, Maria. "Postcolonial Writing and Literary Translation." In *Postcolonial Translation: Theory and Practice*, edited by Susan Bassnett and Harish Trivedi, 19–40. New York: Routledge, 1999.

———, ed. *Translation, Resistance, Activism*. Amherst: University of Massachusetts Press, 2010.

Tymozcko, Maria, and Edwin Gentzler, eds. *Translation and Power*. Amherst: University of Massachusetts Press, 2002.

"Universal Declaration of Human Rights." United Nations. Accessed August 21, 2023. https://www.un.org/en/about-us/universal-declaration-of-human-rights.

Végső, Roland. "Current Trends in Philosophy and Translation." In *The Routledge Handbook of Translation and Philosophy*, edited by Piers Rawling and Philip Wilson, 157–70. New York: Routledge, 2018.

———. "The Parapraxis of Translation." *CR: The New Centennial Review* 12, no. 2 (2012): 47–68.

Venuti, Lawrence. *Contra Instrumentalism: A Translation Polemic*. Lincoln: University of Nebraska Press, 2018.

———. "Local Contingencies: Translation and National Identities." In *Translation Changes Everything*, 116–40.

———. "On a Universal Tendency to Debase Retranslations; or, The Instrumentalism of a Translation Fixation." *PMLA* 138, no. 3 (2023): 598–615.

———. *The Scandals of Translation: Towards an Ethics of Difference*. New York: Routledge, 1998.

———. *Translation Changes Everything: Theory and Practice*. New York: Routledge, 2013.

———. *The Translator's Invisibility: A History of Translation*. London: Routledge, 1995.

Virno, Paolo. *A Grammar of the Multitude: For an Analysis of Contemporary Forms of Life*. Translated by Isabella Bertoletti, James Cascaito, and Andrea Casson. Cambridge: Semiotext(e), 2003.

Walker, Gavin. "The Reinvention of Communism: Politics, History, Globality." In *Communist Currents*, edited by Bruno Bosteels and Jodi Dean, special issue of *South Atlantic Quarterly* 113, no. 4 (2014): 671–85.

Wilder, Gary. *Freedom Time: Negritude, Decolonization, and the Future of the World*. Durham, NC: Duke University Press, 2014.

Xie, Shaobo. "Translation and the Politics of the Universal." *Asia Pacific Translation and Intercultural Studies* 1, no. 1 (2014): 2–11.

Young, Robert J. C. "Philosophy in Translation." In *A Companion to Translation Studies*, edited by Sandra Bermann and Catherine Porter, 41–53. West Sussex, UK: Wiley Blackwell, 2014.

———. *Postcolonialism: An Historical Introduction*. Malden, MA: Blackwell, 2001.

Zerilli, Linda M. G. "This Universalism Which Is Not One." *diacritics* 28, no. 2 (1998): 3–20.

Žižek, Slavoj. "*Da Capo senza Fine*." In Judith Butler, Ernesto Laclau, and Slavoj Žižek, *Contingency, Hegemony, Universality: Contemporary Dialogues on the Left*, 213–62. London: Verso, 2000.

———. *Less than Nothing: Hegel and the Shadow of Dialectical Materialism*. London: Verso, 2012.

———. "Mao Tse-Tung, the Marxist Lord of Misrule." In Mao Zedong, *On Practice and Contradiction*, edited by Slavoj Žižek, 1–28. London: Verso, 2007.

———. *The Ticklish Subject: The Absent Centre of Political Ontology*. London: Verso, 2000.

———. *Welcome to the Desert of the Real: Five Essays on September 11 and Related Dates*. London: Verso, 2002.

Notes

1. Walter Benjamin, "The Task of the Translator," trans. Harry Zohn, in *Selected Writings*, vol. 1, *1913–1926*, ed. Marcus Bullock and Michael W. Jennings (Cambridge, MA: Belknap, 2004), 253–63.

2. Benjamin, "Task of the Translator," 260.

3. Carol Jacobs, *In the Language of Walter Benjamin* (Baltimore: Johns Hopkins University Press, 1999), 84. For the original German, which I included in the excerpted passage of Jacobs's translation, see Walter Benjamin, "Die Aufgabe des Übersetzers," in *Gesammelte Schriften IV/I* (Frankfurt: Suhrkamp Verlag, 1972), 18.

4. On this point, see Jacobs, *In the Language*, 88. See also Paul de Man, *The Resistance to Theory* (Minneapolis: University of Minnesota Press, 1986), 80; Jacques Derrida, "Des tours de Babel," trans. Joseph F. Graham, in *Psyche: Inventions of the Other*, vol. 1, ed. Peggy Kamuf and Elizabeth Rottenberg (Stanford, CA: Stanford University Press, 2007), 200; Eduardo Cadava, *Words of Light: Theses on the Photography of History* (Princeton, NJ: Princeton University Press, 1997), 15.

5. Benjamin, "Task of the Translator," 257.

6. Benjamin, 256, 257. For the German original, see Benjamin, "Die Aufgabe des Übersetzers," 13.

7. On this point, see Gershom Scholem, "Walter Benjamin and His Angel," in *On Jews and Judaism in Crisis: Selected Essays*, ed. Werner J. Dannhauser (Philadelphia: Paul Dry Books, 2012), 233n26; Howard Eiland and Michael W. Jennings, *Walter Benjamin: A Critical Life* (Cambridge, MA: Harvard University Press, 2014), 160; Naomi Seidman, *Faithful Renderings: Jewish-Christian Difference and the Politics of*

Translation (Chicago: University of Chicago Press, 2006), 188. See, relatedly, Gershom Scholem, *Walter Benjamin: The Story of a Friendship*, trans. Harry Zohn (1981; repr., New York: New York Review Books, 2001).

8. The standard English translation of the passage in question reads: "Fragments of a vessel that are to be glued together must match one another in the smallest details, although they need not be like one another. In the same way a translation, instead of imitating the sense of the original, must lovingly and in detail incorporate the original's way of meaning, thus making both the original and the translation recognizable as fragments of a greater language, just as fragments are part of a vessel." Benjamin, "Task of the Translator," 260. As Jacobs points out, this translation "suggests that a totality of fragments are brought together," whereas "Benjamin insists that the final outcome of translation is still 'a broken part.' In the Lurianic doctrine, then, translation would never progress beyond the stage of the *Shevirath Ha-Kelim*." Jacobs, *In the Language*, 127–28n11.

9. Benjamin, "Task of the Translator," 255. For the original German, see Benjamin, "Die Aufgabe des Übersetzers," 12.

10. Benjamin, "Die Aufgabe des Übersetzers," 12. Here I diverge from Jacobs's argument that, for Benjamin, "kinship can *only* be defined negatively." This is also where I would put pressure on de Man's nihilistic (as opposed to messianic) interpretation of Benjamin, which he develops from Jacobs's reading of "The Task of the Translator." See Jacobs, *In the Language*, 80 (my emphasis); de Man, *Resistance to Theory*, 90, 92, 103.

11. Antoine Berman, *The Experience of the Foreign: Culture and Translation in Romantic Germany*, trans. S. Heyvaert (Albany: State University of New York Press, 1992), 13–14.

12. See Berman, *Experience of the Foreign*, 11–12. See, relatedly, Lawrence Venuti, *The Translator's Invisibility: A History of Translation* (New York: Routledge, 2018), 109; Lawrence Venuti, "Local Contingencies: Translation and National Identities," in *Translation Changes Everything: Theory and Practice* (New York: Routledge, 2013), 119, 128.

13. Rudolf Pannwitz as cited in Benjamin, "Task of the Translator," 261–62. For Benjamin's original citation of Pannwitz, see "Die Aufgabe des Übersetzers," 20.

14. "The force of a language is not to reject the foreign, but to devour it." Goethe as cited in Berman, *Experience of the Foreign*, 12.

15. Benjamin, "Task of the Translator," 261.

16. Benjamin, 261.

17. Benjamin, 257.

18. Benjamin, "Die Aufgabe des Übersetzers," 19.

19. Walter Benjamin, "On Language as Such and on the Language of Man," trans. Edmund Jephcott, in *Selected Writings*, vol. 1, 1913–1926, ed. Marcus Bullock and Michael W. Jennings (Cambridge, MA: Belknap, 2004), 72. See, relatedly, Derrida, "Des tours de Babel," in *Psyche*, 191–225; Hent de Vries, "Anti-Babel: The 'Mystical Postulate' in Benjamin, de Certeau and Derrida," *MLN* 107, no. 3 (1992): 441–77.

20. Jacques Derrida, "Roundtable on Translation," trans. Peggy Kamuf, in *The Ear of the Other: Otobiography, Transference, Translation*, ed. Christie V. McDonald (Lincoln: University of Nebraska Press, 1988), 100–101.

21. Derrida, 123.

22. Derrida, 123. The qualification of "good" next to translation is crucial, as not all translations succeed in promising universal reconciliation. For Derrida, "a translation that succeeds in promising reconciliation, in talking about it, desiring it, or making one desire it, such a translation is a rare and notable event." See Derrida, "Des tours de Babel," 213.

23. Jacques Derrida, *Specters of Marx: The State of the Debt, the Work of Mourning, and the New International* (New York: Routledge, 2006), 74, 82, 92. See, relatedly, Maurice Blanchot's discussion of Benjamin and the translator's messianism in "'Translating," in *Friendship*, trans. Elizabeth Rottenberg (Stanford, CA: Stanford University Press, 1997), 57–61. See, in contrast, Michael Löwy's interpretation of Benjamin's messianism in *Redemption and Utopia: Jewish Libertarian Thought in Central Europe* (New York: Verso, 2017), 95–126.

24. This formulation draws from Étienne Balibar's reading of Derrida in *On Universals: Constructing and Deconstructing Community*, trans. Joshua David Jordan (New York: Fordham University Press, 2020), 19–58.

25. See, relatedly, Étienne Balibar, *Secularism and Cosmopolitanism: Critical Hypotheses on Religion and Politics* (New York: Columbia University Press, 2018).

26. Derrida, "Des tours de Babel," in *Psyche*, 199. For the original French, see Jacques Derrida, "Des tours de Babel," in *L'art des confins: Mélanges offerts à Maurice de Gandillac*, ed. Annie Cazenave and Jean-François Lyotard (Paris: Presses Universitaires de France, 1985), 215.

27. For Derrida's related discussion of "the truth of Babel" as a declaration of war on language that nevertheless gives languages, see Jacques Derrida, "Two Words for Joyce," trans. Geoff Bennington, in *Post-structuralist Joyce*, ed. Derek Attridge and Daniel Ferrer (Cambridge: Cambridge University Press, 1984), 145–58.

28. Derrida, "Des tours de Babel," in *L'art des confins*, 215.

29. Derrida, "Des tours de Babel," in *Psyche*, 191. See, relatedly, Balibar's discussion of translation toward the end of *On Universals*, which leads him to envision the political construction of "a certain type of universality," a "universality beyond any unity," that would be "in opposition to others in which multiplicity doesn't have the same constituent role, and in which the relations of domination are consequently less likely to be called into question and challenged." Balibar, *On Universals*, 118–19.

30. For some critical assessments of this tendency, see—among other possible references—Judith Butler, "Restaging the Universal: Hegemony and the Limits of Formalism," in Judith Butler, Ernesto Laclau, and Slavoj Žižek, *Contingency, Hegemony, Universality: Contemporary Dialogues on the Left* (London: Verso, 2000), 11–43; Madhavi Menon, *Indifference to Difference: On Queer Universalism* (Minneapolis: University of Minnesota Press, 2015); Gary Wilder, *Freedom Time:*

Negritude, Decolonization, and the Future of the World (Durham, NC: Duke University Press, 2015), 1–16; Ato Sekyi-Otu, *Left Universalism, Africacentric Essays* (New York: Routledge, 2019); Ilan Kapoor and Zahi Zalloua, *Universal Politics* (Oxford: Oxford University Press, 2022); Marc James Léger, ed., *Identity Trumps Socialism: The Class and Identity Debate after Neoliberalism* (New York: Routledge, 2023).

31. Venuti, "Local Contingencies," 116–40.

32. Victor Hugo as cited in Venuti, "Local Contingencies," 116.

33. Venuti, 116.

34. Venuti, 116.

35. Jacques Derrida as cited in Venuti, 118.

36. Notice how the essay conflates the specific with the general in its discussion of Hugo: "*His universalism* actually reveals the close relationship between his thinking and nationalism. . . . *Universalism* can be useful in criticizing the exclusionary effects of nationalism, but by suppressing linguistic and cultural differences *it* preempts the articulation of theoretical concepts to understand how national identities are formed and what role translation might play in their formation." Venuti, "Local Contingencies," 118 (my emphasis).

37. Venuti, 128.

38. Venuti, 128.

39. Venuti, 128.

40. Venuti, 117.

41. Here I am drawing from Étienne Balibar's discussion of the ambiguity and equivocity of universality in his essay "Ambiguous Universality," in *Politics and the Other Scene*, trans. Christine Jones, James Swenson, and Chris Turner (London: Verso, 2002), 146–75. See also Balibar, *On Universals*, vii–ix.

42. See Lawrence Venuti, *Translation Changes Everything: Theory and Practice* (New York: Routledge, 2013), 215; Venuti, *Translator's Invisibility*, 61, 69, 79, 80, 109, 146; Lawrence Venuti, *The Scandals of Translation: Towards an Ethics of Difference* (New York: Routledge, 1998), 92; Lawrence Venuti, *Contra Instrumentalism: A Translation Polemic* (Lincoln: University of Nebraska Press, 2018), 58, 59, 85, 90; Lawrence Venuti, "On a Universal Tendency to Debase Retranslations; or, The Instrumentalism of a Translation Fixation," *PMLA* 138, no. 3 (2023): 598–615. A notable exception to the antiuniversalist rule can be found in Venuti's *Translation Changes Everything* when he discusses how Alain Badiou theorizes universality in ways that might be useful for thinking about an ethics of translation. See *Translation Changes Everything*, 184–87.

43. Balibar, *On Universals*, 42–43 (emphasis in original).

44. Butler discusses universality as a "site of contest" in "Restaging the Universal," 38. Balibar relatedly discusses universalism as a "site of struggle" in *On Universals*, 4. Here I am combining both formulations to conceive of universality as a site of struggle for different universalisms (that enter into conflict over none other than their different notions of universality). See, relatedly, Linda M. G. Zerilli's discussion of

universality as "a site of multiple significations" in "This Universalism Which Is Not One," *diacritics* 28, no. 2 (1998): 8.

45. For some classic examples, see Susan Bassnett, "Translating for the Theatre: The Case against Performability," *TTR* 4, no. 1 (1991): 99–111; Susan Bassnett, "Still Trapped in the Labyrinth: Further Reflections on Translation and Theatre," in *Constructing Cultures: Essays on Literary Translation*, ed. Susan Bassnett and André Lefevere (Clevendon, UK: Multilingual Matters, 1998), 90–108; Tejaswini Niranjana, *Siting Translation: History, Post-structuralism, and the Colonial Context* (Berkeley: University of California Press, 1992), 9; Maria Tymozcko, "Postcolonial Writing and Literary Translation," in *Postcolonial Translation: Theory and Practice*, ed. Susan Bassnett and Harish Trivedi (New York: Routledge, 1999), 21. For an example outside of translation studies, traditionally construed, see Paul Ricoeur, *On Translation* (London: Routledge, 2006), 9. And finally, for a discussion of the "radically opposed" philosophies of language—universalist vs. monadist—that arguably pave the way for this approach to theorizing translation, see George Steiner, *After Babel: Aspects of Language and Translation*, 3rd ed. (Oxford: Oxford University Press, 1998), 76–77.

46. Naoki Sakai, "The Modern Regime of Translation and Its Politics," in *A History of Modern Translation Knowledge: Sources, Concepts, Effects*, ed. Lieven D'hulst and Yves Gambier (Amsterdam: John Benjamins, 2018), 61–74; Naoki Sakai, *Translation and Subjectivity: On "Japan" and Cultural Nationalism* (Minneapolis: University of Minnesota Press, 1997).

47. Sakai, "Modern Regime of Translation," 61.

48. Sakai, 66.

49. Sakai, 68.

50. Sakai, 70 (emphasis in original). For more on species difference, see Naoki Sakai, "The Regime of Separation and the Performativity of Area," in "The End of Area: Biopolitics, Geopolitics, History," ed. Gavin Walker and Naoki Sakai, special issue, *positions: asia critique* 27, no. 1 (2019): 241–79.

51. Here is how Sakai develops this idea in *Translation and Subjectivity*:

> Let me elaborate on the process in which translation is displaced by its representation, and the constitution of collective subjectivity such as national and ethnic subjectivity in the representation of translation. Through the labor of the translator, the incommensurability as difference that calls for the service of the translator in the first place is negotiated and worked on. In other words, the work of translation is a practice by which the initial discontinuity between the addresser and the addressee is made continuous and recognizable. . . . Only retrospectively and after translation, therefore, can we recognize the initial incommensurability as a gap, crevice, or border between fully constituted entities, spheres, or domains. But, when represented as a gap, crevice, or border, it is no longer incommensurate. (14)

52. Sakai, *Translation and Subjectivity*, 1–17.

53. Sakai, 8.

54. Sakai refers directly to Benjamin on this point in *Translation and Subjectivity*, 5.

55. Sakai, 7.

56. Sakai relatedly discusses particularism and universalism as "oppositional stances that demand one another in their complicity" in *Translation and Subjectivity*, 149.

57. Sakai, 150.

58. Sakai, 149.

59. Sakai, 149.

60. Sakai and Jon Solomon similarly discuss the modern regime of translation as "a globally applicable technique of domination aimed at managing social relationships by forcing them to pass through circuits on the systemic level (such as national sovereignty)." See their essay, "Introduction: Addressing the Multitude of Foreigners, Echoing Foucault," in *Translation, Biopolitics, Colonial Difference*, ed. Naoki Sakai and Jon Solomon (Hong Kong: Hong Kong University Press, 2006), 27.

61. Sakai, *Translation and Subjectivity*, 157.

62. Sakai, "The Modern Regime of Translation," 61.

63. Sakai, *Translation and Subjectivity*, 20, 69, 71, 93, 115, 149, 156.

64. There is one intriguing exception—an exception that perhaps proves the rule—to Sakai's otherwise negative portrayal of universalism. The exception can be found in a different version of his essay "The Modern Regime of Translation and Its Politics," which he coauthored with Sandro Mezzadra to introduce a special issue of *translation: a transdisciplinary journal*. The relevant passage appears just after Mezzadra and Sakai summarize Lydia Liu's contribution to the special issue, which addresses, among other topics, the "competing universals" that are negotiated in and through different translation practices. Mezzadra and Sakai write:

> In brief, we think there is a need to even go beyond the notion of alternative and competing universalisms, which risks ending up reproducing the familiar picture of 'equivalent' (universal) languages, with translation playing the role of arbitrator or mediator among them, thereby restoring the modern regime of translation for national translation rather than undermining it. The point is, instead, to insist that the universal itself . . . has to be produced, and to focus on the necessary roles of translation in this aleatory process of production. These roles cannot but be profoundly ambivalent, and this ambivalence (discussed in this introduction from the point of view provided by the distinction between "homolingual" and "heterolingual" address) shapes universalism as such. Keeping universalism open (open in translation to multiplicity and heterogeneity) means keeping it accessible to the common process of its production, as a basis for the invention of new processes of liberation.

Later in this introduction, I will discuss why I think Liu's conceptualization of competing universals does not fall into the trappings of the modern regime of translation. For now, I just want to underscore some notable tensions at work in the previously cited passage. As in Sakai's other writings, there is a reliance on notions like "the universal itself" and "universalism as such," which often lead to univocal conceptualizations of these ambiguous and equivocal terms. But there is also a brief recognition of a kind of ambivalence internal to universalism, followed by a call to keep universalism open to multiplicity and heterogeneity so that it can serve as the basis for new liberatory processes. These latter suggestions resonate with the aims of the present volume. They also stand in stark contrast with the theoretical maneuver of setting up a rigid opposition between the universal and universalism, on the one hand, and multiplicity and heterogeneity on the other, to then invariably associate any appeal to the universal with the imperialist inscription of difference and any form of universalism with imperialism. See Naoki Sakai and Sandro Mezzadra, introduction to *translation: a transdisciplinary journal*, no. 4 (2014): 26–27. See also Lydia Liu, "The Eventfulness of Translation: Temporality, Difference, and Competing Universals," *translation: a transdisciplinary journal*, no. 4 (2014): 147–70.

65. Dipesh Chakrabarty, *Provincializing Europe: Postcolonial Thought and Historical Difference* (Princeton, NJ: Princeton University Press, 2000), 83–86.

66. Chakrabarty, 85.

67. Chakrabarty, 51–57, 75.

68. Chakrabarty, 82, 83.

69. Chakrabarty, 83, 86.

70. Sandro Mezzadra and Brett Neilson, *Border as Method, or, the Multiplication of Labor* (Durham, NC: Duke University Press, 2013), 275, 298. For their most important references to Chakrabarty and Sakai, see Mezzadra and Neilson, *Border as Method*, 110, 281–84.

71. Mezzadra and Neilson, 275.

72. Mezzadra and Neilson, 281–82, 298.

73. Mezzadra and Neilson, 290–91. Mezzadra and Neilson develop their understanding of the distinction between the common and the universal in conversation with Paolo Virno's *A Grammar of the Multitude: For an Analysis of Contemporary Forms of Life*, trans. Isabella Bertoletti, James Cascaito, and Andrea Casson (Cambridge: Semiotext(e), 2003). For an alternative (and—in my view—far more promising) approach to this distinction, see Cesare Casarino, "Universalism of the Common," *diacritics* 39, no. 4 (2009): 162–76. It is worth noting that elsewhere Mezzadra endorses a similar opposition between the common and the unity of capital's universalizing language of value but goes on—in the very next paragraph— to favorably invoke Judith Butler's theorization of "conflicting notions of universality." It is not entirely clear how to square this moment in Mezzadra's work with the previously cited texts that he coauthored alongside Neilson and Sakai. See Sandro Mezzadra, "Living in Translation: Toward a Heterolingual Theory of the Multitude," in *The Politics of Culture: Around the Work of Naoki Sakai*, ed. Richard Calichman and John Namjun Kim (New York: Routledge, 2010), 134. Mezzadra has in mind Butler's essay "Competing Universalities," in Judith Butler, Ernesto Laclau, and

Slavoj Žižek, *Contingency, Hegemony, Universality: Contemporary Dialogues on the Left* (London: Verso, 2000), 136–81.

74. Much of the work that I have already cited exhibits this approach to translation. For some additional examples, see Eric Cheyfitz, *The Poetics of Imperialism: Translation and Colonization from* The Tempest *to* Tarzan (Oxford: Oxford University Press, 1990); Maria Tymozcko and Edwin Gentzler, eds., *Translation and Power* (Amherst: University of Massachusetts Press, 2002); Emily Apter, *The Translation Zone: A New Comparative Literature* (Princeton, NJ: Princeton University Press, 2006); Michael Hanne, "Metaphors for the Translator," in *The Translator as Writer*, ed. Susan Bassnett and Peter Bush (London: Continuum, 2006), 208–24; Maria Tymozcko, ed., *Translation, Resistance, Activism* (Amherst: University of Massachusetts Press, 2010); Walter Mignolo, "Reflections on Translation across Colonial Epistemic Differences," in *Translatio/n: Narration, Media and the Staging of Differences*, ed. Federico Italiano and Michael Rössner (Bielefeld: transcript, 2012); Ben Conisbee Baer, "What Is Special about Postcolonial Translation?," in *A Companion to Translation Studies*, ed. Sandra Bermann and Catherine Porter (West Sussex, UK: Wiley Blackwell, 2014), 233–45; Christi A. Merrill, "Collaborations at the University of Michigan: Decolonizing Translation Studies," *PMLA* 138, no. 3 (2023): 824–31.

75. For the formulation attributed to Vicente Rafael, see the back cover of *Motherless Tongues: The Insurgency of Language amid Wars of Translation* (Durham, NC: Duke University Press, 2016). A variation of this formulation appears in the book itself on pages 118–19. See also Vicente Rafael, "Targeting Translation: Counterinsurgency and the Weaponization of Language," *Social Text* 30, no. 4 (113) (2012): 55–80; Vicente Rafael, "Linguistic Currencies: The Translative Power of English in Southeast Asia and the United States," *The Translator* 25, no. 2 (2019): 142–58. For Gayatri Chakravorty Spivak's opportune phrase, see "Translating into English," in *An Aesthetic Education in the Era of Globalization* (Cambridge, MA: Harvard University Press, 2012), 270. See, relatedly, Gayatri Chakravorty Spivak, "The Politics of Translation," in *Outside in the Teaching Machine* (New York: Routledge, 2003), 200–225.

76. The inverse position—theorists of universality who are skeptical of or even vilify translation—is far less common, though not inexistent. The reader could turn, for example, to Slavoj Žižek's polemic against the multiculturalism of postcolonial theory in *Welcome to the Desert of the Real*. There he counterposes a notion of universality as "an infinite task of translation" between different cultures to the "actual universality" of a shared antagonism "across the cultural divide." See Slavoj Žižek, *Welcome to the Desert of the Real: Five Essays on September 11 and Related Dates* (London: Verso, 2002), 65–66. See, relatedly, Slavoj Žižek, "Da Capo senza Fine," in Judith Butler, Ernesto Laclau, and Slavoj Žižek, *Contingency, Hegemony, Universality: Contemporary Dialogues on the Left* (London: Verso, 2000), 213–62. This more combative stance can be distinguished from the longstanding tendency within certain philosophical traditions either to ignore questions of language and

translation altogether or to construe them as ultimately unimportant insofar as philosophy, in Barbara Cassin's words, "relates only to a universal logic, identical in all times and all places—for Aristotle, for my colleague at Oxford." As the institutional reference suggests, Cassin associates this approach with analytic philosophy produced in English; however, it could also refer to the Platonism and Pauline universalism of Cassin's French colleague and collaborator, Alain Badiou. See Barbara Cassin's introduction to *Dictionary of Untranslatables: A Philosophical Lexicon*, ed. Barbara Cassin, translation ed. Emily Apter, Jacques Lezra, and Michael Wood (Princeton, NJ: Princeton University Press 2014), xviii; Alain Badiou, "French," in *Dictionary of Untranslatables: A Philosophical Lexicon*, ed. Barbara Cassin, translation ed. Emily Apter, Jacques Lezra, and Michael Wood (Princeton, NJ: Princeton University Press 2014), 349–54; Alain Badiou, *Saint Paul: The Foundation of Universalism*, trans. Ray Brassier (Stanford, CA: Stanford University Press, 2003). See, relatedly, Robert J. C. Young, "Philosophy in Translation," in *A Companion to Translation Studies*, ed. Sandra Bermann and Catherine Porter (West Sussex, UK: Wiley Blackwell, 2014), 41–53; Roland Végső, "Current Trends in Philosophy and Translation," in *The Routledge Handbook of Translation and Philosophy*, ed. Piers Rawling and Philip Wilson (New York: Routledge, 2018), 157–70.

77. Balibar, "Ambiguous Universality," 147 (emphasis in original).

78. Balibar, 147 (emphasis in original). Balibar begins *On Universals* with a summary of "Ambiguous Universality." If, in the earlier essay, Balibar writes about the "insurmountable *equivocity*" of the concept of the universal, in the more recent text he advances a slightly different formulation, insisting on the "*intrinsic equivocity* of the notion of the universal or universality." Balibar's writings, in other words, contain some terminological vacillation, which is not to say terminological imprecision, between the universal and universality (as well as between the insurmountable and the intrinsic). Compare "Ambiguous Universality," 147; *On Universals*, 1. At other moments in his oeuvre, however, Balibar discusses several ways to distinguish the universal from universality and universalism, including in *On Universals*, 44–46, 96. See, relatedly, Güneş Tavmen and Senjuti Chakraborti, "Democracy, Oppression, and Universality: An Interview with Étienne Balibar," *Verso Books* (blog), December 7, 2017, https://www.versobooks.com/blogs/news/3518 -democracy-oppression-and-universality-an-interview-with-etienne-balibar.

79. Balibar, "Ambiguous Universality," 156 (emphasis in original).

80. Balibar, 173.

81. Karl Marx and Frederick Engels, "Manifesto of the Communist Party," in *Collected Works of Karl Marx and Frederick Engels*, vol. 6, *1845–1848* (New York: International Press, 1976), 477–519.

82. See, on this point, Étienne Balibar, *Masses, Classes, Ideas: Studies on Politics and Philosophy before and after Marx* (New York: Routledge, 1994), 204.

83. On the problem of the "missed encounter," see José Aricó, *Marx and Latin America*, trans. David Broder (Chicago: Haymarket Books, 2014); Bruno Bosteels,

Marx and Freud in Latin America: Politics, Psychoanalysis, and Religion in Times of Terror (London: Verso, 2012); Álvaro García Linera, "Indianism and Marxism: The Disparity between Two Revolutionary Rationales," in *Plebeian Power: Collective Action and Indigenous, Working-Class and Popular Identities in Bolivia* (Chicago: Haymarket Books, 2015), 305–21; Jeffrey Gould, "Ignacio Ellacuría and the Salvadorean Revolution," *Journal of Latin American Studies* 47, no. 2 (2015): 285–315. See also Gavin Arnall, "The Missed Encounter of *Turupukllay*: Marxism, Indigenous Communities, and Andean Culture in *Yawar Fiesta*," *Radical Americas* 5, no. 1 (2020): 1–16; Gavin Arnall, "Latin American Marxisms: Reading José Carlos Mariátegui and José Aricó Today," *Journal of Latin American Studies* 29, no. 3 (2021): 489–99. For a related discussion of transforming rather than abandoning institutions, see Conor Tomás Reed, *New York Liberation School: Study and Movement for the People's University* (Brooklyn, NY: Common Notions, 2023).

84. Some other relevant texts that take this same approach—often implicitly or explicitly building upon the work of Balibar, Butler, and Liu—include Saša Hrnjez, "Translational Universality: The Struggle over the Universal," *Labyrinth* 21, no. 2 (2019): 118–37; Kimberly Hutchings, "Universalism in Feminist International Ethics: Gender and the Difficult Labour of Translation," in *Dialogue, Politics and Gender*, ed. Jude Browne (Cambridge: Cambridge University Press, 2013), 81–106; Tze-Yin Teo, *If Babel Had a Form: Translating Equivalence in the Twentieth-Century Transpacific* (New York: Fordham University Press, 2022); Roland Végső, "The Parapraxis of Translation," *CR: The New Centennial Review* 12, no. 2 (2012): 47–68; Shaobo Xie, "Translation and the Politics of the Universal," *Asia Pacific Translation and Intercultural Studies* 1, no. 1 (2014): 2–11.

85. Ernesto Laclau, "Constructing Universality," in Judith Butler, Ernesto Laclau, and Slavoj Žižek, *Contingency, Hegemony, Universality: Contemporary Dialogues on the Left* (London: Verso, 2000), 304. See, relatedly, Ernesto Laclau and Chantal Mouffe, *Hegemony and Socialist Strategy: Towards a Radical Democratic Politics* (London: Verso, 1985).

86. Laclau, "Constructing Universality," 302–3. See also Ernesto Laclau, "Why Do Empty Signifiers Matter to Politics?," in *Emancipation(s)* (London: Verso, 1996), 36–46.

87. Butler, "Competing Universalities," 166–67 (emphasis in original).

88. Michael Hardt helped me think through this "relation without hegemony" after a talk that I delivered at Duke University on January 27, 2023. For a discussion of this passage from Butler and its relevance for thinking about the contemporary Zapatista movement, see Gavin Arnall, "The Many Tasks of the Marxist Translator: Approaching Marxism as/in/with Translation from Antonio Gramsci to the Zapatistas," *Historical Materialism* 30, no. 1 (2022): 99–132.

89. Lydia Liu, "Shadows of Universalism: The Untold Story of Human Rights around 1948," *Critical Inquiry*, no. 40 (2014): 385–417. See also Liu, "The Eventfulness of Translation," 155–68.

90. Liu, "Shadows of Universalism," 388.

91. Liu, 388.

92. Liu, 406.

93. Mezzadra and Sakai overlook this point when they suggest that Liu's notion of competing universals risks "reproducing the familiar picture of 'equivalent' (universal) languages, with translation playing the role of arbitrator or mediator between them, thereby restoring the modern regime of translation for national translation rather than undermining it." Enlightenment and Confucian ideas are not represented as pertaining to separate and self-enclosed traditions of philosophy, which would make them analogous to individuated national languages under the modern regime of translation. Instead, they are conceived as *already* entangled, as *already* bound up with each other and therefore marked by a certain hybridity *before* Chang's practice of translation. It follows that Chang's task, to reiterate, is to establish a new relationship between these radically different yet related traditions, one that would contribute to liberating human rights from its parochialization or provincialization, keeping human rights—in the words of Mezzadra and Sakai— "open in translation to multiplicity and heterogeneity." See Sakai and Mezzadra, introduction to *translation:a transdisciplinary journal*, 26, 27. Compare with Liu's discussion of Chang in "The Eventfulness of Translation," 155–62.

94. Lydia Liu, introduction to *Tokens of Exchange: The Problem of Translation in Global Circulations*, ed. Lydia Liu (Durham, NC: Duke University Press, 1999), 1. Liu implies that this is the case for universalism as such, which is in tension—in my view—with her discussion of "competing universalisms" in another essay for the same volume. See Lydia Liu, "The Question of Meaning-Value in the Political Economy of the Sign," in *Tokens of Exchange*, 19.

95. Liu, "Shadows of Universalism," 408. For expanded discussions of the practice of translingual reworking, see Lydia H. Liu, *Translingual Practice: Literature, National Culture, and Translated Modernity—China, 1900–1937* (Stanford, CA: Stanford University Press, 1995); Lydia H. Liu, *The Clash of Empires: The Invention of China in Modern World Making* (Cambridge, MA: Harvard University Press, 2006).

96. Liu, "Shadows of Universalism," 411.

97. In English, Article 1 of the Universal Declaration of Human Rights reads: "All human beings are born free and equal in dignity and rights. They are endowed with reason and conscience and should act towards one another in a spirit of brotherhood." See "Universal Declaration of Human Rights," United Nations, accessed August 21, 2023, https://www.un.org/en/about-us/universal-declaration-of -human-rights. Liu refers to the precarity of Chang's efforts in "Shadows of Universalism," 389, 406, 408, 410, 412. Liu develops the theoretical and political implications of her thinking about translation as a precarious wager in "The Eventfulness of Translation," 151–55.

98. Liu, "Shadows of Universalism," 411.

99. My interpretation of Liu's argument stems from a passage that can be found in her edited volume, *Tokens of Exchange*: "The articulation of *difference as value* within a structure of unequal exchange thus simultaneously victimizes that

difference by translating it as *lesser value* or *nonuniversal value*. To overcome this conceptual barrier, I propose that we substitute the notion of *competing universalisms* for cultural particularity to help understand the modes of cultural exchange and their genealogies beyond the existing accounts of colonial encounter." See Liu, "The Question of Meaning-Value," 19 (emphasis in original). See, relatedly, Lydia Liu and James St. André, "The Battleground of Translation: Making Equal in a Global Structure of Inequality," *Alif*, no. 38 (2018): 384–87.

100. Balibar, *Secularism and Cosmopolitanism*, 22 (emphasis in original). See, relatedly, Emily Apter, "Cosmopolitics," in *Thinking with Balibar: A Lexicon of Conceptual Practice*, ed. Ann Laura Stoler, Stathis Gourgouris, and Jacques Lezra (New York: Fordham University Press, 2020), 94–116.

101. Balibar, *On Universals*, 27; Balibar, *Secularism and Cosmopolitanism*, xxxi.

102. Balibar is not always consistent on this point; sometimes conflict and competition appear together without clear distinction. This is the case, for example, when he describes antagonisms between the religious and the secular as *"conflicts between competing universalities."* Balibar, *Secularism and Cosmopolitanism*, 21 (emphasis in original).

103. Balibar, *On Universals*, 28 (emphasis in original).

104. Étienne Balibar, "Further Reflections on Exile: War and Translation," in *Conflicting Humanities*, ed. Rosi Braidotti and Paul Gilroy (London: Bloomsbury, 2016), 211–27.

105. Balibar, "Further Reflections on Exile," 213 (emphasis in original). See, relatedly, Étienne Balibar, "Politics and Translation: Reflections on Lyotard, Derrida, and Said," trans. Gavin Walker, in "The End of Area: Biopolitics, Geopolitics, History," ed. Gavin Walker and Naoki Sakai, special issue, *positions: asia critique* 27, no. 1 (2019): 99–114.

106. This is perhaps why Apter intriguingly suggests that, for Balibar, cosmopolitics *"is translation."* To qualify this assertion, she explains that "its politics are flush with acts of translating," which could be restated as *acts that attempt the impossible*. See Apter, "Cosmopolitics," 97 (emphasis in original).

107. In the closing paragraph of his essay *"Vergangene Vergangenheit? (A Past with No Future?),"* Balibar suggests that it was the conflict between liberalism and communism, rather than either side of the conflict, that produced "the most powerful driving forces of democratic progress and advances." This formulation is somewhat enigmatic, raising more questions than it answers, including if, for Balibar, said forces of progress were the product of translation between liberal and communist phrasings of the universal or if they emerged by breaking with both sides of the opposition, by opposing that which united them to form a third way. See Étienne Balibar, *"Vergangene Vergangenheit? (A Past with No Future?),"* in *Europe and the World: World War I as Crisis of Universalism*, ed. Kai Evers and David Pan (Candor, NY: Telos, 2018), 271.

108. Balibar, *Secularism and Cosmopolitanism*, 52, 53.

109. Here it would be tempting to read Balibar as drawing a distinction between a mode of translation bound to particularity (i.e., the negotiation of cultural differences) and a mode of translation bound to universality (i.e., the linking of incompatible religious discourses); however, Balibar maintains that intercultural translation is not solely particularistic, that this mode of translation corresponds to a *multiculturalist horizon of universality*. In this way, his thinking resonates with that of Benjamin and Derrida, as presented in the opening section of this introduction. See Balibar, *Secularism and Cosmopolitanism*, 51–52.

110. Balibar, *Secularism and Cosmopolitanism*, 53.

111. Balibar, xxxi.

112. Balibar writes: "The 'religious' as such always marks *the point of the untranslatable*." Balibar, *Secularism and Cosmopolitanism*, 52 (emphasis in original). For a critical rejoinder to this view, see Judith Butler, *Parting Ways: Jewishness and the Critique of Zionism* (New York: Columbia University Press, 2012), 8–18. Butler is responding to an earlier version of the argument Balibar develops in *Secularism and Cosmopolitanism* that can be found here: Étienne Balibar, "Cosmopolitanism and Secularism: Controversial Legacies and Prospective Interrogations," *Grey Room*, no. 44 (2011): 6–25.

113. Balibar, *Secularism and Cosmopolitanism*, 52.

114. Balibar, 54.

115. See Étienne Balibar, *We, the People of Europe? Reflections on Transnational Citizenship*, trans. James Swenson (Princeton, NJ: Princeton University Press, 2004), 234. See also Balibar's discussion of translators as *"evanescent mediators"* in *On Universals*, 81 (emphasis in original).

116. Balibar, *Secularism and Cosmopolitanism*, 55.

117. Balibar, 53, 54. See, relatedly, Balibar's discussion of how Spinoza and Wittgenstein "translate" across the disjunction between theoretical and practical universalisms in *On Universals*, 65–66.

118. Here I am paraphrasing Balibar, who alludes to "the civilizing (in the sense of civility) of religious antagonisms" and the *"pacification of religious conflicts*, or, still better, their *conversion* or *sublimation* into ideals capable of relativizing communitarian affiliations." See Balibar, *Secularism and Cosmopolitanism*, 51, 52 (emphasis in original). See, relatedly, Étienne Balibar, *Violence and Civility: On the Limits of Political Philosophy*, trans. G. M. Goshgarian (New York: Columbia University Press, 2015).

119. There may in fact be a deeper disagreement between Balibar and Butler (beyond their disagreement concerning the untranslatability of the religious, as mentioned in a previous note). Balibar frequently and sympathetically cites Butler's conceptualization of competing universalities, but he also seems to challenge some of the conclusions that Butler draws from the core example of this phenomenon in the relevant essay from *Contingency, Hegemony, Universality*. As if writing directly to Butler, Balibar states in *On Universals* that

racist or sexist processes of domination (and the violence to which they
lead) naturally tend to instrumentalize not only their respective prejudices
(and thus to mutually reinforce one another) but also *the resistances those
prejudices provoke.* There is a "racist" use of feminism just as there is a
"sexist" use of antiracism, daily examples of which can be found in
contemporary relations between the Euro-American West and the Islamic
world. It is thus impossible to imagine—except in a kind of utopian
communism of emancipatory struggles that is regularly contradicted in
practice—any kind of convergence or fusion of antiracist and antisexist
resistance movements, even if one assumes (as many do) that to a certain
extent they share the "same" enemy.

Here Balibar discredits as a utopian fantasy one of Butler's key claims from
"Competing Universalities": that translation has the capacity to negotiate the tensions
and contradictions between antiracist and antisexist movements—including with
respect to their competing notions of universality—in order to build an alliance or
coalition between said movements. If efforts of this kind have not always succeeded, I
would argue that there are indeed past and present examples of genuine convergence
between antiracist and antisexist movements (e.g., the Zapatista experiment) and
that even if we did not have any examples from which to draw inspiration, this
would not foreclose the possibility of imagining (and fighting for) a different future.
See Balibar, *On Universals*, 7 (emphasis in original). Compare with Butler,
"Competing Universalities," 166–67. On the antiracist and antisexist struggle of the
Zapatistas, see, among other possible references, Hilary Klein, *Compañeras:
Zapatista Women's Stories* (New York: Seven Stories, 2015).

120. See Balibar, *We, the People of Europe?*, 233. Balibar does not go on to specify
what place sublimated religious conflict would have in this new society to come, but
perhaps this is because such an issue cannot be decided in advance without lapsing
into utopian speculation about an unknown future. On the utopian implications of
speculatively mapping what would come after the withering away of a historical
phenomenon, see Vladimir Ilyich Lenin, *The State and Revolution: The Marxist
Theory of the State and the Tasks of the Proletariat in the Revolution*, in *Collected
Works*, vol. 25 (Moscow: Progress, 1964), 385–497.

121. For my use of the term "subterranean," see Louis Althusser, "The
Underground Current of the Materialism of the Encounter," in *Philosophy of the
Encounter: Later Writings, 1978–1987*, trans. G. M. Goshgarian (London: Verso,
2008), 163–207; Emilio de Ípola's *Althusser, The Infinite Farewell*, trans. Gavin
Arnall (Durham, NC: Duke University Press, 2018); Gavin Arnall, *Subterranean
Fanon: An Underground Theory of Radical Change* (New York: Columbia
University Press, 2020), 1–33.

122. See Emily Apter, *Against World Literature: On the Politics of Untranslatability*
(London: Verso, 2013); Jacques Lezra, *On the Nature of Marx's Things: Translation
as Necrophilology* (New York: Fordham University Press, 2018); Mukti Lakhi

Mangharam, *Literatures of Liberation: Non-European Universalisms and Democratic Progress* (Columbus: Ohio State University Press, 2017); Ngũgĩ wa Thiong'o, *The Language of Languages: Reflections on Translation* (London: Seagull Books, 2023).

123. For more nuanced approaches to the relationship between deconstruction and Marxism, approaches that are at the same time very different from and even at odds with each other, see Jacques Derrida, *Specters of Marx*; Fredric Jameson, "The Three Names of the Dialectic" and "Marx's Purloined Letter," in *Valences of the Dialectic* (London: Verso, 2010), 3–70, 127–80. See, relatedly, Michael Sprinker, ed., *Ghostly Demarcations: A Symposium on Jacques Derrida's Specters of Marx* (London: Verso, 2008).

124. Homi Bhabha's *The Location of Culture* (London: Routledge, 1994) exemplifies this approach. When Chakrabarty and Venuti draw from deconstruction, as previously discussed, they also participate in this line of reasoning.

125. Balibar, *On Universals*, 21 (emphasis in original).

126. Along with the texts already cited, see especially the universalist formulations concerning language and translation advanced in Jacques Derrida, *Monolingualism of the Other; or, The Prosthesis of Origin*, trans. Patrick Mensah (Stanford, CA: Stanford University Press, 1998); Jacques Derrida, "What Is a 'Relevant' Translation?," trans. Lawrence Venuti, *Critical Inquiry*, no. 27 (2001): 174–200.

127. The beginnings of this kind of work can be found in David E. Johnson's engaging book, *Kant's Dog: On Borges, Philosophy, and the Time of Translation* (Albany: State University of New York Press, 2012).

128. This was especially the case during the Stalinist phase of the Third International, when incredibly diverse geopolitical conjunctures were grouped together under a series of abstract categorizations (e.g., colonial, semicolonial, and dependent countries) and the same overall strategy was routinely imposed throughout much of the globe based on a unilinear view of historical development. On this point, see Robert J. C. Young, *Postcolonialism: An Historical Introduction* (Malden, MA: Blackwell, 2001). For a discussion of how Marx himself broke with a unilinear view of historical development, see Kevin Anderson, *Marx at the Margins: On Nationalism, Ethnicity, and Non-Western Societies* (Chicago: University of Chicago Press, 2010).

129. V. I. Lenin, "The Junius Pamphlet," in *Collected Works*, vol. 22 (Moscow: Progress, 1964), 316.

130. For more on this point, see Arnall, "Many Tasks of the Marxist Translator," 99–132; Arnall, *Subterranean Fanon*, 6–14; Gavin Arnall, "Hacia una teoría de la práctica teórica: Mariátegui, marxismo y traducción," *Escrituras Americanas* 2, no. 2 (2017): 43–80.

131. From the Latin American context, see—among other recent texts—Mike Gonzalez, *In the Red Corner: The Marxism of José Carlos Mariátegui* (Chicago: Haymarket Books, 2019); Martín Cortés, *Translating Marx: José Aricó and the New Latin American Marxism*, trans. Nicolas Allen (Chicago: Haymarket Books, 2020); Arnall, "Latin American Marxisms." For how this issue gets addressed in other

contexts, see Nergis Ertürk and Özge Serin, eds., *Marxism, Communism, and Translation*, special issue of *boundary 2: an international journal of literature and culture* 43, no. 3 (2016); Rocco Lacorte, "Translation and Marxism," in *The Routledge Handbook of Translation and Politics*, ed. Jonathan Evans and Fruela Fernández (New York: Routledge, 2018), 17–28; Fadi A. Bardawil, *Revolution and Disenchantment: Arab Marxism and the Binds of Emancipation* (Durham, NC: Duke University Press, 2020).

132. In another text that dialogues with the one included in this volume, Cassin acknowledges the problem of evoking "a universal" in the singular yet simultaneously signals her openness to Diagne's approach in doing just that: "If there is such a thing as a universal (I am not convinced that this is the most appropriate word), it is not 'overarching,' but 'lateral,' and it is called translation." Barbara Cassin, "The Energy of the Untranslatables: Translation as a Paradigm for the Human Sciences," *Paragraph* 38, no. 2 (2015): 146. In his contribution to this volume, Diagne cites the French version of this same passage as it appears in the following text: Barbara Cassin, *Philosopher en langues. Les intraduisibles en traduction* (Paris: Éditions Rue d'Ulm, 2014), 10.

133. The latter formulation resonates with Cassin's observation that each language "performs a world; and the shared world is less a point of departure than a regulatory principle." Cassin, introduction to *Dictionary of Untranslatables*, xlx.

134. See, on this point, Slavoj Žižek, *The Ticklish Subject: The Absent Centre of Political Ontology* (London: Verso, 2000), 171–244; Slavoj Žižek, "Mao Tse-Tung, the Marxist Lord of Misrule," in Mao's *On Practice and Contradiction*, ed. Slavoj Žižek (London: Verso, 2007), 1–28; Slavoj Žižek, *Less than Nothing: Hegel and the Shadow of Dialectical Materialism* (London: Verso, 2012), 359–67.

135. For more on this debate as it pertains to universalism, see Balibar, *On Universals*, 88–89.

136. The careful reader can find evidence in Baer's essay of both the stronger and the weaker argument concerning primitive accumulation and diagnostics.

137. In his contribution to this volume, Wilder cites Diagne's use of the phrase, "putting in touch," which is attributed to Antoine Berman. See Souleymane Bachir Diagne, *The Ink of Scholars: Reflections on Philosophy in Africa* (Dakar: CODESRIA, 2016), xx.

138. For a discussion of Gramsci's thinking about translation and concrete universality, see Arnall, "Many Tasks of the Marxist Translator," 100–107.

139. See Asad Haider, *Mistaken Identity: Race and Class in the Age of Trump* (London: Verso, 2018); Massimiliano Tomba, *Insurgent Universality: An Alternative Legacy of Modernity* (Oxford: Oxford University Press, 2019).

140. In my reading, much of Sakai's work could be included in this broader tendency of refusal. If this is the case, then there is arguably some underlying tension between Walker's discussion of universality and his discussion of translation, insofar as the latter relies heavily on certain key ideas borrowed from Sakai. Put another way, I view Walker's theorization of universality as problematizing how

Sakai conceptualizes the modern regime of translation and its mobilization of species or specific difference, even as Walker draws from these same formulations to develop his own thinking about translation.

141. I offer a preliminary response to this question here: Gavin Arnall, "The Idea(s) of Occupy," *Theory & Event* 15, no. 2 (June 2012), http://muse.jhu.edu/journals /theory_and_event/v015/15.2.arnall.html.

142. I also wonder if Walker's discussion of the universal as a Kantian regulative idea might be at odds with his theorization elsewhere of the communist idea and what, borrowing from Hegel, he calls "its process of *actualization*." See Gavin Walker, "The Reinvention of Communism: Politics, History, Globality," in *Communist Currents*, ed. Bruno Bosteels and Jodi Dean, special issue of *South Atlantic Quarterly* 113, no. 4 (2014): 677 (emphasis in original). See, relatedly, Alain Badiou, *The Communist Hypothesis*, trans. David Macey and Steve Corcoran (London: Verso, 2010); Bruno Bosteels, *The Actuality of Communism* (London: Verso, 2011).

"Plus d'une langue": The Paradigm of Translation

Barbara Cassin
Translated by Katie Chenoweth

To begin, allow me to toss out a phrase, as a kind of motto.[1] It was first spoken by Umberto Eco during a lecture and has often been quoted by well-advised ministers in France and elsewhere: "The language of Europe is translation." I would even broaden this phrase to say: "The language of the world is translation." To indicate the direction I would like to take, I would say that translation is what can allow us—what allows me, in any event, and for the moment—to complicate the universal. To complicate the universal: it seems to me that this is what all of us need, politically as well as philosophically.

What does it mean to "complicate the universal"? This entails, in my view, not presupposing that there is only one, a single universal that surmounts and overtakes everything, a universal like the one that Souleymane Bachir Diagne, taking up Merleau-Ponty and reflecting in particular on the postcolonial, calls an "overarching universal" [*universel de surplomb*].[2] There would thus be multiple universals, and we might wonder, along with Heinz Wismann, for example, what to do with a sentence like "my universal is more universal than yours," which is what disagreements between philosophers, or even between politicians, often come down to at bottom.

For it is a matter, in philosophy as well as politics, of articulating differences. Making these differences work or play together, for the better and not for the worse, is the main problem today. This then leads to the question of multiculturalism. You may recall what Angela Merkel said in 2010, that the multicultural approach has "utterly failed."[3] Well, this diagnosis is the diagnosis of a particular person, at a particular moment, just as the universal is always the universal of a particular person, at a particular moment. This diagnosis needs to be relativized. That is what I want to attempt to do, with the help of the paradigm of translation. Indeed, I think that today translation is the best paradigm—I say the best, not at all the only one—for the human sciences. For it allows us to articulate not simply plurality, that is, the plural of singulars like me (*hoi Athēnaoi*, "the Athenians," to say Athens, that oh-so-unique city whose name marks the plural, *Athēnai*), a plurality that is already as such a minimal condition of the political, but also diversity, others and still more others, like me not like me, which is the more challenging condition of a multicultural politics, and perhaps, in the end, of a politics *tout court*. People like me not like me, how is this articulated, together and with me?

Well, this diversity is evidently and from the beginning the condition of languages. Diversity, *Verschiedenheit*, this is the key word for [Wilhelm von] Humboldt, the great German linguist, philologist, philosopher, and diplomat of the late eighteenth century who worked on the "rare" languages Kawi and Basque, whereas his brother Alexander gathered orchids and butterflies; this is his word to describe languages. In *Über der Verschiedenheit*, he maintains that "language manifests itself in reality exclusively as diversity."[4] Humboldt made me realize that we never encounter language [*langage*]; instead, we encounter the diversity of languages [*langues*]. In place of Heidegger's "there is Being," *es gibt Sein*, and the *Sprache*, the language that speaks Being and to which the human, as the shepherd of Being, has to consent, let us take as our point of departure this "there are languages." If we are then in the ontic, and no longer in the ontological, too bad, or so much the better, for it is possible that "ontological difference" is no longer the task of thinking. This diversity is what I believe is essential to think for our world today: beyond plurality, then, diversity.

I would like to begin again from the title "*Plus d'une langue*," which I place in quotation marks: indeed, it is a phrase from Jacques Derrida. Derrida proposes this injunction-observation to define deconstruction, that is, his own work, all of his work, in philosophy. He writes in 1988 in *Memoires for Paul de Man*: "If I had to risk a single definition of deconstruction, one as brief, elliptical, and economical as a watchword, I would say without more words: *plus d'une langue* ["more than one language" and "no more *a* language"].[5] It is remarkable that this idea, "*plus d'une langue*," sums up and defines one of the most contemporary projects to critique and develop the history of philosophy and, by the same token, philosophy itself. What interests me, even more directly than deconstruction, is the way this same injunctive observation is taken up in the insert of a little book written in 1996, *Monolingualism of the Other*. This magnificent oxymoron is perfectly suited to what I am saying here. In *Monolingualism of the Other*, Derrida returns to his own experience as a young Algerian Jewish *pied noir* to whom Arabic was taught, in Algeria, as an optional foreign language, and to his relation to French, the language he speaks. He offers us in the beginning of this book an aporia as fearsome as the very title of his book, *Monolingualism of the Other*. Here is how he utters this aporia, which is, moreover, constructed or "implicated" in a very French syntax:

> *On ne parle jamais une seule langue,*
> *On ne parle jamais qu'une seule langue.*[6]

> One never speaks only one language,
> One only ever speaks only one language.[7]

A pragmatic contradiction if there ever was one, for which German or Anglo-American theorists will reproach him—as a very French philosopher, precisely—and which will in fact contribute to confining Derrida to departments of "French Studies" or "Comparative Literature"[8] rather than philosophy. They will say to him: "'You are a skeptic, a relativist, a nihilist. . . . If you continue, you will be placed in a department of rhetoric or literature. If you keep going . . . , you will be confined to the department of sophistry.'"[9] This threat delights me, of course, as does the diagnosis of relativism. For what magnetized my own work in ancient philosophy, and in philosophy *tout court*, is the relation between sophistry and established, traditional, dominant philosophy, be it that of Parmenides, Plato, or Aristotle. "Speaking for the sake of speaking," *legein logou kharin*, to speak without bending to the principle of non-contradiction—this is indeed Aristotle's criticism of sophistry.[10] To speak "gratuitously," to speak at a "pure loss" as Jacques Lacan says of psychoanalysis, to speak for the pleasure of speaking, and not to speak the truth or seek it out.

Philosophy, generally speaking, knows and professes two very distinct regimes of language: the first is that of "speaking of," in an apophantic mode, to say on the basis of (*apo*) the phenomenon of which one speaks, in the mode of true or false (here, now, I say: "this table, the one I am touching, is light brown," and it's true, you see that it is so); the second is that of "speaking to," what I am doing now, I am addressing you, I am trying to convince you—of what you do not yet know (perhaps I do know in part, but that's not so certain); in short, I'm doing what philosophy calls "rhetoric," and this regime of the persuasive or convincing is, since Plato, left to sophistry. It is ontologically devalued as dealing with the probable, with *doxa*, and not with the true, but it is also devalued politically and linked to "demagogy," in comparison to the action of the philosopher-king who, for his part, aims for the True and the Good.

There is, however, a third discursive regime, precisely that of "speaking for the sake of speaking." In this case it is a matter not of saying what is, nor of creating an effect on/over the other, but of bringing into being what is said, of creating what I call a "world-effect." To make something by speaking, to "perform," if you will, such was the characteristic discourse regime of the sophists who, in fact, produced the Greek city-state, "the most talkative of all" (Jacob Burckhardt), as *agōn*, an intertwining and competition of speech.[11] Plato calls this *epidexis*, a one-man show,[12] a performance, if you will, as distinct from Socratic dialogue. I find the term "performance" to be very appropriate, since it refers to what [J. L.] Austin, in the modern era, calls "speech acts,"[13] and, more especially, what he dubs "performatives." This third dimension of language is what Austin boasts of discovering and inventing. For example: "court is in session" when a judge says it, or "I now pronounce you man and wife" when a mayor says it.[14] These phrases, these little phrases, bring into being what they say. "The utterance is the act," to use [Émile] Benveniste's expression when he comments on Austin.[15] The performative is the most active little act point [*la petite pointe d'acte la plus agissante*] in the performance, or, the performance is a generalized performativity.

Sophistic performance is indeed, for better and not for worse, the discursive regime that allows me to appropriate Jacques Derrida. For each language makes something like its world, and translation is what relates the different worlds and cultures that different languages are. It is on this basis that I understand the injunction-observation *"plus d'une langue."* One never speaks only one language, one only ever speaks only one language: this is why I'm delighted that Derrida has been confined to a department of sophistry.

The second Derrida phrase I would like to add to the same dossier is: "a language is not something that belongs." I would like to read it to you in context, drawn from Derrida's final book, *Learning to Live Finally*, a book published just after his death, the title of which he chose knowing just how mortal he was. *Learning to Live Finally*: that is an oxymoron par excellence when one is dying, when one is dead. Here it is:

> Love in general passes by way of the love of language, which is neither nationalistic nor conservative, but which demands testimonials—and trials. You don't just go and do anything with language; it preexists us and it survives us. When you introduce something into language, you have to do it in a refined manner, by respecting through disrespect its secret law. That's what might be called unfaithful fidelity: when I do violence to the French language, I do so with the refined respect of what I believe to be an injunction of this language, in its life and its evolution. . . . I have only one language, and, at the same time, in an at once singular and exemplary fashion, this language does not belong to

me. . . . A singular history has exacerbated in me this general law: a language is not something that belongs.[16]

Such is the philosophical setting within which I would like to inscribe what I have to say. *"Plus d'une langue"* and "a language is not something that belongs" speak to us as much about politics as about philosophy. If a language is not something that belongs, then what is the relation between language and people, what are the relations between language, culture, and nation? What is a mother tongue exactly? And how might one complicate this idea of the language/people relation with the very idea of translation?

To begin to respond to these questions, I would like to draw on an example and develop it: the *Vocabulaire européen des philosophies*, which should be subtitled *"Dictionnaire des intraduisibles."* This is, fortunately, the title it is taking on in translation: tomorrow I am heading to the US to celebrate the release of the *Dictionary of Untranslatables*.[17]

I would describe this work *sans phrase*, or in one phrase: "Happy after Babel." It is an absolutely unlikely book (the courageous publishers who took it on didn't expect much from it—they ran 1,500 copies and, to their great surprise, it sold close to 15,000). Indeed, it took us much time to complete it—fifteen years since I first came up with the idea—and we worked as a group of 150 scholars from many countries. This dictionary was limited to the languages of Europe, quite simply because were weren't able to work on, or with, Chinese (for example), and we would have inordinately broadened the horizon of our questions; and we were led to deal with the languages that constitute the languages of Europe, especially Greek and Latin, occasionally Sanskrit—though we were not able to deal with Arabic or Hebrew as such—and not only as languages that are passed through or languages beneath languages. In short, as enormous as this work was, it remains very limited and very arbitrary. We tackled around four thousand words, terms, sequences, or language phenomena, drawn from fifteen or so European languages. We selected them because they are the ones we constantly run up against in our reading and scholarship.

The "untranslatables" are symptoms of the difference of languages. It is not a question of sacralizing them, as Heidegger might do or may encourage one to do (as with the translation—the French translation in particular—of his own work!); I will return to this. No, an untranslatable is what never stops (not) being translated. That is the definition I propose. It is what manifests the difference of languages, that is, what shows that languages cannot be superimposed on one another in an exact way, either semantically or syntactically. For example, when I say *"bonjour,"* I am not exactly saying *vale*, the Latin word for "hello" that wishes good health; I am not exactly saying *khaire*, the Greek word for "hello" that wishes you to enjoy or rejoice; I am also not saying *shalom* or *salaam*, I'm not wishing you peace, I am simply wishing you a good day, as with the English "good morning." In this way, each language ushers you, in its way, into the world, into a world. Of course, there are also syntactic symptoms of the difference between languages, for example the order of words, or the way of saying tense and/or aspect. Françoise Balibar, for example, has worked on the gender of words: where is the masculine/feminine difference drawn? Is there a "neuter" or not? Boats are feminine in English, but no one speaks in French of *"une bateau"* [boat] or *"une navire"* [ship], even if *"corvette"* [small warship] or *"chaloupe"* [rowboat] are feminine . . . what does that "say"? If you use Google to automatically translate the phrase *"Et Dieu créa l'homme à son image"* [And God created man in his image], as I attempted to do (you translate into German, then you translate the German translation into French, then the French translation into German, and the translation stabilizes after three times), after three operations you get: *"Et l'homme créa Dieu à son image"* [And man created God in his image]. Wonderful! But we can see just how complicated it is to translate syntax. If you do the same thing in English, you get *"Et Dieu créa l'homme avec son image"* [And God created man with his image]—the meaning of prepositions being yet another example of plurivocity, complexity, very difficult to handle! Actually, you don't get this result anymore, since, as soon as I said this in *Google-moi*,[18] it has been corrected . . .

But this is what is at issue in our work: semantic and syntactic discordances from one language to another. Each language is like a fishing net that, when it is cast, in a particular place, with mesh of a particular size, brings back other fish. This is a lovely image from Trubetzkoy: each language is an "iridescent net" that fishes a world, a "vision of the world." Let us look at several examples so it's more concrete. *"Pravda"*—I am choosing this word because Ukraine is currently in danger and the relation to Russia is problematic. The people I worked with in Ukraine are the very ones who were in Maidan Square, for example Constantin Sigov. You might have read his pieces, and those of his son, in *Le Monde*, for example. They are the ones who wrote the entries in Russian and Ukrainian; they are currently at work on Russian and Ukrainian translations of the dictionary. In other words, there is an interesting and peaceful intellectual circulation here, which, incidentally, is triangulated through French. To wit, *"Pravda,"* Constantin Sigov's entry: he was dead set against having the term fall under the entry for *"Vérité"* ["truth"]. The entry for *"Vérité"* in the *Vocabulaire* deals with *alētheia* (Greek), *veritas* (Latin), *emet* (Hebrew), *Warheit*, and "truth," but not *pravda*. Why? Because *pravda* first means "justice"; it is the word that translates *dikaiosunē*, "justice," in the Bible. So *pravda* does not in the first place, or does not only, mean "truth," or it means "truth" insofar as "truth" means "justice." There is, moreover, another word for saying "truth" as we ordinarily understand it, that is, truth as correctness: it is "*istina.*" So when a Ukrainian or Russian speaker looks at our word "truth," they find it equivocal, since we conflate correctness with truth; and when we look at "*pravda*," from the point of view or our "truth" as "correctness," we find it to be an equivocal term that signifies two things that, for us, are quite distinct, namely, "justice" and "truth."

In this way, we can see that it is necessary to pass by way of another language in order to apprehend the equivocations of our own. It is necessary to "deter-ritorialize" (this is a Deleuzian term) ourselves and look at ourselves from elsewhere in order to understand how we function as a language. A language is one language among others. We speak a language, and not rational and universal *logos*. With *logos*, we run the risk of having others be only "barbar-ians" [*barbares*] with the onomatopoeia of confusion, "babble," "Babel," "blah blah blah" inscribed in their name; unintelligible barbarians about whom we might then ask if they really speak, if they are really humans like me, or humans *tout court*. . . . Understanding that there are multiple languages is, in my view, already extraordinarily consequential both politically speaking and philosoph-ically speaking. There are multiple languages, and I see that what I speak is a language because I can look at myself from the outside, because there is more than one language [*plus d'une langue*]. It is in this way that I can understand and love the functioning of my own language.

Allow me to quote a phrase from Jacques Lacan; usually so difficult, here he is—also, at least—very transparent. Lacan writes, in "L'étourdit": "One language among others is nothing more than the integral of the equivocations that its history has allowed to persist in it."[19] "The integral of the equivocations": each language is characterized by its knots, its homonymies. Let us take a familiar example. "*Sens*" in French generally gives rise to two or three entries in the dictionary—it is already interesting that there can be two, or even three, in what seems to be an arbitrary way! There is "*sens*" in the sense of "sensation," "*sens*" in the sense of "signification," and "*sens*" in the sense of "direction." Yet it is one and the same word. Three entries in the dictionary, sure, but if you look at the history of the word, it is clear that the history of the three entries, the sense of their sense, as it were, is unified. The word "*sens*" comes, by way of the Latin translation *sensus*, from the Greek *nous*, and as always these trans-lations are tested out, or are testable, in the Bible, by way of the Greek of the Septuagint and the Latin of the Vulgate. *Nous* in Greek is both "spirit" and "intuition": thus, god in book lambda of the *Metaphysics* is characterized by

Aristotle as being *noesis noēseōs*, "thought of thought"; as well as, and perhaps first of all, the "sense of smell": thus, when Argos, Odysseus's dog, *noei* his master when he returns after twenty years beneath his beggar's rags, when he "sniffs" him (*"sniffer"* ["snort"] and *"schnouff"* ["dope"] are words in French that refer back etymologically to *nous*), he falls dead on his pile of dung because he "recognizes" him. To smell, intuit, recognize, know: we can see the relation between *sens* as sensibility and *sens* as signification, a relation that indicates the direction of recognition and interpretation. Like *nous* in Greek, *sensus* in Latin marks the "meaning" as distinct from the "letter" of a text. That is what *nous* rendered by *sensus* means. Such that the word *sens*, too, is a knot of equivocations, but for real reasons, fundamental and historical reasons. It is an equivocation produced by history, which history has allowed to subsist in the French language, and it so happens that the history of English—which says "meaning," "sensation," and "direction"—is not the same. French is characterized, then, in relation to English, for example, notably by the fact of this equivocation of *"sens."* Looking back retrospectively at our *Dictionnaire des intraduisibles*, I see that it is constantly dealing with homonyms, precisely: *pravda*, truth/justice; *disegno*, drawing/aim in Renaissance Italian; or, to take another Russian example, *mir*, which means at once "world," "peace," and "country village," in an ambiguity such that Tolstoy in *War and Peace* makes a play on "war" and "world." With this dictionary, then, it is a matter of reflecting on the symptoms of differences between languages, as the crux of languages themselves.

This work is both philosophical and political. Philosophical: it implies that a language is not only a means of communication but that, precisely, it creates a culture and a world; we are comparing visions of the world. And political: I came up with this dictionary as Europe was building itself, with a very precise idea in mind—the idea that, in order for Europe to function and make sense, it was necessary for us not to be reduced to "Globish," or "Global English"; that there would be nothing worse than to have a single language of communication, a *lingua franca*, and then dialects like French, German, Portuguese, and English—real English, a dialect like any other, which few people understand and even fewer speak (in an international conference, you can try this out; we may all speak Globish, but the only one who doesn't understand it is the English scholar from Oxford). Let me say something else about why I refuse Globish so thoroughly: Globish is also, and perhaps first of all, the language of evaluation, what allows everything to be brought down to a common denominator and puts us behind evaluation grids, with keywords to lock us in. It is the language of expertise, a language without authors and without works; the works of Globish are application files in Brussels. I could go on at length about the relation between Globish and search engines like Google, with its "linguistic flavors," to use its own terms; they are bringing into being a world in which quality is nothing but an emergent property of quantity, with no possible perception of invention, at the bottom of the bell curve. It was necessary, then, to work in reverse on Europe's patent diversity and plurality of languages.

I will leave Globish aside to get to my second enemy: "ontological nationalism." Ontological nationalism, as its name suggests, is a philosophers' disease; it has been a particular threat to us in France because we were all formed—or my generation was at least, as was that of my teachers, Derrida's generation, for example—by or with Heidegger. We spoke the "Heideggerian" idiom without always realizing it, and we had to work to distance ourselves from it. The history of philosophy as taught by Heidegger and the Heideggerians is rooted in language, the importance of language and translation. But, precisely, it implies a hierarchy of languages such that all languages would not have the same value, the same thought content. Within the perspective of the history of philosophy as history of Being, Greek, then German—even more Greek than Greek—are languages that are more "thinking" than others, they are *the* languages of philosophy such that the *logos*, the type of universal they propose, forever dominates us. Or even: these are the languages in which Being speaks itself, the languages in which man makes of himself the "shepherd of Being." I would like to read you a phrase I evoke often, and which terrifies me. It is a phrase spoken by Heidegger in 1930:

> *Greek language is philosophical*, i.e., not that Greek is loaded with philosophical terminology, but that it philosophizes in its basic structure and formation [*Sprachgestaltung*]. The same applies to every genuine language, in different degrees to be sure. The extent to which this is so depends on the depth and power of the people who speak the language and exist within it [*Der Grad bemißt sich nach der Tiefe und Gewalt der Existenz des Volkes und Stammes, der die Sprache spricht und in ihr existiert*]. Only our German language has a deep and creative philosophical character to compare with the Greek.[20]

So, neither Globish—Google world, in direct contact with communication and evaluation—nor ontological nationalism, that is, rootedness in a land, a soil, and a race of a superior language. But rather comparison and putting into relation: that is what translation is.

To do this, we need much culture in the Greek and Latin sense of the term, *paideia, cultura animi*, teaching, education of judgment and taste. In France, as in a number of countries, we have a wealth of languages. *"Plus d'une langue"* was the title of a little book that came out of a lecture I gave at the theater in Montreuil at the invitation of Gilberte Tsaï. When I arrived in the theater, which was full of very young children, some with their older siblings, I asked: "Maybe some of you here speak more than one language?" Every hand, almost, went up. Sure, it was Montreuil, but this is much more widespread than is believed. What do we do with these languages? How do we articulate them? We say: "Sit down and be quiet, and now speak French!" This is a very serious error, a denial of civilization. But I must add straightaway that today *la Francophonie*, for example the General Delegation for the French Language and the Languages of France, takes up the motto *"Plus d'une langue."* In my opinion, this marks an essential, inevitable step forward.

So: more than one language in our high schools, and let's not only teach the third one over the lunch hour, or with textbooks that say: "how to go to the pictures,"[21] for basic communication, but rather textbooks that make us read and love works bilingually, even if it's just "Daffodils,"[22] like in the old days . . . For a language, once again, is authors and works. Let's talk about them, let's work on that. And let's learn, by doing so, to read a text. That is what culture is about, that is what translation is about; we read a text well only when we read it in its language, that is, when we know it is written in a language. I find it alarming and scandalous that we persist in ignoring this. The most recent book my children had to read in French class, for example, was *Bilbo le Hobbit* [*The Hobbit*], in translation but without indicating this fact or suggesting to them that something was at issue there. I believe it is truly necessary to be aware of the plurality of languages and their interaction: this is how we will acquire both the possibility of reading a text and the possibility of understanding languages, for the two go hand in hand; it is necessary to understand that a text is a text in a language, written in a language, and that French, too, is a language.

French is one language "among others," it is my own, I love it, it is my mother tongue. But, following here Hannah Arendt, let us refrain from conflating language and people. In a famous interview with Günter Gaus for German television when she had already become American, she said that language was her homeland.[23] A language is not something that belongs, and that is why, after the Nazism that "infused" Germany, Arendt "always" (*immer*, she says) has this language—the language of the songs her mother would sing her at bedtime, that of the poems she knows by heart ("in the back of my mind,"[24] she says in English in the middle of her interview in German)—as a homeland; a language is shared, acquired, learned. It is in the reality proper to this language that one thinks and lives; at the same time, one really only thinks well if one understands that this is one reality among others, if one can "deterrito-rialize" oneself, if one can relativize one's absolute, in other words, if one is not Greek. [Arnaldo] Momigliano's judgment that "the Greeks remained proudly monolingual" is absolutely right: the Greeks thought there was only one way of speaking, namely, one language, their own, *logos*, what the Latins translated both as "reason" and "discourse."[25] A coincidence with enormous consequences: *logos*, *ratio*, and *oratio*, the language that I speak is universal reason. *Hellenizein*, "to speak Greek," simultaneously means to speak correctly, to be cultivated, to think correctly, to be human—and what were others? "Bar-barians" who go "blah blah blah," who jibber and jabber, whose language cannot be understood, who speak unintelligibly, who don't speak like me: are they really speaking? These are not humans like me—are they really humans? I underscored this from the beginning, but I would like to come back to it briefly, since everything returns here. A phrase that Plato attributes in the *Menexenus* to Aspasia, the mistress of Pericles (mistress in every sense of the word, since she supposedly wrote his famous speech): "So firmly rooted and so sound is the noble and liberal character of our city, and endowed also with such a hatred of the barbarian, because we are pure-blooded Greeks, unadul-terated by barbarian stock."[26] National Front talk . . . [27]

This is not the whole of Greece, far from it, and I could speak about Isoc-rates for whom culture and not nature makes Greekness, or Antiphon who uses the word "barbarize" to designate the behavior of one who imagines that others are barbarians. But is it not, after all, the unstoppable remainder of ethnocen-trism to call this "barbarizing" rather than "Hellenizing"? My remedy would be to read texts, texts in their language, and to practice translation. To translate: a good practice, and even a practice that is good, a savoir-faire of difference.

I would like to wrap up by alluding to the next stage of the *Dictionnaire des intraduisibles*.

The *Dictionnaire des intraduisibles* is being translated, that is, it is under-going adaptation, reinvention, in many languages including American English, and, in each case, the language of adaptation decides on the intention. I ex-plained my own intention when I came up with the *Dictionnaire des intraduis-ibles*: neither Globish nor ontological nationalism. The Americans, led by Emily Apter, Jacques Lezra, and Michael Wood, have translated/adapted the dictionary to play English against Globish, to propose an opening onto nonan-alytic "philosophy" or, to put it too quickly, a philosophy not indifferent to languages. The Ukrainians, led by Constantin Sigov, at first wanted to translate the dictionary in order to work on Ukrainian philosophical language, differ-entiating it firmly from Russian, and creating a community of philosophers.

But at the same time, it bears repeating, they are translating into Russian and working with Russian scholars, and publishing in Russian in Kiev. It is a collaboration that transcends conflicts, the necessity of which is worthy of being recognized by Europe with support for this intellectual and intelligent work of peace. Ali Benmakhlouf directed the translation into Arabic of the political section of the dictionary (entries such as "people," "law," or "state") in order to adapt, acclimatize, reflect on the words and practices that are our own, to measure the distance, and the Arabic translation is happening in Lebanon. The Romanians, with Anca Vasiliu and Alex Baumgarten, have translated it in order to think, within their language, about the relationship between the Latin and Slavic traditions. The Portuguese speakers of Brazil, led by Fernando Santoro, are reflecting, by way of their language, on what a postcolonial language is—Brazilian Portuguese in relation to Portuguese, about linguistic "cannibalism" and intermixture with indigenous languages: to use the term of the concretist poets, what is an *"intradução"*? Other adventures are taking shape: Italian, which sets in motion again the relation between philology, history of philosophy, and philosophy; Greek, which takes a step back to reflect on the relation between Ancient Greek and contemporary Greek; Hebrew, which poses the same type of question—a politically urgent question—regarding sacred language and ordinary language; Chinese; and, most recently, Wolof, under the direction of Souleymane Bachir Diagne. In any event, it is clear that there exists, in each case and in a singular way, a political dimension that is indissociable from the dimension of philosophical reflection on language.

I would like to conclude by synthesizing several essential features of translation as a paradigm.

First of all, and I have spoken much about this, it is a matter of consideration for the other, a fellow human, like me not like me: the other is not a barbarian. Languages, says Humboldt, form a pantheon rather than a church: they are gods, plural, and not a single God. What is needed is respect, the very thing the *banlieues* are demanding, as the basis of consideration and the political alike. Translation "takes into consideration" the other and sings the praises of diversity, that is, differentiated plurality.

In addition, or in the same way, each translation—and every translator knows this—engages us in more than one possibility. There is more than one possible translation, and more than one good translation. Not only because it is a matter of knowing when, why, and for whom you are translating; but also because, if each language is a web of equivocations, there are obviously several possible translations. I have experienced this myself in a very violent way with Greek, in particular the translation of Parmenides's poem. Let me give one final example: Parmenides says *esti*, "is." But this one word can mean—because the subject in Greek is included in the verb, in an elliptical or implied way—"he is" or "it is." Now, when one translates in this way (and this is the case for many translators), there are things that, in my view, one no longer understands; one no longer understands the way in which the verb *esti*, "is," produces its subject, *to eon*, "the being," at the end of the poem, how it performs its subject. The poem as it unfolds is effectively a grammatical narrative, a demonstration of the structure of the language [*la langue*] in the process of being made. This is why there is, for me, a good translation, "Is," which leaves the place of the subject open and free; and other translations that are bad, "he is," "it is," or "the being is," which takes for granted what is happening in the poem and through the poem itself.

On the other hand, for another sequence, there are in my view several good translations, and this plurality is even a requirement for really understanding the poem. The initial "is" is said: *muthos hodoio*, we can understand that "is" is the "word of the path"; or rather that it is a "story of the journey." Both work very well. There is absolutely no reason not to translate in these two ways. I would even say: there are many reasons for translating in both ways at once. "The word of the path" describes, precisely, the manner in which, on the basis of the verb "is," one reaches the subject, via a whole series of grammatical and syntactical forms that the poem foregrounds. It is a question, if you will, of the ontology of grammar: by translating as "the word of the path," one retraces the history of the Greek language itself, the way in which it is created throughout Parmenides's poem. With the other translation, "the story of the journey," one expresses how Parmenides's poem is the story of all the great stories, taking up as a palimpsest all the great poems that came before—Homer, Hesiod—and transforming mythemes into philosophemes. One moment shows this brilliantly: the moment when the subject, "the Being," appears, in fragment 8, that is, at the end of the poem. The words used to say it are the same as those that, in Book XII of the *Odyssey*, describe Odysseus tied to his mast passing the Sirens in the open sea. The Sirens sing: "renowned Ulysses, great glory to the Achaeans"; Odysseus is there: *empedon autothi mimno*, "I may abide fast where I am," he says in Homer, his feet planted on the planks of the ship, gripped in the powerful ropes tied around the mast, keeping him from jumping into the sea and thereby succumbing to the charm of the song singing his heroic glory and stating his eternal identity. Now, it so happens that in Parmenides's poem, being is described with precisely the same words, the same sequences! No one notices this, but it is extraordinary . . . or rather it is quite normal, if we understand that Parmenides's poem is the story of all the great stories, and that he is thus rewriting Homer. That is why I want *muthos hodoio* to be able to be translated by both "the word of the path" and "the story of the journey."

There are several good translations, and translation—which is linked in this way to interpretation—teaches what I would call a "consequential or consistent relativism [*relativisme conséquent*]." There is a better translation for—for making x or y understood. Consequential or consistent relativism entails, I believe, passing from the idea of a single Truth, of *the* Truth, and so the idea that there is *a* true and *a* false, to the idea that there is a "more true," a "better for," something like a "dedicated comparative" in a given situation. What Protagoras describes in Plato's *Protagoras* as the know-how of the sophists, and of good teachers more generally: "passing from a less good state to a better state," better for an individual or a city, but not in any way truer . . .

When one translates, when one passes between languages, then, one "de-essentializes" everything. It is always a question of showing that instead of one fixed essence there are interferences, that each language is for another language "*l'auberge du lointain* [the inn of the remote]" (a lovely medieval expression taken up by Antoine Berman). In sum, there are *energeiai*, energies at work, and not merely *erga*, works; and this is how a language defines itself: as an *energeia*, as a perpetual, continuous putting into action; such that the relation between languages, translation, shows how these *energeiai*, these energies evolve and intermix.

To conclude, I would like simply to share a short text by Hannah Arendt. She writes in her *Denktagebuch* [Book of Thoughts], in 1950, a brief excerpt titled "Plurality of languages":

> If there were only one language, perhaps we would be more sure of the essence of things.
>
> What is decisive is: 1. that there are many languages and that they are distinguished not only in their vocabulary, but also in their grammar, and thus in their way of thinking, and 2. that all languages are learnable.
>
> The fact that the object that is there to support the presentation of things can be called *Tisch* or "table"[28] indicates that something of the true essence of what we ourselves produce and name escapes us. . . . Within a homogeneous human community, the essence of the table is named unambiguously by the word "table," and yet as soon as it reaches the border of the community, it totters.
>
> This tottering ambiguity of the world and the uncertainty of the human in it would naturally not exist if it were not possible to learn foreign languages. . . . Hence the folly of the universal language— against the *condition humaine*, the artificial and forcible disambiguation of ambiguity.[29]

It is this "tottering ambiguity of the world" that I wish for us.

Bibliography

Arendt, Hannah. *Denktagebuch*. Vol. 1, 1950–1973, edited by Ursula Ludz and Ingeborg Nordmann. Munich: Piper, 2002.

———. *The Human Condition*. 2nd ed. Chicago: University of Chicago Press, 1998.

———. "What Remains? The Language Remains. A Conversation with Günter Gaus." In *Essays in Understanding, 1930–1954: Formation, Exile, Totalitarianism*. New York: Schocken Books, 1994.

Aristotle. *Metaphysics*. Translated by Hippocrates G. Apostle. Grinnell, IA: Peripatetic, 1979.

Benveniste, Émile. *Problems in General Linguistics: An Expanded Edition*. Vol. 1, edited by Jordan K. Skinner, translated by Mary Elizabeth Meek. Chicago: University of Chicago Press, 2023.

Cassin, Barbara. *Google Me: One-Click Democracy*. Translated by Michael Syrotinski. New York: Fordham University Press, 2017.

———, ed. *Dictionary of Untranslatables: A Philosophical Lexicon*. Translation edited by Emily Apter, Jacques Lezra, and Michael Wood. Princeton, NJ: Princeton University Press, 2014.

———, ed. *Vocabulaire européen des philosophies*. Paris: Éditions du Seuil, 2004.

Derrida, Jacques. *Learning to Live Finally: The Last Interview*. Translated by Pascale-Anne Brault and Michael Naas. New York: Melville House, 2011.

———. *Le Monolinguisme de l'autre, ou, la prothèse d'origine*. Paris: Galilée, 1996.

———. *Memoires for Paul de Man*. Rev. ed. Translated by Cecile Lindsay, Jonathan Culler, and Eduardo Cadava. New York: Columbia University Press, 1989.

———. *Monolingualism of the Other; or, The Prothesis of Origin*. Translated by Patrick Mensah. Stanford, CA: Stanford University Press, 1998.

Diagne, Souleymane Bachir. "Penser l'universel avec Étienne Balibar." *Raison publique*, no. 19 (2014): 15–21.

Heidegger, Martin. *The Essence of Human Freedom: An Introduction to Philosophy*. Translated by Ted Sadler. London: Continuum, 2005.

———. *Gesamtausgabe 2. Abteilung: Vorlesungen 1923–1944. Band 31: Vom Wesen der menschlichen Freiheit: Einleitung in die Philosophie*. Frankfurt: Vittorio Klostermann, 1982.

Humboldt, Wilhelm von. *On the Diversity of Human Language Construction and Its Influence on the Mental Development of the Human Species*. Edited by Michael Losonsky. Translated by Peter Heath. Cambridge: Cambridge University Press, 1999.

Lacan, Jacques. *Autres écrits*. Paris: Éditions du Seuil, 2001.

Momigliano, Arnaldo. "The Fault of the Greeks." *Daedalus* 104, no. 2 (Spring 1975): 9–19.

Plato. *Menexenus*. Edited by David Sansone. Cambridge: Cambridge University Press, 2020.

Weaver, Matthew. "Angela Merkel: German Multiculturalism Has 'Utterly Failed.'" *The Guardian*, October 17, 2010. https://www.theguardian.com/world/2010/oct/17/angela-merkel-german-multiculturalism-failed.

Notes

1. An earlier version of this text was presented at the Gulbenkian Foundation in 2014. It has been modified and supplemented for the present volume.

2. See for example Souleymane Bachir Diagne, "Penser l'universel avec Étienne Balibar," *Raison publique*, no. 19 (2014): 15–21.—Trans.

3. Matthew Weaver, "Angela Merkel: German Multiculturalism Has 'Utterly Failed,'" *The Guardian*, October 17, 2010, https://www.theguardian.com/world/2010/oct/17/angela-merkel-german-multiculturalism-failed.—Trans.

4. Wilhelm von Humboldt, *On the Diversity of Human Language Construction and Its Influence on the Mental Development of the Human Species*, ed. Michael Losonsky, trans. Peter Heath (Cambridge: Cambridge University Press, 1999).

5. Jacques Derrida, *Memoires for Paul de Man*, rev. ed., trans. Cecile Lindsay, Jonathan Culler, and Eduardo Cadava (New York: Columbia University Press, 1989), 15 (translation modified).

6. Jacques Derrida, *Le Monolinguisme de l'autre, ou, la prothèse d'origine* (Paris: Galilée, 1996), 21.

7. Jacques Derrida, *Monolingualism of the Other; or, The Prothesis of Origin*, trans. Patrick Mensah (Stanford, CA: Stanford University Press, 1998), 7 (translation modified).

8. The expressions "French Studies" and "Comparative Literature" are in English in the original.—Trans.

9. Derrida, *Monolingualism*, 4 (translation modified).

10. Aristotle, *Metaphysics*, Book IV, Sections 4–6. [See Aristotle, *Metaphysics*, trans. Hippocrates G. Apostle (Grinnell, IA: Peripatetic, 1979), 59–70.—Trans.]

11. Hannah Arendt cites Burckhardt in *The Human Condition*, 2nd ed. (Chicago: University of Chicago Press, 1998), 26n9.—Trans.

12. In English in the original.—Trans.

13. In English in the original.—Trans.

14. Civil marriage ceremonies in France are typically officiated by the local mayor.—Trans.

15. See Émile Benveniste, *Problems in General Linguistics: An Expanded Edition*, vol. 1, ed. Jordan K. Skinner, trans. Mary Elizabeth Meek (Chicago: University of Chicago Press, 2023).—Trans.

16. Jacques Derrida, *Learning to Live Finally: The Last Interview*, trans. Pascale-Anne Brault and Michael Naas (New York: Melville House, 2011), 36.

17. The *Vocabulaire européen des philosophies*, edited by Barbara Cassin, was first published in France in 2004. The English edition, edited by Emily Apter, Jacques Lezra, and Michael Wood, appeared in 2014 under the title *Dictionary of Untranslatables: A Philosophical Lexicon.*—Trans.

18. See Barbara Cassin, *Google Me: One-Click Democracy*, trans. Michael Syrotinski (New York: Fordham University Press, 2017).—Trans.

19. Jacques Lacan, *Autres écrits* (Paris: Éditions du Seuil, 2001).

20. Martin Heidegger, *The Essence of Human Freedom: An Introduction to Philosophy*, trans. Ted Sadler (London: Continuum, 2005), 36. For the original, see

Martin Heidegger, *Gesamtausgabe 2. Abteilung: Vorlesungen 1923–1944. Band 31: Vom Wesen der menschlichen Freiheit: Einleitung in die Philosophie* (Frankfurt: Vittorio Klostermann, 1982), 50–51.

21. In English in the original.—Trans.

22. In English in the original; a reference to William Wordsworth's lyric poem "I Wandered Lonely as a Cloud."—Trans.

23. See Hannah Arendt, "What Remains? The Language Remains. A Conversation with Günter Gaus," in *Essays in Understanding, 1930–1954: Formation, Exile, Totalitarianism* (New York: Schocken Books, 1994), 1–23.—Trans.

24. In English in the original.—Trans.

25. Arnaldo Momigliano, "The Fault of the Greeks," *Daedalus* 104, no. 2 (Spring 1975): 12.—Trans.

26. Plato, *Menexenus*, 245c–d. [See Plato, *Menexenus*, ed. David Sansone (Cambridge: University of Cambridge Press, 2020), 54.—Trans.]

27. A reference to the Front National, a far-right political party in France.—Trans.

28. In English in the original.—Trans.

29. Hannah Arendt, *Denktagebuch*, vol. 1, ed. Ursula Ludz and Ingeborg Nordmann (Munich: Piper, 2002), 42.

The Philosopher as Translator

Souleymane Bachir Diagne

Introduction

Let me start with an examination of French philosopher Emmanuel Levinas's *Humanisme de l'autre homme*, published in 1972.[1] In particular, the pages under the heading "Before Culture" from the chapter of the book on "Signification and Sense." In those pages, Levinas extolls elevation and verticality as what ordains being and as the only mode of existence of universality. Only from the elevated perspective of a "signification" that "could be detached from . . . cultures" and situated above them is a judgment on those cultures possible.[2] And if one asks about the reality of such a perspective outside of any particular cultural perspective, the answer, Levinas says, is: "Western civilization"; yes, he stresses: "the decried Western civilization . . ."[3] Before I complete the citation, let me ask, in a parenthesis: decried by whom? Obviously, Levinas is speaking of those who, in his words, manifest a "radical opposition, characteristic of our times, against cultural expansion by colonization."[4] And those would be first and foremost the former colonial subjects themselves. But what do they in fact decry? Not "Western civilization" as such, certainly. Rather, they decry the face the "West" presented to the people it colonized, which was not that of civility and civilization. That face is what Mahatma Gandhi was aiming at when he reportedly answered, when asked what he thought of Western civilization: "that would be a good idea." I close the parenthesis and I complete the citation of Levinas: "the decried Western civilization that knew how to understand particular cultures that never understood anything about themselves."[5]

The assumption is that there is a "Western civilization" that is not a culture among cultures, a language among languages, but the Logos itself: Europe

simply cannot be a province of the world. It is naturally endowed with an anthropological vocation (to understand particular cultures that never understood
themselves) because it has had the "generosity . . . [of] liberating the truth
from . . . cultural presuppositions," "purifying thought of cultural alluviums
and *language particularisms*."[6] That is why in fact it could renounce the very
violence of colonialism because "culture and colonization do not [necessarily]
go together."[7]

Now, ours is precisely a time of decolonization: as Levinas writes, it is characterized by "the radical opposition . . . against cultural expansion by colonization."[8] And if that comes to mean that even Western cultural expansion has
no legitimacy anymore, the result of considering that "all cultural personalities
are equally entitled to realize the Spirit [*réalisent au même titre l'esprit*]" is a
loss of "orientation."[9] Playing on the words "occident" and "orient," Levinas
writes: "The world created by this saraband of countless equivalent cultures,
each one justifying itself in its own context, is certainly dis-Occidentalized;
however, it is also disoriented."[10] In a word, this is, in the language of Édouard
Glissant, a *chaos-monde*, a "chaos-world."

Levinas certainly could adopt that expression here and speak of a "chaos-
world." Except of course that it would not have the positive meaning that
Glissant envisions. As we know, the core of Levinas's philosophy, his ethics
more precisely, is that the moral "ought" has its source in the fact that I encounter the naked and vulnerable face of the other person as an absolute transcendence beyond my self-centeredness, and that from that transcendence it
commands me "not to kill," to serve and to protect his or her life. To say that
the other comes to me as a naked face is to say that she does not visit (in the
religious sense of a visitation) against the background of her culture or with it.
By definition, the dyadic I-Thou ethical relationship excludes all appurtenances.
So the absolute respect for the transcendence that the other person is as a naked
face does not translate itself as a command for respect for other cultures or the
other's culture. In a manner that is comparable to the way in which the Immanuel Kant of the *Ethics* is certainly not the one who shows disdain for the
humanity he describes in his anthropology or geography of cultures, Levinas
combines the crucial notion of ethics as hospitality for the Other with the
strong conviction that of course no "other cultural personality is equally entitled to realize the Spirit" as the West, which is unique and exceptional in its
realization of the *translatio studii* from Jerusalem to Athens to Rome.[11] It is the
same conviction that Husserl expressed in his Vienna conference of 1935 on
"Philosophy and the Crisis of the European Man" when he declared that
while the rest of the world should understand that it had to Europeanize itself
as best as it could, a Europe fully aware of its philosophic *telos* could not find

the slightest reason to indianize itself in any respect.[12] The language of phenomenology, Husserl's and Levinas's, is certainly not that of multiculturalism.

Loss of orientation is loss of universality because if signification is tied to language and we are confronted with the plurality of languages in a decolonized or postcolonial world then the verticality and elevation of the universal is simply impossible as the only dimension we are left with is that of laterality or of horizontality where relations between cultures and languages are inscribed. Such a situation will mean "no direct or privileged contact with the world of Ideas," no access to a "universal grammar," but instead going "from one culture [to] penetrate another, as one goes from one's mother tongue to learn another language."[13] And Levinas evokes another phenomenologist, another disciple of Husserl, namely Maurice Merleau-Ponty, as the philosopher who spoke of a "lateral universality," which is, for him of course, a contradiction in terms.

Before I examine what Merleau-Ponty did say and what his "lateral universal" is in order to ask what is wrong with getting out of one's mother tongue to learn another language, let me say a few words about the fact that today in France the virulent opposition voiced against so-called postcoloniality by authors such as Jean-François Bayart or Jean-Loup Amselle, to what Bayart has called "the academic carnival of postcolonial studies,"[14] continues Levinas's lament in the face of a world made of a "saraband of countless equivalent cultures."[15]

Thus, the very first pages of L'Occident décroché by anthropologist Jean-Loup Amselle echo the notion that a dis-occidentalized world is a disoriented world, "a world upside down" witnessing a supposed "crumbling of the West with the concomitant, competing rise of thoughts, of philosophies that contest the intention of Europe and America to dominate the world, which means, according to those who have for them nothing but contempt, questioning their pretention to universality."[16] To paraphrase Derrida paraphrasing Kant, the observation can be made that there is quite an apocalyptic tone recently adopted by many a French intellectual against the chaos-world of the postcolonial.

Amselle considers that the "unhooking" from the West that is, according to him, what postcolonial and subalternist studies amount to means the fragmentation of the world into provinces with the consequence that the untranslatable and what Barbara Cassin has claimed as a "consistent relativism" will reign supreme. Amselle would admit that the machine de guerre against universalism could be justified in a phase of decolonization from a Europe which colonized the rest of the world in the name of the universal. One could think here, for example, of the dramatic gesture of Aimé Césaire writing his famous "Letter to Maurice Thorez" as he resigned from the French Communist Party,

which considered that its own philosophy of emancipation by the universal
class of European proletariat was the solution for people suffering from colonialism as well.[17] This is what led Césaire to the declaration that he refused an
incarcerating conception of one's own sense of a particular identity, but refused
as well the "fraternalism" of the Communist Party and refused to get diluted
in its universalism. For Amselle, that attitude was valid then but is not justifiable anymore because now,

> the prevailing situation in this beginning of the twenty-first century is
> . . . very different from that of the 1950s and 1960s. In the present con-
> text of "clash of civilizations" or rather in what looks more and more
> like a crusades conflict, strategic essentialism has become a problem-
> atic notion as the affirmation of a radical otherness can be perceived
> as the ferment of all fundamentalisms. In the world we are now living
> in, apparently open but in reality perfectly compartmentalized, we
> must abandon any definition or assertion of identity that restrains the
> circulation of enunciations through cultural boundaries, in other
> words, that makes those boundaries exist as such by reinforcing them.[18]

I made clear in the book of dialogue I copublished with Amselle that I am
in agreement with him when it comes to a commitment to the universal.[19] I
do not advocate a world of fragments and insularities, of the untranslatable,
but what Immanuel Wallerstein has called for, after "the era of European universalism": a truly universal universalism and a language for "universalizing
our particulars and particularizing our universals" in an open-ended process
that would "allow us to find new syntheses."[20] I believe that such a truly universal universalism echoes Merleau-Ponty's "lateral universal" and that it is
synonymous with translation. Without the mediation of a universal grammar,
as Levinas said, the possibility of a universal and horizontal circulation of
enunciations is translation.

Here is what Merleau-Ponty says about our postcolonial time:

> The equipment of our social being can be dismantled and recon-
> structed by the voyage, as we are able to learn to speak other lan-
> guages. This provides *a second way to the universal*: no longer the
> *overarching universal* of a strictly objective method, but a sort of *lateral*
> *universal* which we acquire through ethnological experience and its in-
> cessant testing of the self through the other person and the other per-
> son through the self. It is a question of constructing a general system
> of reference in which the point of view of the native, the point of view
> of the civilized man, and the mistaken views each has of the other can

all find a place—that is of constituting a more comprehensive experience which becomes in principle accessible to men of a different time
and country.[21]

First remark: the point made by Levinas (in a dismissive way) that this is
like going "from one's mother tongue to learn another language" is precisely
what is stated here in a positive way.[22] The call is made for the capacity to be
in between languages, to be a translator, and that capacity is the lesson to be
drawn from ethnology: it is important to note that the passage comes from the
text Merleau-Ponty devoted to the reflection on ethnology, entitled "From
Mauss to Claude Lévi-Strauss."

It is important, and this is my second remark, that the lateral universal as
translation does not mean transparency and the elimination of the untranslatable. On the contrary, the untranslatable or the unavoidable misunderstandings
or the "mistaken views about each other" are part of this incessant testing,
marked by the copresence of many different views. So lateral universality does
not have as its horizon the establishment of a universal grammar, nor the end
game of a final reduction of the diversity of the "chaos-world" to the One and
the Same. What does it mean to "learn to speak other languages," thus heeding
the injunction from anthropology?

The Philosopher as a Translator

Speaking to philosophers from the point of view of an anthropologist/linguist,
Edward Sapir had this advice for them:

> Few philosophers have deigned to look into the morphologies of primi-
> tive languages nor have they given the structural peculiarities of their
> own speech more than a passing and perfunctory attention. When one
> has the riddle of the universe on his hands, such pursuits seem trivial
> enough, yet when it begins to be suspected that at least some solutions
> of the great riddle are elaborately roundabout applications of the rules
> of Latin or German or English grammar, the triviality of linguistic
> analysis becomes less certain. To a far greater extent than the philoso-
> pher has realized, he is likely to become the dupe of his speech-forms,
> which is equivalent to saying that the mould of his thought, which is
> typically a linguistic mould, is apt to be projected into his conception of
> the world. Thus, innocent linguistic categories may take on the formi-
> dable appearance of cosmic absolutes. If only, therefore, to save himself

from philosophic verbalism, it would be well for the philosopher to look critically to the linguistic foundations and limitations of his thought.[23]

Let me take as an illustration a particular case evoked by Yvon Belaval, as he precisely called attention to the very "languages" in which philosophers express themselves.[24] In his *Traité des systèmes*, Étienne Bonnot, Abbé de Condillac (1714–1780), philosopher of sensationalism (a Lockian whose starting point is that all knowledge comes from the senses and there are no innate ideas and who himself indicated that his criticism of philosophers amounted to a sheer "teasing" [*badinage*]), critically analyzes an argument made by Cartesian Nicolas Malebranche (1638–1715). A general feature of sensationalist criticism of rationalist and innatist philosophers is to accuse them of verbalism in the sense that they would invoke entities that are in fact the sheer productions of the creative power of language beyond what is actually given. As the French phrase expresses it well, "ils se paient de mots," literally: they reward themselves with words. In this case, Condillac's criticism is different. It is aimed at a particular aspect of Malebranche's core thesis that the ultimate cause of everything is God, so that what we call causes, in the plural, are only *occasions* for God's unique agency: God burns through the occasion of fire. The main objection against occasionalism as the system is known is then to ask: If God is the general cause of all natural inclinations to be found in our minds, how can we account for the possibility of sin?

For Malebranche, the answer to such an objection takes the form of an analogy between the principle of inertia as a natural law of physics and what happens when our natural inclinations are deviated in the direction of wrongdoing. Condillac stresses that this is an aspect of the general analogy established earlier by Malebranche between matter's capacity to receive movement, the understanding's capacity to receive ideas, and the will's capacity to receive inclinations. Which, for Condillac, manifests that, contrarily to his claim, the follower of Descartes has no clear and distinct idea of the notion of will if its explanation is by analogy. The answer to the objection is the following: "in the same way that all movements follow a straight line if they do not encounter some extraneous and particular cause that determine them and change them into curved lines by opposing them, all inclinations that we received from God are straight and could not have any other end than the possession of the good and the truth, were it not for some extraneous cause which would determine what was impressed upon us by nature towards bad ends." To which Condillac simply responds: "What would have Malebranche done if that metaphorical expression, *straight inclinations*, had not been French?"[25]

I will not examine the discussion in any detail, as that is not the point here. What I am interested in are the following two points:

(1) Condillac calls Malebranche's attention to the fact that he is speaking French and that the peculiarities of that language *incline* him to think according to the possibilities they present. However, there is nothing necessary and universal in those peculiarities, by definition. If philosophy does not leave anything unexamined, we need to pay attention to the fact that a given language in which we happen to philosophize inclines us to think in a certain unexamined way.

(2) The second point is implicit in Condillac's criticism. The implication is an invitation to always *translate*, test our arguments by translating them into another language in order to measure how sound they are, in a way that would mean "independently from the particular language we think in." In sum, Condillac is, in some respect, asking Malebranche to translate his statement into a language in which "straight" cannot be used in the metaphorical sense upon which the very meaning of that statement rests. Of course, that does not mean actually performing the translation; the other language can be simply virtual (after all, being monolingual is widespread even among philosophers). The injunction is about just being aware that there are out there many languages where the peculiar use of "straight" is absent.

I generalize that point as the following memento: think in the presence of the plurality of languages! In other words: remember that to philosophize is to speak a language among other languages, and that what you say should undergo the test of translation, the test of the foreign (to evoke Antoine Berman's title).[26] Glissant famously declared: "*J'écris en présence de toutes les langues du monde* [I write in the presence of all the languages of the world]." In a way, that is what Condillac's criticism amounts to. It is also the posture that Merleau-Ponty's notion of "lateral universal" invites philosophers to adopt.

Of course, philosophers have always known that we live in a post-Babel world (to refer here to the biblical myth explaining the origin of our plurilingual condition) and that human languages are many. Nevertheless, they also manifest a strong belief in the *logos* that is both reason and language.[27] To philosophize in what is considered the "Western tradition" is to "speak *logos*" and thus establish one's separation from the Barbarians and their idioms. The plurality of human languages is taken into consideration only when asking whether *the* logos, *the* language of philosophy, can be incarnated in a given language. It is within such a framework that the Heideggerian concept of a historical language and his notion that philosophy naturally speaks Greek and now German are to be understood. Cicero's premise that philosophy can also speak Latin is still a tribute paid to the notion of a "language of philosophy." What he is saying in his *De finibus bonorum et malorum* is that his own Latin language is also or can also be the *logos*.

This is different from the notion coined by Barbara Cassin of "philosophizing in tongues" (a biblical expression that takes seriously our post-Babelian condition), which conveys the double idea that (1) before they are concepts, our concepts are words, they are "words in languages [*mots en langues*],"[28] inscribed in languages; (2) "if there is a universal (I am not so sure that the word is adequate), it is not an 'overarching' one but a 'lateral' one, and its name is translation."[29] When she writes that sentence, Cassin is quoting my own identification of the "lateral universal" with translation. And in fact I am among those who work within the framework established by her *Dictionary of the Untranslatables*, those she refers to in her introduction to *L'énergie des intraduisibles* as "the 150 companions and friends for the journey of more than ten years who explored another kind of freedom and philosophical practice, at once more global and diversified, connected with words, with words in languages."[30] A fundamental assumption that those "companions" share is certainly that there is not such a thing as a *logos* erected in its universal separation.

With the example of Condillac and his criticism of Malebranche, one isolated word was considered. The question of translation is expanded when we consider philosophical *statements* as they involve the very grammar of a language and not just the peculiar use of some words: *Being is and non-being is not* or *I think, therefore I am*, are such statements, for example.

Translation between Indo-European languages can be problematic. It is even more so when we are considering a non-Indo-European language, in particular zero copula languages, when dealing with those ontological statements. When Descartes declares "I am, I exist," thus establishing an equivalence between being and existing, how do we translate his statement in a language where such an absolute use of the verb "to be" does not exist? Or rather, does not exist *in the same way*? When one says "I am" in certain languages, one has to add "what," "where," in "what state," "with whom," and so on. Thus, Rwandan philosopher Alexis Kagamé (1912–1981) has declared that one cannot translate Descartes's *cogito ergo sum* into Kinyarwanda language.[31] In fact, there is always a way of rendering it, but the point he is making is that realizing that "I am" is an untranslatable could have opened up the question of the possibility of making an immediate move from "I think" to "I am," which is precisely a criticism that will be leveled at Descartes's *cogito*.

Logical Analysis of Language and Philosophizing in Tongues

Is this the same as conducting a logical analysis of language according to the Leibnizian program of overcoming the saraband of our post-Babel world by learning to go beyond the *surface grammar* of our languages and retrieve the true *grammar of thought* or of *understanding*, the one that Leibniz called "philosophical," which he believed would be universal? For Leibniz, that philosophical grammar of thought and therefore the universal language is the language of algebra, or rather the *speciose*. And the task of reconstructing the philosophical grammar of all our languages offers a path back to the Adamic language, the pre-Babel condition of *homo loquax*. This task is clearly assumed by two heirs of Leibniz's program of a *lingua characteristica universalis* and a *calculus ratiocinator*, George Boole and Gottlob Frege. Boole writes, for example:

> We could (not) easily conceive that the unnumbered tongues and dialects of the earth should have preserved through the long succession of ages so much that is common and universal, were we not assured of the existence of some deep foundation of their agreement in the laws of the mind itself.[32]

The analogy could be made between that idea of going deep down to the laws of the mind and reconstructing philosophically the language in which all is already translated, and Walter Benjamin's "pure language." Logicians following Leibniz were also seeking the language of all languages, the language of our agreement that would turn any *disputatio* into a *calculemus*.

Philosophizing in tongues means establishing oneself comfortably in our post-Babelian condition; it is not the search for the *philosophical grammar* of our language, but it finds its starting point in the inescapable reality of the *grammatical philosophies* (or the *philosophies of grammar*) that are implicit in our empirical languages, a concept coined by Nietzsche, who considered "grammar as the conceptual matrix of metaphysics"[33] in the often-quoted Article 20 from *Beyond Good and Evil*:

> Philosophizing is to this extent a kind of atavism of the highest order. The strange family resemblance of all Indian, Greek, and German philosophizing is explained easily enough. Where there is affinity of languages, it cannot fail, owing to the common *philosophy of grammar*—I mean, owing to the unconscious domination and guidance by similar grammatical functions—that everything is prepared at the outset for a similar development and sequence of philosophical systems; just as the way seems barred against certain other possibilities of

world-interpretation. It is highly probable that philosophers within the domain of the Ural-Altaic languages (where the conception of the subject is least developed) look otherwise "into the world," and will be found on paths of thought different from those of the Indo-Germanic peoples and the Muslims: the spell of certain grammatical functions is ultimately also the spell of physiological valuations and racial conditions. So much by way of rejecting Locke's superficiality regarding the origin of ideas.[34]

Conclusion

I come back to Levinas. Lateral universality is not to be dismissed in the name of verticality. It is not a contradiction *in adjecto* and therefore an empty phrase. Its meaning is translation. The language of all languages, as Kenyan writer Ngũgĩ wa Thiong'o declares, is translation and not a logos identified with Greek or German.[35] That is the invitation, expressed in the journey of the *Dictionary of Untranslatables*, to discover that every language is always *"une langue, entre autres,"* a language among others.

The lesson drawn by Merleau-Ponty from anthropology (and he indicates that Husserl himself at one point understood the necessity to pay attention to other languages and life forms) is that we have to learn how to think from language to language or between languages.

That has an important pedagogical significance. The reason why mutilingualism is necessary is that it does not just add new linguistic competencies. It teaches the de-centering that is true knowledge. Because to learn is to de-center oneself, that is even truer of the learning of a different language. To Goethe is attributed the declaration that he who does not know a foreign language knows nothing of his mother tongue. That is because monolingualism keeps one enclosed in one's perspective on the world that a language constitutes. In order to be able to step out of a given perspective, of a given way of approaching reality expressed in the structure of one's language, one has to be able to compare it with a different outlook. Obviously, the only outside of a given language is another language.

That is why, as Achille Mbembe rightly says, "colonialism is monolingual." Therefore, people speaking dominated languages are "condemned" to diglossy or heteroglossy. But the truth is that far from being a condemnation, that situation is, should be, a pedagogical blessing. To be condemned to translation is a grace.

Let us then end with a pedagogical utopia. We know that the inscription on the pediment of Plato's Academy read, "Let no one ignorant of geometry enter here." The new Academy of the twenty-first-century global world may command: "Let no one ignorant of a radically other tongue than his own enter here." "Radically other" means from a different family of languages. Utopia? Well, that is the situation of most of us, philosophers from outside Europe and North America, "condemned" to think from language to language, philosophers of plurilingualism, whose experience is that to philosophize is indeed to translate.

Bibliography

Amselle, Jean-Loup. *L'Occident décroché: Enquête sur les postcolonialismes*. Paris: Stock, 2008.

Bayart, Jean-François. *Les études postcoloniales: Un carnaval académique*. Paris: Karthala, 2010.

Belaval, Yvon. *Les philosophes et leur langage*. Paris: Gallimard, 2015.

Berman, Antoine. *L'épreuve de l'étranger: Culture et traduction dans l'Allemagne romantique*. Paris: Gallimard, 1984.

Boole, George. *An Investigation of the Laws of Thought on Which Are Founded the Mathematical Theories of Logic and Probabilities*. New York: Dover, 1958.

Cassin, Barbara. "L'énergie des intraduisibles: La traduction comme paradigme pour des sciences humaines." In *Philosopher en langues: Les intraduisibles en traduction*, ed. Barbara Cassin, 9–20. Paris: Éditions Rue d'Ulm, 2014.

Césaire, Aimé. "Letter to Maurice Thorez." Translated by Chike Jeffers. *Social Text* 28, no. 2 (103) (Summer 2010): 145–52.

Condillac, Étienne Bonnot de. *Traité des systèmes*. Paris: Houel, 1798.

Diagne, Souleymane Bachir, and Jean-Loup Amselle. *In Search of Africa(s): Universalism and Decolonial Thought*. Translated by Andrew Brown. Cambridge, UK: Polity, 2020.

Husserl, Edmund. *Philosophy and the Crisis of the European Mind*. Translated by Quentin Lauer. New York: Harper and Row, 1965.

Ildefonse, Frédérique. *La naissance de la grammaire dans l'Antiquité grecque*. Paris: Vrin, 1997.

Kagamé, Alexis. *La philosophie bantu comparée*. Paris: Présence africaine, 1976.

Levinas, Emmanuel. *Difficult Freedom: Essays in Judaism*. Translated by Sean Hand. Baltimore: Johns Hopkins University Press, 1997.

———. *Humanisme de l'autre homme*. Paris: Fata Morgana, 1972.

———. *Humanism of the Other*. Translated by Nidra Poller. Urbana and Chicago: University of Illinois Press, 2003.

Merleau-Ponty, Maurice. "From Mauss to Lévi-Strauss." In *Signs*. Translated by Richard C. McCleary. Evanston, IL: Northwestern University Press, 1964.

Ngũgĩ wa Thiong'o. *The Language of Languages: Reflections on Translation*. London: Seagull Books, 2023.

Nietzsche, Friedrich. *Beyond Good and Evil*. In *Basic Writings of Nietzsche*. Translated by Walter Kaufmann. New York: Random House, 2000.

Sapir, Edward. "The Grammarian and His Language." In *Selected Writings of Edward Sapir in Language, Culture and Personality*, edited by David G. Mandelbaum. Los Angeles: University of California Press, 1949.

Wallerstein, Immanuel. *European Universalism: The Rhetoric of Power*. New York: New Press, 2006.

Notes

1. Emmanuel Levinas, *Humanisme de l'autre homme* (Paris: Fata Morgana, 1972), has been translated as *Humanism of the Other*, trans. Nidra Poller (Urbana and Chicago: University of Illinois Press, 2003).

2. Levinas, *Humanism of the Other*, 37.

3. Levinas, 37.

4. Levinas, 37.

5. Levinas, 37.

6. Levinas, 37 (my emphasis).

7. Levinas, 37.

8. Levinas, 37.

9. Levinas, 37 (translation modified).

10. Levinas, 37.

11. In *Difficult Freedom: Essays in Judaism*, trans. Sean Hand (Baltimore: Johns Hopkins University Press, 1997), Emmanuel Levinas presents decolonization as "the arrival on the historical scene of those underdeveloped Afro-Asiatic masses who are strangers to the Sacred history that forms the heart of the Judaic-Chistian world" (160).

12. Edmund Husserl, *Philosophy and the Crisis of the European Mind*, trans. Quentin Lauer (New York: Harper and Row, 1965).

13. Levinas, *Humanism of the Other*, 37.

14. Jean-François Bayart, *Les études postcoloniales: Un carnaval académique* (Paris: Karthala, 2010).

15. Levinas, *Humanism of the Other*, 37.

16. Jean-Loup Amselle, *L'Occident décroché: Enquête sur les postcolonialismes* (Paris: Stock, 2008), 7. All translations from this source are my own.

17. Aimé Césaire, "Letter to Maurice Thorez," trans. Chike Jeffers, *Social Text* 28, no. 2 (2010): 145–52.

18. Amselle, *L'Occident décroché*, 7.

19. Souleymane Bachir Diagne and Jean-Loup Amselle, *In Search of Africa(s): Universalism and Decolonial Thought*, trans. Andrew Brown (Cambridge, UK: Polity, 2020).

20. Immanuel Wallerstein, *European Universalism: The Rhetoric of Power* (New York: New Press, 2006). Interestingly, Wallerstein ends on Senghor's concept of a

"rendezvous of give and take" as a metaphor for a "civilization of the universal." See Wallerstein, *European Universalism*, 84.

21. Maurice Merleau-Ponty, "From Mauss to Lévi-Strauss," in *Signs*, trans. Richard C. McCleary (Evanston, IL: Northwestern University Press, 1964), 119–20 (emphasis in original).

22. Levinas, *Humanism of the Other*, 37.

23. Edward Sapir, "The Grammarian and His Language," in *Selected Writings of Edward Sapir in Language, Culture and Personality*, ed. David G. Mandelbaum (Los Angeles: University of California Press, 1949), 157.

24. Yvon Belaval, *Les philosophes et leur langage* (Paris: Gallimard, 2015).

25. "'De même que tous les mouvements se font en ligne droite, s'ils ne trouvent quelques causes étrangères et particulières qui les déterminent, et qui les changent en des lignes courbes par leurs oppositions; ainsi, toutes les inclinations que nous avons de Dieu sont droites, et elles ne pourraient avoir d'autre fin que la possession du bien et de la vérité, s'il n'y avait une cause étrangère qui déterminât l'impression de la nature vers de mauvaises fins.' Qu'aurait fait Malebranche, si cette expression métaphorique, *des inclinations droites*, n'avait pas été française?" Étienne Bonnot de Condillac, *Traité des systèmes* (Paris: Houel, 1798), 63.

26. Antoine Berman, *L'épreuve de l'étranger: Culture et traduction dans l'Allemagne romantique* (Paris: Gallimard, 1984).

27. Barbara Cassin writes that "Latin people translated [*logos*] impeccably as *ratio-et-oratio*." See Barbara Cassin, "L'énergie des intraduisibles: La traduction comme paradigme pour des sciences humaines," in *Philosopher en langues: Les intraduisibles en traduction* (Paris: Éditions Rue d'Ulm, 2014), 10.

28. Cassin, "L'énergie des intraduisibles," 10.

29. Cassin, 10.

30. Cassin, 10.

31. Alexis Kagamé, *La philosophie bantu comparée* (Paris: Présence africaine, 1976), 126.

32. George Boole, *An Investigation of the Laws of Thought on Which Are Founded the Mathematical Theories of Logic and Probabilities* (New York: Dover, 1958).

33. Frédérique Ildefonse, *La naissance de la grammaire dans l'Antiquité grecque* (Paris: Vrin, 1997).

34. Friedrich Nietzsche, *Beyond Good and Evil*, in *Basic Writings of Nietzsche*, trans. Walter Kaufmann (New York: Random House, 2000), 217–18 (my emphasis).

35. Ngũgĩ wa Thiong'o, *The Language of Languages: Reflections on Translation* (London: Seagull Books, 2023).

Babel as Opportunity: Translating Solidarity

Gary Wilder

Internationalism and Translation

On January 18, 2006, a diverse group of alter-globalization activists met in Bamako, Mali, in anticipation of a series of Polycentric World Social Forum meetings in Mali, Venezuela, and Pakistan that same year. Among those gathered were activists, academics, journalists, and politicians from Africa, Asia, Latin America, the Middle East, Europe, and the United States. After two days of intensive discussion among various subcommittees, the group issued "The Bamako Appeal."[1]

Dedicated to the fiftieth anniversary of the Bandung Conference, the Appeal expressed a commitment to "(i) Construct an internationalism that joins the people of the South and North who are ravaged by the dictatorship of financial markets and the uncontrolled global expansion of transnational corporations; (ii) Construct the solidarity of the peoples of Asia, Africa, Europe, and the Americas confronted with the challenges of development in the twenty-first century; (iii) Construct a political, economic and cultural consensus that is an alternative to neoliberal and militarized globalization and the hegemony of the United States and its allies."[2] The authors explicitly linked this call for internationalism, solidarity, and an alternative world order to the creation of "a new popular and historical subject" that is "diverse and multipolar."[3] This subject would be committed to the "radical transformation of the capitalist system," to "harmony in societies by abolishing exploitation by class, gender, race, and caste," and to "a new balance of power between the South and the North."[4] The Appeal declared that the existing world order, organized as it was around imperialism and capitalism, had placed both the future of the planet and the "very existence of humanity" at stake.[5]

The Egyptian political economist Samir Amin was one of the principal authors of the Bamako Appeal. His involvement in the World Social Forum roughly corresponded to a third phase in his intellectual-political itinerary. The latter led from a critique of accumulation on a world scale, imperial underdevelopment, and global polarization, to a program for economic delinking in order to create a polycentric socialist world, to his call for new forms of internationalism able to contest neoliberal capitalism and the imperial division of the world underwritten by American militarism. Throughout this journey—as a student activist in the French Communist Party, an economic adviser in Nasser's Egypt and Keïta's Mali, a university professor, and director of the Third World Forum in Senegal—he remained committed to creating a new socialist and popular democratic world order.[6] This is the perspective from which he declared himself a "universalist internationalist."[7]

When Amin demanded a "humanist alternative to worldwide apartheid" he spoke in the idiom of socialist internationalism, not bourgeois liberalism.[8] Such an alternative, he believed, would depend on non-Western actors' ability to forge a "common front of the South" appropriate to twenty-first-century conditions.[9] This front would have to renounce the comprador role that their national states had assumed in the postcolonial world system. In other words, they would have to politicize contradictions *within* these societies in order to build alliances across regions of the Global South that could stand against both the imperialist West and their own repressive national states and ruling classes. This political orientation would reject nationalist and culturalist fictions about unified societies with pregiven interests. Amin was especially critical of superficially anti-Western political positions that reified "inherited diversities" in ways that intensified social inequalities and diminished democratic possibilities.[10]

In short, Amin argued that this people's front of the South needed to revive the spirit of Bandung solidarity that had been destroyed by neoliberal hegemony after the decline of the postwar order (which had been anchored by Western welfarism, Soviet planning, and Third World developmentalism). Yet, he also insisted that this front abandon the productivist and statist assumptions of Bandung development ideology. The latter, he argued, had uncritically accepted the capitalist law of value that propelled uneven development on a world scale. Accordingly, the Bandung project's misguided attempt to "catch up" to the West actually reproduced the imperial inequalities upon which the postwar world order was founded. If a new "active front of the South" were both to revive the solidarity spirit of Bandung *and* transcend its political economic limitations, it would need to be organized around popular movements and insurgent peoples rather than technocratic elites and national states.[11] Moreover, if it were to have any chance of creating a socialist, internationalist, and humanist alternative to neoliberal apartheid and planetary destruction, it would need to situate itself within an even more expansive "internationalism of peoples." Amin explains,

> the phrase refers to all peoples, North and South, just as it refers not only to the proletariat but to all working classes and strata that are victims of the system, to humanity as a whole, threatened in its survival. This internationalism does not preclude strengthening the solidarity of the peoples of the three continents (Africa, Asia, Latin America) against aggression from the imperialism of the triad. On the contrary, these two internationalisms can only complement and reinforce each other. The solidarity of the peoples of the North and South cannot be based on charity, but on joint action against imperialism.[12]

This internationalism of peoples would be both a means and end of anti-imperial struggle. It would anticipate—call for and call forth—the socialist and polycentric "world we wish to see."[13]

Amin recognized that such an undertaking would face formidable challenges. Wealthy and powerful states would instrumentalize divisions and punish alliances among peoples. Likewise, he warned, reactionary movements in parts of the Global South had a tendency to fixate on "inherited diversities" that appeared to separate peoples, cultures, and civilizations. He argued that these forms of anti-Westernism actually reinforced worldwide Western hegemony. Moreover, he warned that even among progressive forces there existed a wide range of distinct historical situations, political priorities, and degrees of commitment to societal or global transformation. In any given situation, this multiplicity of groups and movements could not be easily aligned. Amin invokes the need "to bring about the convergence of struggles of peasants, women, workers, the unemployed, informal workers, and democratic intellectuals in order to set democratization and social progress as indissoluble objectives for the popular movements as a whole."[14] But how could this be done without abstracting away from concrete situations in the name of a fictive unity? How to construct relations of solidarity without erasing these many axes of difference? Such challenges would be compounded by distance and distinction across geographical or cultural regions.

Amin's response to these difficulties was an underspecified call for "organizing convergence while respecting diversity."[15] The internationalist task was to embrace differences without devolving into a culturalism that would reify them. Likewise, the task was to embrace political diversity without devolving into a liberal pluralism that regarded all movements and positions as equally valid. Amin warned that the mere accumulation of demands should not be mistaken for a coherent movement, vision, or program. He accused alter-globalization militants of just such relativism and misrecognition. On the one hand, he reminded traditional Marxists that internationalist movements could only be strengthened by cultural diversity, internal political debate, and a multiplicity of historical subjects that engage various axes of domination through a mix of immediate interventions and long-term strategies. On the other hand, he reminded left horizontalists that such an internationalism would have to exercise political judgment in determining political criteria for inclusion in the movement. Likewise, the task of creating alternative hegemonic blocs would have to risk exercising leadership, working through traditional militant organizations (like peasant groups and trade unions), and creating novel institutions. This is the perspective from which Amin called for the creation of a new Fifth International that could "gather all peoples' movements of resistance and struggle and guarantee both their voluntary participation in the construction of joint strategies and the independence of their own decision making."[16]

Amin's bold vision of a polycentric internationalism that would contribute to the "advance of socialism, humanism, and universalism" challenges recent currents of postcolonial criticism that dismiss post–Cold War internationalist and cosmopolitan political projects as fundamentally Western, liberal, or idealist justifications for neoimperialist initiatives.[17] Amin certainly understood how internationalism could easily devolve into imperialism, how calls for solidarity could authorize old hierarchies, how opportunities for world-historical transformation could unfold in either progressive or oppressive ways. Indeed, he warned that creating a "front of the South" and an "internationalism of the peoples" would be "a long and difficult process" for which there are no "advance 'recipes'" and "whose outcome is not known in advance."[18]

Organizing convergence while respecting diversity could only proceed concretely, experimentally, and provisionally. On the one hand, it would have to risk compromising unity by embracing difference and disagreement. On the other, it would have to risk eliding differences and suspending conflict by embracing solidarity. Insofar as it pursued the seemingly impossible but necessary task of forging connections across incommensurable differences, organizing convergence while respecting diversity entails some form of translation. Of course, such a statement begs the question of what we mean by translation. In what follows, I will discuss thinkers who help us think about translation as a relational and transformative practice that may inform anti-imperialism, solidarity practices, and internationalist politics.

The Problem of Translation

Any engagement with the politics of translation must recognize the indispensable work done over the past two generations, especially within postcolonial
studies, on translation as an instrument of colonial domination and cultural
hegemony. Such work attends to how, in confrontations between stronger or
majoritarian and weaker or minority languages, especially under conditions
of colonial and racial inequality, translation can reproduce hierarchies. In such
historical situations, the forces of domination seek to "know" subjugated people
in order to better dominate them. The latter are compelled directly or indirectly—through sociocultural arrangements or assimilation policies—to conform to dominant norms.

Epistemologically, this work challenges any notion of translation premised
on an idea that there can be a seamless transparency across texts, languages,
or cultures. Many critics have rightly warned against the epistemic violence
perpetrated by translations across incommensurable languages and lifeworlds
that presuppose the existence of an abstract equivalent or universal metric
through which such differences may be correlated and alterity made legible.
Notably, Dipesh Chakrabarty has persuasively demonstrated that ghostly third
terms supposed to enable neutral transpositions are usually concrete particular
concepts that embody specifically Western historical experiences, norms, and
values. They are false universals that purport to understand but actually erase
difference. At best, such translations will lead to misunderstanding. More
dangerously, they are integral to power/knowledge regimes that subtend forms
of racial and colonial domination.[19]

This critique is on point and indispensable. The question, however, is what
we should conclude from it. Should we reduce dense networks of social relations that often traverse all manner of supposed territorial and cultural boundaries to delimited traditions or forms of life?[20] Should we try to distill what seem
to be universal aspects of social life from what is singular and untranslatable
in order to distinguish between essentially different types of history, one that
is abstract and universal and the other that is concrete and particular?[21] Should
we pursue a program of "epistemic delinking" in order to erect categorical
boundaries between Western and non-Western epistemologies?[22]

I would argue that the tendency to address the problem of translation by
making ontological claims about languages, cultures, and lifeworlds is analytically dubious and politically limiting. Are there modes of thinking and ways
of relating that can attend to entanglement and impurity while respecting
existing and even producing novel singularities? Are there practices of translation that can recognize incommensurables, refuse to posit false equivalences,

renounce the existence of an abstract universal metric while forging mutually illuminating connections across (without erasing) real differences? Can we conceptualize translation as a practice that preserves singularities while forging solidarities within larger differential unities?[23] Might such an attempt to grasp and construct forms of concrete universality allow us to think both translation and internationalism otherwise?

We can usefully route such questions through the remarkable and influential *Dictionary of Untranslatables*, a grand collective project edited by the French philologist and philosopher Barbara Cassin. The *Dictionary* seeks to provincialize supposed universals—in this case, philosophical concepts—from the standpoint of *untranslatability*. It too provides a critique of what we might call the fallacy of misplaced equivalence. Most immediately, Cassin challenges the cultural hegemony of English as the common language of the European Community. More fundamentally, she challenges analytic philosophy's assumption that there are universal concepts that transcend linguistic and historical specificity. In this line of erroneous thinking, because language is supposed to be neutral and concepts universal, the latter can be seamlessly translated into any language without semantic damage or philosophical consequences.

Against global English and analytic philosophy, Cassin underscores that languages do not simply reflect the given world. Rather, "the perspectives constitute the thing; each language is a vision of the world that catches another world in its net, that performs a world."[24] Likewise, words do not simply refer to transhistorical concepts. Cassin argues, "the universality of concepts is absorbed by the singularity of languages."[25] This means that concepts are always embedded in and assume meanings through specific languages, semantic networks and historical situations.[26] On these grounds, Cassin's *Dictionary* seeks to "make perceptible another way of doing philosophy, which does not think of the concept without thinking of the word, for there is no concept without a word."[27] Philosophy must attend to the dynamic relationships between word and world and word and concept. By examining the meaning of supposedly universal concepts in specific languages, as well as the modifications undergone in their movement across languages, the *Dictionary* introduces the problem of translation into the practice of philosophy.

> We have tried to think of philosophy *within* languages. . . . In order to find the meaning of a word in one language, this book explores the networks to which the word belongs and seeks to understand how a network functions in one language by relating it to the networks of other languages. . . . From one language to another, neither the words nor the conceptual networks can simply be superimposed. . . . Each

entry thus starts from a nexus of untranslatability and proceeds to a comparison of terminological networks.[28]

Understanding is not simply a matter of placing meaning in context. It requires us to reconsider context itself by tracing linguistic and semantic "crossings, transfers, and forks in the road . . . turnings, fractures, and carriers.'"[29] It requires attention both to the multiplicity of languages and to multiplicities *within* any given language.

This attention to dynamic processes of crossings, transfers, and fractures distinguishes Cassin's untranslatable from Chakrabarty's seemingly similar conception of the incommensurable. Cassin explains that the *Dictionary* is opposed both to the "logical universalism" of the analytic philosophers that is "indifferent to language" *and* to the kind of "ontological nationalism" promoted by Herder and Heidegger that "essencializ[es] the spirit of language."[30] She writes, "Our work is as far as could be from such a sacralization of the untranslatable, based on the idea of an absolute incommensurability of languages."[31] Cassin underscores, "To speak of *untranslatables* in no way implies that the terms in question, or the expressions, the syntactical or grammatical turns, are not and cannot be translated: the untranslatable is rather what one keeps on (not) translating."[32]

Once again, the question is what we should conclude from Cassin's powerful formulation of translation as *what one keeps on (not) translating*. At one point she declares, "Babel is an opportunity."[33] But she does not adequately develop this promising idea. Indeed, most of her introduction is devoted to how the attempt to translate untranslatables across languages "creates a problem."[34] Her focus, certainly important, is on challenging erroneous assumptions about abstract concepts, neutral language, and transparent equivalence. She wants to interrupt philosophy's misrecognitions and mistaken impositions. The *Dictionary* aims to create friction by giving pause to those who assume that translation is not a problem. But, however implicitly, it still regards translation as a problem—an unavoidable obstacle that always risks eliding the specificity of languages and the singular worlds that they refract.[35] In contrast, I would like to consider a constellation of critical thinkers who treat the dangers of translation as the starting point rather than the aim of analysis. This will help us to embrace the radical possibilities that dwell within the idea of *Babel as an opportunity*.

Babel as Opportunity

Cassin invokes Gilles Deleuze on deterritorialization to support her understanding of the untranslatable as "what one keeps on (not) translating." But we may also read this as a Derridean formulation that displaces any easy binary between territorialized and deterritorialized thinking. Recall that for Derrida, the biblical Tower of Babel story figures translation as both necessary and impossible, as something that God, through the imposition of linguistic plurality among humans, both demands and prohibits.[36] Derrida challenges the conventional dream of translation as seamless equivalence "without remnants."[37] On the contrary, his work suggests that every utterance, even within a given language, must both cross and create the gaps that characterize translation. Demonstrating how singular proper names and iterable common nouns always presuppose one another, Derrida deconstructs the supposed opposition between translation and untranslatability. Demonstrating how each is always the condition of possibility of the other, he figures translation as an inescapable aspect of signification that operates within as well as across languages.[38]

Derrida crystallizes this orientation in seemingly paradoxical declarations such as, "One never writes either in one's own language or a foreign language" and "I only have one language and it is not mine."[39] These abstract philosophical formulations are rooted in concrete historical situations and his own lived experience. In *Monolingualism of the Other*, Derrida relates the singularity of his predicament as an Algerian Jew whose only language is French. He recounts being triply alienated: from his Jewish (linguistic) heritage, his (Arabic- or Berber-speaking) Maghreb milieu, and metropolitan France (which, despite his being a Francophone, remained utterly foreign to him). In the eyes of the French state he was a colonized "native" whose citizenship was conditional and revocable (as was proven during the Vichy Occupation). This situation, shared by colonized peoples and subaltern groups around the world, provides the ground for what Derrida calls the two-sided "law of translation": "1. We only ever speak one language. 2. We never speak only one language."[40]

Derrida's reflections underscore that this "law," along with the predicament it embodies, is both an oppressive burden and a subversive opportunity. He relates how as a student in Algiers and Paris he was driven to master French, a language that could never fully be his own. Paradoxically, his "hyperbolic taste for the purity of language," which included an attempt to erase any hint of idiomatic foreignness from his own speech and writing, led him to develop a signature style that made his written French at once utterly correct and idiomatically singular.[41] In other words, he managed this postcolonial predicament through a kind of excessive correctness. This strategy opened the path to a critical method through which a given language or text may be recognized as, or rendered, other than itself . . . *because* of itself.

In short, the young Derrida developed a kind of polyglot monolingualism that disordered the already impure identities that existed on both sides of the translational exchange. When Derrida recounts, "I always surrender myself to language," he is referring to just this hyperbolic fidelity that transforms both the "translator" (i.e., reader or writer) and the original language or text.[42] This type of subversive surrender was bound up with his desire, regarding French, to "appropriate, domesticate, coax [*amadouer*], that is to say, love by setting on fire, . . . perhaps destroy, in all events mark, transform, prune, cut, forge."[43] His dream was "not that of harming the language" but "perhaps to make something happen to this language" such that "it loses itself by finding itself, by converting itself to itself."[44] Derrida thus appropriated French in a way that was correct yet could not be appropriated. He translated the untranslatable into something legibly untranslatable (even within French). His hyperbolic surrender and transformative appropriation may be understood as a practice of translation that deployed an excessive fidelity to pure French in order to render both his own discourse and the French language more idiomatic, less legible, resistant to easy translation. This is the perspective from which I understand Derrida's claim that all languages or texts are simultaneously translatable and untranslatable, that translation is both necessary and impossible, that every language is, or can be made, foreign to itself.

Derrida's attempt to deconstruct the untenable opposition between translatability and untranslatability is indebted to Walter Benjamin's "Task of the Translator," which he reads closely in "Des tours de Babel." Note that "tour" connotes both a fixed thing (tower) and kinds of movement (e.g., a walk around the neighborhood, taking turns, turning a screw, a turn of events). From the start, Derrida thus embraces Benjamin's understanding of translation as an ongoing practice rather than a fixed object.

Derrida cites Benjamin when he declares that "a text lives only if it lives *on* [*sur-vit*] and it lives *on* only if it is *at once* translatable *and* untranslatable."[45] Recall that for Benjamin the most sophisticated texts—those which are singular and idiomatic, whose deepest meanings can never be simply transferred from one language to another—are the *most* translatable. Challenging the putative superiority of an "original" text, Benjamin declares, "In translation the original rises into a higher and purer linguistic air."[46] This is because translation is a matter of neither "communication . . . of information" nor establishing "likeness to the original."[47] Shifting focus from dead texts and fixed meanings to living languages and the *practice* of translation, Benjamin calls on translators to pay more attention to an original's "way of meaning" than to what is meant.[48] In his view, translation does not aim to recreate the perfect fit between content and language, which he likens to a fruit and its skin. Rather, it seeks to index how that fit is effected in any given language.

For Benjamin, the task of the translator is to illuminate the mediated character of all linguistic exchange in a fallen, which is to say human, world characterized by what he calls the "foreignness of languages."[49] The latter refers not only to the way "natural" languages differ from one another, but to differences within any given language (or text) across different discursive registers (e.g., ordinary, literary, sacred). Accordingly, Benjamin argues that the act of translation elevates and transforms the original text, the original language, *and* the translator's language. Recall the remarkable citation where he notes the "mistaken premise" of translators who "want to turn Hindi, Greek, English into German instead of turning German into Hindi, Greek, English. . . . The basic error of the translator is that he preserves the state in which his own language happens to be instead of allowing his language to be powerfully affected by the foreign tongue."[50] For Benjamin, translation is a (self-)transformative practice that refuses to sacralize either original languages (and texts) or the language of translation (and translated texts). Benjaminian translation thus figures an ethical relation in which, as for Derrida, submission and subversion are conjoined.

Both Benjamin and Derrida challenge the commonplace opposition between translatability and untranslatability, the priority of originals over translations, and the fiction that translation is ever a matter of one-to-one equivalence that erases difference. Each rejects the idea that any signifying practice can exist outside of or apart from translation. Each offers an understanding of translation that explodes identitarian logic. Both figure translation as a transformative practice with subversive possibilities whereby the movement of singular meanings across incommensurable semantic fields may render the strange familiar *and* the familiar strange. Both suggest that translation may function to displace the linguistic hegemony and deform the linguistic certainties of "major" languages. For these reasons, their writings underscore the subversive possibilities of translation as a medium through which to confront a postcolonial predicament and to create non-self-evident solidarities. Their insights may help us to engage the problems and promise of solidarity. For insofar as solidarity practices also seek to create transformative and open-ended relations across singularities, they may be regarded as fundamentally translational.

In short, Benjamin and Derrida figure translation in ways that illuminate how Babel may be an intellectual, ethical, and political opportunity. But they do so at a highly abstract level in order to make general claims about language, texts, and meaning. Benjamin, for example, suggests that translation offers glimpses of a seemingly impossible reconciliation or redemption that, apart from the Messianic end of history, only social revolution could bring about.[51] Derrida asserts that his insight on the impossibility of monolingualism "opens onto a politics, a right, and an ethics."[52] But he never works through the promising links between, on the one hand, his suggestions that all languages differ from themselves and that translation can make language *do things* (i.e., that there is no outside-translation), and on the other, his assertions that the translator's ethical indebtedness points to an internationalist politics founded upon responsibility for and hospitality to the other. Rather, he examines the singular situation of Algerian Jews in order to elaborate what he regards as a universal predicament bound up with signification as such.

Despite these limitations, Benjamin and Derrida illuminate how the irreducibly translational character of language displaces the conventional opposition between abstract universalism and ontological culturalism. Their insights allow us to see how both translation and solidarity practices may embrace singularities in order to produce concrete universality (i.e., differential unities or contradictory totalities). Such an orientation may usefully inform anticolonial politics and internationalist projects. The understanding of translation as an open-ended transformative practice *between and within* languages or peoples conveys just the kind of strategy pursued by many African and Caribbean intellectuals.

The Politics of Translation as an Ethics of Relation

The Senegalese philosopher Souleymane Bachir Diagne has developed a translational understanding of philosophy as an ethical practice that underscores singularity, forges productive connections, and attends to novel configurations. In *The Ink of Scholars* Diagne criticizes Eurocentric assumptions about the nonphilosophical character of African knowledge *and* forcefully critiques ethnological, ontological, or strictly autarchic conceptions of African philosophy. From this perspective, *he argues both that Africans should philosophize in African languages and that Africans should not hesitate to philosophize in non-African languages.* Like Cassin, with whom he has collaborated, he argues that philosophical insights are always rooted, situated, and worldly. But he also insists that their significance may always transcend the linguistic cultural contexts within which they were immediately produced. In his view, philosophy is neither an expression of a historical situation or form of life nor a static body of knowledge; it is a dynamic and open-ended practice. Against the idea that Africans should only seek to produce "an other philosophy, which would keep close to each language's way of speaking," Diagne argues that to "philosophize in African languages" is "a means of thinking philosophically in translation and in crossing perspectives."[53]

This orientation toward philosophy and language frees Diagne from the false oppositions (e.g., origins vs. imitations, or authenticity vs. alienation) which frequently accompany debates about African thought. Such debates often begin with assumptions about linguistic or conceptual purity that disregard entangled histories and polyglot situations. With regard to the question of socialism in Africa, for example, Diagne declares, "only translations exist, without a text that can be claimed as the original one, written in a sacred language."[54] Rather than dispute whether a given philosophy can be adequately translated, he develops an understanding of philosophy itself as a practice of unending translation.

Citing Cassin, Diagne rejects any notion of translation as a matter of finding "equivalents of the same concept in different languages."[55] In contrast, he invokes Hannah Arendt's image of "the faltering equivocity of the world" to embrace what he calls "deterritorialized ways of speaking."[56] Against reductive, appropriative, and ethnocentric types of translation which erase differences, Diagne endorses an understanding of translation as a process or practice of "putting in touch."[57] He beautifully crystallizes this orientation when, contra the Italian commonplace "traduttore, traditore" (translator, traitor), he writes, "Translation is treason? Certainly, but this betrayal is the only fidelity."[58] Through this elegant formulation Diagne demands, first, that we countenance the universal philosophical truths expressed in and through African knowledge and, second, that we recognize the singularity of the African history, modes of understanding, and forms of life that are embedded in—that accompany, haunt, cross, and displace—Africans' use of Western philosophical languages, discourses, frameworks, and genres. For Diagne, neither philosophy nor translation should begin with a will to transparency or a desire to overcome singularities. He regards both philosophy and translation in terms of opening, dialogue, and *métissage*. They are relational and open-ended practices that move back and forth between singularity and universality without an assumed metalanguage. This epistemological understanding also indexes an ethical orientation toward what I have been calling concrete universality.[59]

Diagne's reflections on the translational ethics of "putting in touch" and entering into relation may be usefully placed in dialogue with Édouard Glissant's political-philosophical reflections on the "poetics of Relation." This conception is at once epistemological, aesthetic, ethical, and political. Running through Glissant's reflections on Relation is the problem and promise of translation as a way to overcome the false choice, which so often defines colonial situations, between an abstract universality (which purports to open access to the whole world) and a concrete particularity (which supposedly locks actors in provincial lifeworlds). Glissant challenges the modern imperial dictum that offers colonized peoples wanting to speak their own language an unacceptable choice: "Either you speak a language that is 'universal' . . . and participate in the life of the world; or else you retreat into your particular idiom—quite unfit for sharing—in which case you cut yourself off from the world to wallow alone and sterile in your so-called identity."[60] Conjuring the spirit of his elder inter-locutor Aimé Césaire, Glissant rejects this false alternative between "either . . . seclusion within a restrictive particularity or, conversely dilution within a generalizing universal."[61] Such a logic is unable to recognize, let alone embrace, "relations of multiplicity or contagion" when "mixtures explode into momen-tary flashes of creation."[62]

Against a reductively "monolingual" orientation to the world, Glissant insists, "speaking one's language and opening up to the language of the other no lon-ger form the basis for an alternative."[63] Offering a relational and reciprocal understanding of linguistic plurality, he writes, "'I speak to you in your language voice, and it is in my language use that I understand you.' Creating in any given language thus assumes that one be inhabited by the impossible desire for all the languages in the world. Totality calls out to us."[64] For Glissant, sin-gularity is not reduced to a provincialism, and universality is not abstracted into an underlying or overarching sameness. Rather, when a specific "people speaks its language or languages," it makes its more general "relationship to the world concrete and visible for itself and for others."[65]

Glissant thereby attempts to overcome the false opposition between, on the one hand, a world organized around a united humanity with a universal lan-guage that elides differences and, on the other, a confusion of local languages that partitions peoples from each other and precludes translocal relations. This is the basis for his alternative view of Babel:

> On the other side of the bitter struggles against domination and for the
> liberation of the imagination, there opens up a multiply dispersed
> zone in which we are gripped by vertigo. But this is not the vertigo
> preceding apocalypse and Babel's fall. It is the shiver of a beginning,
> confronted with extreme possibility. It is possible to build the Tower—
> in every language.[66]

This call to build a Tower of Babel in every language conveys a vision of mul-tiple universals, each of which is internally heterogeneous. In this view, every place (or language, or text) is or refracts both *a* world and *the* world.

This embrace of linguistic multiplicity and ceaseless translation reverberates with Glissant's understanding of "the poetics of Relation." The latter indexes an open totality, a transversal (and I would add translational) universality created through ramifying networks of opaque singularities. In contrast to the liberal universal, it is grounded in concrete singularities, sustained not through a will to transparency but through "the right to opacity."[67] In contrast to identitarian ontologies, it is composed of innumerable dynamic singularities entering into endless relations with one another, undergoing all manner of transformation in the process.

For Glissant, opacity facilitates rather than forecloses solidarity. Referring to Relation as an "open totality" whose "poetic force" is "radiant," he writes, "To feel in solidarity with [the opaque other] or to build with him or to like what he does, it is not necessary for me to grasp him. It is not necessary to try to become the other (to become other) nor to 'make' him in my image."[68] He explains, "Opacities can coexist and converge, weaving fabrics. To understand these truly, one must focus on the texture of the weave and not on the nature of its components. . . . This-here is the weave and it weaves no boundaries."[69] Here we might understand the fabric (or Relation) as a concrete universal (always in the process of becoming) and the weaving as practices of translation and solidarity. Elsewhere, Glissant uses the term *donner-avec* (to give-with) to index an epistemology, ethics, and politics that, founded upon offering and opening, challenges any notion of "generalizing universality."[70] We might think of this relational, reciprocal, and interdependent way of knowing and being-together as fundamentally translational.

The Translational Condition

We may usefully place Diagne and Glissant in dialogue with Benjamin and Derrida regarding translation as a relational practice that may transform all elements (languages, cultures, and translators) through the encounter. In their different ways, these thinkers understand translation a practice that displaces the false alternative between abstract universality and concrete singularity. They reject conventional notions of translation that purport to seek perfect equivalence between languages, cultures, or texts—as if there were universal metalanguages through which any particular signification could be neatly transposed from one system or medium to another, as if meaning were not inextricably bound up with the specific language or lifeworld in which it is expressed. Yet they treat the existence of such singularities as evidence that the work of translation cannot be avoided. They remind us that translation always also occurs *within* languages, communities, and groups that are never self-identical. Every utterance both crosses *and* creates the gaps that characterize translation. To the extent that translation illuminates rather than erases singularities, it is an ethical practice that performs and produces reciprocity. As such, translation models and creates concrete pathways for the politics of solidarity. It may be an indispensable aspect of worldwide antiracist, anticolonial, and anticapitalist struggle that also anticipates a world organized around relations of reciprocity and solidarity.

Diagne and Glissant begin with a forceful critique of Eurocentric knowledge, provincial universals, and fictions of intercultural transparency. But their insistence on the fundamentally untranslatable character of singular ways of being and knowing become a charter *for* the practice of translation. Their work helps us to refigure translation as an unavoidable imperative, an ethical responsibility, and a potentially transformational political practice. Their reflections challenge ontological notions of cultures or civilizations as self-identical wholes. They offer us a relational view of social life as mediated by acts of translation in which the prospect of experimental connection and unforeseen creation across seemingly incommensurable differences is always possible. We might call this a translational vision of sociality in which singularity and solidarity are not antithetical to each other. Following their lead, we may employ the optic of translation to challenge conventional assumptions about supposedly self-evident boundaries between us and them, here and there, now and then. Heeding Lenin's revolutionary call to *transform the imperial war into a civil war*, we might say that translation helps us to recognize that what appear to be reified differences between groups, cultures, or languages may actually be ramifying differences *within* them that can facilitate new relations across them.

Translational Politics

Throughout this essay I have used the term "translational" to convey the fact that because singularity, multiplicity, and incommensurability form the very terrain of our thinking and acting, there is no outside of translation. By referring to the translational character of certain currents of philosophy, sociality, and universality, I am underscoring the background condition that makes ongoing translation within and across supposed differences an inescapable imperative. There can be no choosing for or against translation. The question is not whether one supports or opposes translation but whether a specific practice of translation affirms or disrupts existing assumptions and arrangements. What matters is whether a given translation has counterhegemonic potential, whether it helps to create or foreclose emancipatory forms of sociality and political association.

Certainly, we need to challenge any facile positivist or imperialist understanding of translation as transparent equivalence, as an attempt to define one-to-one correspondences. Perhaps such notions may still have currency among technocrats, scientists, analytic philosophers, the global business elite, New York publishing executives, and a monolingual US reading public. Many scenes and forms of translation continue to reproduce relations of racial and colonial inequality. But to regard translation only as an instrument of domination is to miss the transversal practices and projects that have long fueled textual, cultural, and political translation among non-European anti-imperialist Leftists.

Writing about José Rizal, the Filipino anticolonial novelist, Benedict Anderson evokes the polyglot character of late nineteenth-century anti-imperial internationalism:

> Filipinos wrote to Austrians in German, to Japanese in English, to each other in French, or Spanish, or Tagalog, with liberal interventions from the last beautiful international language, Latin. Some of them knew a bit of Russian, Greek, Italian, Japanese, and Chinese. . . . Real communication required the true, hard internationalism of the polyglot. Filipino leaders were peculiarly adapted to the Babelish world.[71]

Within this tradition of polyglot internationalism we can situate Lenin translating Marx into Russian, Langston Hughes translating Nicolás Guillén into English, Paulette Nardal translating Claude McKay into French, and Ali Shariati translating Frantz Fanon into Persian. The anthropologist Fadi Bardawil has recently demonstrated that rapid and collective translations of Marxist and other critical theoretical writings were integral to the work of Lebanese socialists in the 1960s.[72] The fact that these were often translations of translations— Arabic translations of French translations of Russian or German—underscores the open and ramifying character of this practice.

This tradition of translational internationalism is nicely evoked by Ralph Ellison. He describes a scene in the late 1930s where he, not yet a published writer, and Richard Wright, who was about to publish *Uncle Tom's Children*, attended a party in New York where they hoped to raise money for Wright's new literary magazine. Ellison recalls that this was both where he "first heard the folksinger Leadbelly perform" *and* where he met André Malraux, who was there "to make an appeal for the Spanish Loyalists" then fighting Franco in the Civil War. "I had never dreamed that I would be in the presence of Malraux, of whose work I became aware on my second day in Harlem when Langston Hughes suggested that I read *Man's Fate* and *Days of Wrath.* . . . And it is this fortuitous circumstance which led to my selecting Malraux as a literary 'ancestor,' whom, unlike a relative, the artist is permitted to choose."[73]

Here we can see the close affinity between literary translation and international solidarity. Both were bound up with the transversal practice of "choosing ancestors" across inherited territorial, cultural, racial, and national boundaries.

As I have discussed elsewhere, the Martinican poet-activist Aimé Césaire elaborated just such antiprovincial notions of places, cultures, and communities.[74] Consider his strategy of deliberately "inflecting" French as a way of both inhabiting it as his own proper language and rendering it subversively uncanny.[75] We might say that by using French in ways that made the seemingly strange disturbingly familiar and the seemingly familiar disturbingly strange, Césaire and his associates introduced the problematic of translation into the very center of the French language, territory, and polity. This attempt to unthink French and France in ways that pointed beyond the unacceptable alternative of separation or assimilation reverberates with his broader commitment to transcend the false opposition between a "narrow particularism" that would lead to a "walled segregation" and "dilution" in an "emaciated universalism."[76]

Césaire's commitment to concrete universalism informed his approach to solidarity politics. The latter was conjunctural and experimental. Recall that when resigning from the French Communist Party, he rejected its dogmatic insistence that ordinary Martinicans were automatically in solidarity with French workers and the worldwide proletariat. Césaire valued such alliances but challenged the PCF's orthodox injunction to reject "a priori and in the name of an exclusive ideology, men who are nevertheless honest and fundamentally anticolonialist," whether bourgeois Martinicans or African and Caribbean nationalists.[77] He explained, "I do not want to erect solidarities in metaphysics. There are no allies by divine right."[78] Refusing to assign ontological priority to territory, class, or race, Césaire suggested that the contingencies of "place, time, and the nature of things" would determine which balance of solidarities between Martinicans and French citizens, worldwide workers, colonized peoples, and diasporic Blacks would be most politically effective in any given moment.[79] This nexus between (intralingual) translation, anticolonialism, and solidarity politics was crystallized in his vision of an alternative "universal . . . enriched and deepened by all particulars, by the coexistence of all particulars."[80]

Césaire sought to realize this concrete universal vision, to practice translational politics, at the level of political form. After resigning from the PCF, he created an independent Martinican socialist party committed to transforming imperial France into a transcontinental and multinational socialist federation.[81] This new type of polity, he hoped, might point to a world order that was no longer organized around provincial notions of territory, culture, and identity. Césaire's strategy of cultural subversion through intralingual translation—radical literalism—corresponds to this project to abolish France by appropriating it in a transformative way. For Césaire, there was an underlying affinity between "poetic knowledge," cosmopolitan politics, and the utopian prospect of creating a different world.[82] His epistemology, aesthetics, ethics, and politics were grounded in notions of reciprocity and mixture. Running through these domains was a translational attempt to conjugate rooted singularities and translocal solidarities. His subversive relationship to French and his federalist vision of a postnational France can help us to think the relation between anti-imperialism, solidarity politics, and translation.

The epistemological, ethical, and political registers of translation as a catalyst of radical internationalism (and vice versa) converge in the figure of C. L. R. James. In his famous discussion with Trotsky in Mexico, James advised the exiled revolutionary on how to translate Fourth International aims and strategies into a movement to organize African American workers in ways that would transform Marxism itself.[83] This, according to James, was one of the lessons he learned from Lenin, whose "life's work was to translate Marxism into Russian terms for the Russian people"[84] Likewise, James insisted that they could only build a mass party in the United States by reconsidering Marxist theory in relation to American history and conditions. In his plenum address to the 1944 Workers Party national meeting, James declared, *"To Bolshevize America it is necessary to Americanize Bolshevism."*[85] Note that he was not simply advocating an operation of domestication. Americanizing Bolshevism would require a web of transversal translations among James's cohort of US comrades in the New York section of the Workers Party.

Translation was at the very center of this group's friendship, theorizing, and politics. Grace Lee Boggs, a Chinese American militant with a PhD in philosophy, relates how translation was at the center of their productive excitement and exploding insights. She translated Marx's *Economic and Philosophical Manuscripts* from German, while Raya Dunayevskaya, the ex-Trotskyist Russian emigré activist, translated Lenin's notebooks on Hegel from Russian. These translations and ensuing discussions enabled James to write *Notes on Dialectics* (1948). These translations helped them, under the rubric of the "Johnson-Forest Tendency," to grasp the specificity of the American workers' movement in 1947. The point is not that sacred texts gave them access to a transhistorical Marxist truth, but that the practice of translation helped them to develop a conjunctural analysis of *their* specific political situation. Thinking across the semantic networks offered by German, Russian, and English, as well as across the historical experience of the industrial West, the rural East, and the colonized Caribbean, helped them to grasp the form of racial capitalism that they confronted and the possibility of building a revolutionary movement that might be fueled by an autonomous party composed of insurgent Black masses. Here we can recognize translation as a relational and dialogic practice that enables reciprocal transformations in political, ethical, and social domains. Boggs recalls: "CLR, Raya, and I were inseparable. . . . Our energy was fantastic. We would spend a morning or afternoon writing, talking, and eating and then go home and write voluminous letters to one another extending or enlarging on what we had discussed, sending these around to other members of our tendency in barely legible carbon copies."[86] This practice of translation was integral to their attempt to Americanize Bolshevism for the conditions of late twentieth-century capitalism. It also allowed them to anticipate the kind of heterogeneous, polyglot, and translational world that they hoped to build.

Recall that James's cohort hoped to situate an independent US Black people's party within the framework of a postwar Fourth International that was opposed to both Western and Soviet bloc variants of state capitalism. Likewise, Samir Amin called for a Fifth International that would both revive and rework the spirit of Bandung (as well as that of the First International). Amin regarded the new internationalism of peoples as both a means of emancipatory struggle and a substantive feature of the polycentric, socialist, and radically democratic world this struggle would create.

I suggested above that Amin's call for radical internationalists to organize convergence while respecting diversity raised but did not adequately elaborate the possibility of translation as a political practice. Through Derrida, Benjamin, Diagne, Glissant, Césaire, and James, I have indicated some ways that Amin's insight could be further elaborated. In this same spirit, we might usefully place these thinkers "in touch" with Amin's comrade Boaventura de Sousa Santos. This Portuguese social theorist and alter-globalization militant collaborated with Amin in meetings of the World Social Forum. Both were signatories of the 2005 Porto Alegre Manifesto. Santos sought directly to conjugate translation and radical internationalism for the post–Cold War conjuncture.

From the standpoint of "epistemologies of the South," Santos argues that there can be no social justice without cognitive justice.[87] The latter requires the recognition of non-Western forms of knowledge that can only be grasped on their own terms. But it also requires an ongoing practice of what he calls "intercultural translation," which "consists of searching for isomorphic concerns and underlying assumptions among cultures . . . and developing, whenever appropriate, new hybrid forms of cultural understanding and intercommunication."[88] As Santos contends, "translation undermines the idea of original pure cultures and stresses the idea of cultural relationality. . . . Cultures are monolithic only when seen from the outside or from afar. When looked at from the inside or at close range, they are easily seen to comprise various and often conflicting versions of the same culture."[89] Translation, in other words, illuminates the disjunctures *within* as much as between cultures, peoples, and social groups.

Santos develops an understanding of "intercultural translation" as a "living process" that unfolds within the "translational contact zones" created by global capitalism and imperialism.[90] He defines these as zones of historically constituted diversity, inequality, and conflict that compel translation practices. Santos recognizes that in such situations, "mediation, confrontation, and negotiation" may just as likely reinforce as reduce existing hierarchies.[91] This risk is bound up with the fact that these are "relatively uncodified" zones in which there is no singular truth or metalanguage to which translational differences can be referred or in terms of which disagreements can be adjudicated.[92] Under such conditions, "the work of translation is basically an argumentative work, based on the cosmopolitan emotion of sharing the world with those who do not share our knowledge and experience."[93] In this relational and conflictual space, he explains, assumptions about cultural premises become arguments over premises that can never be definitively resolved. Though such spaces are typically organized around structural inequalities, the imperative to translate in the "absence of a general theory" may also provide opportunities "for normative and cultural experimentation and innovation" that could transform actors' understandings and identities.[94] The result may be new kinds of "equality in differences" or "hybrid cultural constellations."[95] Like Diagne's "putting in touch," this approach to translation "aims at reciprocity instead of worrying about source cultures and target cultures."[96]

Santos underscores that intercultural translation, as a "living process" through which "to cope with diversity and conflict," is "not a gesture of intellectual curiosity or cultural dilettantism. It is rather an imperative dictated by the need to broaden political articulation beyond the confines of a given locale or culture."[97] Accordingly, he links intercultural translation to the "interpolitical translation" that is indispensable for "intermovement politics."[98] He thus helps us to refigure translation as a mode of political articulation and solidarity politics in the absence of a "single universal social practice or collective subject to confer meaning and direction to history."[99] Such translation can only be conjunctural, experimental, and strategic. In terms that resonate with Amin's "internationalism of peoples," Santos's interpolitical translation seeks "to identify, in each concrete historical moment or context, which constellations of practices carry more counterhegemonic potential."[100]

Santos's vision of interpolitical translation in the service of intermovement politics is not based on the Comintern model of a central directorate, orthodox ideology, and party line. Rather, it resonates more closely with Césaire's universal enriched by the coexistence of all the particulars, Glissant's vision of Relation as a worldwide network of entangled but irreducible singularities, and Amin's organized but decentralized internationalism of peoples. For Santos, the aim of translation practices and solidarity politics is to create radical blocs that do *not* need to be situated under a single directorate, whose multiple political orientations do *not* need to be standardized within an identical program. As a living process that transforms "subaltern cosmopolitan contact zones" into political solidarities for global struggles against capitalism, colonialism, and patriarchy, Santos's interpolitical translation is a concrete utopian practice that anticipates new forms of being-together.[101] He explains, "The work of translation . . . is a work of epistemological and democratic imagination, aiming to construct new and plural conceptions of social emancipation."[102]

Santos recognizes that "there is no guarantee that a better world will follow or that all those who continue to struggle for it will conceive it the same way."[103] Interpolitical translation risks reproducing existing norms and inequalities. But his work, like Amin's, suggests that this risk cannot be avoided; such future-oriented wagers must be made. This is because the earth is shared. Modern Western forms of domination have created webs of global dependence and subordination, conflict and connection, interdependence and reciprocity, proximity and hybridity. There is no outside of, or spaces that are unaffected by, capitalist and imperialist modernity. There are no pure cultures; all are mutually implicated. Moreover, as Amin insisted, global forms of systemic domination cannot be overcome through local acts of refusal or resistance. Counterhegemonic projects must operate on a worldwide scale. Politically as well as epistemologically, we inhabit a translational world.

To treat Babel as an opportunity is not simply to embrace linguistic or cultural diversity. Babel does not only reject a hegemon's claim to universality. Nor does it only challenge abstract universality from the standpoint of concrete particularity. Rather, as the thinkers I have discussed help us to see, the inescapable fact of Babel, the unavoidable translational condition, may open new horizons of concrete universality—epistemological, ethical, and political orientations that point beyond the false choice between singularity and solidarity. Translation practices, solidarity politics, and internationalist projects forge transversal relations across putative boundaries in ways that illuminate singularity and incommensurability. Translational practices seek to identify the internal heterogeneity of that which appears to be identical and underlying or potential affinities with that which appears to be different. Translational politics may therefore transform all manner of regressive imperial wars into emancipatory civil wars. They are both means and ends of the internationalist struggle for the concrete universal "world we wish to see."

Bibliography

Amin, Samir. *Beyond US Hegemony? Assessing the Prospects for a Multipolar World.* London: Zed Books, 2006.

———. *A Life Looking Forward: Memoirs of an Independent Marxist.* London: Zed Books, 2006.

———. *Re-reading the Postwar Period: An Intellectual Itinerary.* New York: Monthly Review, 1994.

———. *The World We Wish to See: Revolutionary Objectives in the Twenty-First Century.* Translated by James Membrez. New York: Monthly Review, 2008.

Anderson, Benedict. *Under Three Flags: Anarchism and the Anti-colonial Imagination.* London: Verso, 2005.

Asad, Talal. *Formations of the Secular: Christianity, Islam, Modernity.* Stanford, CA: Stanford University Press, 2003.

"The Bamako Appeal." In Samir Amin, *The World We Wish to See: Revolutionary Objectives in the Twenty-First Century,* translated by James Membrez. New York: Monthly Review, 2008.

Bardawil, Fadi. *Revolution and Disenchantment: Arab Marxism and the Binds of Emancipation.* Durham, NC: Duke University Press, 2020.

Becker, Marc. "Report from the World Social Forum VI: Civil Society Meets Chavez's State." *Dollars and Sense* (March/April 2006): 7–8.

Benjamin, Walter. "On Language as Such and the Language of Man." Translated by Edmund Jephcott. In *Selected Writings,* vol. 1, *1913–1926,* edited by Marcus Bullock and Michael W. Jennings, 62–74. Cambridge, MA: Belknap, 2004.

———. "The Task of the Translator." Translated by Harry Zohn. In *Selected Writings,* vol. 1, *1913–1926,* edited by Marcus Bullock and Michael W. Jennings, 253–63. Cambridge, MA: Belknap, 2004.

Berman, Antoine. *The Experience of the Foreign: Culture and Translation in Romantic Germany.* Albany: State University of New York Press, 1992.

Boggs, Grace Lee. *Living for Change: An Autobiography.* Minneapolis: University of Minnesota Press, 1998.

Cassin, Barbara, ed. *Dictionary of Untranslatables: A Philosophical Lexicon.* Translation edited by Emily Apter, Jacques Lezra, and Michael Wood. Princeton, NJ: Princeton University Press, 2014.

Catalinotto, John. "'Bamako Appeal' Promotes Struggle against Market-Driven Society." *Workers World,* January 27, 2006.

Césaire, Aimé. "Letter to Maurice Thorez." Translated by Chike Jeffers. *Social Text* 28, no. 103 (Summer 2010): 145–52.

———. "Poetry and Knowledge." In *Lyric and Dramatic Poetry, 1946–1982,* xlii–lv. Charlottesville: University of Virginia Press, 1990.

Chakrabarty, Dipesh. *Provincializing Europe: Postcolonial Thought and Historical Difference.* 2000; reissued with a new preface, Princeton, NJ: Princeton University Press, 2008.

Chatterjee, Partha. "Nationalism, Internationalism, and Cosmopolitanism: Some Observations from Modern Indian History." *Comparative Studies of South Asia, Africa and the Middle East* 36, no. 2 (2016): 320–34.

Derrida, Jacques. "Des tours de Babel." Translated by Joseph F. Graham. In *Psyche: Inventions of the Other*, vol. 1, edited by Peggy Kamuf and Elizabeth Rottenberg, 191–225. Stanford, CA: Stanford University Press, 2007.

———. "Living On/Borderlines." In *Deconstruction and Criticism*, by Harold Bloom et al., 75–176. New York: Routledge, 1979.

———. *Monolingualism of the Other; or, The Prosthesis of Origin*. Translated by Patrick Mensah. Stanford, CA: Stanford University Press, 1998.

Diagne, Souleymane Bachir. *The Ink of Scholars: Reflections on Philosophy in Africa*. Dakar: CODESRIA, 2016.

Ellison, Ralph. "Hidden Name and Complex Fate." In *The Collected Essays of Ralph Ellison, Revised and Updated*, edited by John F. Callahan, 189–209. New York: Modern Library/Random House, 2004.

Fanon, Frantz. *Black Skin, White Masks*. Boston: Grove, 2008.

Glissant, Édouard. *Poetics of Relation*. Translated by Betsy Wing. Ann Arbor: University of Michigan Press, 1997.

———. *Poétique de la relation: Poétique III*. Paris: Gallimard 1990.

———. *Traité de Tout-Monde: Poétique IV*. Paris: Gallimard, 1997.

Jakobson, Roman. "On Linguistic Aspects of Translation." In *On Translation*, edited by Reuben A. Brower, 232–39. Cambridge, MA: Harvard University Press, 1959.

James, C. L. R. "Education, Propaganda, Agitation: Post-war America and Bolshevism." In C. L. R. James, *Marxism for Our Times*, edited by Martin Glaberman, 3–42. Jackson: University Press of Mississippi, 1999.

Hardt, Michael, and Antonio Negri. *Commonwealth*. Cambridge, MA: Belknap, 2011.

Leiner, Jacqueline. "Entretien avec Aimé Césaire." In *Tropiques, 1941–1945: Collection complète*, v–xxiv. Paris: Jean-Michel Place, 1978.

McLemee, Scott, ed. *C. L. R. James on the "Negro Question."* Jackson: University of Mississippi Press, 1996.

Mignolo, Walter. *The Darker Side of Western Modernity: Global Futures, Decolonial Options*. Durham, NC: Duke University Press, 2011.

Santos, Boaventura de Sousa. *Epistemologies of the South: Justice against Epistemicide*. New York: Routledge, 2014.

Wilder, Gary. "Anticipation." *Political Concepts: A Critical Lexicon*, issue 3. https://www.politicalconcepts.org/category/issue-3/.

———. *Freedom Time: Negritude, Decolonization, and the History of the World*. Durham, NC: Duke University Press, 2014.

Notes

1. This essay is largely drawn from Gary Wilder, *Concrete Utopianism: The Politics of Temporality and Solidarity* (Fordham University Press, 2022). Fuller development of

these themes can be found in chapter 2, "Concrete Utopianism and Critical Internationalism: Refusing Left Realism," and chapter 3, "Practicing Translation: Beyond Left Culturalism."

John Catalinotto, "'Bamako Appeal' Promotes Struggle against Market-Driven Society," *Workers World*, January 27, 2006; Marc Becker, "Report from the World Social Forum VI: Civil Society Meets Chavez's State," *Dollars and Sense* (March/April 2006): 7–8.

2. "The Bamako Appeal," published as appendix 2 in Samir Amin, *The World We Wish to See: Revolutionary Objectives in the Twenty-First Century*, trans. James Membrez (New York: Monthly Review, 2008), 108.

3. "Bamako Appeal," 107.

4. "Bamako Appeal," 107.

5. "Bamako Appeal," 108.

6. See Samir Amin, *A Life Looking Forward: Memoirs of an Independent Marxist* (London: Zed Books, 2006).

7. Samir Amin, *Beyond US Hegemony? Assessing the Prospects for a Multipolar World* (London: Zed Books, 2006), 155; Samir Amin, *Re-reading the Postwar Period: An Intellectual Itinerary* (New York: Monthly Review, 1994), 168.

8. Amin, *Beyond US Hegemony?*, 155.

9. Amin, 160.

10. Amin, 155.

11. Amin, 106.

12. Amin, *World We Wish to See*, 79.

13. On anticipation as a form of concrete utopianism that calls for and calls forth, see Gary Wilder, "Anticipation," *Political Concepts: A Critical Lexicon*, issue 3, https://www.politicalconcepts.org/category/issue-3/.

14. Amin, *World We Wish to See*, 75.

15. Amin, 63.

16. Amin, 79.

17. Amin, 45. See, for example, Partha Chatterjee, "Nationalism, Internationalism, and Cosmopolitanism: Some Observations from Modern Indian History," *Comparative Studies of South Asia, Africa and the Middle East* 36, no. 2 (2016): 320–34.

18. Amin, *Beyond US Hegemony?*, 106, 152.

19. Dipesh Chakrabarty, *Provincializing Europe: Postcolonial Thought and Historical Difference* (2000; reissued with a new preface, Princeton, NJ: Princeton University Press, 2008).

20. In *Provincializing Europe*, Chakrabarty employs an understanding of specific lifeworlds that echo those of Heideggerian phenomenology and early cultural anthropology. For a more nuanced conception of traditions and forms of life defined by internal debate and ongoing transformation, but one which still does not accommodate entanglement or mixture across traditions and forms of life, see Talal Asad, *Formations of the Secular: Christianity, Islam, Modernity* (Stanford, CA: Stanford University Press, 2003).

21. In *Provincializing Europe*, Chakrabarty makes a dubious distinction between what he calls History 1 and History 2.

22. On decolonial or epistemic delinking, see also Walter Mignolo, *The Darker Side of Western Modernity: Global Futures, Decolonial Options* (Durham, NC: Duke University Press, 2011).

23. Following Marx's Hegelian distinction between universal, particular, and singular, I use singularity to mean that which is irreducible and must be grasped on its own terms. The singular is not simply a part of a larger whole. And the term "difference" usually functions to establish boundaries, whether in terms of the binary of sameness vs. difference or between categories of phenomena. In contrast, singularity, as I employ and understand it, typically confounds categorization, classification, and tendencies to ontologize "difference" in determinate ways. My sense of singularities as being capable of entering into endless configurations with other singularities, such that they are transformed and new singularities created, singularities as a source of radical political potential, is informed by the way the concept is employed by Glissant, as discussed in this essay, and Michael Hardt and Antonio Negri in *Commonwealth* (Cambridge, MA: Belknap, 2011).

24. Barbara Cassin, ed., introduction to *Dictionary of Untranslatables: A Philosophical Lexicon*, translation edited by Emily Apter, Jacques Lezra, and Michael Wood (Princeton, NJ: Princeton University Press, 2004), xix.

25. Cassin, *Dictionary of Untranslatables*, xix.

26. "A language . . . is not a fact of nature, an object, but an effect caught up in history and culture, and that ceaselessly invents itself." Cassin, xix.

27. Cassin, xx.

28. Cassin, xvii.

29. Cassin, xvii.

30. Cassin, xviii.

31. Cassin, xviii.

32. Cassin, xvii.

33. Cassin, xix.

34. Cassin, xvii.

35. In her contribution to this volume, Cassin helps us to think further about Babel as an opportunity, although she does not use this formulation, when she figures language as "an *energeia*, as a perpetual, continuous putting into action; such that the relation between languages, translation, shows how these *energeiai*, these energies evolve and intermix."

36. See Jacques Derrida, "Des tours de Babel," trans. Joseph F. Graham, in *Psyche: Inventions of the Other*, vol. 1, ed. Peggy Kamuf and Elizabeth Rottenberg (Stanford, CA: Stanford University Press, 2007), 191–225.

37. Jacques Derrida, "Living On/Borderlines," in *Deconstruction and Criticism*, by Harold Bloom et al. (New York: Routledge, 1979), 119.

38. To this end, he endorses Jakobson's typology of intralingual, interlingual, and intersemiotic translation. See Roman Jakobson, "On Linguistic Aspects of

Translation," in *On Translation*, ed. Reuben A. Brower (Cambridge, MA: Harvard University Press, 1959), 232–39.

39. Derrida, "Living On/Borderlines," 101, and Jacques Derrida, *Monolingualism of the Other; or, The Prosthesis of Origin*, trans. Patrick Mensah (Stanford, CA: Stanford University Press, 1998), 1.

40. Derrida, *Monolingualism*, 10.

41. Derrida, 49.

42. Derrida, 47.

43. Derrida, 50–51.

44. Derrida, 51.

45. Derrida, "Living On/Borderlines," 102.

46.

47. Benjamin, 253, 256.

48. Benjamin, 260.

49. Benjamin, 257.

50. Benjamin, 261–62.

51. See also Walter Benjamin, "On Language as Such and the Language of Man," trans. Edmund Jephcott, in *Selected Writings*, vol. 1, *1913–1926*, ed. Marcus Bullock and Michael W. Jennings (Cambridge, MA: Harvard University Press, 1996), 62–74.

52. Derrida, *Monolingualism*, 24.

53. Souleymane Bachir Diagne, *The Ink of Scholars: Reflections on Philosophy in Africa* (Dakar: CODESRIA, 2016), xx.

54. Diagne, xx.

55. Diagne, xx.

56. Diagne, xx.

57. Diagne, xx. He borrows this phrase from Antoine Berman, who writes that the "ethical aim of translation" is "to be an opening, a dialogue, a cross-breeding, a decentering. Translation is a 'putting in touch with,' or it is *nothing*." Berman, *The Experience of the Foreign: Culture and Translation in Romantic Germany* (Albany: State University of New York Press, 1992), 4 (emphasis in original). Berman's original formulation is "mise en rapport," a placing in relation that, in addition to "being in touch," connotes connection, understanding, affinity, and ongoing relationship.

58. Diagne, *Ink of Scholars*, xx. Diagne makes this point in dialogue with Léopold Senghor, who reminds readers that Birago Diop understood this Italian warning when he "translated" African folktales into written form. Rather than seek word to word equivalences, Senghor explains, Diop was a creative artist who rethought and reworked them.

59. Cf. Diagne's contribution to this volume, in which he reworks Merleau-Ponty's conception of a "lateral universal" in order to understand translation as a practice of "incessant testing, marked by the copresence of many different views," whose aim is neither "transparency and the elimination of the untranslatable" nor to establish a universal grammar.

60. Édouard Glissant, *Poetics of Relation*, trans. Betsy Wing (Ann Arbor: University of Michigan Press, 1997), 103. Gavin Arnall usefully suggests that Glissant here may be invoking and reworking, which is to say "translating," Fanon's passage from *Black Skin, White Masks* in which he suggests that Antillean students in Paris are faced with only two choices: "either support the white world" by speaking French or "reject Europe" and retreat into Creole. Frantz Fanon, *Black Skin, White Masks* (Boston: Grove, 2008), 20.

61. Glissant, *Poetics of Relation*, 103.

62. Glissant, 103, 105.

63. Glissant, 107. Note that Derrida first presented the paper that would become *Monolingualism of the Other* at a conference organized by Glissant. In it, he invokes Glissant's conception of Relation but does not take it up in ways that might have helped him to displace rather than reproduce the old antinomy between universality and particularity.

64. Glissant, *Poetics of Relation*, 107–8.

65. Glissant, 108. This dialectical understanding of place and world is further developed in Édouard Glissant, *Traité de Tout-Monde: Poétique IV* (Paris: Gallimard, 1997).

66. Glissant, *Poetics of Relation*, 109.

67. Glissant, 190.

68. Glissant, 192, 193.

69. Glissant, 190.

70. Édouard Glissant, *Poétique de la relation: Poétique III* (Paris: Gallimard 1990), 156, 206. Betsy Wing, who translates this as "giving-on-and-with," emphasizes the contrast Glissant makes with "comprendre" as a seizing or grasping form of knowing that seeks to incorporate difference into sameness. "Donner-avec" emphasizes a relation of giving rather than taking. Glissant, *Poetics of Relation*, xiv, 212. I would suggest that for Glissant this formulation is meant to convey not only a different mode of understanding but an alternative conception of (translational) sociality (that may be source and product of solidarity). It reverberates productively with Diagne's ethico-epistemological conception of "putting in touch."

71. Benedict Anderson, *Under Three Flags: Anarchism and the Anti-colonial Imagination* (London: Verso, 2005), 5.

72. Fadi Bardawil, *Revolution and Disenchantment: Arab Marxism and the Binds of Emancipation* (Durham, NC: Duke University Press, 2020).

73. Ralph Ellison, "Hidden Name and Complex Fate," in *The Collected Essays of Ralph Ellison, Revised and Updated*, ed. John F. Callahan (New York: Modern Library/Random House, 2004), 205.

74. Gary Wilder, *Freedom Time: Negritude, Decolonization, and the History of the World* (Durham, NC: Duke University Press, 2014).

75. Césaire discusses this inflection in Jacqueline Leiner, "Entretien avec Aimé Césaire," in *Tropiques, 1941–1945: Collection complète* (Paris: Jean Michel Place,

1978). Elsewhere I analyze this as a strategy of "radical literalism" akin to immanent critique. See Wilder, *Freedom Time*, 33.

76. Aimé Césaire, "Letter to Maurice Thorez," trans. Chike Jeffers, *Social Text* 28, no. 103 (Summer 2010): 152. Note here the source of Glissant's later formulation.

77. Césaire, 148.

78. Césaire, 151.

79. Césaire, 151.

80. Césaire, 152.

81. On this vision and project see Wilder, *Freedom Time*.

82. Through poetic knowledge, Césaire offers a (poetic) critique of realist, rationalist, empiricist, and positivist ways of knowing from an aesthetic, embodied, and concrete standpoint. He suggests that these conventional ways of knowing mistakenly presuppose the subject-object binary and focus more on reified elements than on dynamic relations, being rather than becoming, actuality rather than potentiality. See Aimé Césaire, "Poetry and Knowledge," in *Lyric and Dramatic Poetry, 1946–1982* (Charlottesville: University of Virginia Press, 1990).

83. C. L. R. James, "Preliminary Notes on the Negro Question (1939)" and "Notes Following the Discussion (1939)," in *C. L. R. James on the "Negro Question,"* ed. Scott McLemee (Jackson: University of Mississippi Press, 1996).

84. C. L. R. James, "Education, Propaganda, Agitation: Post-war America and Bolshevism," in C. L. R. James, *Marxism for our Times*, ed. Martin Glaberman (Jackson: University of Mississippi Press, 1999), 16.

85. James, "Education, Propaganda, Agitation," 16–17.

86. Grace Lee Boggs, *Living for Change: An Autobiography* (Minneapolis: University of Minnesota Press, 1998), 58–61.

87. Boaventura de Sousa Santos, *Epistemologies of the South: Justice against Epistemicide* (New York: Routledge, 2014).

88. Santos, 212.

89. Santos, 228.

90. Santos, 215, 216.

91. Santos, 112.

92. Santos, 219.

93. Santos, 232.

94. Santos, 213, 219.

95. Santos, 217, 218.

96. Santos, 214.

97. Santos, 214.

98. Santos, 213.

99. Santos, 222.

100. Santos, 222.

101. Santos, 227.

102. Santos, 233.

103. Santos, 233.

Primitive Accumulation, Again

Ben Conisbee Baer

In a 2019 interview with Dana Perino on Fox News' *The Daily Briefing*, Facebook chairman and CEO Mark Zuckerberg (whose estimated net worth was then about one hundred billion dollars) responded as follows to the question of whether billionaires should exist: "I don't think that in some cosmic sense that anyone deserves to have billions of dollars. There are a lot of people who do really good things and kind of help a lot of other people. And you get well compensated for that."[1] Ideology moves past us quicker than thought. It is thus reasonable to pause and read for a moment the CEO's spoken formulation, examining the apparent non sequitur that hangs in the paratactic void between Zuckerberg's first sentence and the following two. There is an unconditional ("cosmic") nonjustification for the existence of billionaires. So why should they exist? The gulf of this unconditional undeservingness must be leaped across by a judgment. Thus, what conditions the unconditionally unjustifiable into recognizable legitimacy is doing "good things," giving *help*.[2] The justification for being "well compensated" is that one is helping a lot of other people, a fantastical narrative that posits a causal relation between a flow of help (one way) and a flow of value (back to the helper). The power to help brings compensation: the weights and balances of an economy. The more help given ("*a lot* of other people"), the more value received ("*well* compensated"). What is the moral of this socioeconomic fable? What lesson does it teach?

At the end of the first volume of *Capital*, Marx analyzed and criticized the story of "primitive accumulation" prevailing in his times. Primitive accumulation is in fact Marx's own shorthand name for the *Ausgangspunkt*—the "point of departure"—of the capitalist mode of production.[3] In Marx's day, dominant commonsense and theoretical explanations of the preconditions and beginnings of this remarkable technique for concentrating, organizing, and commanding the labor of others for profit framed it as a tale of natural winners and losers. Of winners who help the losers to live because the latter cannot help themselves. Marx shows that behind the phenomenon of the losers' dependency (and its remedy through productive employment) lie heterogeneous processes of separation and violence that produce a proletarian condition.[4] Dependency codes the juridical "freedom" of the proletarian-becoming-worker, free to sell its capability for work and thus both structurally predicated as labor-power and—"hurled onto the labor-market"—dependent on the apparent benevolence of a purchaser (employer) who possesses sufficient money and means to capitalize the combination of these elements (C1, 876). Marx's essential teaching is that, precisely because of the underlying relation that posits the worker as "bearer" of labor-power, the working class is the agent of capital; but it cannot appear that way from within popular ideology or academic economic theory. He therefore provides a supplementary corrective or revision to a universalizing story that both divides humanity into different natural types and assigns their socioeconomic dominance or dependent subordination as the result of belonging to one or other of these defined groups.

This story, which seems necessarily to take on narrative and even mythographic form, is universalizing because it claims to apply to humanity as such. It appears and reappears as an account of the human condition. Yet as its anthropologistic division translates into specific examples (by classifying named groups, for instance), it both discloses an interest and encounters problems of translatability. In the broadest possible terms, two of the major codes of this anthropological difference are race and gender, which unevenly commensurate large groups on one or other side of the fault line. For obvious reasons it is both inadequate and provisionally necessary to frame these divisions as such abstract codes. Race-effects and gender-effects permeate the formal abstraction of modern class-formations precisely because sedimented histories of the division of labor and group-formations are residual in industrial capitalism and can become functional for it. When it is abstracted into a general schema, the ideologeme of natural winners and losers, helpers and helped, looks simplistic in the extreme. Why, you might ask, expend any effort to dispel it? One reason is that the schema as I have just outlined it (or as Marx himself summarizes it) rarely, if ever, appears as a doctrinal theoretical statement. The schema abstracts and renders formulaic what remains untheorized, presupposed, or even unconscious within the pervasive common sense of a particular cultural and social situation.[5]

We cannot assume that an ideology practiced and lived in the element of common sense is automatically dislodged by either one-time rational correction or technoscientific development. Correspondingly, in spite of Marx's apparently decisive criticism, the primitive accumulation story's axiomatics remain intact in the common sense of Mark Zuckerberg's statement a century and a half later: one group of people is well compensated for *doing good*, for helping another, dependent, group that cannot help itself.

Marx's discussion of primitive accumulation takes place in a number of different registers, and follows an unstable, multifaceted, and sometimes confusing itinerary. First, it designates an ideological, "common sense" schema of a natural difference between human types, a schema that, as already noted, "must be reconstructed after the fact" in critical epistemological work. Second, it designates the narrative, descriptive, mediatized, and institutional forms, both quotidian and academic, in which variants of the ideologeme are manifest. This is the "material," so to speak, that a critical epistemology must work to interrupt and revise. The ideologeme is not an ideal semantic content prior to or independent of the forms or media in which it manifests, but rather a schema that can adapt to any number of cultural scripts that code human difference. The schema may tend to universalize, but it is not universal (its power of universal*ization* demands an unceasing work of translation that limits and plays interference with the process, hence producing sites of struggle). Critical epistemological work is necessarily repetitive precisely because translation, narrativization, and phenomenalization are themselves persistent, recurrent. Their representations keep painting big, broad-brush pictures that effect homogenizing commensurations of many types of histories and positions by assigning them to an originary human default: an anthropological difference that rationalizes the gap between rich and poor, dominant and subordinate, and sustains the idea that the winners help the losers. Alternatively, and perhaps even more perniciously, a recent twist in this ideological schema proposes that *everyone can be a winner.*

Serge Latouche characterizes this latter claim as a "logic of self-interested benevolence" on the part of those who have already "won" (and will keep winning). As he points out, the coercive and powerful mythology of universal success is a deep-seated apology for global capitalist development controlled from above.[6] The hitherto unsuccessful must be helped to develop by "us" (this logic speaks in the first-person voice of the self-recognized global winners), entrapping the subjects of development in an unending game of catch-up fueled by the seductive carrot of individualized entrepreneurialism and the disciplinary stick of State and para-State interventions. It is quite possible to turn the desperation and understandable self-interest of the poor into a desire for, or even a *"passionate attachment* to forms of capitalist development imbued with a streak of capitalocentric orientalism," write Anjan Chakrabarti and Anup

Dhar, underlining the significance of a "struggle over mindset" in formerly colonized areas subsumed in development regimes.[7] The logic that incorporates benevolent strategies of "poverty management" and "sustainable development" implicates the schema of benevolence that we saw in Mark Zuckerberg's statement.[8] India, which is the major focus of Chakrabarti and Dhar's study, also has the world's largest number of users of Meta's (formerly Facebook's) WhatsApp messaging application. It so happens that WhatsApp is pioneering its digital payments function in India (peer-to-peer value transfers), which is a significant move within the auto-entrepreneurial shift in top-down strategies of sustainable development. The symbiosis of powerful entrepreneurialism at the top and philanthropic intervention for its victims at the bottom remains latent in Zuckerberg's remarks, but it is clear that "everyone can be a winner" translates in practice into "win-win" for capital. In the words of a representative: "not only do corporations tap into a vibrant market, but by treating the poor as consumers they are no longer treated with indignity; they become empowered customers."[9] Echoing Marx's terms, but inverting the values, the entrepreneur as social activist will create a "harmony in the interests of the winners and the losers" because, in the psychological presuppositions of this theory, "everyone has . . . overlapping preferences" such that what is good for the winners is also good for the losers.[10] At such moments it is possible to discern how this mindset reprises a rather older colonial axiomatics: *we* can save the lives of *millions of children who die* each year in poor countries. . . . And back home in the United States or Europe, it is *we* who must find ways to *make our education systems work for every child.*" Frantz Fanon long ago commented on this colonial value-system: *they* are dying masses ("millions of children"); *our* children are individuals who must be carefully nurtured (quality "education . . . for every child").[11]

Across many registers, in multiple idioms, such representations and narratives determine widely diffused elements of epistemic formation in societies touched by capitalist development, and today there are none that are not. In a given instance, the figure of default will find its force and shape in inherited, sedimented idioms of social differentiation. Yet for obvious reasons of untranslatability, this does not give rise to a substantive homogeneity in which the idioms of capitalistic subjectivization and sociality are entirely common (neither universal nor uniform).

The third disposition of Marx's "primitive accumulation" designates a process, "the separation of the conditions of labor from labor," which is the condition of the capital-*relation* and, downstream from that, its activation and management as capital*ism*. Thus, it forms part of the "concept" of capital itself.[12] Most theoretical treatments focus on the third item, treating primitive accumulation as a diagnostic category with which to name and classify: first, the correct historical sequence and causal chain of the transition from feudalism to capitalism; and second, all manner of baleful and expropriative phenomena, from old enclosures to new, theft of indigenous knowledges, resource extraction, mass indebtedness, deracination, population control, and so on. In the present chapter, however, I am interested in the relation between the first two items: the quotidian or commonsensical (epistemic) sets of presuppositions and the manifold narrative and figurative formulations in which they appear. Rather than treat primitive accumulation as an instrumental diagnostic category with which to classify phenomena, I bring out Marx's construction of a critical epistemology, the point of which is to outline a practice of disrupting—or redirecting—the uneven inscription of capitalist subjectivity. This is part of Marx's great intended lesson: the worker is not the victimized recipient of help from above, but the collective agent of capital.

The concerns of the present volume are translation and universality as sites of struggle. To reflect briefly on these terms and their relation: An allegorical figuration of the relation comes via the Abrahamic tradition in the Babel story, where the sons of Shem undertake a vast colonial project of making the entire world translate itself into their language (thereby ending the need for translation). By imposing their language as universal, "the Semites want to bring the world to reason [*mettre à la raison le monde*], and this reason can signify simultaneously a colonial violence (since they would thus universalize their idiom) *and* a peaceful transparency of the human community."[13] An irreducible and violent desire of translation, then, is a self-obliterating one: a transcoding of meaning without loss that could only annihilate the practice of translation itself. And this for better *and* worse: colonial violence and peaceful transparency. *Pax translatione.* I remark here that the desire called socialism also harbors a version of this wish. As a planned socialization that in theory encompasses the world, socialism must organize on the basis of fostering unification, integration, and calculation, inevitably pushing against the variegation of languages in the interest of efficient association. Hence the concern within socialist movements from the nineteenth century onward for the potential of an international or universal language (an interlanguage or world language).

"Translation, a system of translation, is only possible if a permanent code allows a substitution or transformation of signifiers while retaining the same signified, always present, despite the absence of any specific signifier," writes Derrida.[14] Linguistic translation's impossible yet constitutive economic dream of a one-for-one equal conversion across languages fantasizes the carrying of meaning (a signified) across the difference of signifiers: a simulacrum of equal *exchange*. Thus, "as soon as one puts two or three words in the place of one, translation becomes an analytic explicitation; that is, it is no longer strictly speaking a translation."[15] As Derrida points out, few theorists have yet explored these economic dimensions of the problem. One may question the strictness of this formula of translation economics, but it does describe an impossible ideal without which "translation" as we know it would not be. Signifier for signifier, carrying meaning over ideally, translation wagers "on a received truth, a truth that is stabilized, firm and reliable (*bebaios*), the truth of a meaning that, unscathed and immune, would be transmitted from one so-called language to another in general, with no veil interposed, without anything sticking or being erased, and resisting the passage." But something does stick: "the warp" of the text that "remains forever . . . untranslatable." Not only the idiom but sonority, "the braid of phonemes" given in the "irreplaceable tunic of consonants" as lip movements.[16] Or in an earlier text:

> a word-body [*un corps verbal*] does not permit itself to be translated or transported into another language. It is precisely this that translation must put aside. Put aside the body [*corps*], such is the essential energy of translation. When it reinstalls the body, it is poetry. In this sense, the body of the signifier as the body of the signifier constitutes the idiom of every dream scene, dreams are untranslatable.[17]

What resists translation simultaneously solicits translation's forceful universalizing energy and limits the fulfillment of its desire. How does this relate to the question of primitive accumulation?

In a remarkable chapter of his book *Provincializing Europe*, Dipesh Chakrabarty suggests, first, that "grasping the category 'capital' entails grasping its universal constitution," a proposition with which Marx would have been fully in agreement.[18] Thus for Marx, "the tendency to create the *world market* is directly given in the concept of capital itself. . . . There appears here the universalizing [*universelle*] tendency of capital, which distinguishes it from all previous stages of production . . . it strives towards the universal development of the forces of production."[19] Capital as concept is general and abstract; the universalizing tendency (manifest initially in terms of world market) is produced by its need to realize these predicates by instituting the same measure of exchange across unevenly developed social formations (I do not assume a normative standard of "development" in saying this: it is merely most efficient and convenient for capital to standardize exchange as far as possible, with the violent and disruptive effects this restructuring entails on the ground). This pushes "universal development of the forces of production" because "the surplusvalue created at one point requires the creation of surplusvalue at another point, *for which it may be exchanged.*"[20] Correspondingly, Chakrabarty focuses on abstract labor as "universal category"—posited through labor-power as the common and uniform measure that maximizes efficiency and calculability in production for exchange, the secret of the "universal industriousness" of "production founded on capital" that generates "the most total and universal social product."[21] This "civilizing influence of capital," I repeat, is due to the "creation . . . of labor with a new use-value" (i.e., labor-*power*, the use-value of which is used by capital for the results I just detailed).[22] And as Chakrabarty observes with Marx, this universality is coemergent with the juridico-political values of "bourgeois" society—liberty, equality, equal right, and equal exchange—such that "the equality and equivalence of all kinds of labor . . . could not be deciphered until the concept of human equality had already taken on the fixity of a popular assumption" (C1, 152).[23] Before following the next move of Chakrabarty's argument, I note that for Marx the capital-relation is thereby haunted by the specter of justice, if only in the antinomies of bourgeois juridical forms. Consequently, the double bind within what Étienne Balibar has called "equaliberty" cannot be bypassed but must rather be applied (or translated) to the conflicted potentials of labor-power as commodity.[24]

The haunting of capital by an aporetic figure of justice brings us to the second gesture of Chakrabarty's argument, which additionally introduces the other main substantive of the present collection: translation. In what ways is capital translated into capital*ism*, he asks? The term translation here is perhaps resonant rather than satisfyingly elaborated; nevertheless, it is sufficient to indicate sites of struggle or friction that emerge as capital encounters, in part by producing, its own differences from itself (or its own limits). These differences and limits are at one level the class relations needed to manage and develop capital and to produce surplus-value. "Capital posits every such limit [*Grenze*] as a barrier [*Schranke*] and hence gets ideally [*ideel*] beyond it."[25] The ideal or ideational (fantasmatic) getting over the barrier or out of the cage, however, is not necessarily "real" (*real*). "The universality toward which it [capital] irresistibly strives encounters barriers in its own nature" that push it toward either sublation (*Aufhebung*) or dissolution (*Auflösung*).[26] On the way to its self-dissolution or self-sublation, however, capital needs differences in order to function as capital: they provide the material traction to "translate" it into a capital*ism* driven by its own dialectic of self-resistance. A "transition/ translation to capital*ism*" from the capital-concept involves negotiation and struggle with what Chakrabarty calls "History 2," elements that are not essentially functional for the capital-concept (the logically functional elements presupposed for capital are termed "History 1"). Hence, "Marx accepts . . . that the total universe of pasts that capital encounters is larger than the sum of those

elements in which are worked out the presuppositions of capital."[27] The differences from its concept that capital encounters are not the same everywhere
and at all times, which occasions a historical variety of capitalisms.

Oskar Negt and Alexander Kluge give a longer view than Chakrabarty's,
though it is centered on European (and especially German) history. "The
historical struggle of capital," they write, "goes against the incalculable of the
historical and moral element of labor-power."[28] Incalculable because of the
shadow of the longue durée of development from upper-primate to human
characteristics, including bodily structure, cognitive capability, psychic formations, and psycho-physical processes; cultural and ethical systems; technique
and technologies. All this comprises an abyssal and diversified historical sedi-
ment. This material can "appear to capital" as *Umständlichkeit*—fastidiousness
or circuitousness, a kind of unnecessary fuss of tradition or the "residual"—yet
it is also the contingent and incalculable element in which capital gets traction
as capitalism.[29] *Geschichte und Eigensinn* may be read as a treatise on what
Negt and Kluge call the "permanence of primitive accumulation," which is
the long-term effect of underived *Trennungen* (separations).[30] Species-history
as such emerges from underived separations (tracking back to evolutionary
cell-divisions and organic specialization from microorganisms on up), condition
for the appearance and development of the human and its differentiated "labor-
capacities" (not yet labor-power). Primitive accumulation (a specific social
separation) marks a derivation from general separation-processes. At one level,
its permanence is manifest as a "principle of social change" as "a beginning
[that] has thickened into a principle of ever-renewed upheavals."[31] At the more
original level of Negt and Kluge's analysis, "permanence" also names a "mode
of unfolding" (*Entfaltungsweise*) of the results of separation in specific situations, each of which leaves its own "imprint" (*Prägung*) and "code" (*Chiffre*)
on the resulting system.[32] This thesis of an imprinting and coding of capital
into capitalism—in essence a kind of writing that inscribes social subjects
through previously separated-out and heterogeneous (human and other) materials at hand—complements Chakrabarty's suggestive turn to translation. For
Negt and Kluge, translation is inscription *of* and *by* capital as it becomes a
variety of capitalisms: the "originary [primitive] imprint" (*ursprüngliche Prägung*) of separation and expropriation in each case conditions the development
(i.e., integration or not) of the separated elements as capitalist accumulation
expands.[33] The "historical imprinting of labor-power" thereby determines the
shape of capitalist sociality, and permanence is in the trace of the originary
process: "All later imprints of labor-power take on these separation-codings
[*Trennungschiffre*]. But the separation-process has a different figure [*Gestalt*]
in each country."[34] Tightly focused on Germany, Negt and Kluge argue that

in that country primitive accumulation is a kind of purloined letter, or water-mark, irregularly distributed in time and space. Traces of the process are un-evenly scattered across the space-time of the modern social formation for those who can read them. It is a mistake to take the "one-sided image" of Marx's English example as a norm from which "another figure" may emerge as "mea-surable deviation" (as we shall see, Marx attempted to rectify himself on this point). The diversity of separation-figures is much more complex and "dispersed over the entirety of [Germany's] historical time."[35] Nachträglichkeit of primitive accumulation: "the individual moments of separation-processes [are] really only later in retrospect posited together and identified in results as a process of primitive accumulation, *dispersed over the entire history of feudalism and capitalist formation in Germany*."[36] Reading such figures evidently entails a new task of translation itself, especially if we leave the national outlines of German or British history.

Thus, while translation could resemble something like transcoding into universal categories that render all situations and histories into commensurable terms (the terms of the dominant), it is in the struggle between Chakrabarty's Histories 1 and 2 that the untranslatable idiomaticity of heterogeneous elements forces a "translation" from concept-logic into capitalist practice. The friction of the untranslatability involved is what makes translation both necessary and impossible, the work of which involves, for example, whatever mindsets, prac-tices, and institutions there are to hand that take on the task of managing capital and producing surplus-value. These can be, for better and worse, in-competent, indifferent, rapacious, benevolent, skilled, etc. (The process of "real subsumption" begins to redesign those mindsets, practices, and institutions for ever-closer conformity with capital logic, but this is an interminable task.[37]) Like Negt and Kluge (and Marx himself), Chakrabarty writes of the "double possibilities" presented to capital by the relations and "other histories" it en-counters.[38] Which is to say that capital is itself pharmakontic, susceptible of different uses that twist its logic and concept; and that social direction of capital can push it in a more or less capital*ist* or social*ist* direction—though "double-ness" might also imply other options entirely (clearly the recent historical dominant has been an industrial-capitalistic use of capital). In terms that I will reprise later in this chapter, Chakrabarty suggests that doubleness is manifest in "pasts" that "interrupt and punctuate," that are "constantly interrupting" the process, narrativization, and translation of capital logic.[39]

My general argument in this chapter expands the scene of translation in the senses suggested by Chakrabarty and Negt and Kluge. I follow the trans-lation of the capital-relation into a scenographics of anthropological difference that purports to explain that relation. This shows how Marx's "primitive accumulation" argument is an epistemological intervention into the subjective-ideological practices of classification used both spontaneously and theoretically to diagnose, name, and control social groups and their relations. The resulting ideological schemas and the concrete subjectivities that are their condition and effect—idiomatically at work everywhere capital is on the move—themselves translate a different kind of Marxian generality, which is a human relation to unconditional surplus.

We are examining the ideological schema of an anthropological difference. It is a kind of discursive value-form transcoding statements and phenomena, bodies and practices, for capital logic across the unequal cultural and epistemic terrain of social formations. As a form, it is empty enough both to accommodate a wide range of cultural contents and to make use of preexisting cultural typologies. The ideological schema identified by Marx translates and abstracts (reduces) the way in which a social formation (or a segment of one) relates generally to an unconditional surplus. This unconditional surplusity is—in Marx's definition— an irreducible characteristic of the human, its self-difference in productive capacity as always-more-than-itself. It is important to acknowledge that our position on surplusity excludes exceptional circumstances associated with very extreme poverty or disaster such as prolonged famine or malnutrition that, for example, prevent generational replacement. The same would go for the phenomena that are gathered under the heading of genocide. Such conditions, though they can in fact even be "normalized" for certain highly precarious and deprived groups, are nevertheless almost always artifactual *social* products. Moreover, their perpetuation tends to rely on precisely the kinds of anthropological, dehumanizing group distinctions that are at issue in this chapter.

Drawing on Marx, but upping the stakes, Georges Bataille will posit an extrahuman unconditional surplusity as such ("cosmic," in the language of the Facebook CEO) in the "excess energy" gifted to the globe by the sun.[40] This is an energy-surplus that, partially captured, delayed, and differentiated, sustains all of the terrestrial general surplusity of "life." Hence, Bataille proposes that this excess "*translates* to the effervescence of life" and opens to the incalculable, that is, to what he calls "general economy."[41]

In Marx, labor, coemerging with the human and "to a certain degree socialized"—minimally encompassing forms of division, sharing, cooperation—produces an excess that makes it possible for a relation to exist in which "the surplus labor of one person becomes a condition of existence for another" (C1, 647). Labor itself, therefore, is in the mode of human auto-excess: *surplus* labor is in the species, for example allowing it to rear new generations who are themselves helpless at birth and can only live on the excess of others. (This invites theories of sexual difference and gendering that Marx ceased exploring in an explicit way early on.[42]) This also—and Bataille is preoccupied by this point—possibilizes luxury and sumptuary excess of all kinds, which become the dominant cultural-economic signatures of various social formations (the hallmarks of "civilizations" in an earlier intellectual lexicon). Pharmakon of the surplus, then: this excess that is, definitively humanly, created above the needs of "one person" is supplementary in structure. That is, it outlines a space in which the incalculable "development" of self and other may happen, conditioned for better or worse by the systems that are being supplemented. Childbearing, childrearing, education, care of the old and sick, welfare in general, the gift, culture: these could not take place without it. By exactly the same supplementary logic, it is also the very possibility of greed, selfishness, plunder, hoarding, privilege, theft, enslavement, predation, exploitation. And, of course, profit. The wild anthropology of primitive accumulation gives a form of appearance to the "capital-relation" because the latter's relation of separation (*Trennung* or *Scheidung* in Marx's lexicon) is as such nonphenomenal. You can of course visibilize people being deprived of resources, evicted, etc., but the capital-relation, the social relation as such, cannot appear save in the supplementary form of a cultural coding. The (now obsolete) form of the "family wage" as a code for the wage-form, which is one possible expression of the capital-relation, shows how closely this coding is linked to gendered norms and cultural representations. It is the capital-relation that allows surplus labor to appear as surplus-product and be realized as surplus-value: a restricted rationalization and social quantification of general surplusity. The industrialization and socialization of surplus-value production also announces the possibility for the social control, use, and re-generalization of surplus that Marx thinks of as socia*lism*. A control that, if used to sustain relations of surplus production, appropriation, and distribution that create a "situation in which objective wealth is there to satisfy the worker's own developmental needs" and not "the valorization-needs of the values at hand," would use the calculable in the service of the incalculable. How, in the unprogrammable interest of social justice, might it be possible to produce subjectivities angled or vectored in this way? To produce subjectivities that might desire to practice and even institutionalize forms of responsibility for which "the worker's own developmental needs"—as also the needs of others—may not be immediately identical with what the *I* wants for itself right now? (C1, 772).[43] Here, it is Marx's *epistemological* intervention that points toward a double bind that his own work could not yet unravel. As George Padmore was to put it nearly a hundred years after *Capital* appeared, "Socialists are, in effect, the manipulators of capital free of capitalist aims. . . . They want to invest capital for social aims rather than for private profit." But on the other hand, he writes, "you cannot build socialism without socialists." Marx's epistemological intervention merely hints at the problem of how socialists are to be produced.[44]

We saw in the words of Mark Zuckerberg the trace of a schema of anthropological difference in the common sense of today's ruling class. This common sense recasts profitably commodified data extraction as a kind of philanthropic gift to those who need the help of the "free services" of the powerful. One could say that this imaginary pattern figures compensation as a peculiar new form of tribute from life-information-stripped cyberserfs to their superhuman benefactor.

Let us backtrack again to Marx's day and look at the relay that carries the (binarizing) schema, though not its exact contents, to the present. Seen from below, though here relayed in the words of a pioneering upper-class activist, this schema of helper and helped can look like this:

> I wanted to speak to all those whom I met and make them understand what it was to constitute the working class—the right to work, etc.— Not one was able to comprehend a single one of these questions.— They all answered me in a crass way: "Well, there certainly must be rich people to give poor people work; otherwise how would the poor live?"—It is clear that their priests continually repeat that to them. "There must be rich and poor; the first enable the second to live."[45]

"There must be rich and poor; the first enable the second to live." This configures the self-understanding of the social agents of surplus-production as recipients of help. It is drawn from Flora Tristan's account of her conversations in 1844 with workers in the French city of Nîmes. Her attempt to reconfigure this epistemic sensibility apparently misfired here (the counterposition of her forceful "right to work" alternative did not take, though experience shows that structures of feeling take much time and effort to turn around and that longer-term subjective engagement is required). Naturally, Tristan met with more class-conscious and militant workers on her travels as well. But let us take the assumptions she rages against here as representative—in the broadest possible terms—of a certain quasi-subalternized normality. Accepting the risks of such a move, if one transposes the Nîmes workers' theory of their situation into the realm of heteronormative relations of dependency between the sexes (love, duty, loyalty, care of the other's sense of well-being) one perhaps obtains a different impression of both how tenaciously internalized and how routine it is. And also on what levels subjective engagement might be necessary. The fact that it yet remains somewhat plausible to make the transposition to gendering also demonstrates the power of ideological value-forms to shift between discursive formations even as they might also articulate, for the individual, unlivable tensions between those formations.[46] Tristan's entire journal remains instructive about the types of problems encountered and produced for the well-meaning activist-vanguard in the class or gender field.

Let us read at last Marx's portrayal of the general doctrine of primitive accumulation justifying making money off the work of others. Recall that "primitive accumulation" as I consider it here is Marx's double name for a circulating ideological schema and a critical epistemology of it:

> This primitive accumulation plays approximately the same role in political economy as original sin in theology. Adam bit the apple, and thereby sin fell upon the human race. Its origin is supposed to be explained when it is told as an anecdote about the past. In a long-gone time, there was on the one hand a diligent, intelligent, and above all frugal elite and on the other lazy shreds [*faulenzende . . . Lumpen*] who wasted all they had and more. The legend of the theological Fall may tell us how mankind was thereby cursed to eat its bread in the sweat of its brow; but the history of the economic Fall reveals to us how it is that there are people for whom this is not at all necessary. Same old same old. So it was that the former accumulated wealth, and the latter had finally nothing left to sell but their own skins.[47] (C1, 873)

Marx tells us this schema of two groups is a fabular construction, a story with a moral precept, a pedagogy that stages within its narrative design the justification of a specific social and economic relationship. What is *taught* by this legend, inasmuch as Marx characterizes its lesson, is that the good group profits by giving the bad group the jobs it needs to keep body and soul together. Lesson learned: "Well, there certainly must be rich people to give poor people work; otherwise how would the poor live?"

It might seem bizarre that an ideologeme manifest in long-outdated discourses (nineteenth-century political economy, theological doxa)—or indeed Marx's steam-age critical account of it—could have any purchase in today's socioeconomic world. Marx names a genre in which it could be corrected: "history" (though we shall see that such correction cannot be completed). His satirical and mocking tone perhaps discloses an attempt to contain a disquiet and uncertainty about the tenacity of these axioms and schemas sustained by pre- or noncapitalist signifiers of everyday subordination and social inequality. While the capital-relation as socialized is for Marx a new thing that represents a possible stepping-stone to socialism, it is established in social and discursive landscapes that encode it in heterogeneous (pre-)histories of work, domination, lifeways, and culture that a logic of commodification alone could never fully sublate. This raises the disturbing question concerning the degree to which the developmental logic of capital is capable of sublating other (older) class processes. Emmanuel Terray recently wrote that "Marx overestimates somewhat, in my view, the specificity of the capitalist mode of production and the discontinuities that separate bourgeois society from all those that precede it."[48] In some of his final notes, Althusser asked his readers to imagine the "bourgeoisie" not as the dialectically "contrary product of feudality" but as the "culmination . . . highest form . . . perfection" of feudality.[49] Capitalism as a way of making feudality run more efficiently inasmuch as feudality's achievements were built on a much less technically efficient mode of producing and distributing surplus. Cedric Robinson argues that capitalism is an "extension" of feudal relations because it does not fully sublate distinctions between humans that derive from the long history of enslaved and customarily obligatory labor. For Robinson, this makes race itself the main value-form that commensurates the logics of domination and exploitation between modes of production: for "each historical moment," he writes, "race was its epistemology, its ordering principle, its organizing structure, its moral authority, its economy of justice, commerce, and power."[50] "Race" here may overgeneralize signifiers differing across conjunctures (by a translation arguably positing a stable semantic content in every context), but something like a race-effect enters into all capitalist-affected class formations precisely because of the sedimented history of compulsory or extorted (surplus) labor practices.

For race as a discursive value-form, the commensurating element in its modern modality is "biology" (genetics, heredity). This was not always the case.[51] In Robinson's flexible and strategic usage, "race" itself is the commensurating term between the older hierarchies and the class formations of modern capitalism:

> Social divisions and habits of life and attitude that predated capitalist production continued into the modern era and extended to the working classes located in Britain specific social sensibilities and consciousness. . . . The negations resultant from capitalist modes of production, relations of production, and ideology did not manifest themselves as an eradication of oppositions among the working classes. Instead, the dialectic of proletarianization disciplined the working classes to the importance of distinctions: between ethnics and nationalities; between skilled and unskilled workers; and, as we shall see later in even more

dramatic terms, between races. The persistence and creation of such oppositions within the working classes were a critical aspect of the triumph of capitalism in the nineteenth century.[52]

As with other critics such as Jack Forbes and Colette Guillaumin, this manner of historicizing racism is compatible with Marx's characterization of primitive accumulation. The modern racial code reads backward from the effect of racial subordination to a cause in some irreducible human difference, whether attributed to biology, ethnos, or an essentialized "culture."[53] The structure of feeling in which it is universalizable for group formation resembles a "They," in some way, are "not like us." Hence the idiomatic coding of surplus labor is different for all class societies; it is not always racialized in the modern scientific sense, but in each of them it nevertheless takes place:

> Capital did not invent surplus labor. Wherever a part of society possesses the monopoly of the means of production, the worker, free or unfree, must add to the labor-time necessary for his own maintenance an extra quantity of labor-time [*überschüssige Arbeitszeit*: labor-time in excess] in order to produce the means of subsistence for the owner of the means of production. (C1, 344)

The ideologeme from so-called primitive accumulation effects a telescoping commensuration of these histories of the "excessive" by attributing them to an originary human default: the conditioning, production, distribution, appropriation of unconditional surplus is assigned to an anthropological difference with a range of subjectifying effects. This default can be encoded in terms of race, ethnos, caste, sexual difference; or indeed according to what is perhaps most irreducible, the differentiation of human from animal.[54] It happens in some way in every formation. It can mobilize and shape affects such as loyalty, fealty, duty, and love (a feudal-gendered system).[55] Marx dreams of undoing the social relations and practices that determine the resulting diagnostic names and their effects.

The schema Marx outlines is his own formalization of the way in which this situation and process translate into the most common traits he can decipher: the figuration of an originary human default that gives rise to a social hierarchy conditioned by its relation to surplus (excess) and the latter's coding. In the Abrahamic framework Marx assumes, this default is displaced from an originary lapse in the human as such (a theology of sin) into a jagged fissure *within* humanity (a fissure that communicates with a super-/subhuman distinction shared by modern racial and gender ideologies). As its argument advances, the chapter on primitive accumulation suggests that the anthropological difference—as a learned, internalized, affective and effective (subject-forming) classification and not necessarily an objective reality—recurs as one ramifying *condition* of capitalist development and stability. The precept about capitalism's origins folds over to become a condition of its indefinite prolongation as it becomes real, is taught formally and informally, translated into languages, statements, and representations, institutionalized as an epistemic horizon. This, I suggest, is an important site of struggle over the "permanence of primitive accumulation."[56]

Rather than using "primitive accumulation" only as a diagnostic instrument to phenomenalize and classify various disparate and nonequivalent bad extractive capitalist practices (land grabs, incarceration, DNA patenting, etc.), it is possible to take it as critical epistemology: a persistent work of interrupting and undoing the figures and names taught by gendered, raced, and classed normalities that classify and control social groups in ways that sustain those "bad" things. Rather than providing endless diagnoses of the evils of capitalism, epistemological work can be directed toward epistemic and subjective change.

In *Capital*, Marx is not writing a history of industrial capitalism. His qualifiedly historical analysis of its beginnings at the end of volume 1 instead addresses a theoretical lacuna. There is something missing in the logical pattern of his own theoretical construction of the system. Having given, in the previous several hundred pages, an analysis of the industrial capitalist system as a process of production and expanded reproduction (accumulation), Marx steps back to look at the "presuppositions" involved in the key moments of that process and finds a faulty circuit of logic (*fehlerhaften Kreislauf*) in his presentation (C1, 873). Philosophically, the system cannot be explained by its component parts. All the elements of the functioning system presuppose each other in a tautologous way, so how does it get moving? What is the *"Ausgangspunkt,"* or point of departure, of the capitalist mode of production (C1, 873)? In the context of the tautology, primitive accumulation appears at first to supply a lack in Marx's own presentation of capitalism as it has been broken into its elements of accumulation, surplus-value, production, and "the availability of huge masses of capital and labor-power in the hands of commodity producers" (C1, 873).

The specificity of primitive accumulation, then, does not refer to the fact that once upon a time some people seized hold of more money or material resources than others. This social fact is immemorial, and only has to do with capitalism to the extent that predatory greed and rapaciousness may be counted as human universals (itself no trivial consideration). Rather, primitive accumulation names the translation, *in* figures of anthropological difference, of the installation of something otherwise nonphenomenal: the capital-relation

and the resulting definitive casting of the worker as (bearer of) labor-power as
the effect of identifiable but site-specific separation-processes. I underline processes in the plural here, as Marx indicates a complex and open-ended chain
that possibilizes not just the capital-relation as such but the fact that it becomes
systemic, sticks or "takes" as Althusser will put it. Preconditions for industrial
capitalism have historically existed in various times and places without industrial capitalism being the effect of their conjuncture.[57] In Marx's account, the
preconditions include the eviction of small peasants and rural workers for the
creation of livestock megafarms and leisure parks; corrupt and speculative real
estate deals on stolen lands (with analogous evicting and property-consolidating
effects); legal and coercive interventions by the State to control the movements
of those turned into deterritorialized vagabonds by these evictions; capitalization of land and agriculture generally (agribusiness); the accumulation of wealth
in a rapacious colonial trade including chattel slavery (mercantile capitalism,
not yet industrial); home market and foreign trade; trade tariffs; international
credit systems; and national indebtedness. William Clare Roberts underlines
the instrumentality of the State for primitive accumulation: it neither intends
capitalism as such, nor constitutes a specifically industrial capitalist institution.
From its own dependency on money-revenue, it rather develops the preconditions—legal and social—that enable the translation of capital into *industrial*
capitalism.[58] State and crown investments in maritime exploration, leading to
the competitive colonial process from the fifteenth century onward, were, for
example, a significant factor in the stockpiling of large amounts of monetary
and material wealth in Europe; but this was not yet industrialized in Marx's
sense. He writes that the "moments" (genealogically diverse levers) of primitive
accumulation are, by the seventeenth century, "systematically combined"
(*systematisch zusammengefasst*) by the agency of a State that nevertheless had
no plan to establish an industrial capitalist system (C1, 915).

If you convert your disinhibited violent crimes into legally sanctioned actions
by the agency of the State, then economic greed has become politicized, too.
It has become a matter of legislation, of legal sanction, of State support. At a
certain point, writes Marx, "the law itself now becomes the instrument by
which the people's land is stolen" (C1, 885). Yet, to repeat, none of this was
intended or even destined to give rise to industrial capitalism, and we will
probably never get a decisively watertight empirical account of exactly why, in
this specific context, a contingent conjuncture of risk-taking "men with money"
and available working hands *did* engender industrial capitalism.[59]

Thus, when Marx writes that "force [*Gewalt*] . . . is itself an economic power
[*Potenz*]," he formulates a condensed theorization of the contingency of the
processes we are discussing (C1, 916). Which is to suggest that violently pursued

projects can potentialize economic effects far beyond whatever the authors of such projects might have intended or been able to imagine; for example, the *systematic* installation of the capital-relation as the possibility of generalized industrial capital*ism* as an effect of *Gewalten*—violences or forces—that had other aims entirely.

Philosophical protocols do not permit a logically articulated system's origins to be located inside that system, thus the emergence of industrial capitalism cannot be explained by the combination of its functional elements. More simply put, Marx is obliged to shift genre gears because an account of transition (birth of the system—itself a charged metaphor) requires a minimally narrative form that stages a process.[60] If we take Chakrabarty's thesis of a "translation" from capital to capitalism at its word, this is a process that implicates languages and idioms. The site of this "originary" (*ursprünglich*) process is already occupied by signifying fragments of the ideologeme Marx seeks to revise. A blunt theoretical correction follows: "The capital-relation presupposes the separation [*Scheidung*] between the workers and ownership of the conditions of realization of their work." It is this separation that makes possible the definition of the worker as "bearer of labor-power" (*Träger der Arbeitskraft*) (C1, 874). Everything hangs on this. Consequently, as we have already seen, "the subject is predicated as structurally super-adequate to itself, definitively productive of surplus labor over necessary labor."[61] Or, in Negt and Kluge's words, "so-called *primitive* accumulation [is] the pivot- and breakout-point for each modern production of labor-power."[62] Surplus *value* is the way surplus *labor* appears in this industrial system, and this is the *Ursprung* of the possibility for capital *value* to become "the *subject* of a process" of expansion, of "self-valorization . . . the occult ability to add value to itself" (C1, 255, my emphasis).

We are primarily concerned, however, with the picture that Marx is attempting to deconstitute. In a discussion of primitive accumulation, Jason Read has argued that "the fantasy of the thrifty protocapitalist, whatever its function as nursery tale may be within the schoolbooks and ideologies of capital, is wholly inadequate to the task of accounting for the formation of the capitalist mode of production."[63] Of course it is. But questions persist: Inadequate for whom? What desires do they nevertheless solicit? Why do these kinds of intellectually derisory explanations remain more tenacious and widespread than the critical theory of *Capital*? With transformations that must be accounted for, they persist within techniques of subjectivation relayed by such far-reaching insights as that of Michel Foucault into the structure of the neoliberal subject as "an entrepreneur of himself."[64] Such entrepreneurialism (and the market order posited as its condition and effect) is far from a spontaneous phenomenon. It demands massive inputs and interventions by the State and other agencies concerning

educational, rearing, and training conditions as well as other institutional arrangements. This is in addition to the harsh nonformal pedagogy of the organized social and working environment.

Marx's apparent haste to dismiss the pitifully puerile kinds of narratives and
explanations indicated above is conditioned by his own class-specific educative
and intellectual formation (philosophy, classics, law, radical journalism) and
by his enlightenment confidence in the power of rational explanation to install
the critical knowledge that will allow, in Gramsci's words, that the "entire
work-force . . . should conceive itself as a 'collective worker,'" therefore as the
agent of social production, and therefore as in a position to transform social
relations.[65] Yet his confidence in such a transformation as an inevitability of
social evolution, supplemented by correct theory and political organization,
weakened over time. The eschatological conclusion to the first volume of
Capital—the rhetorical climax of the "primitive accumulation" section with
which we are concerned here—brings its implicit tension of agent and subject
to an extreme point by staging revolution in the passive voice: "the centraliza-
tion of means of production and the socialization of labor reach a point where
they become incompatible with their capitalist husk. *It is* blown apart. . . . The
expropriators *are* expropriated" (C1, 929, my emphases).[66] Marx ascribes the
determinants of this revolution to the inexorable conjuncture of working-class
poverty and anger, and the fact that this class is trained (*geschult*, schooled),
unified and organized by the "mechanism" of the capitalist production-process
itself. (This assumes, without stating it, a *critical* as well as technical knowledge
of the way capitalism works as a machine for extracting surplus labor, i.e., the
secret of capital's productivity, the very knowledge Marx was trying to impart
in *Capital*). In more systematizing formulations in the deeply influential *Anti-
Dühring* (1878), Engels posits the question of the formation of a mass *will*-to-
change as an automatism emerging from systemic contradiction. In a striking
analogy between military and industrial mobilization of the masses (prefiguring
the famous "military-industrial complex" of a century later), he suggests that
the modern history of mass military enrollment represents a collective learning-
process that trains the people in the use of (forcible) means to transform the
State once they have a will with the correct content: "this moment will arrive
as soon as the mass of the people . . . *will have* a will . . . militarism collapses
by the dialectics of its own evolution."[67] The military machine here *is* the industrial machine; or, more precisely, is a metonym of it at the site of its most
extreme contradictions. Its industrial apparatus (means of *production*) is literally
a means of producing means of *destruction* (weapons of war); and not only that,
it is *self*-destructive: "militarism . . . brought to doom [*zugrunde*] in consequence
of its own development" because with the development of ever-better weaponry,

all military advances ensure the self-defeat of mutual destruction.[68] Progress in social productivity parallels progress in means of destructivity and gives the working class the training with which to overthrow this system if only the masses' "will" arrives at a "*content* [that] would be in accord with their class position." "Socialism will infallibly effect [*erwirken*]" the content of this will— precisely the thing that failed in the revolutions of 1848 (where the content turned out to be bourgeois). It is significant that we have moved explicitly to the question of a popular *will*, where the epistemological supplement it needs is cast as a "content" that socialism effectuates.[69] Closer to our own time, Negt and Kluge will respond thus: "The expectation on the part of theoreticians goes as far as to say that the propertyless, driven by misery, will inevitably force themselves to appropriate the means of production; under the supervision of this philosophy, an emancipatory process will materialize. Observations from the last one hundred and fifty years have yet to support these expectations. . . . These processes do not function automatically."[70]

Marx (critical epistemology) and Engels (creation of a will-to-socialism) have brought us to the site of a problem. Marx's account of primitive accumulation delineates the problem of figuring out the "transition," as it were, between an ideologeme embedded in the idioms of dispersed common sense and the leveraging of critical knowledge out of the elements and logic of the ideologeme's expressions in such idioms. The problem pivots on how to turn the latter's terms, which are the medium of popular assumptions, into a knowledge that rectifies the popular episteme from within. And how then does this knowledge become something that engages the will and desire of the working class? Gramsci later sets up the problem in slightly different terms: "men attain consciousness of fundamental conflicts on the terrain of ideology" in a way "not psychological or moralistic in character, but structural-gnoseological [*organico gnoseologico*]."[71] The terrain of ideology is the surface at which class conflicts appear, but a critical "structural-gnoseological" consciousness—a critical understanding of the ideological forms of appearance—is far from automatic. Indeed, it is produced interactively and site-specifically; there is no given formula or fail-safe technique. This is why Gramsci argues for a dynamic educative process that recasts prevailing vanguard models of political pedagogy by positing a supplement in which the "teacher" is asked to become student of the "environment" (that is, student of those s/he would instruct, in an expanded sense that includes the relevant cultural-social-economic scripts). Gramsci calls for work that involves the self-translation of the teacher into the idiom of a given ideological terrain so as to learn to draw out a kind of diagnostic knowledge from its articulations or "structural" (*organico*) features (what Gramsci always means by "organic" is the laid-out-ness, organ-ization, articulation, of elements). Yet diagnosis runs the risk of premature closure along such lines as these: ideological representations are idiotic; here is the correct diagnosis; real history / our theory is the cure; socialism will supply the correct content. We see some of this in Marx and to an extent in Gramsci (it remains a huge, inherited failing of Left vanguardism). On the other hand, if Marx's text is followed carefully we see that the critical intellectual's own knowledge (and ability to diagnose) is parasitic upon, organ-ized by, the ideological frame-works attached to the relations of production. Entering into this messy terrain is self-implicating and open-ended. The ideologeme is nothing if not recurrent, and the instantiations and translations of its schema seem inexhaustible.

To clarify here: diagnosis involves classification of phenomena into a set or typology to enable such statements as "x is an example of primitive accumula-tion." Diagnostic activity is thus on the side of calculation, and as such is in-dispensable for any socialist practice. However, what Marx points to, and where Gramsci follows and supplements him, is an intimation that extradiagnostic work is also needed to bring about lasting change, and that this will involve tinkering with the symbolic and imaginary orders, entering the thickets of subject-production.

It is therefore worth pressing a little further on the protocols of Marx's treat-ment of the ideologeme, not least because "primitive accumulation" has become an object of greatly renewed interest and application in radical diagnosis today.[72]

We return to the fable I quoted above, the story of the "diligent, intelligent, and above all frugal elite" who accumulated capital before capitalism, and the "lazy shreds who wasted all they had and more." According to this story, the propertied minority "previously" accumulated its starter-capital by virtue of that anthropological difference. The constitutionally unable were given jobs by the others. Forms of the story of this difference then *recur* as an explanation within developed capitalism. I have suggested that its cluster of figurations communicates and is compatible with modern race-thinking. Accordingly, meditating upon the vicissitudes of extreme anti-Indian racism in Bolivia's ruling class from the period of founding the oligarchic state to the 1950s, René Zavaleta Mercado ponders whether "natural selection was an inevitable myth or ideologeme of the circumstances of originary accumulation."[73] This is nat-ural selection in the Spencerian social Darwinist sense of "survival of the fit-test," articulating a conviction of biological (hereditary) "originary inequality."[74] If, at the level of pervasive ideologemes, some variant of a racializing classifi-catory reflex is common to capitalist formations, then it is also "juridically and morally contradictory, if not inconceivable" for societies that recognize them-selves in "bourgeois" terms as national formations constituted upon human equality of birth and instantiating other "bourgeois" universalisms.[75] (The

Bolivian dispensations discussed by Zavaleta took an exclusionist—and more or less genocidal and hyperexploitative—attitude to their indigenous population considered as subhuman).

Bolivia's "process of originary accumulation without a national orientation" is, moreover, a situation illegible from within Marx's tendential nation-state norm for endogenous industrial capitalist formation: a bourgeois national State at work to sustain the hegemonic conditions for home market, colonial power, national debt, trade protectionism.[76] Looking at Bolivia's recent past, Zavaleta is depicting a situation where capitalism is *not* the dominant point of reference, and this gives a uniquely disarticulated, "motley" (*abigarrado/a*) figure to the social formation. Paradoxically, it is the racialized "social Darwinist" ideological form that offers a superstructural (cultural) class continuity within the cosmopolitical "xenophilia" of a Bolivian State oligarchy that did not dedicate itself to capitalist development.[77] "It is also," writes Zavaleta, "possible to imagine a process of originary accumulation without a national orientation in its discourse, that is, not all originary accumulation produces a nation."[78] This is a notable divergence from Marx's main account in which national systems "all employ State power" (all "without exception," as he writes in the French edition of *Capital*) to move to industrial capitalism (C1, 915–16).[79] Zavaleta thereby offers a way to understand the codes of primitive accumulation as an epistemological instrument for disclosing that which is out of joint with the efficient national coding of social development through a capital-State complex; and this in turn supports our view that Marx's epistemological argument supplements—or interrupts—diagnosis. Zavaleta's unfinished allegory of the present history of Bolivia offers an alternative account of the political unconscious of primitive accumulation wherein the past is not the prehistory of capital, and the capitalist mode of production plays at best a bit part in the drama of Bolivian modernity.

Joseph Schumpeter returns this relay to metropolitan economic theory on the cusp of neoliberal ascendance. Among the most significant precursors of the capitalist vanguard's rhetoric of "disruption" in its current forms, Schumpeter polemically but symptomatically reverses Marx's argument. He does this precisely by affirming the literal truth of the fable. "Supernormal intelligence and energy," he writes, "account for industrial success"; and even if accumulation of riches is achieved by theft and robbery, "successful robbery must rest on the personal superiority of the robbers."[80] This of course perversely confirms the pertinence of Marx's argument that the distended "beginning" of capitalism demands some narrative and figurative form of appearance that ascribes its emergence to a difference in human types. It is a small, though nonetheless significant, slide from ascriptions of individualized "personal superiority" to more general typologies of group difference; yet this is the form taken by the displacement that racializes, genders, ethnicizes, or castes the class differentials of "industrial success." The sentiment that success as such demonstrates the personal superiority of the successful, *even if the metric is the success of getting away with crimes*, is now such a generalized structure of feeling that it is virtually undocumentable. We could cite the fetishization of "smartness," documented by Karen Ho in her ethnography of Wall Street as a performative system of class signifiers:

> What constitutes "smartness" is explicitly dependent on school pedigree as well as race. . . . On Wall Street, "smartness" means much more than individual intelligence; it conveys a naturalized and generic sense of "impressiveness," of elite, pinnacle status and expertise, which is used to signify, even prove, investment bankers' worthiness as advisors to corporate America and leaders of the global financial markets. . . . Smartness must be represented and reinforced by a specific appearance and bodily technique.[81]

This line of discussion brings us to the bottomless sedimentation of histories of the distinction between mental and manual labor, a relevant topic that I can only note here.

I have been arguing that in Marx's usage, primitive accumulation may be read not as a diagnostic category but as critical epistemology. As such, it must remain provisional—perhaps not even attached to its own name—inasmuch as parasitically bound to the idioms and narratives that fill a discursive value-form with content. As I show later, Marx's treatment and translation of the name "primitive accumulation" indicates this orientation toward epistemological practice. Correspondingly, the economic historian Philip Mirowski, in his analysis of the neoliberal paradigms that both determined the economic catastrophe of 2007–8 and were generally accepted as the solutions to it, suggests that the success of neoliberalism as a pervasive episteme may be ascribed to the power of "stories": artifactual narrative constructs that interpellate the subject with, in Althusser's terms, "imaginary solutions to real problems." In Mirowski's words, this is "a set of images, causal scenarios, and precepts that begin to add up to something approaching a worldview" if taken as "spread over a lifetime." He contends that such fabulae have a real—though I would add not always necessarily predictable—systemic effect on economic and social behavior, and that this helps explain the general acceptance of neoliberal "solutions" to the very problems neoliberal practices have engendered, such as the global financial crisis of 2007–8.[82] Thus, as I have been arguing, epistemological work must remain a site of translation problems: struggles between a systemic desire to universalize (translation's desire to carry an unharmed semantic content between any languages) and the conditions that make any translation nonidentical with what is translated (the unique body of the signifier, for example). I have also argued, following Chakrabarty, that the translation of capital into capitalism(s) involves varieties of conflict and complicity with the idioms of surplusity wherever this translation occurs. It follows that the "separation" indispensable for installing the capital-relation and positing the worker as producer of surplus-*value* may take many forms on the ground, with effects that redefine social groups that disrupt and exploit *in-situ* codings of surplusity.

Finding a certain common element in the archive of transition, Silvia Federici can think the persecuted "witch" as a type case of capitalist "separation." What the transition to capitalism meant in general terms for working women in early modern Europe was a deterritorialized "great confinement," to use Foucault's term; a dispersal of women into isolated (familial) points organized around a reproductive function. This offers many rich lines of investigation that challenge and enrich prevailing Marxist accounts. If we track the fault lines of this gendered separation in the longue durée up to the social-mediatic starting point of the present chapter, we can discern a particular capitalization of gendered affect.[83] Facebook was initiated on the basis of the circulation and capitalization of gendered affect. As "Facemash," its prototype was an application that facilitated the comparison of the faces of pairs of female college students in order to rate their sexual attractiveness. Thus, underlying today's seemingly more neutral "like" and other "reactions" functions—themselves extracting monetizable data in the affect-form from users—we can find the trace of a much older seam of gendered class-formation as the sequestering, class-ification, and exchange of women in rated groupings. Groupings of women that consolidate the identities of male-run social units.[84] (Ultimately, we could add that such gender systems are historically large enough to hold capitalism in their vise, and not the other way around).

In his own account of the ideologeme, Marx names several powerful rhetorical registers in which the unit of anthropological difference appears in narrative form. For political economy—which is in Marx's day the academic theorization and apologia of capitalist operation—the new social relation has a biblical analog. By positing this analogical relation, Marx implies that academic theory borrows the resources of a more diffuse perceptual and signifying system that holds human differences to be essential traits with a moral coding. At this level, Marx's epistemological approach discloses the presuppositions of "theory" held on an epistemic level. The theoretical account of the difference that explains capitalism resembles, structurally or functionally, the theological *legend* of the Fall of Man (into sin, the *Sündenfall*). This event took place before the historical movement and development of peoples, but it was at the same time the origin of that history's program, predicated upon the knowledge of good and evil. Expulsion from the garden on the basis of a double transgression entails generations and genealogy, suffering, death, fratricide, human diffusion, economy, agriculture, industry, urbanization, antagonism, gender hierarchy. Marx underlines the analogous function (*Rolle*) of the legend rather than its thematic content: "This primitive accumulation plays approximately the same role in political economy as original sin in theology" (C1, 873). Tracking this loose analogic of the legend clues us into what Marx is after: the differentiation that plays out in human history as *effect* of the transgression in fact minimally assumes that very fault in the predisposition of Adam, and especially the woman (she is not named "Eve" until after their exile), to transgress on the basis of a desire.[85] (Any quasi-racial anthropological fault line is thus itself fissured by sexual difference from the start; from before the start.) The condemnation of these male and female beings to toil and pain is already inscribed in the flawed characteristics of their humanity as cause. As with racism and sexism's classifications and partitions of humans, the effect becomes its own cause. This is the effective analogy—a metaleptic ideological substitution of cause for effect—that Marx tells us takes place in the dominant accounts of capitalism's beginnings.[86]

The biblical analogy is well chosen inasmuch as scripture was *the* common text across all social strata in nineteenth-century Europe. Indeed, Bible translations in Germany, England, and France played a key role in the grammatization and standardization of their respective languages as *national* languages, as did even more widely known texts such as *The Book of Common Prayer* in England.[87] Translation takes on a certain modernizing and universalizing role in this context. Until recently, then, scripture represented the most general narrative resource for living in terms of, as Gramsci writes (in Catholic Italy, admittedly, but looking beyond his locality), "religion taken not in the confessional sense but in the secular sense of a unity of faith between a conception of the world and a corresponding norm of conduct."[88] That is to say, it works at both epistemic and epistemological levels for subjects "modernized" in this way. If we honor Marx's choice of words here and notice that the legend plays a "role" (*Rolle*), then the abstract structure of analogy is both given a theatrical dimension (representation) and set in a circular pattern of repetition-substitution (rotation). It is then legitimate to suggest that this role-play brings in descriptive resemblance as well as substitution and is therefore an epistemological indication that academic theories of the beginning of capitalism are governed by a more general theological "conception of the world." The translation of scripture plays its part here, supplying within a mythographic figurative system the language, norms, and ethics that constitute the terms and presuppositions of theoretical economics. Marx is reading this as the provisionally localizable source from which the epistemic value-form draws its terms of commensurability.

It is at this point that Marx's epistemological approach points the way for work at the epistemic level, a kind of work tasked with exceeding its own epistemological grounding. It returns us to the scene of Flora Tristan's despair over the hapless conditions of the Nîmes workers (summed up as "the rich are necessary for the poor to live"), but also to all the quotidian binary formulae (winners and losers, helpers and helped, innovators and imitators, us and them) that contain the traces of heterogeneous group formations.

Primitive accumulation "plays . . . [a] role" in the theatrical scenography of political economy. The latter's theater requires figures of human actors, since it puts on stage the drama of intrinsic human differences that result in social and economic inequality.[89] This part of *Capital* instantiates a structural irony of parasitism by intercepting the terms of the main narrative. If we understand parabasis, in the critical sense given it by Paul de Man, as the "interruption of a discourse by a shift in the rhetorical register," it does not need to be defined exclusively in the form of breaking with a syntactical pattern.[90] Irony in the mode of parabasis can also operate semantically. Some figure steps in from a space external to the coherent and systematic tropological functioning of a main narrative line, interruptively disclosing another story, another logic, another system, or another set of references incompatible with it. When de Man cites Friedrich Schlegel's definition of the disruption of a figural chain by a system incompatible with it, the term used is *"aus der Rolle fallen,"* to drop out of one's role, to drop the act, pause the play; the "interruption of a discourse."[91] In de Man's terms, parabasis should be thought as "permanent," not as a periodic interruption, but as something possible at all points. "At all points the narrative *can be* interrupted."[92] Note he says "can be," and not "is." "You have to imagine the parabasis as *being able to take place at all times.*"[93] For de Man, this "being able" is finally perhaps confined to a machinicity of language itself that persistently undoes its own attempts at reflexivity as much as reference. With Marx we have to shift the levels a bit and think about the parabasis as the imaginative work of epistemological shifting, intervening in a metaleptic political and anthropological narrative and initially altering the references. In the face of systemic, micro- and macrological propagation of stories that tie social difference to intrinsic human typology, Marx enters into a kind of wild and unguaranteed empiricism—what he called "the *history* of the economic fall." Here, wild empiricism means following the trail of separation and accumulation processes across several hundred years in one country to see where they go. This is another reason Marx's conceptual intervention is parasitical; it calls for a permanent parabasis that works from within a local history as well as the prevailing ethical and epistemic scripts. The "anecdotal" stories of anthropological difference will always pop up, and so this task of undoing and reinterpreting is necessarily unending and fragmentary, linked as it is to the perpetual generation of theatrical narratives, great and small, that give coherent figure to the contingent patterns of capitalist development.

Marx, as is now widely recognized, revised his own *avant la lettre* political unconscious argument about the homogeneity of the pattern of capitalist development in the French translation of *Capital*. At the end of the first part of the revised "primitive accumulation" chapter, he strongly qualifies earlier formulations of capitalist development that implied a uniform, even universal, Euronormative and urban-centric pattern for the rest of the world. In 1881 he receives a request for a prognosis about capitalist development in Russia by a group of Russian exiles—a question that implicitly asked whether British-style primitive accumulation was "historically necessary" for Russia to pass through capitalism to socialism.[94] At stake is the "communal" rural form of socioeconomic life in a vast agrarian society and whether its dislocation and dissolution by industrial capitalism must be diagnosed as an inevitability from the most developed industrial capitalist area. Marx's response is terse and minimal, but he writes the following, quoting his own revised version of the passage in the French *Capital*:

> At the core of the capitalist system, therefore, lies the complete separation of the producer from the means of production. . . . The basis for this whole development is the *expropriation of the agricultural producer*. To date this has not been accomplished in a radical fashion anywhere except in England. . . . But *all the other countries of Western Europe* are undergoing the same process.[95]

> Hence the "historical inevitability" of this process is *expressly* limited to *the countries of Western Europe*. . . . Hence the analysis in *Capital* does not adduce reasons either for or against the vitality of the rural commune, but the special study I have made of it . . . has convinced me that this commune is the fulcrum of social regeneration in Russia.[96]

The question from outside allows Marx to *détourne* a reading of the narrative of development that his own theory had made possible.

Marx himself is doing critical epistemological work on an ideological form that constructs a universalizing figure for surplus-ing across time and space, a figure that makes it appear as if the social relation that determines the possibility of surplus-*value* is fixed in the intrinsic difference of human types. Because there is surplus-ing in all social formations, the "capitalist" translation can be imposed upon them in ways that mobilize existing idiomatic binaries and classifications in terms of two types of humanity, one of which is capable of the accumulation that appears as aid to the incapacitated other.

Back in nineteenth-century Europe, Marx argues that in his situation the dominant coding of this division works through a representation of human default depicted in Genesis—a twist on the Augustinian doctrine of original sin. As we have noted, in other areas and languages, especially outside western Europe, this might receive a different cultural coding. Self-translation into the possibility of engaging with these idioms on a subjective level would be a task for an International worthy of the name. Even though Marx is restricted to the mythographic scriptural example, however, he indicates the internal margin at which epistemic continuity fades out. That is, he shows where this most common text—that configures localized ideological units of epistemic reconciliation and commensurability—ceases to have traction. The ideologeme of primitive accumulation as he has described it comes undone, not in a necessarily felicitous way (since it simply ceases to signify), but in a way that discloses fault lines within the "same" culture and thus assigns another kind of task to the activist intellectual.

In an earlier chapter of *Capital* titled "The Working Day," Marx looks at limit-cases of exceptional exploitation to illustrate the normal operation of capitalism. Child workers can be employed both to lengthen the working day (by easing adult work) and to depress the value of labor-power (because the infrastructure of lower-paid children makes it appear as if the adult male workers are being paid the value of labor-power, whereas their work is being subsidized by that of the children at a lower rate). Marx brings us to the most subaltern example he can find in the official record: the testimony of a ten-year-old girl called Jane Murfey, whose interview had been included as evidence for the British government's Children's Employment Commission published as Marx was finishing *Capital*: "This girl spelt God as dog, and did not know the name of the queen" (C1, 370).[97] Divine and terrestrial sovereignty lose their proper names on this border of subalternity.

But what is at stake in Marx's invocation of this loss? His outrage at the preemptive cognitive destruction and epistemic underdevelopment of the child workers is palpable, but this leads to other considerations. Drawing attention to "the level of education of these 'labor-powers,'" Marx cites numerous other testimonies from the Children's Employment Commission's *Fifth Report* showing that, among child workers, the common cultural text that gives the official script of primitive accumulation its content has become meaningless: "'Have heard say that God made the world, and that all the people was drowned but one; heard say that one was a little bird.' William Smith, age 15"; "'The devil is a good person. I don't know where he lives.' 'Christ was a wicked man'" (C1, 370). These are only a fraction of the instances in one year's report. There are more examples just as blunt: "Never heard of Jesus Christ. . . . Don't know what the Bible is," not to speak of the absence of other more mundane kinds of knowledge[98] The children are shown to be lacking in basic literacy, arithmetic competence, and general knowledge (including that of scriptural narrative). This anticipates multiple implications as far as primitive accumulation is concerned. For the sake of concision, I underline only the following. First, and most important for the present argument, the children do not accede to the figurative scheme as scripturally articulated. Its terms are garbled by them at best, and Marx's intended reader does not share this confusion. It is a "worldview" that points toward the space of an upbringing that has not been filled with the elements that would constitute the hegemonic threshold (what Zavaleta called the "social optimum") required for the successful simulacrum of consensual integration into a bourgeois industrial nation-state. (While a variety of philanthropic and religious primary school institutions existed in 1860s England, the gradual construction of a State-mandated and nationally coordinated elementary system did not begin until the 1870s). This is not to say that there were no means of exacting obedience and subordination from child workers, or of instilling in them norms and some basic theory of their dependency: one can speculate that these might be full of parental and community coercion as well as affection, intergenerational pressures, desperation, untheorized solidarity, and so on. None of that is documented, but Marx's sense that the *Sündenfall* story is an analogy (playing a functional role to sustain a commonsense binary) rather than supplying a universal figurative content is a useful insight here. A different functional narrative of a fault line of human in/capability could play the same role, implying that the imaginative activist must dig yet deeper to bridge the communication gap and locate the frames in which these "labor-powers" have a subjective self-representation of their situation; why and how it figures their normality in the absence of the scriptural instance. This also points toward the discontinuities of class formation and the latter's idioms, however distant from translation into recognizably Marxist terms. For the activist, this opens a different site of struggle precisely because the epistemic apparatus of "these labor-powers" has not been shaped effectively by the most general narrative formulae (they are, then, beyond generalization).

As Richard Halpern has shown in his insightful account of the relation between primitive accumulation processes and education in early modern

England, there was no shortage of moralizing pedagogy and educational theory from the fifteenth century onward that sustained scripturally inflected ideologemes of "two sorts of people" with differing intrinsic capacities that determine their ultimate wealth or poverty. This does not simply appear at the level of the content of moral lessons, but is systemically and structurally installed in what Halpern calls the "demonstrative function" instituted by Renaissance schooling. This mechanism correlates educational results to the student's innate capacities or aptitudes in a metaleptic reversal of cause and effect. The paradigm assumes what it seeks to "demonstrate": the high-achieving student was always intrinsically more capable as shown by their high achievement. . . . In the crisis of an increasing wealth gap in sixteenth-century England, "the schools helped create an ideological climate in which economic success and failure were understood through the categories of diligence and laziness, self-discipline and excess, talent and the lack of it."[99] This Erasmian, humanistic educational philosophy carried, therefore, its own shadow of feudalism and the three (or four) estates.[100] The very poorest fell out of this educational system in any case, and J. L. Vives's 1526 lament about the proletarianized children of early modern Europe seems ironically to apply to those interviewed by the Factory Inspectors in the mid-1860s:

> Children of the needy receive a deplorable upbringing. Together with their brood, the poor are cast out of the churches and wander over the land; they do not receive the sacraments and they hear no services. We do not know by what law they live, nor what their practices or beliefs.[101]

Yet the important difference is that the children discussed by Marx are exorbitant instances of *workers* — occupying a liminally subaltern position in industrial production — and therefore they must somehow be considered as agents of capital and included in the itinerary of Marxist theory and practice. While the child workers' testimonies may seem abject and even tragic, Marx's monitoring of their formation is precisely not about presenting them as the most pathetic victims of exploitation in need of benevolent assistance. The effort is rather to indicate that here too is a place at which collectivities must be imagined and constructed.[102] The alternative is the perhaps unsurprisingly pessimistic prognosis given later in the primitive accumulation chapter:

> As capitalist production moves forward, a working class develops that by education, tradition and habit looks upon the requirements of that mode of production as self-evident natural laws. The organization of the formed capitalist process of production breaks every resistance. (C1, 899)

Echoes of Flora Tristan. Bringing this sharply up to date with respect to capi-talist development in contemporary India, Chakrabarti and Dhar observe a long-term effect of capitalcentric development embedded in policy and practice: "the targeted populace remains outside the domain of policy making."[103]

Let us return to Marx's breakdown of how the ideological schema of primitive accumulation appears in the way he considers typical. The second narrative form of this ideologeme is *anecdote*. The "origin" is "narrated as an anecdote about the past" (*als Anekdote der Vergangenheit erzählt wird*) (C1, 873). This is now a discursive explanation rather than the previously discussed analogy. For the Marx trained in Classics, an anecdote is not just any story. It is the narrative revelation of an unpublicized (literally: not given-out) episode, often carrying the connotation of salacious or prurient gossip.[104] Marx proposes that the cap-italist concept-narrative appears as the disclosure of a secret. In this case, unlike Procopius's claim to personal testimony in the *Anekdota*, it has the troubling, because unaccountable, anonymous phenomenality of gossip or rumor. Marx's first chapter-section is titled "The Secret of So-Called Primitive Accumulation." So, like an unctuous meme or an inexplicit, murmured insinuation that is as powerful as—and less easily confronted than—any officially sanctioned prej-udice (Jim Crow, apartheid); or, like the micrological and indirect manifestation of implicit, everyday racism, the secret spread abroad in capitalist society is that economic humanity is made up of two quasi-racial groups, idle *Lumpens* and thrifty entrepreneurs. The secret that an essential anthropological difference necessarily engenders a social system spreads with all the force of the imper-sonal and spontaneous.

This is a first unveiling; a first disclosure. Like the biblical story that it pro-longs and modernizes, it is a tale of primal hierarchy leading to primal shame; revelation of the naked incapacity of the proletarians-who-must-be-helped, who cover their shame with the shredded rags (*Lumpen*) they wear; rags that of course only reveal even more clearly their nakedness in the very act of trying to conceal it. Commenting, not without some irony, on Alain David's attempt to find the "true historical weight of this artifact without consistency called race," Jacques Derrida tracks David's discussion of the anthropological differ-ence at work in this same biblical narrative.[105] At the limit of reflexive con-sciousness, we enter the terrain of affect, "shame and the human experience of nudity" from which David "deduces the 'feeling that governs the division of races.'"[106] This immeasurable weight, experienceable therefore only as affect, he terms "primitive humiliation" (*humiliation primitive*), as projective effect of the constitution of an anthropological difference of superiority and inferiority.[107] While social class is neither an affect nor an identity, the role of affect in

constructing norms of conformity and obedience as well as energies of insur-
rection and struggle remains on the margins of Marxist discourse. "We suspect
that the discrediting of labor, which in antiquity is a matter for slaves, must
have far-reaching consequences for the imprinting [*Prägung*] of labor-power
and the norms bound to it."[108]

> Unto Adam also and to his wife did the LORD God make coats of
> skins, and clothed them. . . . Therefore the LORD God sent him forth
> from the garden of Eden, to till the ground from whence he was
> taken.[109]

> That letter (D) is N; that is A; that (Y) is T. Don't know what DAY
> spells, nor what SUN spells. Don't know how many months there are
> in the year. August is the first month in the year. Christmas day comes
> in May. Don't know what happened on that day. Think I have heard
> about Jesus Christ; don't know anything he did, or how he died. Have
> not been to Sunday school since I was ever so little—that high (about 5
> years old). Have no clothes but these to go in (mere rags).

> Don't go to Sunday school. Have not got any other clothes but what I
> have on—(very ragged).[110]

Marx brings this to hyperbolic conclusion. The most disorganized and marginal
section of the proletariat gets its nickname by metonymy from the *Lumpen*
(rags) it wears to cover its nakedness and that paradoxically emphasize its radical
exposure. Yet even this nakedness does not belong to it: "the latter had finally
nothing left to sell but their own skins" (C1, 873).

> . . . he put his naked hand into the furnace and pulled the pipe out. It
> took the skin off his fingers.[111]

This is undoubtedly why, in a following section titled "The Genesis of the
Industrial Capitalist," Marx evokes both the "hunting of blackskins" (*Schwar-
zhäute*, i.e., African slaves) and the extermination of the "redskin" (*Rothaut*,
indigenous American) as "chief moments of primitive accumulation" (C1,
915–18).[112] Each group is defined as a chromatically classified exposed skin—
Marx is ventriloquizing a harsh racial reductionism—for sale one way or the
other. Black African slave labor, and cash rewards for Native American prisoners
or scalps. As part of the *same* sequence, these "moments" extend at growing
levels of abstraction into contemporaneity with the modern fiscal system and
the introduction of world-spanning financial networks of credit that indebt
entire nations. "The public debt becomes one of the most powerful levers of
primitive accumulation . . . [a condition of] violent expropriation" (C1, 919;

921). "A great deal of capital that pops up today in the United States without a birth certificate was yesterday in England capitalized child-blood" he tells us in the same section (C1, 920). This is abstraction as seen from the capital side: "the use of [the (child-)worker's] labor-power is labor itself" (C1, 283). That was yesterday; today it is identity-less capital in transnational movement. Value in the money-form or in the data-form may indeed, per Marx's Ovidian idiom, "metamorphose" as it traverses the circuits of money-capital, production, and commodity-capital. But it cannot really be translated back into its "original." *Pecunia non olet* is the motto of this mode of universalized laundering.

Displacing (that is, transposing and not deleting but setting to work in an-other system) the schema and logic of the biblical story, Marx will go on to tell of the expulsions and wanderings of the proletarianized. Their systematic re-territorialization—as rural and then urban *workers*—begins with agribusiness: "the flax looks exactly as it did before. Not a fiber of it is changed, but a new social soul has entered into its body. It is now part of the constant capital of the master-manufacturer" (C1, 909). (An analysis of expanded capitalist agri-culture, fully subsumed, might today investigate the plant "fiber" now adjusted for maximum efficiency with chemical fertilizers and pesticides as well as genetic modification; but this supports Marx's larger argument.) But in turning to the conjuncture that produces the capital-relation, Marx stages a second unveiling: one that reveals the secret of the first (a second "secret of primitive accumulation," but a second secret that is logically the *first* or originary secret: the secret veiled by the story of an intrinsically segregated humanity). The secret of the secret is not the process of accumulation of material wealth at one pole of society by theft or hard work on the part of a naturally superior (or stronger and more violent) race of humans. It is rather the specific conjuncture of processes that made a systemic social *relation* possible, that also gave it trac-tion, such that, when set to work in a particular way, its elaborated effect may be industrial capitalism.

In *Reading Capital*, Balibar indicated that the "mythic" function of the ideol-ogeme is a "*retrospective projection* of the forms of capitalist production and of the forms of exchange and law which correspond to it."[113] The effect becomes its own condition in the "fabulous retroactivity" instantiated by all narrative recounting.[114] The effect is both the performative construction of a collectivity *and* a difference. In Balibar's terms, the form of appearance of this retrospective projection is "memory." "The memory of the [capitalist] mode of production" represents the "continuing present of an origin homogenous with the current process" in the double form of the right to property in personal labor (individual production for exchange or accumulation) and the right of the owner of the conditions of production (the capitalist) to appropriate the product (which negates the first law by separating property from individual labor).[115] Therefore, "the memory inscribed in this law of appropriation is a purely fictive one," an imaginary resolution to a real contradiction.[116] As I am arguing, the identification of a fiction of this type does not necessarily attenuate its force. Memory does not primarily designate for Balibar the retentions of an individual psyche but the para-individual space of ideology as a collective, imaginary specularization of "separation." Yet first, such a memory-figure is not automatically produced; or if it is, we must ask about the mechanism of its automaticity. And second, as Bernard Stiegler never ceased to remind us, it is nevertheless recurrently produced, repeated, materialized, transmitted, taught in externalized (written, spoken, imaged, institutionalized) forms that entail further narrativizations, externalizations, and technical mediations in order to develop and make appear classificatory differentiations between human "types."

Thus, continuing his enumeration of the media and institutions carrying the ideologeme of primitive accumulation, Marx writes that in spite of the "insipid childishness" of the economic narratives, their "standpoint of the child's primer [*Kinderfibel*]" prevails generally when "the defense of property" is at stake (C1, 873–74).[117] An allusive but insistent thread of Marx's argument is that the ideologeme is set in place by the institutions and practices of education and childrearing in school and home from the very start of life and in each generation raised in a capitalistic society.

Marx shifts to the sphere of political discourse from the maelstrom of 1848 to find a discursive instance of the pervasive notion of essential anthropological difference in action. He writes that Louis Adolphe Thiers produces a prodigious "*Kinderfibel*," alluding to Thiers's *De la propriété* (1848), a book of popular political wisdom designed to manage social crisis (C1, 874).[118] Such manuals continue to appear. The French statesman seeks to demonstrate that property is both a universal fact and a natural right grounded on the differential faculties of each individual. These faculties are themselves the first unconditional property, basis for the coded property-right over whatever surplus the faculties can subsequently appropriate from nature or produce through work. Thus, "the inequality of man's faculties necessarily engenders [*nait forcément*] an inequality of goods."[119]

"Is it really true," asks Thiers,

> that one man has great physical strength, another very little? that one is strong but awkward, another weak but clever? that one will do but little work, another much? Is it true that, setting aside the traditional inequalities of birth and fortune, taking two workmen in any

manufactory, one will exhibit extreme skill, indefatigable diligence, earn three or four times more than the other, accumulate his first gains, and form a capital with which in turn he will speculate and become immensely rich? These happy faculties, moral or physical, are certainly his own. This will not be denied; and with no misapplication of language, it may be said they are his property. But this property is unequal; for with certain faculties this man remains poor all his life, with certain others that man becomes rich and powerful. They are the essential cause that one has much, the other little.[120]

Thiers constructs interminable anthropological stories to support his claim that social inequality in property is grounded on intrinsic differences in human capacity:

Even before the time when long-accumulated labor, and transmission from generation to generation, has added conventional inequalities to the first natural inequalities, you will acknowledge that even in the savage state the highly gifted man possesses great advantages. In the chase, if he be more skillful, he has twice as much food as his neighbor. In self-defense, if he be stronger, he has twice the means of resistance. Inequality appears, therefore, at the very commencement of social existence; it is manifested on the first day. And the ulterior inequalities of the richest society are but the lengthened shadow of a body already highly elevated.[121]

This participates in a widely shared presupposition that there have never existed in any social formation equalizing mechanisms, laws, and institutions to regulate the effects of the real and inevitable differentials in the capabilities of individual human beings.[122] Marx's later sketch of a form of justice configured by practices *transgressive* of statistical equalization was not grounded on the assumption that all human beings are or should be made exactly the same, or that "outcomes" should be made artificially identical; nor did he extrapolate social classes, inequalities, and hierarchies from an anthropological fact of differentiated individual capabilities or characteristics. However, this latter line of argument is deployed in Thiers to support the admirable liberal notion of a divinely ordained "unity in diversity, and diversity in unity" (DP, 29). This (imaginary) solution to the (real) problem of social classes is not only that they reflect insurmountable and essential distinctions in human types, but that their existence is condition and effect of felicitous diversity—and should be desired rather than criticized. These lessons are still being taught.

Marx made a footnoted addition to the end of this paragraph in the French edition of *Capital* (1872–75). As if to assure himself that the point about schooling should be re-marked, he returns us to the scene of the classroom. "Goethe," he writes, "irritated by these nonsensicalities, mocked them in the following dialogue."[123] He quotes in its entirety Goethe's short dialogue-poem *Katechisation*. I translate from Marx's French translation in *Le Capital*, as it makes visible his own emphases:

Schoolteacher: So tell me, where did your father's fortune come from?

Child: From grandfather.

Schoolteacher: And how did he get it?

Child: From great-grandfather.

Schoolteacher: And how did that one get it?

Child: He snatched it.[124]

Catechization: rehearsed question-and-answer exercise to check that the child has internalized a fixed moral code. The questions are not real questions, since the answers are preformulated and presupposed by them (a valid teaching method as used in the learning of multiplication tables, verbal conjugations, etc.). Here, pushed to recite the formula leading to the "originary" moment, the child scandalously repeats Thiers's lesson as the law of the strongest, he snatched it, *il l'a prise* (Goethe's prescient irony in a commercializing, emergently capitalist society). It is as if this discloses in advance the uncensored fantasy of Thiers, a secret transcript of an originary autonormative power of taking, seizing, or grasping a surplus, creating a short circuit between economic inequality and a certain sovereignty.

However, the lesson here is that of unintended consequences. Marx's real point is that the child (and indeed his father and grandfather) is the contingent beneficiary of a *gewaltsam* event that occurred generations ago. Even Thiers acknowledges that the system of patrilineal inheritance does not reflect superior individual capacities on the part of the heir. The Goethe poem echoes Marx's earlier observation that the industrial capitalists were themselves beneficiaries of processes in which they played no active role. The industrial capitalists took advantage of propitious circumstances; they succeeded by "exploiting events that owed absolutely nothing to them" (C1, 875). If it was the corruption and greed of the landed gentry that destroyed feudalism from within, and if it was the State that taught vagabond masses the meaning of work through the criminalization of movement and legalized torture for vagrancy, then the entrepreneur may step in between landed gentry and proletariat to take advantage of a situation that exists for entirely unrelated reasons. (For instance, the entrepreneur uses the gentry's extensive stolen lands in exchange for rent in money, and employs on this land those persons who have no other way of making a living. Entrepreneur: literally one who takes-from-between, giving rise to enter-prise; *il l'a prise*.) Hence, at least in Marx's example, the "capitalist *farmer*" is a pathbreaking figure on the way to the industrial production of surplus-value (C1, 905–13).

The child in Goethe's poem—the great-grandson—is the analogue of the capitalist inasmuch as he is in a position to capital*ize* upon a fortune that is merely a contingent inheritance seized by an unknown person in unknown circumstances generations ago.

Katechisation introduces the symbolic institution of patrilineal inheritance, both name and property passing intact down the male generational sequence (from great-grandfather to child). It brings us back to the question of the gendering of these processes, wherein the asserted autonormativity of the male line (the "same" thing, infinitely repeatable and inheritable without loss) covers up the contingency of lineage and inheritance. Inheritance of family wealth has been largely naturalized; inheritance and transmission of the name in the male line is a cornerstone of the symbolic order. If, by this logic, it seems "right" that—because of his name—a great-grandson should inherit wealth that he neither worked for nor even stole for himself, then this illustrates precisely Marx's intimation that these social processes "take" at the level of everyday sensibilities and attitudes. The general formula for capital itself, in its most ideologically blinding and commonsense iteration, exemplifies this: M-C-M′: that is to say, *money* (M) that *makes more money* (M′) by a process of commodity-exchange (C).[125] Because value is in the same form (money) at either end of the formula, the sum that has "grown" in the meantime can appear as sharing a "familial" identity with the money advanced. It seems as if it has automatically reproduced and grown itself like a patrilineal family tree, whereas—as Marx's effort was to prove—the extra, the surplus(-value) is in fact *produced* using a specific technique.

What the *autos* of an autonormative formal identity (money in—more-money out) conceals is the fact of its own heteronomy, its dependence on the hetero-norms (and indeed laws) of a valorization-process in which the value of what is formally the "same" money is "grown." In fact, a particular commodity is *used* to produce the excess, the more-value. Here is the heteronomy: money does not "grow" by itself. A heterogeneous implement is organized and exploited to make it "more." And there is something other than an analogy here with the autonormativity of patrilineal family trees, name-forms, and inheritance-structures when one considers that the hetero-norms of familial propagation involve gender-specific practices and functions in which gendered bodies are *used* to produce *more* of something that will carry the same (name) into the future; a narrow example being childbearing, but this is not the exclusive instance.

So it is that Thiers, political architect of the massacre of the Parisian communards and sloganeer of "unity in diversity," has marked the transition in Marx's discussion to a different sort of investigation of violence and force in the constitution and maintenance of the capitalist mode of production.

In showing that industrial capitalism can be the long-term effect of entirely unrelated forms of force or violence, therefore, Marx does not affirm that "property is theft" in the zero-sum Proudhonian sense. As Roberts has indicated, Marx is pointedly targeting positions on the relation between property, force and violence that characterized the mainstream socialist movement of his day.[126] If a "fortune" gained by theft is an above-average excess, there must already have been a surplus-in-others'-production for the taking. Forcible appropriation ("he *snatched* it") therefore presupposes an extra something for the taking, minimally a potential surplus; and the production, circulation, and destination of surplus in different forms (value, labor, product) is a decisive element of Marx's larger argument. It is precisely what distinguishes Marx's position from political theories that only examine the distribution and possession of political power in social formations.[127] In a footnote to the "Commodity and Money" chapter of *Capital*, Marx rectifies a simplistic theory of living by theft, by "taking": "Truly comical is M. Bastiat, who imagines that the ancient Greeks and Romans lived by plunder alone. For if people live by plunder for centuries there must, after all, always be something there to plunder; in other words, the objects of plunder must be continually reproduced. It seems, therefore, that even the Greeks and the Romans had a process of production, hence an economy, which constituted the material basis of their world as much as the bourgeois economy constitutes that of the present-day world" (C1, 175). If what is stolen—expropriated—is reproducible by the victims, then it is by definition a surplus. This is why Marx theorizes the capitalist wage as an averaged calculus of the amount necessary to sustain, that is, *reproduce*, the worker's labor-power at its prevailing normal level (this is the "value" of labor-power). In capital-logic, everything it can produce in excess of that value-level counts as surplus-value. Surplus, then, marks both the contingency of social relations and group formations, and the incalculable element in social production itself. Capital must calculate on this incalculability; its deployment of averages is its way of finessing the incalculable; and formal-to-real subsumption is the effect of this need for ever-more-reliable calculation that is condition and effect of technoscientific advance.

Buried in a footnote, and slight as the gesture may be, Marx's addition of the Goethe poem also reminds us that at the margins of his theoretical cognizance there remains a concern for the question of generationality and its formal and informal learning-processes. It is an indication of work to be done, and even of the sites in which that work could take place (the educational apparatus, the family). Patrimonial wealth transmitted generationally is certainly a "pre-capitalist" element, part of a gendered class process that has been condition and effect of the development of capitalism. Likewise, the rise of wealthy social strata through violence and crime that are legalized and sanitized as the generations turn over. In addition to this, the sanitizing and normalization of wealth-creation based upon capitalism's uniquely obscured mode of theft—the exploitation of *surplus* labor—is now part of ordinary middle-class intergenerational epistemic formation in a global capitalist economy. It is reflected in the titles of current children's books such as *Growing Money: A Complete Investing Guide for Kids* (2010); *Go! Stock! Go! A Stock Market Guide for Enterprising Children and Their Curious Parents* (2014); *Kidpreneurs: Young Entrepreneurs with Big Ideas* (2017); *The Startup Club* (2017); *Blue Chip Kids: What Every Child (and Parent) Should Know about Money, Investing, and the Market* (2015); *Jasmine Launches a Startup* (2018). The list could go on.

The books just cited represent the training of children from the most highly developed capitalist formations in how to be "good" at managing and directing money. This means thrifty and efficient, able to defer gratification; but also instrumental and opportunistic enough to "grow" their capital. Karen Ho's ethnography of Wall Street reminded us that this can become a "way of life," even a "lifestyle," for some. Neoliberal appropriations of the concept of "human capital" beginning in the 1960s develop the lessons into the individual life in a related manner. Once the self is defined as a capital asset in which to invest, then being an entrepreneur of oneself becomes a possible way to imagine one's life, possibly even soliciting an auto-primitive-accumulation of human capital (for which the gendered history of family relations would provide the first textbook . . .). It is not for nothing that the classic text on human capital is subtitled "with Special Reference to Education."[128] Exactly *how* the capital grows—exceeds itself—is not part of the lesson. "The circuit of money capital is . . . the most one-sided, hence most striking and characteristic form of appearance of the circuit of industrial capital, in which its aim and driving motive—the valorization of value, money-making and accumulation—appears in a form that leaps to the eye."[129] This blindingly obvious (*in die Augen springend*) phenomenality is precisely a *formal* identity: the money-*form* at either end of the circuit such that it really seems as if money engenders more of itself. The uncanny conjuncture of generationality (parents training their children) and the pervasive figuration of growing money as if it were a crop to fertilize or livestock (or indeed children) to breed returns us to Marx's unraveling of the emergence of the capital-relation above. The "form of appearance" of value (i.e., money) defines the circuit that "starts and finishes with actual money" and both "expresses money-making, the driving motive of capitalist production, most palpably" and also makes it seem as if the process actually is one of "money *breeding* money" (*Geld heckendes Geld*) (C2, 137–38, my emphasis). This is for Marx exactly what makes the circuit of money-capital "irrational," when "part of a sum of money appears as the mother [*als Mutter*] of another part of the same sum of money" (C2, 131). It is not the motherhood as such that Marx thinks of as aberrant, but rather the appearance of autogenesis obscuring the heteronomy by which "productive capital [is] the only function in which capital value *breeds* value [*Wert heckt*]" (C2, 131). Production uses something heterogeneous to value to extrude more-value, giving rise to another "irrational" form, the wage: "labor as the value-forming element cannot itself possess any value" (C2, 113). "Labor . . . has no value itself" (C1, 677). To think that the wage (a sum of value in the money form) buys labor (a non-value) is irrational, *but the form makes it seem to make sense* as "the characteristic feature of a 'money economy'" (C2, 113).

This is all to say that, in a nonthematic way, Marx's text discloses the intertwined logics of a gendered reproductive symbolic system and the expanding (re-)production of capital, the system of which finds perspectival forms of representation (*Darstellung*) that make it appear as this or that. It can appear, be experienced as, just the exchange of one useful thing for another, or as money procreating itself. As parthenogenesis or as the progeny of a copulation. *Geld heckendes Geld*, *Wert hecken*, this verb roots "hatch" but is also related to terms for a stud bull, genitals, and the *coup* of a blow or stroke. These are epistemic ingredients that make up how capital accumulation (making-itself-more) is seen, both in common sense and in academic theory. So ingrained are these connections in very general and pervasive gender norms that they are barely isolable and only appear in a symptomatic way in Marx's text, in a sort of translation by other means.

Sandro Mezzadra writes that "for Marx, primitive accumulation is not a concept, it is rather a phrase borrowed from others." Balibar formulated this twist likewise: "the name has been retained, but it now designates a completely different [*tout autre*] process."[130] Neither captures the specificity and sheer strangeness of the textual procedure: a procedure that reflects the difficulty of grasping and undoing ideological schemata and proceeding from their protocols and imagery to a critical reinscription that supplements diagnostics.

Right at the start of the chapter, Marx writes that you can get out of the vicious circle "by assuming a 'primitive' accumulation (the 'previous accumulation' of Adam Smith) which precedes capitalist accumulation" (C1, 873).[131] Note Marx's quotation marks, parentheses, and citation of an English-language source for his own translation. Marx does not offer a source for the phrase from Smith. Marxological research has traced a likely possibility in the introduction to Book II of *An Inquiry into the Nature and Causes of the Wealth of Nations*, where Smith is positing a moment prior to, but necessary for, the division of labor. The story there is perhaps as banal as the one about human difference already discussed. Before the division of labor, which is Smith's main object here, everyone provided for themselves and met their own needs as and when necessary: "When he is hungry, he goes to the forest to hunt; when his coat is worn out, he cloaths himself with the skin of the first large animal he kills: and when his hut begins to go to ruin, he repairs it, as well as he can, with the trees and the turf that are nearest it."[132] (Truly, *Robinson Crusoe*, poorly read, is the reference-text of political economy's anthropology!) With the division of labor, "men" must accumulate enough both for subsistence and to be able to exchange for the things they need but cannot make. Smith proposes that "previous" accumulation is both a necessary ground for the division of labor and that the more division of labor there is, the more "previous accumulation" becomes necessary to facilitate exchange.[133] Those who have previously accumulated more (due, one supposes, to their thrift, diligence, and intelligence—or perhaps luck or rapaciousness) would in theory be able to exchange for more with others and thereby accumulate yet more and faster. While Halpern rightly points out that Smith's system makes social differences between human beings an *effect* of the division of labor, the anthropological difference we have been discussing is latent in Smith's account.[134]

What seems to happen is that Marx borrows Smith's appellation ("previous accumulation"), translates it into German (*ursprüngliche Akkumulation*), and gives it a new content (the process of separation by which the capital-relation comes about). Marx quotes what he gives out to be Smith's phrase, "previous accumulation." Yet "previous accumulation" is not exactly Smith's phrase— Marx has already edited and reordered the syntax of the universally cited source for his term, the phrase "as the accumulation of stock must, in the nature of things, be previous to the division of labour" from the "Introduction" to Book II of *Wealth of Nations*.[135] It is plausible to argue, therefore, that Smith is displaced from the phrase attributed to him, and that Marx also keeps a distance from it with his hedging quotation marks. Does this mean that the phrase, henceforth stripped of the proper name "Smith," becomes the placeholder for an "originary" ideologeme that, as Halpern also suggests, is general, unattributable, and that by definition cannot have an individual author? Marx's own editing distils a name for an ideologeme from an implied, general textual dispersion. At the very least, the conduct of Marx's own text tells us that if we go looking for a punctual origin by tracking down a quotation from Smith, we will not find it. The patronym is a feint, and the name of the father (*Adam*, of course) is a derivation that tries to exert symbolic control over the unstable and unmasterable general field from which it derives.

Second, while *ursprüngliche* is certainly a plausible translation for "previous" in the philosophical lexicon, it names something other than a mere temporal antecedence. Indeed, in its sense of something "originary" it designates a repeated but differential emergence of that which springs up from a before that is not necessarily accessible as such, but that must be posited (assumed) *as a before* in every capitalism structured as a logically self-moving system. It is the site at which logic and chrono-logic come apart.

Marx's German "translation" of Smith's English word is then translated back into English as "primitive." The problems with this English paraphrase are now well-known. It first appeared in the Aveling and Moore translation of *Capital* in 1887 and was followed in the now-standard translation by Ben Fowkes. Yet preceding this, we must acknowledge that Marx appears to endorse the rendering of *ursprüngliche* as "primitive" in the 1872–75 French translation by Joseph Roy, the details and revisions of which he carefully supervised.[136] There the phrase appears as *"accumulation primitive"* from Roy/Marx, and it is likely that Aveling and Moore were following this example.

The name, then, has not been retained; it has been altered several times in feints of translation and syntactical mutilation. Marx hereby practices an artificial paleonymy of "primitive accumulation," paleonymy being "the 'strategic' necessity that requires the occasional maintenance of an *old name* in order to launch a new concept." Paleonymy names a critical supplementarity, the marking of an irreducible complicity with the structure or system being criticized: "the name X being maintained as a kind of *lever of intervention*, in order to maintain a grasp on the previous organization, which is to be transformed effectively"[137] Marx's is an *artificial* paleonymy because it pretends to keep the old name while in fact substituting one reworked by a ruse of translation. "So-called," indeed. "Primitive accumulation," leveraged out of Adam Smith's lexicon to deconstruct a more pervasive generality, is neither completely innovative nor anyone else's actual term but Marx's. If we are concerned by the violence of this gesture, recall that Marx's parasitic work here is a strike against diagnosis (classifying types of people by essential differences) and its social effects. *Ursprüngliche Akkumulation* may be a name, but it operates so as to destabilize diagnosis.

Yet the name, for Marx, is a pharmakon. It can be used to heal or to poison. At the end of the third volume of *Capital*, and following the account of political economist Charles Neate, Marx writes that a certain principle of renaming had applied to English feudal tenures. If the feudal tenure system once functioned on the basis of a personal relation of dependency, loyalty, service, and protection, the early modern period witnessed the emergent capitalization of land and a shift from service obligations to cash payments on the part of the tenant. Yet "the bond of fealty and allegiance was retained, *at least in name*," including eventually "knight-service" to the sovereign.[138] (As remains true today, therefore, it was effectively possible to *buy* a knighthood without any other real obligation to the crown.) Because of the way the relations were named and ritually sealed, they could appear feudal even if in fact they were emergently market or commercial relations with no responsibility of personal bond; that is, they were invisibly subsumed in another system.

Illustrating the revamping of this pharmakontic naming, Marx then shows that it is possible to make any mode of production appear congruent with capitalism by subsuming its "form of production" under capitalist "forms of revenue"; a process that works by the "analogy" operated by a renaming.[139] If it is chopped up and transcoded, "subsumed under [capitalist] Revenue-forms," the noncapitalist thing sustains "the illusion [*Schein*: index of the fetish] that capitalist relations would be the natural relations of every mode of production" (C3, 1015). This is precisely what takes place in the construction of "the worker himself as a sort of enterprise for himself . . . an entrepreneur of himself."[140] The individual—in its specific capacities—is seen as a capitalist *by nature*, as a proprietor of its own means of production, as its own "capital" that generates a "revenue"; and for Marx "to a certain degree this is not incorrect" because for the "analogy" to work, there must be a signifying system in place that makes the transcoding both functional and subjectively acceptable (by a sort of violent translation) (C3, 1015). If subsumption is the incorporation of one thing under the form, rule, or law of another, this works on the basis of a third element of commensurability between the two heterogeneous items. Marx points to the commonality that makes this and other modes of subsumption possible: not the social forms, but the *Grundlagen*, the sedimentary foundations, that are "communally shared by all social modes of production" (*allen gesellschaftlichen Produktionsweisen gemeinschaftlich sind*) (C3, 1015). Capitalism's mode of translation imprints its own social form at the site of the irreducible *Grundlagen* such that this form appears as the correct—the exclusive—rendition of the "original." His illustration of an analogic capitalist subsumption is the "small peasant," a non-capitalist producer, made to appear as his own capitalist employer.

It was a prescient choice for today's world in which global capital has unmediated access to "peasants and petty producers" through the destruction of national and local State-level "measures of protection and promotion." The "agriculture sector (and more generally petty production) becomes open to encroachment by big capital, including metropolitan capital, from outside, and hence to the classical form of 'primitive accumulation of capital,'" and "peasants and petty producers [are] made to enter into a direct relationship with multinational agribusiness and multinational retail giants."[141] As Michael Watts has shown in the context of the West African peasantry, a paradoxical effect of this situation is that "resiliency" to these dislocations and disruptions of life becomes a new metric and *name*, not simply for development but for survival.[142] The calculus of resiliency is made "appropriate to *any* form of perturbation and uncertainty: extreme weather events are analogous to coping with recurrent financial shocks."[143] And it is within the entrepreneurial self-coding of adaptability to economic and environmental shock that "the idea of a spontaneous market order"—figured in the Hayekian framework of a species of natural selection—"has become, ironically, a form of sustainable development" in which the West African peasant becomes "a sort of hedge-fund manager for his own impoverished life."[144] Entrepreneurship = resiliency = survival (of the fittest) in an increasingly hostile world. Two types of humanity.

In the same passages I quoted above from the end of the third volume of *Capital*, Marx additionally indicates the possibility of a socialist subsumption of capitalism. But that's a story for another occasion. In the meantime, still on the question of names, he returns us to a site of epistemic and epistemological struggle: "This girl spelt God as dog, and did not know the name of the queen."

Bibliography

Allen, Sheila, and Carol Wolkowitz. *Homeworking: Myths and Realities*. Houndmills, UK: Macmillan Education, 1987.

Althusser, Louis. "Ideology and Ideological State Apparatuses (Notes towards an Investigation)." In *Lenin and Philosophy*. Translated by Ben Brewster. New York: Monthly Review, 1971.

———. "Underground Current of the Materialism of the Encounter." In *Philosophy of the Encounter: Later Writings, 1978–1987*. Translated by G. M. Goshgarian. New York: Verso, 2006.

Althusser, Louis, and Étienne Balibar. *Reading Capital*. Translated by Ben Brewster. London: New Left Books, 1977.

Amin, Samir. *Unequal Development: An Essay on the Social Formations of Peripheral Capitalism.* Translated by Brian Pearce. Hassocks, UK: Harvester, 1973.

Anderson, Kevin. "The 'Unknown' Marx's *Capital*, Volume I: The French Edition of 1872–75, 100 Years Later." *Review of Radical Political Economics* 15, no. 4 (1983): 71–80.

Arendt, Hannah. *Imperialism.* Orlando, FL: Harcourt Brace, 1968.

Baer, Ben Conisbee. *Indigenous Vanguards: Education, National Liberation, and the Limits of Modernism.* New York: Columbia University Press, 2019.

———. "Schiz-ability." *PMLA* 129, no. 3 (2014): 484–90.

———. "What Is Special about Postcolonial Translation?" In *Wiley-Blackwell Companion to Translation Studies*, ed. Sandra Bermann and Catherine Porter, 233–45. Hoboken, NJ: Wiley-Blackwell, 2014.

Bal, Mieke. "Sexuality, Sin and Sorrow: The Emergence of the Female Character (A Reading of *Genesis* 1–3)." *Poetics Today* 6, no. 1–2 (1985): 21–42.

Balibar, Étienne. "Bourgeois Universality and Anthropological Differences." In *Citizen Subject: Foundations for Philosophical Anthropology.* Translated by Steven Miller. New York: Fordham University Press, 2017.

———. "Class Racism." In Étienne Balibar and Immanuel Wallerstein, *Race, Nation, Class: Ambiguous Identities.* Translated by Chris Turner. London: Verso, 1991.

———. *Equaliberty.* Translated by James Ingram. Durham, NC: Duke University Press, 2014.

———. "In Search of the Proletariat." In *Masses, Classes, Ideas: Studies on Philosophy and Politics before and after Marx.* Translated by James Swenson. New York: Routledge, 1994.

———. *On Universals: Constructing and Deconstructing Community.* Translated by Joshua David Jordan. New York: Fordham University Press, 2020.

———. "Possessive Individualism Reversed." *Constellations* 9, no. 3 (2002): 299–317.

Bataille, Georges. *The Accursed Share: An Essay on General Economy.* Translated by Robert Hurley. New York: Zone, 1991.

Becker, Gary S. *Human Capital: A Theoretical and Empirical Analysis, with Special Reference to Education.* Chicago: University of Chicago Press, 1993.

Bonefeld, Werner. "The Permanence of Primitive Accumulation: Commodity Fetishism and Social Constitution." *The Commoner*, no. 2 (September 2001). https://thecommoner.org/wp-content/uploads/2019/10/The-Permanence-of -Primitive-Accumulation-Bonefeld.pdf.

Brown, Tony C. "The Time of Globalization: Rethinking Primitive Accumulation." *Rethinking Marxism* 21, no. 4 (2009): 571–84.

Caffentzis, George. *In Letters of Blood and Fire: Work, Machines, and the Crisis of Capitalism.* Oakland, CA: PM, 2013.

Chakrabarti, Anjan, and Anup Dhar. *Dislocation and Resettlement in Development: From Third World to the World of the Third.* New York: Routledge, 2009.

Chakrabarty, Dipesh. "The Two Histories of Capital." In *Provincializing Europe: Postcolonial Thought and Historical Difference*. Princeton, NJ: Princeton University Press, 2000.

Cixous, Hélène, and Jacques Derrida. *Veils*. Translated by Geoffrey Bennington. Stanford, CA: Stanford University Press, 2001.

Coulthard, Glen Sean. *Red Skin, White Masks: Rejecting the Colonial Politics of Recognition*. Minneapolis: University of Minnesota Press, 2014.

De Angelis, Massimo. "Marx and Primitive Accumulation: The Continuous Character of Capital's 'Enclosures.'" *The Commoner*, no. 2 (September 2001). https://thecommoner.org/wp-content/uploads/2019/10/Marx-and-primitive -accumulation-deAngelis.pdf.

———. "Marx's Theory of Primitive Accumulation: A Suggested Reinterpretation." University of East London, Department of Economics, Working Paper no. 29, May 2000. https://www.academia.edu/3132423/Marxs_theory_of_primitive _accumulation_A_suggested_reinterpretation.

Deleuze, Gilles, and Félix Guattari. *Anti-Oedipus: Capitalism and Schizophrenia*. Translated by Robert Hurley et al. London: Athlone, 1983.

de Man, Paul. *Allegories of Reading: Figural Language in Rousseau, Nietzsche, Rilke, and Proust*. New Haven, CT: Yale University Press, 1979.

———. "The Concept of Irony" In *Aesthetic Ideology*. Minneapolis: University of Minnesota Press, 1996.

Derrida, Jacques. *The Animal That Therefore I Am*. Translated by David Wills. New York: Fordham University Press, 2008.

———. "Declarations of Independence." Translated by Tom Keenan and Tom Pepper. *New Political Science* 7, no. 1 (1986): 7–15.

———. "Des tours de Babel." Translated by Joseph F. Graham. In *Psyche: Inventions of the Other*, Vol. 1. Edited by Peggy Kamuf and Elizabeth Rottenberg. Stanford, CA: Stanford University Press, 2007.

———. *Dissemination*. Translated by Barbara Johnson. Chicago: Athlone, 1981.

———. *The Ear of the Other: Otobiography, Transference, Translation*. Lincoln: University of Nebraska Press, 1988.

———. "La forme et la façon." Preface to Alain David, *Racisme et antisémitisme: Essai de philosophie sur l'envers des concepts*. Paris: Ellipses, 2001.

———. "Freud and the Scene of Writing." In *Writing and Difference*. Translated by Alan Bass. London: Routledge, 1981.

———. *Positions*. Translated by Alan Bass. Chicago: University of Chicago Press, 1981.

Engels, Friedrich. "Anti-Dühring." Translated by Emile Burns. In *Marx-Engels Collected Works*, vol. 25, 1873–1883. London: Lawrence and Wishart, 1987.

Fanon, Frantz. *The Wretched of the Earth*. Translated by Richard Philcox. New York: Grove, 2004.

Febvre, Lucien, and Henri-Jean Martin. *The Coming of the Book: The Impact of Printing, 1450–1800*. Translated by David Gerard. New York: Verso, 1976.

Federici, Silvia. *Caliban and the Witch: Women, the Body, and Primitive Accumulation*. New York: Autonomedia, 2004.

Forbes, Jack D. *Africans and Native Americans: The Language of Race and the Evolution of Red-Black Peoples*. Urbana: University of Illinois Press, 1993.

Foucault, Michel. *The Birth of Biopolitics: Lectures at the Collège de France, 1978–1979*. Translated by Graham Burchell. New York: Palgrave, 2008.

Fraad, Harriet, Richard Wolff, and Stephen Resnick, *Bringing It All Back Home: Class, Gender, and Power in the Modern Household*. London: Pluto, 1994.

Genette, Gérard. *Métalepse: De la figure à la fiction*. Paris: Éditions du Seuil, 2004.

Giridharadas, Anand. *Winners Take All: The Elite Charade of Changing the World*. New York: Vintage, 2019.

Goethe, Johann Wolfgang von. *Poems of Goethe*. Edited by Ronald Gray. Cambridge: Cambridge University Press, 1966.

Gramsci, Antonio. *Selections from the Prison Notebooks*. Edited and translated by Quintin Hoare and Geoffrey Nowell Smith. London: Lawrence and Wishart, 1998.

Guillaumin, Colette. *Racism, Sexism, Power, and Ideology*. New York: Routledge, 1995.

Halpern, Richard. *The Poetics of Primitive Accumulation: English Renaissance Culture and the Genealogy of Capital*. Ithaca, NY: Cornell University Press, 1991.

Hardt, Michael, and Antonio Negri. *Assembly*. Oxford: Oxford University Press, 2017.

———. *Empire*. Cambridge, MA: Harvard University Press, 2000.

Harootunian, Harry. *Marx after Marx: History and Time in the Expansion of Capitalism*. New York: Columbia University Press, 2015.

Harris, Marvin. *The Rise of Anthropological Theory*. New York: Columbia University Press, 1968.

Harvey, David. "The 'New' Imperialism: Accumulation by Dispossession." *Socialist Register* 40 (2004): 63–87.

Ho, Karen. *Liquidated: An Ethnography of Wall Street*. Durham, NC: Duke University Press, 2009.

Ince, Onur Ulas. "Primitive Accumulation, New Enclosures, and Global Land Grabs: A Theoretical Intervention." *Rural Sociology* 79, no. 1 (2014): 104–31.

Jameson, Fredric. *The Political Unconscious: Narrative as a Socially Symbolic Act*. Ithaca, NY: Cornell University Press, 1982.

Kazanjian, David. "Dispossession Reimagined from the 1690s." In *A Time for Critique*, edited by Didier Fassin and Bernard Harcourt, 210–29. New York: Columbia University Press, 2019.

Latouche, Serge. *In the Wake of the Affluent Society: An Exploration of Post-development*. Translated by Martin O'Connor and Rosemary Arnoux. London: Zed Books, 1993.

Leroi-Gourhan, André. *Gesture and Speech*. Translated by Anna Bostock Berger. Cambridge, MA: MIT Press, 1993 [1964].

Luxemburg, Rosa. "The Mass Strike, the Political Party, and the Trade Unions." Translated by Patrick Lavin. In *The Essential Rosa Luxemburg*, edited by Helen Scott, 111–81. Chicago: Haymarket, 2008.

Marx, Karl. *Capital: A Critique of Political Economy*, vol. 1. Translated by Ben Fowkes. London: Penguin, 1976.

———. *Capital: A Critique of Political Economy*, vol. 2. Translated by David Fernbach. London: Penguin, 1978.

———. *Capital: A Critique of Political Economy*, vol. 3. Translated by David Fernbach. London: Penguin, 1981.

———. *Le Capital*. Translated by J. Roy. Paris: Garnier-Flammarion, 1969.

———. *Grundrisse*. Translated by Martin Nicolaus. London: Penguin, 1993.

———. "Letter to Vera Zasulich." In *Marx-Engels Collected Works*, vol. 24, 1874–83, 370–71. London: Lawrence and Wishart, 1989.

———. "Results of the Direct Production Process." Translated by Ben Fowkes. In *Marx and Engels Collected Works*, vol. 34, 1861–64, 355–471. London: Lawrence and Wishart, 2010.

———. *Theories of Surplus Value*, vol. 3. Translated by Jack Cohen and S. W. Ryazanskaya. Moscow: Progress, 1971.

McCloskey, Donald. "Storytelling in Economics." In *The Uses of Storytelling in the Sciences, Philosophy, and Literature*, ed. Christopher Nash, 5–22. New York: Routledge, 2005.

Mezzadra, Sandro. *In the Marxian Workshops: Producing Subjects*. Translated by Yari Lanci. New York: Roman and Littlefield, 2018.

Mies, Maria. *The Lace-Makers of Narsapur: Indian Housewives Produce for the World Market*. London: Zed Books, 1982.

Mirowski, Philip. *Never Let a Serious Crisis Go to Waste: How Neoliberalism Survived the Financial Meltdown*. New York: Verso, 2013.

Mitter, Swasti. *Common Fate, Common Bond: Women in the Global Economy*. London: Pluto, 1986.

Morris, Rosalind. *"Ursprüngliche Akkumulation*: The Secret of an Originary Mistranslation." *Boundary 2* 43, no. 3 (2016): 29–77.

Neate, Charles. *Two Lectures on the History and Conditions of Landed Property*. Oxford: J. H. and Jas. Parker, 1860.

Negt, Oskar, and Alexander Kluge. *Geschichte und Eigensinn*. Frankfurt am Main: Zweitausendeins, 1981.

———. *History and Obstinacy*. Translated by Richard Langston et al. New York: Zone, 2014.

Nichols, Robert. "Disaggregating Primitive Accumulation." *Radical Philosophy*, no. 194 (November–December 2015): 18–28.

Padmore, George. "A Guide to Pan-African Socialism." In *African Socialism*, edited by William Friedman and Carl G. Rosberg Jr., 223–37. Stanford, CA: Stanford University Press, 1964.

Patnaik, Utsa. "Capitalism and the Production of Poverty." *Social Scientist* 40, nos. 1–2 (January–February 2012): 3–20.

Patnaik, Utsa, and Prabhat Patnaik. *Capital and Imperialism: Theory, History, and the Present*. New York: Monthly Review, 2021.

Perelman, Michael. "A Short History of Primitive Accumulation." *CounterPunch*, April 16, 2013. http://www.counterpunch.org/2013/04/16/a-short-history-of -primitive-accumulation/.

Procopius. *Anecdota*. Translated by H. B. Dewing. Cambridge, MA: Harvard University Press, 1935.

Prügl, Elizabeth. *The Global Construction of Gender: Home-Based Work in the Political Economy of the 20th Century*. New York: Columbia University Press, 1999.

Read, Jason. "Primitive Accumulation: The Aleatory Foundation of Capitalism." *Rethinking Marxism* 14, no. 2 (Summer 2002): 24–29.

Resnick, Stephen A., and Richard D. Wolff. *Class Theory and History: Capitalism and Communism in the USSR*. New York: Routledge, 2002.

Roberts, William Clare. "What Was Primitive Accumulation? Reconstructing the Origin of a Critical Concept." *European Journal of Political Theory* 19, no. 4 (2017): 532–52.

Robinson, Cedric. *Black Marxism: The Making of the Black Radical Tradition*. Chapel Hill: University of North Carolina Press, 2000.

Rubin, Gayle. "The Traffic in Women: Notes on the 'Political Economy' of Sex." In *Toward an Anthropology of Women*, edited by Rayna R. Reiter, 157–210. New York: Monthly Review, 1975.

Sanyal, Kalyan. *Rethinking Capitalist Development: Primitive Accumulation, Governmentality, and Postcolonial Capitalism*. New Delhi: Routledge, 2013.

Sassen, Saskia. "A Savage Sorting of Winners and Losers: Contemporary Versions of Primitive Accumulation." *Globalizations* 7, nos. 1–2 (2010): 23–50.

Schumpeter, Joseph. *Capitalism, Socialism and Democracy*. 3rd ed. New York: Harper Collins, 2008 [1950].

Sheshadri, Kalpana Rahita. *HumAnimal: Race, Law, Language*. Minneapolis: University of Minnesota Press, 2012.

Shilliam, Robbie. "Hegemony and the Unfashionable Problematic of 'Primitive Accumulation.'" *Millennium: Journal of International Studies* 32, no. 1 (2004): 59–88.

Smith, Adam. *An Inquiry into the Nature and Causes of the Wealth of Nations*, vol. 1. Oxford: Clarendon, 1979.

Spivak, Gayatri Chakravorty. *A Critique of Postcolonial Reason: Toward a History of the Vanishing Present*. Cambridge, MA: Harvard University Press, 1999.

———. "Global Marx?" In *Knowledge, Class, and Economics: Marxism Without Guarantees*, edited by Theodore A. Burczak, Robert F. Garnett, and Richard P. McIntyre, 190–205. New York: Routledge, 2018.

———. "Limits and Openings of Marx in Derrida." In *Outside in the Teaching Machine*, 97–120. New York: Routledge, 1993.

———. "Scattered Speculations on the Question of Value." In *In Other Worlds: Essays in Cultural Politics*, 154–78. New York: Methuen, 1987.

Staples, David E. *No Place Like Home: Organizing Home-Based Labor in the Era of Structural Adjustment.* New York: Routledge, 2006.

Stiegler, Bernard. *The Age of Disruption: Technology and Madness in Computational Capitalism.* Translated by Daniel Ross. Cambridge, UK: Polity, 2019.

Sweney, Mark. "Facebook Boss Mark Zuckerberg Joins Centibillionaire Club." *The Guardian*, August 7, 2020. https://www.theguardian.com/technology/2020/aug/07 /facebook-boss-mark-zuckerberg-joins-centibillionaire-club.

Terray, Emmanuel. "Exploitation and Domination in Marx's Thought." Translated by Joseph Serrano. *Rethinking Marxism* 31, no. 4 (2019): 412–24.

Thiers, Louis Adolphe. *De la propriété.* Paulin, L'Heureux, 1848.

———. *The Rights of Property: A Refutation of Communism and Socialism.* London: R. Groombridge and Sons, 1848.

Tomba, Massimiliano. "Layered Historiography: Re-reading the So-Called Primitive Accumulation." In *Marx's Temporalities*, 159–86. Leiden: Brill, 2013.

Tristan, Flora. *Le tour de France: État actuel de la classe ouvrière sous l'aspect moral, intellectuel, matériel.* Paris: Éditions Tête de Feuilles, 1973.

———. *Flora Tristan, Utopian Feminist: Her Travel Diaries and Personal Crusade.* Edited and translated by Doris Belk and Paul Belk. Indianapolis: Indiana University Press, 1993.

von Werlhof, Claudia. "'Globalization' and the 'Permanent' Process of 'Primitive Accumulation': The Example of the MAI, the Multilateral Agreement on Investment." *Journal of World-Systems Research* 6, no. 3 (Fall/Winter 2000): 728–47.

Walker, Gavin. "Primitive Accumulation and the Formation of Difference: On Marx and Schmitt." *Rethinking Marxism* 23, no. 3 (2011): 384–404.

———. "Primitive Accumulation and the State-Form: National Debt as an Apparatus of Capture." *Viewpoint*, October 29, 2014. http://viewpointmag.com/2014/10/29 /primitive-accumulation-and-the-state-form-national-debt-as-an-apparatus-of -capture/.

Watts, Michael J. *Silent Violence: Food, Famine, and Peasantry in Northern Nigeria.* Athens: University of Georgia Press, 2012.

Williams, Raymond. "Social Darwinism." In *Problems in Materialism and Culture.* New York: Verso, 1997.

Wilson, Tamar Diane. "Primitive Accumulation and the Labor Subsidies to Capitalism." *Review of Radical Political Economics* 44, no. 2 (2012): 201–12.

Zasulich, Vera. "Vera Zasulich: A Letter to Marx." In *Late Marx and the Russian Road*, edited by Teodor Shanin, 98–99. New York: Monthly Review, 1983.

———. "Vera Zasulic an Marx." In *Marx-Engels Archiv: Zeitschrift des Marx-Engels-Instituts in Moskau*, edited by D. B. Riazanov, vol. 1. Frankfurt am Main: Verlag Sauer & Auvremann, 1969.

Zavaleta Mercado, René. *Towards a History of the National-Popular in Bolivia, 1879–1980.* Translated by Anne Freeland. Calcutta: Seagull Books, 2018.

Notes

1. I would like to thank the editors and anonymous reviewers of the present volume, the participants in the 2016 Political Concepts workshop at NYU, the participants at the 2016 Modern Language Association session "Political Concepts in Translation" organized by Emily Apter and Sangeeta Ray, Cate Reilly, and the participants in a Princeton departmental works-in-progress workshop, especially the respondent, Mari Jarris, for their comments on earlier versions of the present chapter. This remains as much a map of ongoing directions for work as a finalized argument.

Quotation from Mark Zuckerberg taken from the partial transcript of his interview with Dana Perino at https://finance.yahoo.com/news/mark-zuckerberg -interview-key-moments-192443958.html. The full interview can be viewed at https://www.youtube.com/watch?v=LJDANzTzIoo. The interview first aired on October 18, 2019. As of the interview, Zuckerberg's net worth was around seventy billion. At the time of revision, less than a year later, it had climbed by over twenty billion during the COVID-19 pandemic and in part due to the pending bans on the social media company that owns the TikTok app and the rollout of Facebook's copycat version. Mark Sweney, "Facebook Boss Mark Zuckerberg Joins Centi-billionaire Club," *The Guardian*, August 7, 2020, https://www.theguardian.com /technology/2020/aug/07/facebook-boss-mark-zuckerberg-joins-centibillionaire-club.

2. Note also that Zuckerberg quickly turns to his philanthropic foundation and states at the end of the interview that his company offers "social services."

3. Karl Marx, *Capital: A Critique of Political Economy*, vol. 1, trans. Ben Fowkes (London: Penguin, 1976), 873. Cited hereafter in the text as C1 with page number following. I have silently modified translations where appropriate. Marx's German for "primitive accumulation" is *ursprüngliche Akkumulation*, which can also be rendered as "originary accumulation." I comment on this in conclusion.

4. In this section of *Capital*, the classically trained Marx's usage makes the term "proletarian" resonate with its Servian signification: those outside Rome's propertied classes, mere "begetters of children," to translate *proletarii* literally. It is subtly but insistently differentiated from the working class here, raising the question of the (re-)production of exploitable human material: proletariat signifies deterritorialized groups—separated from any proprietorship over their conditions of work and deprived of technical know-how—prior to their reterritorialization as workers for capitalist employers who own and control—and unknowingly socialize—the conditions of work. For relevant discussion, see Étienne Balibar, "In Search of the Proletariat," in *Masses, Classes, Ideas: Studies on Philosophy and Politics before and after Marx*, trans. James Swenson (New York: Routledge, 1994), 125–50.

5. As Fredric Jameson puts it, an ideologeme as such is "never given directly in primary verbal form, but must always be reconstructed after the fact, as working hypothesis and subtext." Fredric Jameson, *The Political Unconscious: Narrative as a Socially Symbolic Act* (Ithaca, NY: Cornell University Press, 1982), 185. Jameson

further specifies an ideologeme as a minimal ideological "unit" with the "possibility to manifest itself either as a pseudoidea—a conceptual or belief system, an abstract value, an opinion or a prejudice—or as a protonarrative, a kind of ultimate class fantasy about the 'collective characters' which are the classes in opposition" (87). Pseudoidea and narrative are obviously not categories that exclude each other. They feed each other.

6. Serge Latouche, *In the Wake of the Affluent Society: An Exploration of Post-development*, trans. Martin O'Connor and Rosemary Arnoux (London: Zed Books, 1993), 78.

7. Anjan Chakrabarti and Anup Dhar, *Dislocation and Resettlement in Development: From Third World to the World of the Third* (New York: Routledge, 2009), 19, 13, original emphases.

8. "The 'third world' must not simply be seen as an evil other, but also a victim other. This realization brought with it a sea change in the technology of power, whereby a new strategy evolved in the form of intervention within the domain of world of the third so as to persuade the subjects therein to give consent to its own existence as devalued, that is third world-ist, and hence in want of the proposed *hegemonic need* construed and forwarded by the development paradigm. An array of development practices involving national and international flows of social surplus enabled, in one turn, the ideological production of the subjects as devalued 'third world' selves and also allowed them additional space (through various projects) to articulate their 'liberation' from their self-proclaimed devalued state." Chakrabarti and Dhar, *Dislocation and Resettlement*, 168.

9. Management scholar C. K. Prahalad quoted in Anand Giridharadas, *Winners Take All: The Elite Charade of Changing the World* (New York: Vintage, 2019), 38. This is a "popular" bestselling book that is a fine survey of recent configurations of the doing-good-and-helping mindset that has become the dominant figure of global capital leadership's accounts of its just rewards.

10. Giridharadas, *Winners Take All*, 45, 48. The second quotation uses the words of Greg Ferenstein, a journalist who summarizes a "new ideology" that he calls "Optimism."

11. Matthew Bishop and Michael Green, *Philanthropocapitalism: How the Rich Can Save the World* (2008), quoted in Giridharadas, *Winners Take All*, 46, my emphases. Fanon's take on the axiomatics of colonial proportionality may be found in Frantz Fanon, *The Wretched of the Earth*, trans. Richard Philcox (New York: Grove, 2004), 4–6, 43. For relevant commentary on this, see Ben Conisbee Baer, *Indigenous Vanguards: Education, National Liberation, and the Limits of Modernism* (New York: Columbia University Press, 2019), 14–17.

12. Karl Marx, *Theories of Surplus Value*, vol. 3, trans. Jack Cohen and S. W. Ryazanskaya (Moscow: Progress, 1971), 311. Marx writes here that "it is this separation which constitutes the concept of capital and of *primitive* accumulation" (Marx's emphasis).

13. Jacques Derrida, "Des tours de Babel," trans. Joseph F. Graham, in *Psyche: Inventions of the Other*, vol. 1, ed. Peggy Kamuf and Elizabeth Rottenberg (Stanford,

CA: Stanford University Press, 2007), 199. This and the following paragraph of my text draw on material in Ben Conisbee Baer, "What Is Special about Postcolonial Translation?" in Sandra Bermann and Catherine Porter, eds., *Wiley-Blackwell Companion to Translation Studies* (Hoboken, NJ: Wiley-Blackwell, 2014), 233–45.

14. Jacques Derrida, "Freud and the Scene of Writing," in *Writing and Difference*, trans. Alan Bass (London: Routledge, 1981), 210.

15. Jacques Derrida, *The Ear of the Other: Otobiography, Transference, Translation* (Lincoln: University of Nebraska Press, 1988), 155.

16. Hélène Cixous and Jacques Derrida, *Veils*, trans. Geoffrey Bennington (Stanford, CA: Stanford University Press, 2001), 55, 56–57.

17. Derrida, "Freud and the Scene of Writing," 210.

18. Dipesh Chakrabarty, "The Two Histories of Capital," in *Provincializing Europe: Postcolonial Thought and Historical Difference* (Princeton, NJ: Princeton University Press, 2000), 70.

19. Karl Marx, *Grundrisse*, trans. Martin Nicolaus (London: Penguin, 1993), 408, 540.

20. Marx, *Grundrisse*, 407, my emphasis. "The exact development of the concept of capital [is] necessary, since it [is] the fundamental concept of modern economics, just as capital itself, whose abstract, reflected image [is] its concept [*dessen abstraktes Gegenbild sein Begriff*], [is] the foundation of bourgeois society" (331).

21. Chakrabarty, "Two Histories of Capital," 58; Marx, *Grundrisse*, 409.

22. Marx, *Grundrisse*, 409. Marx is being comparative (with other modes of production) and not ironic in this remark, though his critique is of course oriented to showing the price paid for progress in the capitalist form. "Civilizing influence of capital" is in English in the original.

23. This is, argues Marx, why Aristotle, living in a slaveholding society that by definition could not think human equality of birth, could not fully decipher the value-form.

24. Étienne Balibar, *Equaliberty*, trans. James Ingram (Durham, NC: Duke University Press, 2014). The irresolvable double bind of liberty and equality engenders insurrectional *and* exclusionary politics from emphases on either term, each time also in the name of a certain universality.

25. Marx, *Grundrisse*, 410.

26. Marx, *Grundrisse*, 410, 540. The relation between *Aufhebung* and *Auflösung* in the *Grundrisse* is fascinating but beyond my scope here. It suggests at the least that capitalism's tendency could be purely destructive or entropic in the long run.

27. Chakrabarty, "Two Histories of Capital," 63–64.

28. Oskar Negt and Alexander Kluge, *Geschichte und Eigensinn* (Frankfurt am Main: Zweitausendeins, 1981), 30. All translations are my own. The phrase "historical and moral element" is from Marx, *Capital*, vol. 1, where he writes that "in contrast, therefore, with the case of other commodities, the determination of the value of labor-power contains a historical and moral element" (276). This is an instance of Marx glossing over a vast terrain of determining differences (and especially sexual difference) so as to make his point, for better and worse.

29. Negt and Kluge, *Geschichte und Eigensinn*, 30.

30. Negt and Kluge, 37.

31. Negt and Kluge, 36.

32. Negt and Kluge, 544–55.

33. Negt and Kluge, 545.

34. Negt and Kluge, 30.

35. Negt and Kluge, 38, 688.

36. Negt and Kluge, 557. Emphasis in original.

37. I cannot comment further on this here. Marx's most elaborated discussion of subsumption occurs in passages that he chose not to include in *Capital*. The best English translation is "Results of the Direct Production Process," trans. Ben Fowkes, in *Marx and Engels Collected Works*, vol. 34, 1861–64 (London: Lawrence and Wishart, 2010), 355–471.

38. Chakrabarty, "Two Histories of Capital," 64, 70.

39. Chakrabarty, 64, 66.

40. Bataille's account has a highly interesting relationship with the pharmakontic supplementarity of surplus that Marx perceived when thinking through the possibility of socialism. I will elaborate this relation in forthcoming work. Georges Bataille, *The Accursed Share: An Essay on General Economy*, trans. Robert Hurley (New York: Zone, 1991), 9–41 and *passim*.

41. Bataille, *Accursed Share*, 10, my emphasis.

42. The most extensive thematic treatment of sexual difference and the division of labor in Marx is in *The German Ideology*, a manuscript cowritten with Engels. I have begun a reading of this in Ben Conisbee Baer, "Schiz-ability," *PMLA* 129, no. 3 (2014): 484–90.

43. Gayatri Spivak's innovative discussions of the relation between the capital-relation and the possibility of socialism have shaped my thinking here. See for example Gayatri Spivak, "Limits and Openings of Marx in Derrida," in *Outside in the Teaching Machine* (New York: Routledge, 1993), 97–120, and also by Spivak, "Global Marx?," in *Knowledge, Class, and Economics: Marxism without Guarantees*, ed. Theodore A. Burczak, Robert F. Garnett, and Richard P. McIntyre (New York: Routledge, 2018), 190–205.

44. George Padmore, "A Guide to Pan-African Socialism," in *African Socialism*, ed. William Friedman and Carl G. Rosberg Jr. (Stanford, CA: Stanford University Press, 1964), 234, 231. I have attempted a preliminary discussion of the vanguard/educational paradox that you need socialists to make socialists (i.e., *who* will do the teaching and making here?) in Baer, *Indigenous Vanguards*.

45. Flora Tristan, *Le tour de France: État actuel de la classe ouvrière sous l'aspect moral, intellectuel, matériel* (Paris: Éditions Tête de Feuilles, 1973), 207. English translation in Flora Tristan, *Flora Tristan, Utopian Feminist: Her Travel Diaries and Personal Crusade*, ed. and trans. Doris Belk and Paul Belk (Indianapolis: Indiana University Press, 1993), 162. For relevant commentary on this passage see Colette Guillaumin, *Racism, Sexism, Power, and Ideology* (New York: Routledge, 1995),

162–63. Tristan was moving around France to propagate and publicize among workers the arguments she had presented in *Workers' Union* (1843). The diary of this journey is an extraordinary document of early socialist-feminist activism.

46. An example is the discontinuity between household class-formation ("feudal") and capitalist class process as discussed in Harriet Fraad, Richard Wolff, and Stephen Resnick, *Bringing It All Back Home: Class, Gender, and Power in the Modern Household* (London: Pluto, 1994). For an indicative sentence: "feudal surplus labor production appears as a 'natural' outgrowth of female love" (13). An elaborated analysis by Fraad discusses anorexia as a "hunger strike" that negotiates and expresses an impossible double bind between the respective class processes and their demands on women: feudal (household, private, noncapitalist) and capitalist (workplace, public), where the former runs on an affective value-system (112–31).

47. Marx continues, "And from this Fall dates the poverty of the great masses who still, in spite of all their labor, have nothing to sell but themselves, and the riches of the few, that constantly grows, though they have long given up work."

48. Emmanuel Terray, "Exploitation and Domination in Marx's Thought," trans. Joseph Serrano, *Rethinking Marxism* 31, no. 4 (2019): 412–24.

49. Louis Althusser, "Underground Current of the Materialism of the Encounter," in *Philosophy of the Encounter: Later Writings,1978–1987*, trans. G. M. Goshgarian (New York: Verso, 2006), 201.

50. Cedric Robinson, *Black Marxism: The Making of the Black Radical Tradition* (Chapel Hill: University of North Carolina Press, 2000), 9, xxxi. Robinson does not universalize the modern, biological race ideology, which is the notion that groups are defined by inherited biological-somatic characteristics, genetically distinct and internally homogenous. The most vivid account of the biological ideology may be found in Guillaumin, *Racism, Sexism*, 29–98 and *passim*. Robinson's looser definition allows us to accommodate the modern displacement to biological determinism while honoring the cross-contamination of racializing or ethnocentric group formations, and indeed the historical depth of discourses that define the *anthropos* against an undifferentiated animality that Guillaumin also discusses.

51. Jack D. Forbes, *Africans and Native Americans: The Language of Race and the Evolution of Red-Black Peoples* (Urbana: University of Illinois Press, 1993) analyzes racial classification on the ground in the colonial Americas, disclosing it as subject to a polysemous and confusing array of practical transformations. This effectively deconstructs the alignment between somatic appearance and heredity. Hannah Arendt's "Race-Thinking before Racism" resonates with Guillaumin in its (intra-European) account of the ethnocentric, or even autocentric, structure of group-formation and differentiation as its structures are exploited for civilizationism and ultimately scientific racism. Akin to what Marvin Harris called "folk racism," ethnocentrism, which is not necessarily grounded on perceptible somatic difference, is possibly an anthropological irreducible. According to Leroi-Gourhan, "ethnocentrism is in fact what best defines the prescientific vision of the human being," where other groups "not like us" may appear on the far side of a highly

elastic human/animal limit. Hannah Arendt, *Imperialism* (Orlando, FL: Harcourt Brace, 1968), 38–64; Marvin Harris, *The Rise of Anthropological Theory* (New York: Columbia University Press, 1968), 81; André Leroi-Gourhan, *Gesture and Speech*, trans. Anna Bostock Berger (Cambridge, MA: MIT Press, 1993 [1964]), 5.

52. Robinson, *Black Marxism*, 42.

53. My use of the language of "anthropological difference" overlaps in certain ways with Étienne Balibar's recent work on this terminology in the field of citizenship, community, race, and gender. In particular, Balibar has written vividly of the ways in which discourses that posit a universal human essence themselves become the occasions for the definition and norming of naturalized differences between humans, and for the idea of a human essence from which some may be excluded. The shifting site of anthropological divisions brings us once more to an interminable task of translation and epistemological work. See in particular, Étienne Balibar, "Bourgeois Universality and Anthropological Differences," in *Citizen Subject: Foundations for Philosophical Anthropology*, trans. Steven Miller (New York: Fordham University Press, 2017), 275–302; and Balibar's recent essays on the topic now collected in *On Universals: Constructing and Deconstructing Community*, trans. Joshua David Jordan (New York: Fordham University Press, 2020).

54. Jacques Derrida, *The Animal That Therefore I Am*, trans. David Wills (New York: Fordham University Press, 2008) does not address the racialized aspect of this configuration in detail, but he leaves enough clues for the reader to be able to join the dots if so inclined. Kalpana Rahita Sheshadri, *HumAnimal: Race, Law, Language* (Minneapolis: University of Minnesota Press, 2012) helps us to bring out some lines of connection.

55. In this connection, see again Fraad, Resnick, and Wolff, *Bringing It All Back Home* on the gendered domestic mode of production that runs on affect in a feudal manner.

56. See my comments above on Negt and Kluge, *Geschichte und Eigensinn*, 36–40. There are many other modalities in which the permanence, repetition, recursiveness, etc. of primitive accumulation are discussed. I mention some of these below and address this question at more length in forthcoming work.

57. Althusser: "We can . . . suppose *that this encounter occurred several times in history before taking hold in the West*, but for lack of an element or a suitable arrangement of the elements, failed to 'take.'" "Underground Current," 198. Deleuze and Guattari are more adventurous on this point, suggesting that "precapitalist social machines" constantly push away the abstraction of capital and live in "dread of a decoded flow" (capital is decoded flow). The fearsome abstraction of a decoded flow (the possibility of capital itself) is not in itself foreign to those "pre-capitalist" social formations: "It cannot be said that the previous formations did not foresee this Thing that only came from without by rising from within, and that at all costs had to be prevented from rising." Gilles Deleuze and Félix Guattari, *Anti-Oedipus: Capitalism and Schizophrenia*, trans. Robert Hurley et al. (London: Athlone, 1983), 153.

58. William Clare Roberts, "What Was Primitive Accumulation? Reconstructing the Origin of a Critical Concept," *European Journal of Political Theory* 19, no. 4 (2017): 532–52.

59. Althusser, "Underground Current," 197–203. Samir Amin's innovative thesis is that feudal European society, more "backward" and underdeveloped than the large Asian and Arab imperial formations that surrounded it, was also looser in economic structure, less centralized, and therefore able to be more innovative, flexible, and disinhibited in methods of exploitation and extraction. "This weakness, this peripheral character" of the European socius in comparison with the great "tribute-paying" empires "was to become its strength." Samir Amin, *Unequal Development: An Essay on the Social Formations of Peripheral Capitalism*, trans. Brian Pearce (Hassocks, UK: Harvester, 1973), 9–58.

60. Many commentators have observed the fissure between logic and chrono-logic here and drawn various conclusions. The "relationship between the logical and historical order of exposition in Marx's method" precludes the construction of a linear narrative, and this perhaps translates a situation of disarticulated temporality: if the "first *time*" of capitalism's historical origins "must logically repeat itself every day," then at the very least we are not dealing with a "linear and progressive" historical time. Sandro Mezzadra, *In the Marxian Workshops: Producing Subjects*, trans. Yari Lanci (New York: Roman and Littlefield, 2018), 105, 103, my emphasis.

61. Gayatri Chakravorty Spivak, "Scattered Speculations on the Question of Value," in *In Other Worlds: Essays in Cultural Politics* (New York: Methuen, 1987), 161, my emphasis.

62. Negt and Kluge, *Geschichte und Eigensinn*, 35, original emphasis.

63. Jason Read, "Primitive Accumulation: The Aleatory Foundation of Capitalism," *Rethinking Marxism* 14, no. 2 (Summer 2002): 28.

64. Michel Foucault, *The Birth of Biopolitics: Lectures at the Collège de France, 1978–1979*, trans. Graham Burchell (New York: Palgrave, 2008), 226. The transformations are important, of course. The implicit neoliberal theory of the subject is the thesis of its plasticity and level of risk-taking disinhibition, such that it can use markets to maximize its advantages. It thus displaces anthropic difference (and of course all the baggage of class-formation) to the level of radical individualism. Good relevant discussion of this latter aspect may be found in Philip Mirowski, *Never Let a Serious Crisis Go to Waste: How Neoliberalism Survived the Financial Meltdown* (New York: Verso, 2013), especially chapters 2 and 3.

65. Antonio Gramsci, *Selections from the Prison Notebooks*, ed. and trans. Quintin Hoare and Geoffrey Nowell Smith (London: Lawrence and Wishart, 1998), 202.

66. For an illuminating discussion of Marx's eschatological tone, see Étienne Balibar, "Possessive Individualism Reversed," *Constellations* 9, no. 3 (2002): 307–11. More generally, Étienne Balibar, "The Messianic Moment in Marx," in *Citizen Subject*, 143–54.

67. Friedrich Engels, "Anti-Dühring," trans. Emile Burns, in *Marx-Engels Collected Works*, vol. 25, 1873–1883 (London: Lawrence and Wishart, 1987), 158.

68. Engels, 161.

69. Engels, 158, translation modified. This supplement will be formulated in the Leninist tradition as the party's task ("conscious leading group") that enters into what Gramsci conceives as a reciprocal "educational" relation with the "spontaneous" movements already happening, i.e., that are "formed through everyday experience illuminated by 'common sense.'" It is above all imperative for Gramsci that the "conscious leadership" resonate with and be merely different in degree from the spontaneous currents in which it must learn to swim. Gramsci, *Prison Notebooks*, 196–99. Rosa Luxemburg rethinks the party's vanguard role in yet another way, tasking it with "adaptability" to the inscription of its "conscious direction" in the "incalculable" of the revolutionary conjuncture (including the affective currents of working-class struggle). Connection, representation, and attempted commensuration such that points of upheaval may be generalized. Rosa Luxemburg, "The Mass Strike, the Political Party, and the Trade Unions," trans. Patrick Lavin, in *The Essential Rosa Luxemburg*, ed. Helen Scott (Chicago: Haymarket, 2008), 148, 147, 129. In conclusion, Luxemburg suggestively writes of the working masses as "the operative chorus" (*handelnde Chorus*) in the theater of struggle, alluding to the understanding in German theory (Schlegel) of parabasis in Attic comedy (interruption of the main discursive line of a drama by the chorus) (181, translation altered). The place of consciousness occupied by "leadership" is displaced into the site of the *translator* (*Dolmetscher*, oral translator, interpreter) of the very collective will that intermittently steps forth to interrupt leadership's own "speaking personae" or roles ("*sprechenden Personen*," 181). I return to parabasis in conclusion. For a related consideration of some of these questions in the Soviet context, see Cate Reilly's chapter in the present volume.

70. Oskar Negt and Alexander Kluge, *History and Obstinacy*, trans. Richard Langston et al. (New York: Zone, 2014), 419. This passage appears in a new appendix prepared only for the heavily edited English version of their 1981 *Geschichte und Eigensinn*. A key impetus for writing the book was the experience of the relative defeat of the German workers' movements of the 1960s and '70s. This English edition remains inexplicably—and disappointingly—truncated, and does not make accessible to the non-German reader the authors' extensive treatment of primitive accumulation, among many other things.

71. Gramsci, *Prison Notebooks*, 164, translation altered. Gramsci is parsing part of the famous "Preface" to Marx's *Contribution to A Critique of Political Economy* (1859). Commenting on a passage similar to this from elsewhere in the *Prison Notebooks*, Gayatri Spivak has remarked upon the translation of *gnoseologico* as "epistemological" rather than, as literality would demand, "diagnostic." See Spivak, "Global Marx?"

72. Following is a list of just some of the many excellent articles, chapters, and books not otherwise cited in the present chapter that have directly thematized the

question of primitive accumulation in recent years. A striking commonality across their many differences is interest in the diagnostic usefulness of primitive accumulation. Massimo De Angelis, "Marx and Primitive Accumulation: The Continuous Character of Capital's 'Enclosures,'" *The Commoner*, no. 2 (September 2001), https://thecommoner.org/wp-content/uploads/2019/10/Marx -and-primitive-accumulation-deAngelis.pdf; Massimo De Angelis, "Marx's Theory of Primitive Accumulation: A Suggested Reinterpretation," University of East London, Department of Economics, Working Paper no. 29, May 2000, https:// www.academia.edu/3132423/Marxs_theory_of_primitive_accumulation_A _suggested_reinterpretation; Werner Bonefeld, "The Permanence of Primitive Accumulation: Commodity Fetishism and Social Constitution," *The Commoner*, no. 2 (September 2001), https://thecommoner.org/wp-content/uploads/2019/10/The -Permanence-of-Primitive-Accumulation-Bonefeld.pdf; Michael Perelman, "A Short History of Primitive Accumulation," *CounterPunch*, April 16, 2013, http://www .counterpunch.org/2013/04/16/a-short-history-of-primitive-accumulation/; Onur Ulas Ince, "Primitive Accumulation, New Enclosures, and Global Land Grabs: A Theoretical Intervention," *Rural Sociology* 79, no. 1 (2014): 104–31; David Harvey, "The 'New' Imperialism: Accumulation by Dispossession," *Socialist Register* 40 (2004): 63–87; Tony C. Brown, "The Time of Globalization: Rethinking Primitive Accumulation," *Rethinking Marxism* 21, no. 4 (2009): 571–84; Robbie Shilliam, "Hegemony and the Unfashionable Problematic of 'Primitive Accumulation,'" *Millennium: Journal of International Studies* 32, no. 1 (2004): 59–88; Gavin Walker, "Primitive Accumulation and the Formation of Difference: On Marx and Schmitt," *Rethinking Marxism* 23, no. 3 (2011): 384–404; Gavin Walker, "Primitive Accumulation and the State-Form: National Debt as an Apparatus of Capture," *Viewpoint*, October 29, 2014, http://viewpointmag.com/2014/10/29/primitive -accumulation-and-the-state-form-national-debt-as-an-apparatus-of-capture/; Saskia Sassen, "A Savage Sorting of Winners and Losers: Contemporary Versions of Primitive Accumulation," *Globalizations* 7, nos. 1–2 (2010): 23–50; Robert Nichols, "Disaggregating Primitive Accumulation," *Radical Philosophy*, no. 194 (November– December 2015): 18–28; Claudia von Werlhof, "'Globalization' and the 'Permanent' Process of 'Primitive Accumulation': The Example of the MAI, the Multilateral Agreement on Investment," *Journal of World-Systems Research* 6, no. 3 (Fall/Winter 2000): 728–47; Massimiliano Tomba, "Layered Historiography: Re-reading the So-Called Primitive Accumulation," in *Marx's Temporalities* (Leiden: Brill, 2013), 159–86; Utsa Patnaik, "Capitalism and the Production of Poverty," *Social Scientist* 40, nos. 1–2 (January–February 2012): 3–20; Tamar Diane Wilson, "Primitive Accumulation and the Labor Subsidies to Capitalism," *Review of Radical Political Economics* 44, no. 2 (2012): 201–12; David Kazanjian, "Dispossession Reimagined from the 1690s," in *A Time for Critique*, ed. Didier Fassin and Bernard Harcourt (New York: Columbia University Press, 2019), 210–29. Beside Silvia Federici's *Caliban and the Witch* (see below), the most important book-length intervention in the current discussion of primitive accumulation is Kalyan Sanyal, *Rethinking*

Capitalist Development: Primitive Accumulation, Governmentality, and Postcolonial Capitalism (New Delhi: Routledge, 2013). Other notable recent contributions include Harry Harootunian, *Marx after Marx: History and Time in the Expansion of Capitalism* (New York: Columbia University Press, 2015), which emphasizes the subsumption argument; George Caffentzis, *In Letters of Blood and Fire: Work, Machines, and the Crisis of Capitalism* (Oakland, CA: PM, 2013); Glen Sean Coulthard, *Red Skin, White Masks: Rejecting the Colonial Politics of Recognition* (Minneapolis: University of Minnesota Press, 2014), which renews this discussion for indigenous North America begin by Roxanne Dunbar-Ortiz and others in the 1970s. Note that Antonio Negri and Michael Hardt in their *Empire* series move away from the explanatory value of primitive accumulation (because anachronistic) in favor of the real/formal subsumption pair. If these concepts are to be used diagnostically, then I tend to agree with them. For comparison, see the difference between Michael Hardt and Antonio Negri, *Empire* (Cambridge, MA: Harvard University Press, 2000), 256–59 and Hardt and Negri, *Assembly* (Oxford: Oxford University Press, 2017), 178–82. All this covers a vast field of investigation. If there is a further step that I am suggesting in this direction, it is for intellectual activism to try to expand or transform the limits of the "concept" as given (proving its "permanence" is necessary but insufficient). A starting point would be to investigate the names classifying group and anthropological differences in the idioms of the world, an exercise that if pursued could strike against diagnosis. Intellectual activists must be able to follow and translate the singular and collective cathexes of classifications and process-names for a world map of the investment of their conceptual and narrative articulations—in all languages and the desiring-structures entangled with them. Thus, deep language-learning, collective work, and sociocultural literacy of a rare type. And a new *savoir-faire* of translation.

73. René Zavaleta Mercado, *Towards a History of the National-Popular in Bolivia, 1879–1980*, trans. Anne Freeland (Calcutta: Seagull Books, 2018), 190. "Originary accumulation" = primitive accumulation as per the Spanish translation of *Capital* (*acumulación originaria*).

74. Zavaleta Mercado, *Towards a History*, 192.

75. Étienne Balibar, "Class Racism," in Étienne Balibar and Immanuel Wallerstein, *Race, Nation, Class: Ambiguous Identities*, trans. Chris Turner (London: Verso, 1991), 209. Balibar gives a detailed conspectus of the interpenetration of racial and class discourses and imagery in modern western Europe.

76. Zavaleta Mercado, *Towards a History*, 231–32, and 190–283 for the elaborated argument.

77. Zavaleta Mercado, 200.

78. Zavaleta Mercado, 231.

79. Karl Marx, *Le Capital (Livre 1)*, trans. J. Roy (Paris: Garnier-Flammarion, 1969), 557. See also, and notably for my argument in this chapter, Zavaleta Mercado's treatment of the topic of "surplus," which provides a striking defetishization of the

Marxian concept from within a Marxist perspective (*Towards a History*, 17–97, and especially 39–41).

80. Joseph Schumpeter, *Capitalism, Socialism and Democracy*, 3rd ed. (New York: Harper Collins, 2008 [1950]), 16–18. Schumpeter's theory of "creative destruction," the "essential fact about capitalism" (83), articulates a long history of what Peter Sloterdijk and Bernard Stiegler call "disinhibition." Bernard Stiegler, *The Age of Disruption: Technology and Madness in Computational Capitalism*, trans. Daniel Ross (Cambridge, UK: Polity, 2019), 106–31. Reconstruction of the full argument is not possible here. The emergence of a will-to-risk-taking (disinhibition) through the making-*calculable* of risk probabilities becomes the dominant modern coding of "innovation," producing the affect and "sense of a permission to commit crimes" (122). It is not an accident that the credo of Facebook is "move fast and break things." The thieves and robbers in Marx's account are of course not necessarily even the ones who became capitalists. They were instead responsible for creating the wandering proletariat through corrupt or greedy (or both) theft of land, eviction, etc. This theft is underived; it does not depend on an imputed codification of prior personal property in the stolen items except, as Marx points out, to the extent that private property is retrospectively projected onto the "expropriated." Capital*ism*'s mode of systemic theft ("exploitation")—calculated by probabilistic averages—adds another twist. A sense of some of the intellectual relays between Marx and Schumpeter on the issue of the natural superiority of innovative swindlers may be found in Raymond Williams, "Social Darwinism," in *Problems in Materialism and Culture* (New York: Verso, 1997), 86–102.

81. Karen Ho, *Liquidated: An Ethnography of Wall Street* (Durham, NC: Duke University Press, 2009), 56, 40–41. See also *passim*, but especially chapter 1, "The Culture of Smartness." Ho, herself a former finance recruit from Princeton, moves somewhat toward a critical articulation of her own ideological production as investigator of the system that produced her.

82. Philip Mirowski, *Never Let a Serious Crisis Go to Waste*, 154–55.

83. Federici, *Caliban and the Witch*.

84. The "set of arrangements by which a society transforms biological sexuality into products of human activity, and in which these transformed sexual needs are satisfied" is an institutionalized general system of exchange that produces equivalences and differences. "Woman" can occupy multiple coordinates on that grid of equivalences and differences: "is the woman traded for a woman, or is there an equivalent?" Such systems "may be implicated in the evolution of social strata . . . [and] intersect with large-scale political processes." Gayle Rubin, "The Traffic in Women: Notes on the 'Political Economy' of Sex," in *Toward an Anthropology of Women*, ed. Rayna R. Reiter (New York: Monthly Review, 1975), 159, 207, 209.

85. "Und das Weib sah, dass von dem Baum gut zu essen wäre und dass er eine Lust für die Augen wäre und verlockend, weil er klug machte." Genesis 3:6 (Luther's translation, which would have been in Marx's mind). "And when the woman saw that the tree was good for food, and that it was pleasant to the eyes, and a tree to be

desired to make one wise" (King James Version). The solicitation, and thus the existence, of desire (for knowledge or wisdom—as well as sustenance and aesthetic pleasure) is clear here. Mieke Bal points out that woman is the originary seeker of knowledge and wisdom in her compelling reading of these passages in "Sexuality, Sin and Sorrow: The Emergence of the Female Character (A Reading of *Genesis* 1–3)," *Poetics Today* 6, no. 1–2 (1985): 21–42.

86. Gérard Genette, *Métalepse: De la figure à la fiction* (Paris: Éditions du Seuil, 2004). Rosalind Morris has noted the gendered dimensions of this inversion in her "*Ursprüngliche Akkumulation*: The Secret of an Originary Mistranslation," *Boundary* 2 43, no. 3 (2016): 38–39. This metaleptic figure is a general and highly diffuse ideological pattern, perhaps definitive of ideology as such, especially in its Althusserian formulation.

87. This is obviously a highly complex situation, but in the most general terms scripture was the great common textual reference point (for or against, secularizing or not, it doesn't matter) across classes. Marx is addressing the discursive level of figurations simple and general enough to move between common sense and academic theory (recall why Universities existed in the first place). A starting point for fleshing out these issues remains Lucien Febvre and Henri-Jean Martin, *The Coming of the Book: The Impact of Printing, 1450–1800*, trans. David Gerard (New York: Verso, 1976), especially 148–332. The specifically Christianizing scriptural relay continues in the modern European colonies, where it was missionaries and their printing operations that were typically responsible for producing the beginnings of grammatized and standardized vernaculars.

88. Gramsci, *Prison Notebooks*, 326. Althusser's more systematizing formulation is that prior to the system of capitalisms necessarily anchored to nation-states (and thus requiring national education systems), the dominant Ideological State Apparatus was the Church. It is highly interesting that his most elaborated description of interpellation (the ideological structure par excellence) is the "Christian religious ideology." This may have been determined by Althusser's own background, but it also confirms the only partial success of the supposedly secularizing missions of European national education systems. Or perhaps that so-called secularization resembles a translation of religious idioms. Louis Althusser, "Ideology and Ideological State Apparatuses (Notes towards an Investigation)," in *Lenin and Philosophy*, trans. Ben Brewster (New York: Monthly Review, 1971), 127–86.

89. Donald McCloskey, "Storytelling in Economics," in *The Uses of Storytelling in the Sciences, Philosophy, and Literature*, ed. Christopher Nash (New York: Routledge, 2005), 5–22, offers a thoughtful starting point for further analysis as to the relation between the scientificity and narrativity of this discipline.

90. Paul de Man, "The Concept of Irony," in *Aesthetic Ideology* (Minneapolis: University of Minnesota Press, 1996), 178.

91. Paul de Man, *Allegories of Reading: Figural Language in Rousseau, Nietzsche, Rilke, and Proust* (New Haven, CT: Yale University Press, 1979), 300.

92. De Man, "Concept of Irony," 179.

93. De Man, 179. I have learned from Gayatri Spivak's suggestive remarks that critically détourne de Man's argument about parabasis in Gayatri Spivak, *A Critique of Postcolonial Reason: Toward a History of the Vanishing Present* (Cambridge, MA: Harvard University Press, 1999), 84, 171, 350, 377, 445.

94. Vera Zasulich, "Vera Zasulich: A Letter to Marx," in *Late Marx and the Russian Road*, ed. Teodor Shanin (New York: Monthly Review, 1983), 99. The original in French is published as Vera Zasulich, "Vera Zasulic an Marx," in *Marx-Engels Archiv: Zeitschrift des Marx-Engels-Instituts in Moskau*, ed. D. B. Riazanov, vol. 1 (Frankfurt am Main: Verlag Sauer & Auvremann, 1969).

95. Marx, *Le Capital*, 315.

96. Karl Marx, "Letter to Vera Zasulich," in *Marx-Engels Collected Works*, vol. 24, *1874–83* (London: Lawrence and Wishart, 1989), 370. The extensive drafts of Marx's ultimately very short letter supply openings for more work on these questions. All I need to do here is show how Marx limits the ostensible universality of the prevailing form of capitalist development.

97. Marx does not give the name and age of the girl, who worked at Mr. Simpson's box factory as a paster. See Children's Employment Commission, *Fifth Report* (London: HMSO, 1866), 55. The report contains a comparable example of this inversion among children in a London textile factory: "The best among them read the words, 'My God, I love thee,' on this wise, 'My, my, God, dog'" (96). One could also ask how this plays with the abject last words of Kafka's *The Trial* or with Derrida's *The Beast and the Sovereign*.

98. Children's Employment Commission, *Fifth Report*, 91. George Ballard, age 9 years 5 months.

99. Richard Halpern, *The Poetics of Primitive Accumulation: English Renaissance Culture and the Genealogy of Capital* (Ithaca, NY: Cornell University Press, 1991), 94. The first two chapters of the book are especially relevant to my own line of argument.

100. Halpern, *Poetics*, 93.

101. Juan Luis Vives, *On Assistance to the Poor* (De subventione pauperum), quoted in Halpern, *Poetics*, 74.

102. The same is true of two other modalities of capitalist work that have vastly inflated since Marx's era: what he calls "Modern Domestic Industry" and "Piece Wages," pieceworking and homeworking (C1, 595–99, 692–700). These are inflection points between labor-power (formed within capital logic) and subalternity (the heterogeneity outside capital-logic) that for this very reason are nonetheless sites of hyperexploitation and intolerable clashes between capitalist and affective modes of production. It is not possible in the present chapter to fully interpret this in light of the fact that Marx's text persistently points to such instances of exception on the threshold of an archetype of capitalism as "a closed self-contained system" or "ideal average." One can but agree with Utsa Patnaik and Prabhat Patnaik that "the very existence and expansion" of capitalism "is conditional upon . . . [its] interaction"

with a vast noncapitalist "setting." Utsa Patnaik and Prabhat Patnaik, *Capital and Imperialism: Theory, History, and the Present* (New York: Monthly Review, 2021), 7. I believe that the Patnaiks' argument is supported by Althusser's analysis of the "ideal average" of capitalist production as Marx's conceptual object. The strongest implication of Althusser's reading is that the conceptuality of the "ideal object" is an epistemological instrument with which to think how different social formations are constituted, and not a *diagnostic metric* with which to classify and plot them on a developmental graph. This is more useful than arguing that every capitalistic society tends asymptotically toward realizing the abstract concept, since the empirical actualization of this concept in its purity is strictly impossible (and Rosa Luxemburg was among the first to indicate this). Hence, the conceptual *Kerngestalt* that Marx attempted to produce is not best suited to diagnose normative deviations, even though this is one of the major uses certain Marxist traditions have made of it by folding the (empirical English) example into the concept (measuring the divergence of any specific social formation from a conceptual ideal and organizing "developmental" policy accordingly). However, while Althusser is generative here, I hope that this chapter has shown that I cannot ultimately endorse such a radical break between concept and example. Louis Althusser and Étienne Balibar, *Reading Capital*, trans. Ben Brewster (London: New Left Books, 1977), 194–98. For relevant scholarship in the area of homeworking and pieceworking, see Maria Mies, *The Lace-Makers of Narsapur: Indian Housewives Produce for the World Market* (London: Zed Books, 1982); Sheila Allen and Carol Wolkowitz, *Homeworking: Myths and Realities* (Houndmills, UK: Macmillan Education, 1987); Swasti Mitter, *Common Fate, Common Bond: Women in the Global Economy* (London: Pluto, 1986); Elizabeth Prügl, *The Global Construction of Gender: Home-Based Work in the Political Economy of the 20th Century* (New York: Columbia University Press, 1999); David E. Staples, *No Place Like Home: Organizing Home-Based Labor in the Era of Structural Adjustment* (New York: Routledge, 2006).

103. Chakrabarti and Dhar, *Dislocation and Resettlement*, 4.

104. The classic example being the *Anekdota* of Procopius (c. 550), the tell-all supplement to his official histories of Justinian and the wars of the eastern Roman Empire, only published following the deaths of the emperor and his entourage. The introductory section of this work is a fascinating example of self-justification for the disclosure of what remained concealed in the official chronicles. Procopius, *Anecdota*, trans. H. B. Dewing (Cambridge, MA: Harvard University Press, 1935).

105. Jacques Derrida, "La forme et la façon," preface to Alain David, *Racisme et antisémitisme: Essai de philosophie sur l'envers des concepts* (Paris: Ellipses, 2001), 24. All translations mine.

106. Derrida, 24–25.

107. Derrida, 25. This returns us to the denegation of nudity in clothing and the role of animality as defining a difference internal to, or a difference from, the human.

108. Negt and Kluge, *Geschichte und Eigensinn*, 560. My trans. The authors' frame here is too big to be any more than conjectural, as they concede; but it is

precisely the shifting figurations and schemas of historical processes, their unknowable weight and manifestations, that are of interest here. Georges Sorel, Walter Benjamin, Rosa Luxemburg, and Antonio Gramsci are four figures who have attempted to theorize the effects of currents of affect in Marxist ways.

109. Genesis 3:21, 23, King James.

110. Children's Employment Commission, *Fifth Report*, 92, 162. Jonathan Giddings, age 11; John Morse, age 12.

111. Children's Employment Commission, *Reports of the Commissioners. Fourth Report* (London, 1865), 259. Mother of fifteen-year-old boy injured in glass-blowing factory.

112. I am grateful to Monica Stanton, a graduate student in my Marx seminar in 2017, for calling attention to the imagery of skins in *Capital*.

113. Althusser and Balibar, *Reading Capital*, 276.

114. Jacques Derrida, "Declarations of Independence," trans. Tom Keenan and Tom Pepper, *New Political Science* 7, no. 1 (1986): 7–15. The "we the people" analyzed by Derrida in these terms, for instance, both asserts the identity of a collective "us" and distinguishes that "us" from a "them" as an act of postcolonial self-emancipation in nationalist form. The "we" of the signatories fabulously preexisted the signature that founds the "we" itself—a move that always depends on some *"coup de force."* Derrida identifies a force or power to use the first-person pronoun (to say "we" or "I") that antecedes the utterance yet appears as its originator. I come back to the question of this power below.

115. Althusser and Balibar, *Reading Capital*, 277.

116. Althusser and Balibar, 278.

117. Fowkes's translation choice changes the significance of this point by rendering *Kinderfibel* as "nursery tale" and the allusion to the space of the schoolroom as "all age groups" (for *Altersklassen*, classes for older students).

118. Louis Adolphe Thiers, *De la propriété* (Paulin, L'Heureux, 1848); translated anonymously as *The Rights of Property: A Refutation of Communism and Socialism* (London: R. Groombridge and Sons, 1848). I have modified translations where appropriate. The attack on "property" represented by the revolutions of 1848 haunts Thiers in the figure of Proudhon (*Qu'est-ce que la propriété? ou Recherche sur le principe du Droit et du Gouvernement* [1840]), who, however, is not directly mentioned or cited in the text.

119. Thiers, *De la propriété*, 26.

120. Thiers, 19–20.

121. Thiers, 26.

122. Marx addresses formal equalization (equal *exchange*) within the "narrow horizon of bourgeois right" in "Critique of the Gotha Program" [1875], in *Karl Marx, Frederick Engels Collected Works*, vol. 24 (New York: International, 1989), 87. This produces the paradoxes of the "first phase of communist society," since equal exchange would produce the very structure Thiers describes: unequal distribution of the social product based on differentiated individual capacities for work. At this

point in his argument, the construction of an ethic of production and distribution *for others* as well as selves remains full of "defects," pinned within the legal figure of "right" and the "economic structure of society and the cultural development that it determines" (87). Marx's suggestion that this will open up into an incalculable relation between "abilities" and "needs" points toward the unraveling of rights coded by diagnostic metrics.

123. Marx, *Le Capital*, 687, my trans.

124. Marx, 687. For the 1773 German original see Johann Wolfgang von Goethe, *Poems of Goethe*, ed. Ronald Gray (Cambridge: Cambridge University Press, 1966), 78. Marx's translation of the last line is: "*il l'a prise*": he took, grabbed, seized, or stole it. Goethe: "*der hats genommen.*"

125. The general formula may be found in *Capital*, vol. 1, 247–57. The most intensive and detailed deconstruction of the formula occurs in volume 2 of *Capital*.

126. Roberts, "What Was Primitive Accumulation?" shows that the general socialist position in Marx's day up to Proudhon was a theory of capitalistic extortion that amounts to a direct and violent theft from the working class. This is exactly what the Marxian analysis of exploitation is supposed to correct (thus, theft of *produced* surplus-value, not of the existing material property of the poor). It is also supposed to have the effect of saving socialist theory from a moralizing condemnation of the law of the strongest. Hence Marx's efforts to demonstrate a dialectic of capitalist socialization rather than sustaining a nostalgic argument for "restoring what was rightfully ours and was stolen from us." Thus, the genealogy of cruelty that makes industrial capitalism possible is not properly internal to the capital-relation. This does not preclude, however, consideration of the violence and cruelty (structural and sanguinary) that are the effects of capitalist development. And as I have been arguing, it is possible that Marx himself marginalizes the repetitions within the historical rupture of capitalism.

127. Stephen A. Resnick and Richard D. Wolff, *Class Theory and History: Capitalism and Communism in the USSR* (New York: Routledge, 2002), 104–29. This book recalibrates the debate about the Soviet Union (and Marxist theory more generally) away from a prevailing focus on classes defined by their relation to political power and toward analysis of the diffusion of class positions in relation to the production, appropriation, and distribution of social surplus (-labor). Their argument for thinking in terms of a general surplusity and its divisions has informed my own here.

128. Gary S. Becker, *Human Capital: A Theoretical and Empirical Analysis, with Special Reference to Education* (Chicago: University of Chicago Press, 1993). The first edition appeared in 1964.

129. Karl Marx, *Capital: A Critique of Political Economy*, vol. 2, trans. David Fernbach (London: Penguin, 1978), 140. The "deception" (*Taüschung*) or "illusory character" of the circuit is precisely that "what is emphasized is not the valorization of the value, but the *money form* of this process" (141). Cited hereafter in the text as C2 with page number following.

130. Sandro Mezzadra, "The Topicality of Prehistory: A New Reading of Marx's Analysis of 'So-Called Primitive Accumulation,'" in *In the Marxian Workshops*, 105. Althusser and Balibar, *Reading Capital*, 277, translation modified.

131. The German reads, "eine der kapitalistischen Akkumulation vorausgehende „ursprüngliche" Akkumulation ("previous accumulation" bei Adam Smith)." All critical editions and commentators refer us to this same passage in Smith. Marx does not give more than the parenthetical ("previous accumulation" bei Adam Smith).

132. Adam Smith, *An Inquiry into the Nature and Causes of the Wealth of Nations*, vol. 1 (Oxford: Clarendon, 1979), 276.

133. "As the accumulation of stock is previously necessary for carrying on this great improvement in the productive powers of labour, so that accumulation naturally leads to this improvement." Smith, *Wealth of Nations*, 277.

134. Halpern, *Poetics*, 85–86. Halpern ingeniously argues that "Marx's misattribution [of the ideologeme to Smith] produces an interesting result: a collective social discourse anterior to Smith and which he positively rejects is nevertheless foisted onto him. The historical product of a social class is thereby rewritten as the fault of an individual's shortcomings or dishonesties. The rhetoric of *Capital* thus reenacts or performs the myth of primitive accumulation itself, in that Adam Smith, like the poor, comes to bear a moral burden that is not rightfully his," 86.

135. Smith, *Wealth of Nations*, 277. I have learned from Rosalind Morris's insightful reading of Marx's textual practice in "*Ursprüngliche Akkumulation*," 33–35. Morris observes that Marx's usage is a "rendering" of Smith's phrase, which can be taken as translation or—in the spirit of Marx's own theory of abstract labor— a violent boiling down as in rendering animal bones into glue (homogenization) (33). I say this because, as Morris recognizes, the Smithian phrase is not Smith's phrase, and is "rendered" into its usable form by a justifiable textual violence. These arguments resonate with Halpern's as discussed in the previous note.

136. Marx's correspondence regarding the French translation is a litany of complaints about the amount of revision he had to do on Roy's manuscript. While Kevin Anderson is correct to suggest that the French edition is in certain ways the most developed version incorporating new material, clarifications, and formulas, there is clearly an element of damage control also involved in Marx's active reworking of the translation. The edition should also be read in this light. See Anderson's illuminating discussion in "The 'Unknown' Marx's *Capital*, Volume I: The French Edition of 1872– 75, 100 Years Later," *Review of Radical Political Economics* 15, no. 4 (1983): 71–80.

137. Jacques Derrida, *Positions*, trans. Alan Bass (Chicago: University of Chicago Press, 1981), 71, original emphasis. I believe that *paleonymy* is a Derridean neologism—and thus a *new* name to designate the strategic preservation of the old. In this sense, it is not so far from Marx's own textual practice. Discussing paleonymy at the beginning of *Dissemination*, Derrida alludes to Marxism as "a certain philosophical deconstruction" precisely concerning the term "matter." Jacques Derrida, *Dissemination*, trans. Barbara Johnson (Chicago: Athlone, 1981), 4.

138. Charles Neate, *Two Lectures on the History and Conditions of Landed Property* (Oxford: J. H. and Jas. Parker, 1860), 22–23, my emphasis. Marx quotes from this passage in *Capital*, vol. 3, 1015. Neate's lectures take as their point of departure Thiers's *De la propriété* discussed above. He wishes to continue—and critically enrich—Thiers's argument for the natural rights of property by accounting for the structure of the right to property in land and its derivatives (such as the right of its alienation and inheritance). This is in the context of an acknowledged class strife, a "wide-spread and ever-smoldering feeling of discontent" that is calling the rights of property into question (3). Remarking that under England's feudal system "the land which made the man should also give him his name," Neate laments that this "system of nomenclature" has a ruinous effect upon "natural principle" and "the truth of history," since the honor of long-standing hereditary names of "successful or eminent men" is thereby devalued (21–22).

139. Karl Marx, *Capital: A Critique of Political Economy*, vol. 3, trans. David Fernbach (London: Penguin, 1981), 1015. Cited hereafter in the text as C3 with page number following.

140. Foucault, *Birth of Biopolitics*, 225–26.

141. Patnaik and Patnaik, *Capital and Imperialism*, 274. The Patnaiks' examples are almost exclusively drawn from modern India, though the problems they call attention to are resonant for many postcolonies. The self-entrepreneurial structure is much more widely effective at different levels and in varying institutional and subjective formats depending on the society in which it operates.

142. Michael J. Watts, *Silent Violence:Food, Famine, and Peasantry in Northern Nigeria* (Athens: University of Georgia Press, 2012), lxxx–lxxxii. I refer here to Watts's introduction to the new 2012 edition of his book, first published in 1983.

143. Watts, lxxxi. Emphasis in original.

144. Watts, lxxxii.

Psychoanalytic States: Translating from Lenin to Freud and *Au-delà*

Cate I. Reilly

Psychoanalysis, it's like the Russian revolution, you can't tell when it starts to go bad.

—GILLES DELEUZE AND FÉLIX GUATTARI, *ANTI-OEDIPUS*

One has the right to wonder if what is called psychoanalysis supposes in some way, inscribes at the heart of its own possibility, the memory, the conscious or unconscious archive of the French Revolution and a few other revolutions, all European, that followed it in February and then in June of 1848, then during the Commune, then in 1917. An enormous, bottomless memory where the worst cruelty . . . go[es] side by side indissociably, as if the two processes were inseparable, with the invention of human rights.

—JACQUES DERRIDA,
"PSYCHOANALYSIS SEARCHES THE STATES OF ITS SOUL"[1]

The first and only Russian-language translation of Jean Laplanche and Jean-Bertrand Pontalis's well-known psychoanalytic dictionary, *Vocabulaire de la psychanalyse* (1967), begins with an unusual claim. "This is a French dictionary of psychoanalysis," the Moscow translator writes in Russian, before launching into an array of further, no less paradoxical, clarifications.

> [The *Vocabulaire*] does not, however, present a particularly distinctive French point of view or position on psychoanalytic discussions (at least to the extent such a perspective exists in any kind of unity). This is a French dictionary of German psychoanalysis, specifically

[psychoanalysis] in the classically Freudian form. Indeed, that is
what determines the precise nature and scope of the Dictionary,
[which is] highly regarded in Europe.[2]

The contortions necessary to clarify the specific nature of the undertaking—a
translation of a translation—combined with the thirty-year gap separating the
1996 Russian edition from the original, speak at once to the fate of psychoanalysis in the Soviet Union and larger problems at the conceptual core of psychoanalysis and translation. Most obviously, the passage alludes to the way in
which, in the course of the twentieth century, the psychoanalytic encounter
with place has been largely mediated by translation, as psychoanalysis spread
outside Central Europe by way of languages other than German. As is by now
familiar, the diverse and asynchronous linguistic transformation of the psychoanalytic corpus that made Freud's work a global phenomenon in the twentieth
century was also accompanied by varying levels of national receptivity or hos-
tility to psychoanalytic practice. For example, the fact that a Russian-language
edition of the *Vocabulaire* appeared only in 1996 pays tribute to the long-
standing censure of psychoanalysis within the USSR, lifted predominantly by
dint of the Soviet Union's collapse in 1991. Yet if political contingencies play
as great a role in determining psychoanalysis's linguistic movements as the
practice of translation itself, one wonders—following on Deleuze, Guattari,
and Derrida's own remarks—how the psychoanalytic revolution should be
conceptualized in relation to the political upheavals that both produced and
precluded the possibility of psychoanalysis outside Austro-Hungary.

The problem of just what one is speaking about when discussing psychoanalysis and translation is further complicated by another factor. The linguistic
dissemination of Freud's work has also been accompanied by the emergence
of an analytically specific cartography. As psychoanalysis spread internationally,
it produced its own institutional imagination of the globe. One need only turn
to the various national and international psychoanalytic bodies, of which the
International Psychoanalytic Association (IPA) is perhaps the most prominent,
to see evidence of a psychoanalytic worlding. This is, on the one hand, what
Derrida designates "geopsychoanalysis" (in a 1981 article describing the IPA's
"psychoanalytic colonization" of the "rest-of-the-world") and, on the other, the
central topic organizing the many postcolonially inspired works about Freud's
anthropological biases and psychoanalysis's colonial abuses.[3] As these texts
collectively make clear, thinking in terms of psychoanalysis *and* translation,
not merely psychoanalysis *in* one translation or another, requires attending to
the psychoanalytic construction of place. Here again, the Russian text is a case
in point. The *Slovar'* legitimates its endeavor by referring to the high regard

in which Laplanche and Pontalis's dictionary is held in Europe. Citing collaboration with the French Foreign Embassy in Moscow, the French Ministry of
Foreign Affairs, and the Sorbonne, the translator implicitly sketches an outline
of center and periphery.[4] France and Europe are hubs in clinical cartography.
Post-socialist Russia is an aspirational, but decidedly provincial, outlier.

Finally, there is the matter of translation within psychoanalysis. As Hungar-
ian psychoanalyst Nicholas Abraham pointed out in a 1968 review of the *Vocabulaire*, its encyclopedism, its authors' insistence on pinning down Freud's
notoriously elusive concepts, is at odds with both the antisemantic nature of
the analytic "kernel" and psychoanalytic resistance to being a system of reference more generally. In "The Shell and the Kernel: The Scope and Originality
of Freudian Psychoanalysis," Abraham observes that the *Vocabulaire*'s attempt
to "define the status of the psychoanalytic 'thing'" misses that Freud's writing
is an invitation to exegesis and not a bid for the construction of an analytic
corpus juris.[5] Similarly, Pakistani-British analyst M. Masud R. Khan does not
hesitate to comment on the "completely new language gradually crystalliz[ing]
in Freud's hermeneutics of human epistemology," in the editorial preface to
the 1973 English edition of the *Vocabulaire*.[6] What thus appears in the 1996
Russian edition as the tricky problem of finding Russian-language equivalents
for German terms in French translation turns out to be only the tip of the
iceberg. Beneath it, haunting efforts to translate Freud's work, lies the far
thornier issue of defining those terms in any language whatsoever.

Three paths thus collide in the 1996 Russian translation, which can also be
thought of as critical axes crisscrossing the uneven terrain of psychoanalytic
universalizability. Speaking of psychoanalysis "and" translation minimally
entails speaking of the field's linguistic transformations alongside (1) those
wrought on psychoanalysis by the political and cultural exigencies of specific
geospatial contexts; (2) psychoanalysis's evolving relationship to the meaning
of the term "world"; (3) a certain "foreignness" (to cite Abraham) of the psychoanalytic endeavor unto itself. Indeed, only when regarded as a triplicate
effort to facilitate psychoanalysis in Russia(n), to mark Russia's reemergence as
a distinct zone on the psychoanalytic map, and to recognize the (potentially)
anasemic quality of the psychoanalytic lexicon does it makes sense to write,
in Cyrillic, "this is a French dictionary of psychoanalysis."

Without intending to, the Russian version thereby hints at a niggling phenomenon for which there is neither entry nor name in any technical lexicon
of Freud's work, but which nevertheless organizes the entire matrix inscribed
by psychoanalysis "and" translation. How would it be possible to describe, and
so think, the interplay between sovereign dominion, psychoanalytic worlding,
and the unusual analytic relationship to signification that becomes apparent

as soon as one asks about psychoanalysis and translation? What kind of meta-psychological concept does or might their mutual entanglement propose? And, if such a concept existed, in what language would one speak of it?

In his late writings on psychoanalysis, Derrida repeatedly refers to a "sovereign cruelty" (*souveraine cruauté*). I read in this abstruse phrase an attempt to formulate such a concept. Building on and adapting the idea of sovereign cruelty offers a way to think psychoanalysis and translation in the expanded sense. At best equivocally defined by Derrida and absent from the various dictionaries of deconstruction, "sovereign cruelty" takes up Freud's own sporadic references to *Grausamkeit* (meaning brutality or ferocity in German) in order to map, without locating, the intersection of geopolitical dominion, institutional-analytic cartography, and language. Through it, Derrida presents psychoanalysis as a condition of being open to that which is nominally outside of or marginal to the psychoanalytic endeavor. In *États d'âme de la psychanalyse* (Psychoanalysis Searches the States of Its Soul), delivered as an address to an international gathering of psychoanalysts in 2000, the phrase specifically indicates the peculiar position of psychoanalysis at the turn of the millennium: uncomfortably stretched between the intimacy of clinical practice, globalization, and issues of sovereignty and human rights. To strive toward what Derrida terms the "impossible beyond of a sovereign cruelty" (l'impossible au-delà d'une souveraine cruauté) would mean, he proposes, for psychoanalysis to embrace responsibility for a hitherto absent engagement with the geopolitical and historical cruelties that structure (and have structured) its global situatedness: war, genocide, crimes against humanity, the death penalty, and innumerable further traumas of the public sphere. Even if such acknowledgment were to come at the price of psychoanalysis itself. "Sovereign cruelty," a kind of death-drive internal to the psychoanalytic project that is refracted in the instability of its own lexicon, thus comes to name the "state" of a psychoanalysis legitimated by its unique capacity for self-undoing.

Yet Derrida's idea of sovereign cruelty is already anticipated by, and to a certain extent the inheritor of, a prior Soviet insight about psychoanalysis dating from the 1920s. Widely available Russian translations of Freud's work published during the brief period of psychoanalytic viability in Communist Russia resulted in a chance overlap between Freud's vocabulary and key Marxist-Leninist concepts, opening the same equivocal intersection of the psychological and political spheres that Derrida would seek to describe some eight decades later. As a result, the very geographic region so self-declaredly bereft of a psychoanalytic tradition as to require a Russian translation of the *Vocabulaire* turns out instead to be integral to understanding the relationship between psychoanalysis and translation that configures the *Vocabulaire*, but which it can neither grasp

nor name. Placing Soviet psychoanalysis in dialogue with Derrida's formulations not only suggests a new way of thinking about the Freudo-Marxist tradition, but also implies that regions allegedly peripheral to the psychoanalytic
endeavor, those to which psychoanalysis must be "imported," are already its
most robust points of specification.

Revolutionary Psychoanalysis, 1789–2000

The unusual setting at which Derrida delivered the address that would become
États d'âme de la psychanalyse is an integral point of reference for that piece.[7]
His talk at once problematizes and repudiates the national specificity of the
event hosting it. The 2000 Paris gathering known as the Estates-General of
Psychoanalysis (États Généraux de la Psychanalyse, EGP) was named after the
1789 French revolutionary Estates-General (États Généraux) that led to the
execution of Louis XVI and the overthrow of the French monarchy. The brain-
child of French psychoanalyst René Major, the EGP was organized as a deliberate departure both from nationally specific psychoanalytic congresses (e.g.,
the Berlin Psychoanalytic Association, Asociación Psicoanalítica Argentina,
the Indian Pyschoanalytical Society) as well the International Psychoanalytic
Association (IPA). Unlike these venues, Major intended for EGP to speak to
"all those who, whatever their institutional membership or reason for refusing
institutional membership, were ready to engage in a collective reflection . . .
on the general state [*l'état général*] of psychoanalysis . . . at the beginning of
the twenty-first century."[8]

The project was three years in the making. Between 1997 and 2000, a committee of 160 members located in different countries worked to organize the
event. Major invited Derrida and the Chilean writer Armando Uribe as guest
speakers based on their work's relevance to the conference topic and his
collaboration with each at prior events focusing on psychoanalysis in Latin
America.[9] The final conference placed a heavy emphasis on the symbolic value
of the French revolutionary timeline. Scheduled to take place in July 2000, the
EGP coincided exactly with the 211th anniversary of the French Revolution.
It convened, moreover, during the same four-day period, from July 8 to 11,
during which the 1789 Estates-General convoked and authorized by Louis XVI
ceased to exist and was replaced by the self-authorizing National Constituent
Assembly, which became the new French government after the storming of the
Bastille.

The significance of these dates helped Major bring home that the EGP was,
like its historical predecessor, intended to institute a new form of self-authorizing
republican governance that would speak directly on behalf of the psychoanalytic

population. Its punning title conveyed that the participants would anticipate "a new imperative" for psychoanalysis by dispensing with hierarchical structures in favor of republican decision-making. Just as the Third Estate had declared itself a representative of the people, rather than a class-based subsection of the population, Major presented the EGP as a supranational psychoanalytic body that would eliminate inequalities in the psychoanalytic *peuple* on a global scale and unambiguously align psychoanalytic practice more closely with the pursuit of *droits* (rights/laws) by explicitly considering the ethical, juridical, and political issues of the postwar era. In christening his conference with the same title as the gathering that had heralded the outbreak of the French Revolution, Major also alluded to the fact that the Estates-General had produced its own destruction in 1789, bringing with its collapse the execution of the monarch and the end of an entire system of rule. The 2000 conference thus placed psychoanalytic participants at the crossroads of a past deeply implicated in history of human rights and an unformulated future that ran the risk of psychoanalysis's own self-annihilation, if only by analogy.

At the same time, the EGP's stated goal of producing a *"general* state [*l'état général*] of psychoanalysis," was in tension with its own nationally specific coordinates, all French. The history on which it drew presupposed both a linguistic and a geopolitical particularity at odds with the conference's commitment to international pluralism. While bringing together 1,200 attendees from thirty-two countries and officially being conducted in four languages, the subsequent French-language publication of the proceedings (*États généraux de la psychanalyse, juillet 2000* [Aubier, 2003]) regretfully acknowledged the impossibility of accommodating such polyglossia in print. The event's declarations and resolutions, included in an appendix to the published proceedings, were similarly monoglot. The Institute for Advanced Study in Psychoanalysis (Institut des Hautes Études en Psychanalyse, IHEP) it created, still operative today, was likewise based in France. Considerations of the class politics of psychoanalysis and class composition of the Paris gathering similarly played little role in this version of the general psychoanalytic state, despite a long-standing history of protests against psychoanalysis as for-profit endeavor (as in 1969 when a subset of analysts at the IPA's Rome meeting characterized it as a "Congre$$" and created their own event).[10] While a second gathering of the EGP did take place in Rio de Janeiro in 2003, headlined by major figures from critical theory, one of the primary organizers of the Paris event later characterized this second Latin American iteration as little more than an embarrassing "failure" before going on to portray the Parisian EGP's success as singular.[11] Her comments provoked dismay among Brazilian organizers, some of whom subsequently published their own analysis of the Estados Gerais in response.[12]

A third meeting in Brussels planned for July 2006 never progressed beyond the initial planning stages owing to a lack of participation.[13] In France, while philosophical discussions of psychoanalysis and cruelty continued apace (driven both by September 11 and by the beginning of the American War on Terror), the conversation shifted away from global psychoanalytic representation to the question of cruelty within democracy, leaving the earlier problems of analytic republicanism and language seemingly unresolved.[14]

Neither the EGP's focus on the psyche and the state nor its struggle to balance between local and universal were unique to that gathering, however. On the one hand, the Paris conference extended a basic question about psychoanalysis and universality operative since Freud's attempts at a psycho-anthropology in works like *Totem and Taboo, Civilization and Its Discontents*, and *Moses and Monotheism*, and his rather lesser-known publication *Why War?* (1933).[15] The last, an exchange of letters with Albert Einstein (on the topic, "Is there any way of delivering mankind from the menace of war?"), had been arranged by the League of Nations' Permanent Committee for Literature and the Arts, as part of a project to publish open letters in English, French, and German on issues serving "common interests of the League of Nations." In it, both Freud and Einstein actively speculated about the existence of a universal human aggression, the eradication or regulation of which might change the nature of conflict on an international scale.

On the other hand, the EGP was more proximately the culmination of some two decades of prior work by René Major. Beginning with a psychoanalytic lecture series entitled "Confrontation" in the late 1970s, Major sought to articulate how a theory of the psyche might transgress the individual and familial sphere, and interface with sociopolitical concerns at large. He accordingly defined the 2000 gathering's goals much like those of his earlier lecture series: it was an effort to understand where psychoanalysis stood at the beginning of the twenty-first century in terms of "clinical practice, transmission, institutional existence, the social and political, philosophy, art, literature, law, neurosciences, biology and genetics."[16] As with the reflections on the USSR that dot the pages of the publishing apparatus for "Confrontation" and feature more prominently in Major's 1986 book, *On Election: Freud in the Face of American, German, and Soviet Ideologies*, the Paris conference similarly took note of recent upheavals in Eastern Europe. Elizabeth Roudinesco stated in her introductory remarks that one of the issues facing participants was how to think about psychoanalysis "in the various countries where it has not yet been rooted and in Europe where it is enjoying a new success, notably after the fall of Communist regimes."[17] Any interrogation of psychoanalysis's global role in the millennium would need to reckon, she proposed, with the comparatively recent crumbling of the Soviet Union, which was presumably felt even more keenly when Major's call for participants went out in 1997.

Derrida's *États d'âme de la psychanalyse* draws simultaneously on these sources, weaving together Freud's anthropology, the 1932 Einstein correspondence, and Major's prior work. Not only does *États d'âme* invoke the EGP by name (through its reference to *états* or "states" of the soul), but it also does so on the level of source matter, going so far as to allude to a prior publication Major had edited on the topic of "L'état freudien" (the Freudian state) and to Major and Roudinesco's own writings. *États* offers a condensation of the same issues of representation and rights that the EGP's own historically circumscribed name invoked. The title addresses, in a literal sense, whether psychoanalysis has a stable identity and object, that is, whether it is something that *can* be addressed. The innovative English rendering, "Psychoanalysis Searches the States of Its Soul," pales with what the French can be read to imply. If the word *état* is taken in the sense of "condition" (in good condition [*en bon état*], in poor condition [*en mauvais état*]), the title would mean "The Conditions of the Soul of Psychoanalysis." If, by contrast, *état* implies "state" or "nation state," one is dealing with a "National Composition of the Soul of Psychoanalysis" or, perhaps, in an echo of the ancien *régime's* three estates, the "Estate of the Soul of Psychoanalysis." There is yet a further possibility. The phrase *états d'âme* can be an idiomatic expression referring to having qualms, hesitations, or misgivings (*avoir des états d'âme*), mixed with a whiff of culpability, even guilt. Hence a "Soul-Searching of Psychoanalysis" or "Qualms of Psychoanalysis." Finally, as seen in Major's "L'état freudien," a sense of profession or trade is also feasible here, alluding to the question of psychoanalytic professionalization versus lay or wild analysis.

Derrida's equivocal lack of differentiation between these multiple possible variant readings of his title is symptomatic of their inseparability. The overall questions at stake are roughly: In what type of *condition* does psychoanalysis find itself and what *responsibilities* does (or should) it bear given its evolving *national* composition and relationship to the *state* and to state violence? Lurking here is the yet older consideration of the relative universality (or lack thereof) of the psychoanalytic subject. So too, the problem surrounding the establishment of governing bodies (institutions with sovereign power) by psychoanalysis for itself, in light of its own structural and methodological opposition to paternal mastery.

Perhaps unsurprisingly, *États d'âme* embraces the problematic national specificity of the EGP by beginning with a "digression" on French grammar, as if to highlight, not withdraw, from the question of translation.

> If I say right now, . . . "Yes, I am suffering cruelly" [*je souffre cruelle-ment*] or again 'You are being *made* or *allowed* to suffer cruelly' [*On vous* fait *ou on vous* laisse *cruellement souffrir*] or yet again, "You are making *her* or you are letting *him* suffer cruelly" [*Vous* la *faites ou on vous* le *laissez cruellement souffrir*] . . . all these possible modifications leave the adverb intact, an invariant that seems, once and for all, to qualify a state of suffering, namely, cruelty, "cruelly."[18]

These idiomatic expressions throw the intending subject into question. Because lacking an agent or perpetrator, the French phrase "I am suffering cruelly" (*je souffre cruellement*) leaves it grammatically unclear just who or what is responsible for causing harm. Likewise, "on vous fait/laisse cruellement souffrir" presents no distinct source for the suffering in question. This opening allows Derrida to ask whether such cruelty—in its syntactical agentlessness; its links to the work of Nietzsche, Sade, and Artaud; its refusal of rational egoism—might be the "horizon most proper to psychoanalysis," if not the "ultimate ground on which one day its figure took shape."[19] In this case, the untranslatability of the French phrases reflects, as symptom, a more foundational intractability in language potentially also determinative for psychoanalysis. Such cruelty would not be something done by self-aware actors intent on harm, but an anterior phenomenon that precedes conscious intentionality and can be glimpsed in linguistic expressions that elide an agential doer.[20] Using Einstein's remarks in the 1932 Freud-Einstein correspondence as a bridge, *États d'âme* goes on to discuss American autonomy, cruel and unusual punishment, and the death penalty in the United States, situating psychoanalysis as the science best equipped to address these topics, being the only one to take cruelty as its object. The piece closes with potential implications of his interpretation for the EGP and for psychoanalysis more generally. An enigmatic postscript (dated after the conference) brings the address's initial grammatical digression full circle, pitying the translator faced with the task of rendering French expressions for cruelty such as *avoir mal, faire mal* (to feel hurt, to cause hurt) into another language.

While Derrida's talk is laced with references to his prior work (on representation, communication circuits, logocentrism), he largely frames it in terms of single question. "Is there . . . for psychoanalytic thought to come . . . a beyond [*au-delà*], that would stand beyond [*au-delà*] . . . *both* the pleasure and reality principles *and* the death or sovereign mastery drives [*maîtrise souveraine*], which seem to be at work whenever cruelty is on the horizon?"[21] Put slightly differently, *États d'âme* interrogates the proper name of psychoanalysis and the tradition conjoining "might and right," in La Fontaine's phraseology. Recognizing psychoanalysis's historical resistance to engaging with politically sovereign claims, and political theology's tendency to downplay or disregard psychology, Derrida proposes cruelty as the overlooked common denominator between the psychic economy and sovereign authority, insofar as the latter configures a relationship between *Gewalt* (violence) and *Recht* (right). "Sovereign cruelty," then, seems to point to a horizon that is paradoxically in excess of psychoanalysis yet also already contained within it, at once self-authorizing and self-destructive. Initially framed as little more than a citation of *Grausamkeit* in Freud's work, the term "cruauté" gradually comes in *États d'âme* to designate the peculiar movement of a joint psychoanalytic and sovereign self-devouring, a kind of autophagy, that serves as the central provocation and so too the central enigma of *États d'âme*. The wager throughout is that any study of the proper boundaries of the psychoanalytic revolution must simultaneously explore the way in which revolutionary upheavals, defined by the self-authorization of a new order as it displaces an older form of authority, may entail psychoanalytic principles. Whence the impossibility of the 2000 Paris event repeating its 1789 precursor, save as farce.

Indeed, for all the stress that Major placed on the French backdrop for the event, the full implications and meaning of Derrida's sense of cruelty become clearest by observing where *États* opens beyond the French Revolution. Just as Derrida extracts an element from Freud's work to which Freud does not explicitly attend, but to which he nevertheless consistently refers, Derrida's own commentary on psychoanalytic cruelty is shaped by elements at once inside and outside the scope of *États d'âme* and perhaps of psychoanalysis itself. One of these is the 1917 Russian Revolution. The passing references to 1917 in *États d'âme* help disclose Major's own silent debt to a Russo-Soviet dimension of the psychoanalytic tradition that repeatedly creeps in despite Major's numerous outward disavowals of the USSR's significance for psychoanalysis. A visual image on the cover of Major's earlier 1984 publication "L'état freudien" exposes its unlikely significance. As a kind of primal scene for both the EGP and Derrida's address, this image poses a question about the relationship between the paternal function and sovereign political authority, forcing the issue of whether state power ultimately regulates and controls the terms of psychoanalytic inquiry or whether such inquiry discloses laws that transcend every merely instituted order. In so doing, the image illuminates Derrida's talk while reconfiguring what it would mean to consider psychoanalysis "after" the fall of Communist regimes or in all those places "where it has not yet been rooted."

The Freudian State: *Homo Homini Lupus*

The French journal *Cahiers Confrontation* served as the publishing apparatus for Major and Dominique J. Geachan's seminar series "Confrontation" (1979–89), which studied questions outside the purview of any single discipline. Ranging from "art and disorder" and "Latin America" to "male sexuality" and "accident and catastrophe," the various seminar topics all foregrounded a connection to psychoanalysis. *Cahiers Confrontation* used a clever typographic parapraxis, a kind of slip of the pen, repeated on the cover of every issue to emphasize the psychoanalytic link. The word "Confrontation," printed in black, appears with a shadow behind it, which is actually the letters "e-u-d," printed in gray. In addition to being called Confrontation, the series thus carries a second title, Confreudtation, showing the palimpsestic shadow that psychoanalysis literally and figuratively casts on the seminar series.

The visual dimension was an important component of the *Cahiers Confrontation* overall. Working in a minimalist style, the Italian artist Valerio Adami condensed each issue's theme into a calligraphic line drawing featured on the cover. Issue 11, "L'État freudien" (The Freudian State, Spring 1984) was no exception.[22] The cover featured an illustration of a single sewing pin and a large pair of scissors. Adami depicts the scissors cutting along a line drawn in tailor's chalk that runs horizontally across the page. This chalk line separates the vertically stacked words of the issue's title, isolating *l'État* above it, and *freudien* below. Superficially, the image plays on the dual meaning of *état* as "state" and as "profession or trade," as in *tailleur de son état* (a tailor by trade), in order to visually interrogate the divide separating the profession of psychoanalysis from the concerns of state, and thereby preface the 1984 issue's contents.

As Major notes in its introduction, one of the issue's central concerns was to assess the IPA's 1977 Constitution. This constitution had formally "distinguish[ed] between *terra psychanalytica* and *incognita*" by separating the IPA's allegedly primary spheres of geographic concern from "the rest of the world" (already the subject of Derrida's critical text on geopsychoanalysis).[23] The other was a consideration of what psychoanalysis might contribute to an understanding of *droits* and the state. "L'État freudien" included, in addition to Major's reflections on psychoanalysis and human rights, a reprint of work by Austrian political philosopher Hans Kelsen from the 1920s, contributions from exiled Chilean writer Armando Uribe (also a participant in the 2000 Paris event), and writing by a number of legal scholars, sociologists, and psychoanalysts. Reflections on the IPA's 1981 resolution against nuclear war abutted commentary on

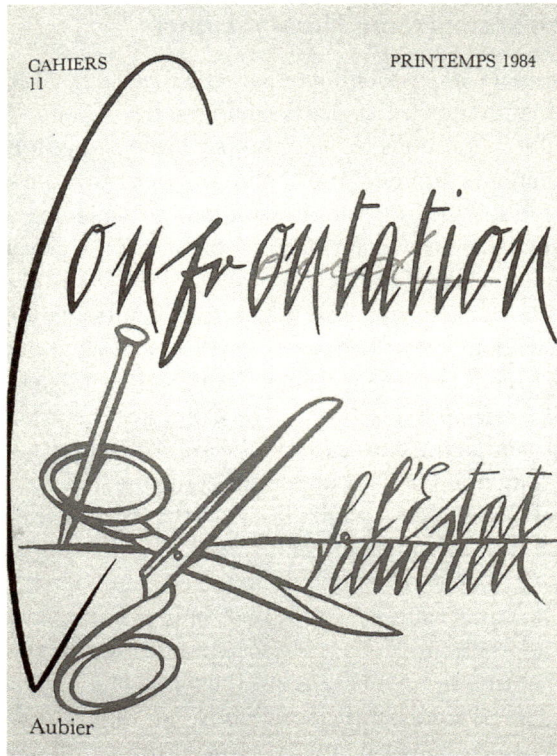

Cover of "L'État freudien" (1984), issue 11 of *Cahiers Confrontation*

the recent deinstitutionalization of Italian psychiatry. In keeping with the unspoken consensus that Soviet psychoanalysis was an oxymoron, however, the USSR's place in the IPA's cartography and its possible contributions to the topic of human rights had no outward role. Barred from the text proper, Eastern Europe nevertheless returns in Adami's cover image, which symptomatically calls attention to the centrality of the Russian Revolution for any consideration of "L'État freudien" by referring to the case history of the Russian aristocrat known as the Wolf-Man.

The horizontal chalk line on the cover graphically places "the state" and psychoanalysis in a relationship of tense mutuality, enhanced by Adami's choice of font. His dense cursive makes it look as though the words on either side of the chalk line are mirror images of one another. Slicing between them, the line visibly recalls the Saussurian bar, emphasizing the importance of language to the study of *l'état freudien* and seeming to pose a question about signifier and signified. Is *l'état* representing *freudien* or vice versa? The issue of who or what is on top resonates with the ways in which the cover also stages a primal scene. At points, the cursive script of the issue's title suggestively transgresses the chalk line, begging the question of its ability to truly separate the two. Thrusting upward from below, the phallic "f" of *freudien* penetrates the territory of *l'état*, where it mimics the loop of the "l." A little further on, the top of "d" jabs into the triangular crevice created by the cursive connector linking the capital "É" to the "t" in *État*.

The typographic copulation on the right side of the cover is doubled by a pictographic one on the left. There, a deliberately oversized sewing pin plunges through the hole of the scissors' handle. Because the pin is angled parallel to the scissors' upper blade, and because it is (physically and metaphorically) on the same side of the line as *l'état*, it functions jointly as a sword and as a phallus. The pin's equivocality reinforces the complexity of the paternal function, as it operates both politically and psychologically. Importantly, these two "scenes" (the scissors and pin on one side, the stacked text on the other) are interrupted by the scissors' blades. Given that Adami's drawing is done in red ink, and plays out an act of cutting, it is easy to see the allusion to castration therein.

Adami's design, with its simultaneous emphasis on intercourse and the loss of the phallus, is a picture of *the* primal scene par excellence: Sergey Pankeyev's—the Wolf-Man's—childhood experience of witnessing his parents' coitus *a tergo*. The drawing is not only a representation of key psychoanalytic concepts (castration, penis envy) but also a rebus of one of Freud's most celebrated cases, a case at once intimately bound up with the question of sadism and aggression, and involving a Russian aristocrat whose life and fortunes were transformed by the events of 1917. The case contributed substantially to Freud's understanding of child psychosexual development and was the origin of his theory of the *Urszene*: the child's real or inferred observation of his/her parents' intercourse and subsequent conclusion that their behavior entailed a violent act. Freud relied on this case specifically to prove the import of infantile sexuality to psychoanalysis against critiques from Carl Jung and Alfred Adler, and to conclusively demonstrate—or at least so Freud believed at the time—the key axioms of psychoanalytic treatment. Reviewing the Wolf-Man's case history sheds additional light on how Adami's image stages the return of a region of the world allegedly both topically and geographically outside the scope of the Freudian state.

"From the History of an Infantile Neurosis" (1918) documents a fragment of Pankeyev's treatment connected to the latter's childhood development of an obsessional neurosis involving a fear of animals. The case famously pivots around Pankeyev's childhood dream about a number of threatening wolves perched in a tree. In the dream, Pankeyev's wolves all have prominent bushy tails. Freud quickly concludes that his patient's early fear of animals was in some way related to a fear of castration. (The connection makes sense especially because the German term for tail, *Schwanz*, may also refer to the penis). Yet Freud could not determine the precise nature of the link until Pankeyev remarked that the dream reminded him of a story he had once heard from his grandfather. In it, a tailor (*der Schneider*, lit. a cutter) is startled by a wolf suddenly leaping through the window of his workshop. He nevertheless manages to catch the animal by its tail and pull it off entirely. While walking in the forest some time later, the tailor encounters an entire pack of wolves, which happens to include his (now-tailless) intruder. He ascends a nearby tree to escape, but the wolves, not to be deterred, climb on top of one another trying to reach him. The tailor finally saves himself by crying out "Catch the gray one by his tail [*Schwanz*]!" which sufficiently frightens the tailless wolf, standing at the base of the stack, that he runs away and causes the others atop him to tumble down as well.

In Freud's reading, the bushy tails in the Wolf-Man's dream are, as the German suggests, representatives of the penis, while the tailor (or "cutter") from Pankeyev's grandfather's story ends up fused with the wolves. These dream-wolves are thus threatening not merely by nature of their being wolves, but because they carry the symbolic weight of the tailor's cut, leading Freud to assert that his patient's fear of castration is based on an unconscious connection between this children's story and a forgotten primal scene Pankeyev witnessed between his parents, a scene in which "the tail" seemed to disappear. Freud speculates that the young Sergey must have, while sleeping in his parents' bedroom, awoken to find his mother and father in a position where "he was able to see his mother's genitals as well as his father's organ."[24] Several years later, the unconscious recollection of this scene no doubt generated the anxiety-provoking dream about wolves. When Pankeyev saw his father situated behind his mother in bed, the child must have interpreted his father's actions as aggressive to the point of sadism. At the same time, the boy presumably experienced profound fear as a result of the (seeming) disappearance of his father's penis, which looked as if it had been cut off.

Adami's illustration for *Cahiers Confrontation* captures the essential components of the Wolf-Man's case with remarkable concision, pointing out its key importance for a consideration of "the Freudian state" and simultaneously reaffirming its significance to Freud as a prototype for psychoanalytic treatment. The stacked organization of the words in Adami's drawing recalls both the stacked wolves of the story, and the position of Pankeyev's father, who appeared to the child to have climbed on top of his mother. The "f" and "d" (in *freud-ien*), which must cross the chalk line from below to penetrate the space of *l'état*, typographically reproduce the copulation the boy allegedly witnessed. The fact that the stems of these letters are also cut off by a tailor's chalk line, and that the entire title is represented as if about to be swallowed up by the scissors' open mouth, succeeds in visually condensing the grandfather's story, the fear of castration it occasioned, and Freud's subsequent theorization of the primal scene.

Whereas Eastern Europe is consistently an afterthought in Major's work, something that must be superadded to psychoanalytic inquiry because sup-posedly external to it, Adami's drawing discloses the disingenuousness of this position, illuminating psychoanalysis's conceptual debt to a Russian émigré who conducted his analysis in translation, and with whose case history Freud never ceased to struggle. Moreover, the drawing unintentionally alludes to the fact that the Wolf-Man played a role in Freud's life and writing well be-yond the 1910–11 analysis that produced the 1918 case history. Far from con-cluding their interaction, the initial analysis was merely a prelude to a set of ongoing interactions between the two men that unfolded in large part as a direct result of the Bolshevik victory. The history of the Wolf-Man's flight from Communist Russia is thus inscribed in psychoanalysis's own development, first via Pankeyev's lifelong pursuit of psychoanalytic treatment for symptoms that never fully resolved, and then through Freud's persistent return to his case in later writings.

Pankeyev records in his memoirs that his first analysis with Freud concluded with the "assassination of the Austrian Crown Prince, and World War I, which followed this event."[25] As he documents, he returned home to Russia only to witness the effects of the Russian Revolution firsthand in Odessa and have his life turned upside down by them. When he next met Freud in Vienna in 1919, he was no longer a landed member of the Russian nobility able to travel, when-ever he pleased, in great luxury all over Europe, but a landless, penniless, and stateless émigré trapped in interwar Austria. Having paid Freud lavishly for the first analysis, he was so impoverished in 1919 that Freud undertook the second analysis free of charge and even started a collection among his psychoanalytic colleagues to support the Wolf-Man.

Notably, however, the patient whose case Freud had held up as a resounding example of psychoanalysis's curative power in 1918 was still experiencing the same anal complaint in 1919, much to Freud's dismay. What could this patient's return with a near-identical problem suggest other than that Freud's trium-phant conclusion—that adult neuroses could be fully cured by returning to disturbances in infantile sexuality—had been wrong? Torok and Abraham postulate that the Wolf-Man's failure to recover never stopped haunting Freud.[26]

It is for this reason, they suggest, that references to his case continue to reappear, albeit unnamed, in texts including *The Uncanny* (1919), *Fetishism* (1927), *Analysis Terminable and Interminable* (1937) and *The Splitting of the Ego in the Process of Defense* (1938). The persistence of these references reflects Freud's ongoing effort to work out the mystery of the same case he already defended as the definitive model for psychoanalytic practice.

Subsequent analyses of the Wolf-Man conducted by Ruth Mack Brunswick, Muriel Gardiner, and several others provide further evidence of the case's significance to the psychoanalytic tradition in the longue durée, if only by way of its apparent irresolvability.[27] The Wolf-Man never fully recovered. This mystery is famously the basis for Torok and Abraham's notion of the Wolf-Man's cryptonomy, or his possession of a set of words kept secret ("encrypted") and so withdrawn from the space of analysis. Yet the anasemic or nonreferential dimension that Torok and Abraham ascribe to his case is also bound up with Abraham's earlier remarks on psychoanalytic language's fundamental resistance to definition, translation, and systematization. The cryptic inaccessibility of the Wolf-Man's lexicon as Torok and Abraham describe it in *The Wolf-Man's Magic Word* thus merges with psychoanalysis's own, obscuring the boundary between this Russian case and the "non-presence of self to itself" Abraham ascribes to the psychoanalytic kernel.

The "*L'État freudien*" issue of *Cahiers Confrontation* silently continues this Russo-Soviet psychoanalytic genealogy despite itself. Published against the backdrop of the Soviet crisis that was occasioned by the sequential deaths of, first, Yuri Andropov, the same year, and then Konstantin Chernenko in 1985, the issue cannot be separated from the fallout of events that contributed to the Wolf-Man's massively extended analysis in the first place, although never mentioning them. Like the wolf through the window, this Russian dimension leaps in unbidden. A threat to be mastered, a tailless beast who is nevertheless all too potent. In the face of outward statements to the contrary, Freud, and Major like him, never manage to have done with either the Wolf-Man's case history or a region supposedly external to the analytic project. The case's emphasis on jointly psychological and political forms of cruelty connects with, but also jaggedly refuses to be flattened into Freud's universalizing anthropological claim that man is a wolf to man: *homo homini lupus*.

Through the Window:
On Cruelty and Two Senses of the Beyond

Derrida's address to the EGP is similarly built around a series of unexpected encounters that epistemologically mimic the wolf's leap through the window.

All are intended to illuminate the ways in which psychoanalysis contains—like self-authorizing revolutionary movements—the dangerous but necessary seed of its own excess and (self-)transcendence. The limit that psychoanalysis reaches at this moment is not an endpoint, but a way of eliciting the specter of an as yet unrealized and not strictly psychoanalytic alternative.

The first such encounter is Derrida's own: the nonanalyst asked to address a group of analysts. *États d'âme* is full of references to "greeting" or "saluting" the Estates-General, in which the author seeks to determine the conditions for recognizing the body of representatives gathered before him at the Sorbonne. Without being able to claim a proper object for psychoanalysis, he addresses the group in the name of the "beyond [*au-delà*] of the beyond of the pleasure principle." This "beyond" (the same in both the phrases "beyond of the beyond" and the "impossible beyond of a sovereign cruelty") has a double meaning. The first is Freud's *jenseits* of *Beyond the Pleasure Principle*, in which Freud goes past his earlier claims about the reality and pleasure principles in formulating the notion of the death drive. The second, however, is Derrida's own proposition that Freud's intuition be taken a step further and used to consider the existence of something structurally anticipated by the death drive, but no longer a part of psychoanalytic terminology, something that might be said to govern psychoanalysis. To discuss it, a second interruption is necessary. A knock comes at the door:

> Before I begin, assuming that I ever begin, I must . . . settle my choice
> on two common nouns. They have just struck a knock at the door, or
> struck period; we will answer them without yet being able to answer
> for them [*sans pouvoir encore en repondre*]; they are the nouns "cruelty"
> [*cruauté*] and "sovereignty" [*souveraineté*].[28]

The cruelty that unexpectedly arrives at this point is Albert Einstein's unlikely reference to the word in his 1932 correspondence with Freud. Much to Freud's surprise, the analytically naïve Einstein managed to land on a topic not only of significant interest for psychoanalytic thought, but also one already a manifest part of Freud's own work. Einstein, not Freud, is the first to speculate on the existence of a universal force of "human aggression" (*menschliche Aggressivität*) in the correspondence. War, the physicist writes, is merely one manifestation of this aggression, "the most representative and most cruel [*unhielvollste*], because uncontrollable, form of conflict within human communities." [29] Regulating it offers the best chance of preventing armed conflict on an international scale.

Yet this very idea of a universalized aggression is already present in Freud's work in discussions of *Grausamkeit* that occur as early as *Studies on Hysteria*

(1893) and as late as *Moses and Monotheism* (1939).[30] Most numerous in *Three Essays on the Theory of Sexuality* (1905), *Grausamkeit* is connected to the drive for mastery (*Bemächtigungstrieb*) there and forms part of the sexual instinct, expressed either actively (in sadism) or passively (in masochism). The term reappears in major case histories (Dora, the Rat Man, and the Wolf-Man), where Freud uses it in much the same manner: to describe a repressed sadistic instinct displaced into other behaviors/fantasies. *Thoughts for the Times on War and Death* (1915), commenting on the outbreak of World War I, takes a slightly different tack. Here *Grausamkeit* describes human regression to so-called primitive impulses that are out of sync with possessors' (supposed) level of civilization. As in the anthropological writings, *Grausamkeit* in this sense is presented as a dangerous relic from mankind's phylogenetic past that breaks through into the present. *Totem and Taboo* (1913) proclaims that the "savage and half savage races are guilty of uninhibited and ruthless cruelty [*Grausamkeit*] towards their enemies," while *Group Psychology* (1921) presents cruelty as the regressive source of the mob's frenzy.[31] In the mob, "individual inhibitions fall away and all the cruel [*grausamen*], brutal and destructive instincts, which lie dormant in individuals as relics of a primitive epoch" come to the fore.[32] Cruelty in this sense is closer to a phantasmatic state of nature, something rigidly opposed to the "work of civilization," as Freud puts it in *Future of an Illusion* (1930). Similarly, *Civilization and Its Discontents* (1930) describes a force of "cruel aggressiveness" (*grausame Aggression*) perpetually pent up and ready to strike at the slightest provocation.[33]

For all the frequency with which cruelty appears in Freud's work, however, it is not part of the recognized psychoanalytic lexicon. Moreover, Freud never reflects specifically on cruelty per se. Neither do the various psychoanalytic dictionaries attempt to flesh out a definition under that heading. At times, Freud also appears to blend cruelty with his equally complex formulations on aggression (*Aggression, Aggressivität*), as in the "grausame Aggression" of *Civilization and Its Discontents*. Derrida carries this ambiguity further in *États d'âme*, augmenting these already diverse psychoanalytic meanings with Einstein's reflections on the term, in addition to those of Sade, Nietzsche, and Artaud (not to mention a number of postwar philosophical responses engaging those writers).[34] He freely connects Artaud's famous insistence that theater recover a more primal life force by becoming "cruel" (i.e., by attending on the physical properties of the stage and a "poetry of space," not language), with Sade's notion that cruelty is a kind of primary energy possessed by man before being corrupted by civilization.[35]

Introducing this enormous plurality of sources helps Derrida develop cruelty outside the scope of any single discourse, whether psychoanalytic, philosophical, scientific, or juridical. It also situates his usage beyond performative utterances and constative declarations equipped with the capacity to found, make, and delimit. "Sovereign cruelty" as it appears in États d'âme sketches, without declaratively instituting, a terrain that is common to analytic aggression and political authority and nevertheless prior to both. Sharing a debt to a violence that would establish mastery, psychoanalysis and sovereignty are at the mercy of this same power, called cruelty, which Derrida presents as possessing the capacity to cannibalize them from within. This self-destructive "sovereign cruelty" is also a way of thinking psychoanalysis and translation. Seen in light of a background cruelty, translation in psychoanalysis ceases to be about finding referential equivalency and instead turns on acknowledging psychoanalysis's own insistence on a terminological instability and associative cross-lingual slippages that make its terms—like the analysand's language—radically open to interpretation, if not interminable context-specific redefinition. "The reading of a symbolic text does not in reality stop at the observation of a one-to-one correspondence between terms. . . . To understand a symbol is to place it back into the dynamism of an intersubjective functioning," Derrida quotes Abraham as remarking in 1961.[36]

In both the psychological and linguistic domain, psychoanalysis's "definitive" characteristic is then its innate resistance to constative, foundational acts, its own foremost among them. Acknowledging this limit—a kind of philosophical escape hatch or eject button—that is at once an integral part of psychoanalysis *and* a mechanism allowing it to supersede itself, makes it possible to think the impact of geopolitically specific contexts on psychoanalysis, its internal resistance to worlding (apart from whatever psychoanalytic associations may propose), and its terminological flexibility in tandem. "It is through its power to put in crisis that psychoanalysis is threatened and thus enters its own crisis," Derrida remarks.[37] Yet the same openness to revolutionary transformation that makes psychoanalysis resist even itself is also the basis of the translational project, where it cannot help but cause the translator pain. "*Avoir mal, faire mal, vouloir du mal, en vouloir à quelqu'un* . . . I already imagine the sufferings of the translator," Derrida writes in the postscript of États d'âme.[38] What in translation studies has come to be known as "untranslatability," following Barbara Cassin, here grows indissociable from the psychoanalytic and political sphere, which are likewise sustained, likewise undone, by a cruelty prior to all three.

At the same time, the concept of cruelty articulated in États d'âme is not instituted by that text, merely reflected there. The type of cruelty Derrida describes also appears in (and helps makes sense of) a translational peculiarity within Soviet psychoanalysis of the 1920s and 1930s. During that time, an overlap between new terminology introduced by Marxism-Leninism and Russian translations of Freud's psychoanalytic terms made psycho-political theories drawing on both possible. While often characterized as being erroneous interpretations of Freud, these hybrid forms of Freudo-Marxism *avant-la-lettre* show the same semantic flexibility Derrida would only begin to imagine decades later and embody the idea of psychoanalysis as science paradoxically defined by its own capacity for self-undoing.

Off with His Tail! The Russian Revolution

At least outwardly, there is little basis for connecting the events of 1917 to Freud's work. Freud's and Lenin's recorded comments on the question of the link between psychoanalysis and the Russian Revolution appear to give a definitive answer: there isn't one. To whatever degree Freud may initially have been a supporter of 1917, by 1930 he was thoroughly pessimistic about the revolution's prospects. Writing in *Civilization and Its Discontents*, he remarked that historical materialism's faith in the creation of a new man was deeply at odds with basic human nature.

> I have no concern with any economic criticism of the communist
> system; I cannot enquire into whether the abolition of private property
> is expedient or advantageous. But I am able to recognize that the psy-
> chological premises on which the system is based are an untenable
> illusion. In abolishing private property . . . we have in no way altered
> the difference in power [*Macht*] and influence [*Einfluss*] which are
> misused by aggressiveness [*die Aggression*], nor have we altered any-
> thing in its nature. Aggressiveness was not created by property.[39]

Here and elsewhere in that text, Freud presents the Bolshevik project as little more than the opportunistic expression of the same type of unavoidable, inborn human aggression to which Einstein would also draw attention several years later.

For his part, Lenin appeared similarly skeptical about Freud. In a famous remark about psychoanalysis to Clara Zetkin, one of his only recorded comments on the topic, Lenin seems to dismiss Freud entirely:

> The expansion [of women comrades' interest in the question of sex
> and marriage] through Freudian hypotheses seems "educated," even to
> arise from science, but it is only the stuff of incompetent amateurs.
> Freudian theory is the fashion these days. I mistrust the sexual theories
> of the articles, treatises, pamphlets, etc., in short, the specific literature

that flourishes luxuriantly in the dirty soil of bourgeois society. . . . It seems to me that these sexual theories springing up like weeds, which for the large part are arbitrary hypotheses, arise from the personal need to justify personal abnormality or hypertrophy in sexual life before bourgeois morality and to solicit its tolerance of them. . . . No matter how wild and revolutionary it thinks itself, it is still really quite bourgeois. . . . There is no place for it in the Party, in the class-conscious, fighting proletariat.[40]

Freud's and Lenin's comments jointly solidify a position that has only grown more prevalent over time: psychoanalysis and the Soviet Union are as oil and water. Whether one looks at the rise of Pavlovian behaviorism or the formal closure of the state-sponsored Russian Psychoanalytic Institute in 1930, the dominant Soviet narrative about psychoanalysis, at least until the Brezhnev era, was that it was incompatible with Marxism-Leninism because it structurally endorsed a bourgeois, individualist perspective. This is also the position that Freudo-Marxist theory in France took as it emerged in the 1970s in the context of the anti-psychiatry movement. In a 1977 issue of *Semiotext(e)* dedicated to *Anti-Oedipus*, French theorist Sylvère Lotringer characterized the situation as one of opposite extremes. Whereas in Europe, the libido was little more than a patch designed to disguise "the increasingly obsolete structure of the family," in the USSR, the libido's revolutionary energy had been "crushed . . . under the heel of the State-Nation-Family."[41] The sociologist Jacques Donzelot put it even more succinctly: "The Soviets have Pavlov, the Americans will have Freud; Stalin by the way prefers, adores, stimuli."[42]

Yet, between 1920 and 1930, a small body of Soviet texts emerged that sought to combine communist doctrine and psychoanalysis, seeing each as an asset, not an impediment, to the other. While this period has been largely overlooked due to its brevity and the failure of the resulting theories to gain traction either in the Soviet Union or abroad, it nevertheless represents an unusual example of psychoanalysis's direct and willing integration into a political movement, and, for a time, that movement's active embrace of psychoanalytic theories and resources, with unusual consequences.

The postrevolutionary synthesis of Freud and Marx was unquestionably helped by the fact that psychoanalysis was already well-established in imperial Russia. Beginning with the publication of the *Interpretation of Dreams* in Russian in 1904—the first translation into any language—a psychoanalytic fever swept the country that was temporarily interrupted by the Russian civil war but not significantly diminished by it. Efforts to organize local psychoanalytic societies at different sites in Russia began as early as 1921, with the foundation of a psychoanalytic group for the study of artistic creativity in Moscow. This served as the basis for the larger and more topically diverse Russian Psychoanalytic Society, also in Moscow, the following year. Organized by Freud's disciple Mosche Wulff (1878–1971) and the Russian psychiatrist Ivan Dmitriyevich Ermakov (1875–1942), whose work had appeared earlier in Freud's journal, the new society's purview included clinical analysis and pedagogy, alongside the study of literature and art. One of Jung's students and a member of Freud's inner circle between 1911 and 1912, the Russian psychoanalyst Sabina Spielrein not only published the first research paper by a Russian contributor in Freud's *Jahrbuch*, but also wrote extensively on a destructive drive opposed to self-preservation before Freud had formulated the death drive. Returning to Soviet Russia in 1923, she taught popular courses on child psychoanalysis at the State Psychoanalytic Institute.

The pedagogical dimension of psychoanalysis was particularly important, given the Communist Party's focus on the need to abolish the old imperial educational system and form the citizens of the future. Extensive support by party leaders meant that Ermakov was even able to set up a Moscow-based "Children's Home and Laboratory" in 1921, a highly innovative psychoanalytic orphanage for "mentally disturbed and homeless young victims of the postrevolutionary era," which was housed in Gorky's former residence in Moscow.[43] Mikhail Etkind points out that the majority of these children were actually the offspring of party executives who, having supposedly given all of their time and energy to the state, were unable to care for their children. (There is even anecdotal evidence that Stalin's son Vasiliy attended for a time.) In 1922, the children's home began receiving support from Narkompros (The People's Commissariat for Education) headed by Lunacharsky and cofounded by Nadezhda Krupskaya, its deputy director as well as Lenin's wife. It is almost certain that Krupskaya was aware of and supported the activities of the school to some degree. She worked closely at Narkompros with two individuals (Stanislav Shatskiy, 1878–1934, and Pavel Blonskiy, 1884–1941) whose names appear on the list of members of the Russian Psychoanalytic Society published by the IPA in 1924.

As Wulff and Ermakov were putting together the Moscow society, the neurophysiologist Alexander Romanovich Luria (1902–1977) was simultaneously organizing the formation of a similar group in Kazan, several hundred miles due east. His efforts and quick success made it possible for the two groups to merge into what was to become the State Psychoanalytic Institute in 1923. As its name suggests, this unique endeavor possessed both the formal backing of the Communist Party and official recognition by the International Psychoanalytic Association. When accepted into IPA, it was one of only three such institutes in the world at the time, and of course the only one with Communist support.[44] Historian Martin Miller sums up the scenario as follows: "It can safely be said (with all the implied ironies, given what was to come later) that no government was ever responsible for supporting psychoanalysis to such an extent, before or after."[45]

Wulff and Ermakov put a provision for a Russian series of Freud's work into the charter establishing the State Psychoanalytic Institute. Intended to make the full set of Freud's German publications readily accessible to a Soviet audience, the thirty-two proposed titles would serve as a Russian standard edition, thereby replacing the more heterogeneous array of translations from the prerevolutionary period. The resulting series, titled the "Psychological and Psychoanalytic Library," was released by Gosizdat, the State Publishing House of the Soviet Union, between 1923 and 1929. Wulff appears to have done the majority of the translations and Ermakov to have written the introductions. Only fifteen of the books actually appeared, however, a number that reflects a changing political environment as the decade progressed. While Ermakov's introductions initially lauded Freud's innovations, in the waning years of the 1920s, following Lenin's death, they increasingly reflected pressure by Soviet authorities to fit psychoanalysis into an ever-narrowing vision of Marxism-Leninism.[46]

There is a good deal of secondary scholarship in Russian and in English on this period for psychoanalysis, but most commentators tend to conclude that the era's psychoanalytic vanguard was a fascinating curiosity doomed from the outset who made only sporadically accurate use of Freud's ideas. This narrative, supported by Freud's and Lenin's own comments, regards the State Psychoanalytic Institute as a last stand for psychoanalysis before the onslaught of Pavlovian behaviorism, a phenomenon possible only within the dying gasps of intellectual and creative freedom under the New Economic Policy. A related version interprets Soviet psychoanalysis as the scientific correlate of Trotsky's political rise and fall. Given Trotsky's well-known support for Freud's work, it makes sense that Trotsky's political fortunes should match Soviet psychoanalysis's own. Indisputably, by the time Freudo-Marxist philosopher Wilhelm Reich arrived in Moscow in 1929, the situation was already dire for psychoanalysis. The last publication by the Psychological and Psychoanalytic Library (Freud's *Future of an Illusion*) appeared in 1930 and the Institute's final report to the IPA the same year.

Yet little attention has been paid to the unusual use Soviet psychoanalysis made of Lenin's theory of spontaneity (*stikhiynost'*) and consciousness (*soznatyel'nost'*), first laid out in *What Is to Be Done? Burning Questions of Our Movement* (1902) and a key concept in Marxism-Leninism. Trosky as well as

Marxist psychoanalysts such as Ermakov (the State Psychoanalytic Institute's founder), Vera Schmidt (director of the psychoanalytic children's home), and Georgiy Malis (a psychiatrist who wrote *The Psychoanalysis of Communism* in 1924), however, all notably used the term "consciousness" *(soznatyel'nost')* in ways that bizarrely fused the Marxist-Leninist idea of class consciousness with an allusion to the psychoanalytic unconscious, translated as "bessoznatel'noye" (lit. that which is without awareness) in Russian. This duality additionally appears in the writing of figures as prominent as Nadezhda Krupskaya.

The Russian common noun *soznatyel'nost'* (derived from *soznaniye*, "consciousness") means awareness in the sense of sensitivity to one's surroundings. It is also the technical term Lenin employs in *What Is to Be Done?* to describe the level of political class-consciousness needed by the revolution's leaders. There he presents the idea that true revolution can only be carried out by an industrial proletariat, not the peasantry, and argues that this proletariat must be trained in a specific way. A worker's daily struggle against exploitation by his or her immediate working environment, and that worker's participation in wider, organized struggles against groups of employers, will provide basic insight into the nature of class, a position Lenin characterizes as "spontaneous" *(stikhiyniy,* meaning "elemental" or "natural"). While the worker will learn a number of important things from involvement in these conflicts— the existence of class divisions, antagonism of the bourgeoisie, tendency of the government to side against the workers, need for political activity—this knowledge will only be sufficient for "militant" action, not for truly revolutionary activity.

In order to ascend from spontaneity to *soznatyel'nost'* (consciousness/awareness), something else is needed. As Lenin put it, "Class political consciousness can be brought to workers *only from without,* that is, only from outside the economic struggle, from outside the sphere of relations between workers and employers."[47] The acquisition of *soznatyel'nost'* had to involve the proletariat's transcendence of their own class economic concerns and arrival at a position that could account for the wider organization of all classes of society and grasp the forces structuring it. *Soznatyel'nost',* in other words, would be the position from which an individual would be able to view the totality of social relations. It involved being able to respond to all instances of "tyranny, oppression, violence and abuse no matter what class is affected." Rather than this constituting an elitist position, as later caricatured, Lenin's stance implied that the proletariat's natural spontaneity would need to be supplemented by consciousness in a process of *Bildung.*[48] Spontaneity was a necessary but not sufficient condition for revolution.

In several works from the mid-1920s, however, Marxist-Leninist class consciousness began to shade into a Freudian account of the psyche, and vice versa. In *Literature and Revolution* (1923), Trotsky repeatedly equates the Freudian unconscious with an elemental state of class-political spontaneity that he indicates should be overcome. The Freudian unconscious in Trotsky's usage is something to be suppressed or surmounted en route to a higher form of psychological existence, poetic expression, and social organization. As Trotsky puts it, human beings' ability to conquer their feelings and raise their instincts to the pinnacles of class-political consciousness (*soznatel'nost'*) will determine the extent to which they can become psychological exemplars of a new "sociobiological type."[49] Describing futurism as the first "conscious" (*soznatel'noye*) form of art in history, he goes on to discuss how the new urban language of tramcars and electricity prompts poets to write works that "penetrate the dark shell of the unconscious [*bessoznatel'nogo*]" and so to reflect a mass psychological transformation that complements the transformation in the social environment.[50] Trotsky frames "social construction and psychological self-education" as aspects of the same process to such an extent that he does not hesitate to describe the 1917 Revolution as the process of driving "the unconscious [*bessoznatel'noe*] out of politics by overthrowing monarchy and class . . . with clear and open Soviet dictatorship."[51] Time and again, *Literature and Revolution* aligns the Freudian unconscious with a state of class-political ignorance or situates it as an evolutionary antecedent to Communism. While insisting the unconscious must be vanquished, Trostky nevertheless remains firmly committed to a psychoanalytic framework.

Georgiy Malis's short book *Psychoanalysis of Communism* repeats the gesture, even citing a line from Trotsky as its epigraph. "What, then, is our revolution if not a mad rebellion against the elemental [*stikhiynogo*], senseless, biological automatism of life— . . . in the name of a conscious [*soznatyel'nogo*], rational, purposeful, and dynamic beginning to life?"[52] Trotsky is quoting Lenin in the passage, but his tendency to slip between a psychological and political register, combined with Malis's placement of the quote immediately below his title, makes the reference to a "conscious" beginning of life take on an added analytic dimension. Like Trotsky, Malis begins from the premise that psychoanalysis is the means whereby Marxism can be extended to the study of the psyche. He reasons that if, as per Marx, "social existence determines consciousness" (*bytie opredeliayet soznanie*), psychoanalysis is important because it shows the manner in which unconscious tendencies collide with social reality to shape human mentality.[53] Citing Trotsky's claim about the need for every person to master the "element of the unconscious" in their soul, Malis also carries this idea significantly further in his work, presenting repression as a means of generating useful psychological energy for society.

Through sporadic references to Freud's *Totem and Taboo*, Malis contends that human phylogenetic development roughly aligns with Freud's understanding of individual psychosexual development. The human species has progressed from a primary narcissism, embodied in the "savage's animism," to the libido's selection of an object, represented by the establishment of religion, and—at least in Communist society—to being on the brink of a momentous "third stage" that will involve a free choice of object no longer determined either by religion or by the Oedipus complex. To reach this third stage, Malis proposes the Soviet educational system be reorganized with psychoanalytic principles in mind. Instead of teaching children facts and figures, educators should seek to tap into the innate energy all children possess by virtue of having repressed their infantile experiences. In bourgeois society, such energy is wasted through displacement into fantasy, art for art's sake, and other "asocial" behaviors. Soviet education, by contrast, should curate the sublimation process so as not to leave any "undischarged reserves of psychoenergy" that might express themselves on an individual level.[54] Future workers trained to sublimate their desires in activities for the common good would have no need to pursue pleasure privately, as the social system would satisfy all their psychical needs. In this third stage, Malis claims there will, in effect, no longer be any conflict between the pleasure and reality principles, as man's unconscious world, rife with unbridled desires, would grow indecipherable from a lived reality capable of fulfilling them.

This declaration that the social system of the future would conform to man's unconscious world attempts to make the Marxist philosophy of history, with its massive critique of the intending subject, compatible with agential desire. Among other things, psychoanalysis offered thinkers in the Soviet Union of the 1920s an opportunity to cut the Gordian knot between individual psychology and historical materialism. Since the psychoanalytic subject was not an intending one, writers like Malis could frame this subject as uniquely compatible with historical materialism's nonagential perspective and suggest the subject's capacity to be psychologically optimized for a new social reality. While reflecting Lenin's claims, Malis's conflicted presentation of a self-determining subject simultaneously at the mercy of forces beyond him or herself, also cuts to the very core of Lenin's and others' investigations into the conditions for revolution. It addresses how class-political consciousness, or any other formation necessary for revolution, will come about, opening the question of whether it is something that can be intentionally instilled or must emerge through a more indirect route, lacking an agent. Malis ultimately concludes, for example, that the profession of "educator" will disappear over time, as all members of society will be capable of serving in that role. Without naming Lenin outright, Derrida identifies the same problem in *États d'âme*, offering a covert reference to the 1902 text along the way: "How an authentic auto-nomy . . . institutes itself and *must* do so, on the basis of a hetero-nomy that still survives what survives it . . . this is one of the forms of the question "What is to be done?" that I would like to take . . . beyond all possible sovereignty and cruelty."[55]

This link between the psychological and political senses of *soznatyel'nost'* reappears in other educational treatises written by Marxist psychoanalysts of the time, all of whom were focused on how to shape the mindset of the new man. Ermakov's introduction to a 1922 collection of Freud's articles (*Basic Psychological Theories in Psychoanalysis*) includes a set of remarks on the particular value of psychoanalysis for pedagogy. Observing that the "most interesting" area of Freud's research concerned the "realm of the child's soul," Ermakov goes on to suggest that psychoanalysis is of fundamental import for teachers because it enables them to gain deeper knowledge of "their charges' psyches and particularities of thinking" and thus to "grow closer to them."[56] He presents Freud's theories as an opportunity to revise and partially de-hierarchize the relationship between teacher and student. In a Rousseauian version of the educative project, Ermakov—like Malis—seems to suggest psychoanalysis as the royal road to a new Soviet learning environment because of its ability to provide educators with abstract methodological principles, not clinical interventions. Even dream analysis can be harmlessly incorporated into this project: "When we familiarize ourselves with a child's dreams, we acquire very important data for assessing that area of the unconscious [*bes-soznatel'nogo*] which it is the teacher's task, by way of pedagogical techniques, to translate into consciousness [*soznanie*]."[57] Ermakov presents psychoanalysis as a tool with which to bring repressed phenomena to light in the service of the formation of a new man. While he describes a transition from the unconscious to consciousness or *soznanie*, meaning the mental state of being conscious (related to, but not the same as, Lenin's *soznatel'nost'*), there is, as in Malis's and Trotsky's texts, a certain degree of ambiguity about whether such consciousness is strictly psychological.[58] Ermakov implies that an educator's knowledge of children's dreams will allow them to convert the latent content of pupils' dreams into manifest content. In the Soviet educational context, where teachers were responsible for cultivating new citizens, the line also suggests that dream interpretation plays some kind of role in preparing young minds to become socially aware in Lenin's class-political sense.

The ambiguity reappears in Nadezhda Krupskaya's 1932 remarks to the Communist Academy on pedology. There, Krupskaya singles out psychoanalysis for praise as an educational endeavor. Like Ermakov, she presents it as a key resource in forming the new man. "It would be wrong," she declares "to throw the baby out with the bathwater in the heat of critique of the Freudians, to abandon the use of valuable material on the issue of translating subconscious impulses into conscious [*soznatel'nye*] ones, which is an extremely important pedagogical task for us." Although garbling the distinction between the subconscious and unconscious, Krupskaya nevertheless frames psychoanalysis as valuable primarily because of what it offers Soviet pedagogy: the opportunity to bring children's nonconscious psychological experience to light. A variation of this move appears in Vera Schmidt's report to the IPA on the psychoanalytic children's home.[59]

Soviet psychoanalysts' attribution of a jointly psychoanalytic and ideological meaning to *soznatyel'nost'* reconfigures the divide between "Freud" and "the state" as metaphorically staged by the scissors on Major's 1984 issue of *Cahiers Confrontation*. By upsetting the standard narrative about psychoanalysis and the Soviet Union's antithetical relationship, in favor of one about their innate compatibility, these writers' works—like the Wolf-Man's better-known case history—also dramatically reconfigure what it means to speak of a psychoanalytic "terra incognita."

Writing in 1996, the Russian translator of the *Vocabulaire* is content to declare the total lack of "any stable tradition of the translation of psychoanalytic terminology" in the Russian language, and to cite both that deficiency and the genesis of new body of psychoanalytic literature in the West as the primary motivations for undertaking the translation.[60] The suggestion is, much as in Roudinesco's comments, that psychoanalysis is essentially alien to the former Eastern Bloc. "All citations of Freud's work have been translated anew, although, of course, the translator considered the attempts of both old Russian translations of Freud, and the English and German editions of Laplanche and Pontalis' book."[61] Yet emphasizing the need for psychoanalysis to be brought or imported to Russian-speaking regions overlooks its prior existence there, and simultaneously reinforces a tired narrative of center and periphery. Such an account is at odds with psychoanalysis's presence within imperial Russia and the Soviet Union from the outset, as well as with those regions' role within (and influence on) psychoanalysis. Moreover, this style of thinking misses that both the Wolf-Man's case history and Soviet psychoanalysis are, in fact, sources for imagining the synthesis of "state [*état*]" and the "psychoanalytic profession [*état*]" that Major, the EGP conference, and Derrida frame as a crucial part of imagining psychoanalysis's future.

The idea of a Russo-Soviet dimension of the analytic project is nevertheless one for which recent critical literature on psychoanalysis and Marxism has yet to account. Without constituting a unified canon, Freudo-Marxism might be described as the roughly cohesive line of inquiry, identifiable by its double paternity, within the significantly larger field of scholarship that relates the "interiority" of consciousness to the "exteriority" of communal life by attending to questions of place, politics, economics, and un/translatability. A potential influence on Austrian psychoanalytic renegade Wilhelm Reich's work (rather than an inheritor of it), Soviet psychoanalysis is nevertheless typically framed both outside the recognized temporal and geographical coordinates of Freudo-Marxist scholarship. It might easily, however, be seen as part of the tradition addressing psychopolitical questions that extends from the Frankfurt School and the antipsychiatry movement to research on psychoanalysis and de/colo-niality, and Žižek's Lacanian Marxism. Positioned in this way, Soviet psycho-analysis, and other "misapplications" of the psychoanalytic method in a politicized context, would cease to be an irrelevant footnote, and represent a site of potential dialogue with recent publications by figures such as Franco "Bifo" Berardi, Bruno Bosteels, Todd McGowan, Samo Tomšič, and Alenka Zupančič, among many others.[62]

Beyond this, however, the Russo-Soviet psychoanalytic tradition illustrates an example of "sovereign cruelty" in which psychoanalysis is defined by its capacity to be open to new horizons by way of an auto-destructive, auto-resistant, even auto-revolutionary function that produces its own beyond. Both the Wolf-Man's encrypted lexicon and the level of flexibility between political and psy-chological understandings of "consciousness" in the Soviet context help point to the anasemic, or nonreferential, dimension of psychoanalytic terminology, in which it is a question not of establishing determinative definitions but of actively engaging a wide array of interpretive possibilities. Cruelty here describes an innate linguistic resistance to systematization that is common to both the psychoanalytic lexicon and the patient's own. Conversely, the impossibility of ever arriving at a perfect translation between languages in any context, is, Derrida suggests, itself evidence of a cruelty that is prior to either translation or psychoanalysis. Once again: "*Avoir mal, faire mal, vouloir du mal, en vouloir à quelqu'un* . . . I already imagine the sufferings of the translator."

The idea of such a cruelty, which interrogates the ground of sovereignty, shifting it from the state of exception (where the sovereign is he who transcends the law) to one in which power is derived from a capacity to produce one's own undoing, makes it possible to think of Soviet psychoanalysis as an opening onto the same "impossible horizon" that Derrida's later formulations in *États d'âme* suggest. The "beyond" of psychoanalysis is the beyond, the *jenseits*, that Freud actively intends and the beyond, the *au-delà*, that exceeds Freud's control, spilling into a future prefigured by psychoanalysis but not limited to it in any doctrinal sense. Thinking in this way necessitates reimagining the meaning of psychoanalysis "elsewhere" and doing so in a manner with which postcolonial critique has long been familiar.

Acknowledging psychoanalysis as a colonial discipline structured around the consolidation of a white European national self through positing a primitive anthropological "other," Ranjana Khanna nevertheless proposes a reconfigured psychoanalysis, one read "against the grain." In *Dark Continents*, she suggests psychoanalysis as a means through which "contingent postcolonial futures can be imagined ethically."[63] In *Unconscious Dominions: Psychoanalysis, Colonial Trauma, and Global Sovereignties*, the volume's editors note the paradox whereby psychoanalysis was "practiced and elaborated in colonial settings" but also became a powerful critique of colonialism, in the works of figures like Ashis Nandy, Frantz Fanon, Homi K. Bhabha. The closing essay to that work, also by Khanna, observes that "the international demands of psychoanalysis a new version of itself, as it did of Marxism some time earlier," and pushes to think how the global space of late capitalism changes how analysis might be understood.[64] In the same vein, the group of contributors writing in "What Is the Future of Psychoanalysis in the Academy?" question how an acknowledgment of the unconscious might shape the telling of history as such (Omnia El Shakry), speculate on psychoanalysis as a way of addressing life in the face of the finitude in a globalized twenty-first century (Zahid Chaudhary), and present it as a site of disputation for the neoliberal tendency within the academy to reduce knowledge to its "instrumental and functional dimension" (Eli Zaretsky). Perhaps tellingly, the latest mission statement by the IPA is organized around the platform "IPA and the World."[65]

These thinkers collectively engage with psychoanalysis as a phenomenon that is at once politically and psychologically resistant. This cruel resistance also extends to the matter of translation. Lamenting the difficulty of identifying "equivalents" for fundamental psychoanalytic concepts such as *Besetzung*, the Russian translator of the *Vocabulaire* observes the equal inadequacy of the French *investissement*, the English "cathexis," and the Russian *vlozhenie*. She concludes that the best way to help Russian readers avoid confusion arising from inevitably problematic Russian-language translations of Laplanche and Pontalis's French is to simply omit the passages that pose exceptional translational difficulty. In the resulting Russian text, such elisions are marked as "[. . .]" in consequence. These gaps bear out a cruelty within language that is also within and beyond psychoanalysis. They make clear that translational economy—the game of finding just the right way of saying the same thing in a different language—does not exist in and of itself but must be actively *instituted*.

Bibliography

Abraham, Nicolas. "The Shell and the Kernel: The Scope and Originality of Freudian Psychoanalysis." In Nicolas Abraham and Maria Torok, *The Shell and the Kernel: Renewals of Psychoanalysis*, edited and translated by Nicholas T. Rand, 79–98. Chicago: University of Chicago Press, 1994.

Abraham, Nicholas, and Maria Torok. *The Wolf Man's Magic Word: A Cryptonymy.* Translated by Nicholas Rand. Minneapolis: University of Minnesota Press, 1986.

Almeida, Andréa Carvalho Mendes de, Bela Sister, Cristiane Sammarone, et al. "Entrevista: Elizabeth Roudinesco—(In)fidelidade à aventura freudiana." *Percurso*, no. 37 (2006). https://www.freudiana.com.br/sem-categoria/elizabeth -roudinesco-in-fidelidade-a-aventura-freudiana.html.

Anderson, Warwick, Deborah Jenson, and Richard C. Killer, eds. *Unconscious Dominions: Psychoanalysis, Colonial Trauma, and Global Sovereignties.* Durham, NC: Duke University Press, 2011.

Baudrillard, Jean, and Jacques Derrida. *Pourquoi la guerre aujourd'hui?* Edited by René Major. Paris: Lignes, 2015.

Bauer, Raymond Augustine. *The New Man in Soviet Psychology.* Cambridge, MA: Harvard University Press, 1952.

Berardi, Franco "Bifo." *The Soul at Work: From Alienation to Autonomy.* South Pasadena, CA: Semiotext(e), 2009.

Bosteels, Bruno. *Marx and Freud in Latin America: Politics, Psychoanalysis, and Religion in Times of Terror.* New York: Verso, 2012.

Damousi, Joy, and Mariano Ben Plotkin, eds. *The Transnational Unconscious: Essays in the History of Psychoanalysis and Transnationalism.* New York: Palgrave Macmillan, 2009.

Deleuze, Gilles, and Félix Guattari. *Anti-Oedipus: Capitalism and Schizophrenia.* Translated by Robert Hurley, Mark Seem, and Helen R. Lane. Minneapolis: University of Minnesota Press, 2000.

Derrida, Jacques. "Fors: The Anglish Words of Nicholas Abraham and Maria Torok." Translated by Barbara Johnson. Foreword to Abraham and Torok, *The Wolf Man's Magic Word*, xi–xlviii.

———. "Geopsychoanalysis: '. . . and the Rest of the World.'"*American Imago* 48, no. 2 (Summer 1991): 199–231.

———. "Psychoanalysis Searches the States of Its Soul: The Impossible Beyond of a Sovereign Cruelty." In *Without Alibi*, edited and translated by Peggy Kamuf, 238–80. Stanford, CA: Stanford University Press, 2002.

Desgroseillers, René. "En son nom propre: La carrière et l'œuvre de René Major." *Filigrane* 11, no. 2 (2002): 157–84.

Donzelot, Jacques. "An Antisociology." *Semiotext(e)* 2, no. 3 (1977): 27–44.

Einstein, Albert, and Sigmund Freud. *Why War?* Translated by Stuart Gilbert. International Institute of Intellectual Cooperation, League of Nations, 1933.

Freud, Sigmund. *Gesammelte Werke*, vol. 1. Frankfurt am Main: Fischer Taschenbuch
Verlag, 1999.
———. *Gesammelte Werke*, vol. 9. Frankfurt am Main: Fischer Taschenbuch Verlag,
1999.
———. *Gesammelte Werke*, vol. 12. Frankfurt am Main: Fischer Taschenbuch Verlag,
1999.
———. *Gesammelte Werke*, vol. 14. Frankfurt am Main: Fischer Taschenbuch Verlag,
1999.
———. *Gesammelte Werke*, vol. 17. Frankfurt am Main: Fischer Taschenbuch Verlag,
1999.
———. *Osnovyye psikhologicheskiye teorii v psikhoanalize: Sbornik statey*. Moscow:
Gosizdat, 1923.
———. *Standard Edition of the Complete Psychological Works*, vol. 17. Translated by
James Strachey. London: Vintage, 2001.
———. *Standard Edition of the Complete Psychological Works*, vol. 21. Translated by
James Strachey. London: Hogarth, 1993.
Hartnack, Christiane. *Psychoanalysis in Colonial India*. New York: Oxford
University Press, 2001.
Heimann, Paula. "Entwicklungssprünge und das Auftreten der Grausamkeit." In
Bis hierher und nicht weiter: Ist die menschliche Aggression unbefreidbar?, edited
by Alexander Mitscherlich, 105–7. Munich: Piper, 1969.
Herzog, Dagmar. *Cold War Freud: Psychoanalysis in an Age of Catastrophes*.
Cambridge: Cambridge University Press, 2017.
Khan, M. Masud R. Editorial Preface. In J. Laplanche and J.-B. Pontalis, *The
Language of Psycho-analysis*, v. Translated by Donald Nicholson-Smith. New
York: W. W. Norton, 1973.
Khanna, Ranjana. *Dark Continents: Psychoanalysis and Colonialism*. Durham, NC:
Duke University Press, 2003.
Laplanche, J., and J. B. Pontalis. *Slovar' po psikhoanalizu*. Translated by N. S.
Avtonomova. Moscow: Vysshaya shkola, 1996.
Lenin, Vladimir Ilych. "What Is to Be Done?" In *Collected Works*, vol. 5. Moscow:
Progress, 1961.
Lih, Lars. *Lenin Rediscovered: What Is to Be Done? in Context*. Chicago: Haymarket
Books, 2008.
Lotringer, Sylvère. "Libido Unbound: The Politics of 'Schizophrenia.'" *Semiotext(e)*
2, no. 3 (1977): 5–10.
Major, René. "Des conditions psychanalytiques d'une référence aux droits de
l'homme." *Cahiers Confrontation*, no. 11 (Printemps 1984): 9–22.
———. *La démocratie en cruauté*. Paris: Galilée, 2003.
———. *États d'âme de la psychanalyse: Adresse aux États Généraux de la
Psychanalyse*. Paris: Galilée, 2000.
———, ed. *États généraux de la psychanalyse*. Paris: Aubier, 2003.
Malis, Georgiy. *Psikhoanaliz kommunizma*. Khar'kov: Kosmos, 1924.

Matza, Thomas. *Shock Therapy: Psychology, Precarity, and Well-Being in Postsocialist Russia*. Durham, NC: Duke University Press, 2018.

McGowan, Todd. *Capitalism and Desire: The Psychic Cost of Free Markets*. New York: Columbia University Press, 2016.

Miller, Martin A. *Freud and the Bolsheviks: Psychoanalysis in Imperial Russia and the Soviet Union*. New Haven, CT: Yale University Press, 1998.

Milnitzky, Fátima, Gisela Haddad, Mario Pablo Fuks, Paulina Rocha, and Sidnei Goldberg. "Quem escreve História da Psicanálise?" *Percurso*, no. 38 (June 2007). http://revistapercurso.uol.com.br/index.php?apg=artigo_view&ida=231&ori =edicao&id_edicao=38.

Mitscherlich, Alexander. "Zwei Arten der Grausamkeit." In *Toleranz: Überprüfung eines Begriffs*, 168–89. Frankfurt: Suhrkamp Taschenbuch, 1974.

Roudinesco, Elizabeth. "Introduction to the Estates General of Psychoanalysis (July 8, 2000)." *Journal of European Psychoanalysis*, no. 10–11 (Winter–Fall 2000).

Said, Edward W. *Freud and the Non-European*. London: Verso, 2003.

Schmidt, Vera. *Psychoanalytische Erziehung in Sowjetrussland*. Leipzig: Internationaler Psychoanalytischer Verlag, 1924.

Tomšič, Samo. *The Capitalist Unconscious*. New York: Verso, 2015.

Trotsky, L. *Literatura i revoliutsiya*. Moscow: Krasnaya nov', 1923.

Wolfe, Harriet. "IPA in the World." International Psychoanalytic Association. Accessed December 1, 2021. https://www.ipa.world/IPA/en/IPA1/our_mission _2021.aspx

The Wolf-Man by the Wolf-Man. Edited and translated by Muriel Gardiner. New York: Basic Books, 1971.

Zetkin, Clara. *Erinnerungen an Lenin*. Berlin: Dietz, 1961.

Notes

1. I am grateful to both Gavin Arnall and Katie Chenoweth for the invitation to participate in this volume and for their feedback along the way, as well as that of the anonymous reviewers. Earlier versions of the chapter were presented at a symposium on neurodiversities at Duke University (October 2018); at a Modern Language Association Convention panel on "Ideologies of Health in Soviet Literature Politics" (January 2019); and at an American Comparative Literature Association seminar on "Psychoanalysis in the Vernacular" (March 2019). My thanks to Jill Jarvis for her insights outside those contexts. The first epigraph is from Gilles Deleuze and Félix Guattari, *Anti-Oedipus: Capitalism and Schizophrenia*, trans. Robert Hurley, Mark Seem, and Helen R. Lane (Minneapolis: University of Minnesota Press, 2000), 55. The second epigraph can be found in Jacques Derrida, "Psychoanalysis Searches the States of Its Soul: The Impossible Beyond of a Sovereign Cruelty," in *Without Alibi*, ed. and trans. Peggy Kamuf (Stanford, CA: Stanford University Press, 2002), 266. In instances where no translator is specified, the translation is my own.

2. N. S. Avtonomova in J. Laplanche and J. B. Pontalis, *Slovar' po psikhoanalizu*, trans. N. S. Avtonomova (Moscow: Vysshaya shkola, 1996), 5.

3. Jacques Derrida, "Geopsychoanalysis: '. . . and the Rest of the World,'"*American Imago* 48, no. 2 (Summer 1991): 199–231. On psychoanalysis and colonialism see, for example, Warwick Anderson, Deborah Jenson, and Richard C. Killer, eds., *Unconscious Dominions: Psychoanalysis, Colonial Trauma, and Global Sovereignties* (Durham, NC: Duke University Press, 2011); Joy Damousi and Mariano Ben Plotkin, eds., *The Transnational Unconscious: Essays in the History of Psychoanalysis and Transnationalism* (New York: Palgrave Macmillan, 2009); Christiane Hartnack, *Psychoanalysis in Colonial India* (New York: Oxford University Press, 2001); Ranjana Khanna, *Dark Continents: Psychoanalysis and Colonialism* (Durham, NC: Duke University Press, 2003); Edward W. Said, *Freud and the Non-European* (London: Verso, 2003).

4. Laplanche and Pontalis, *Slovar'*, 20.

5. Nicolas Abraham, "The Shell and the Kernel: The Scope and Originality of Freudian Psychoanalysis," in Nicolas Abraham and Maria Torok, *The Shell and the Kernel: Renewals of Psychoanalysis*, ed. and trans. Nicholas T. Rand (Chicago: University of Chicago Press, 1994), 79–98.

6. M. Masud R. Khan, editorial preface to J. Laplanche and J.-B. Pontalis, *The Language of Psycho-Analysis*, trans. Donald Nicholson-Smith (New York: W. W. Norton, 1973), v.

7. *États d'âme de la psychanalyse: Adresse aux États Généraux de la Psychanalyse* (Paris: Galilée, 2000) appeared as a stand-alone work before the conference proceedings were published. Major's edited volume, *États généraux de la psychanalyse* (Paris: Aubier, 2003), reproduces Derrida's text as it is found the Galilée edition. In the English, Peggy Kamuf refers to the *États Généraux de la Psychanalyse* as the "States General," not the "Estates-General," which is the typical English phrase (and punctuation) used for the 1789 event. This is presumably to avoid English-language readers' resulting confusion with a conference called the "Estates-General of Psychoanalysis," which would not make it clear that the French term *état* may refer equally to a nation-state and to the three estates of the realm under the ancien régime, among a number of other possibilities. I have retained use of Estates-General here to highlight the important connection of Major's title to the French Revolution, but I also discuss the multiple meanings of *état* later in the piece.

8. Major, *États généraux*, 9 and 12.

9. Uribe delivered a paper entitled "Le fantasme Pinochet" in 2000. On Major and Derrida's earlier collaboration, see René Desgroseillers, "En son nom propre : La carrière et l'œuvre de René Major," *Filigrane* 11, no. 2 (2002): 157–84.

10. Described in Dagmar Herzog, *Cold War Freud: Psychoanalysis in an Age of Catastrophes* (Cambridge: Cambridge University Press, 2017), 5–7.

11. Sérgio Paul Rouanet, Antonio Negri, and Tariq Ali were the main speakers. Derrida was diagnosed with pancreatic cancer in 2003 and did not attend the Rio gathering. The comment was made by Elizabeth Roudinesco in an interview with

the Brazilian journal *Percurso*. See Andréa Carvalho Mendes de Almeida, Bela Sister, Cristiane Sammarone, et al., "Entrevista: Elizabeth Roudinesco—(In) fidelidade à aventura freudiana," *Percurso*, no. 37 (2006), https://www.freudiana.com .br/sem-categoria/elizabeth-roudinesco-in-fildelidade-a-aventura-freudiana.html.

12. Fátima Milnitzky, Gisela Haddad, Mario Pablo Fuks, Paulina Rocha, and Sidnei Goldberg, "Quem escreve História da Psicanálise?" *Percurso*, no. 38 (June 2007), http://revistapercurso.uol.com.br/index.php?apg=artigo_view&ida=231&ori =edicao&id_edicao=38.

13. Almeida, "Entrevista: Elizabeth Roudinesco."

14. René Major, *La démocratie en cruauté* (Paris: Galilée, 2003); Jean Baudrillard and Jacques Derrida, *Pourquoi la guerre aujourd'hui?*, ed. René Major (Paris: Lignes, 2015).

15. Freud and Einstein corresponded in German between July and September 1932. Their exchange was published in English in 1933. See Albert Einstein and Sigmund Freud, *Why War?*, trans. Stuart Gilbert (International Institute of Intellectual Cooperation, League of Nations, 1933).

16. Major, *États généraux*, 9.

17. Elizabeth Roudinesco, "Introduction to the Estates General of Psychoanalysis (July 8, 2000)," *Journal of European Psychoanalysis*, no. 10–11 (Winter–Fall 2000). The original French of Roudinesco's talk can be found in Major, *États généraux*, 31–42.

18. Derrida, "Psychoanalysis Searches," 238. Emphasis Derrida's.

19. Derrida, 239.

20. In this sense, it is the opposite of German psychoanalyst Alexander Mitscherlich's discussion of Freudian *Grausamkeit* in "Two Types of Cruelty" from 1974. There Mitscherlich establishes cruelty as the human being's defining characteristic, before going on to argue for a distinction between "cruelty as pleasure" (which merely satisfies personal ends) and "cruelty as work." He defines a remorselessly destructive form of bloodlust openly sanctioned by society and at the root of tragedies such as the death camps at Treblinka and Auschwitz and the massacres at Katyn and My Lai. See Alexander Mitscherlich, "Zwei Arten der Grausamkeit," in *Toleranz. Überprüfung eines Begriffs* (Frankfurt: Suhrkamp Taschenbuch, 1974), 168–89, and Herzog's discussion in *Cold War Freud*, 123–50. Herzog notes that Mitscherlich's training analyst, Paula Heimann, also wrote on the topic of *Grausamkeit* in her "Entwicklungssprünge und das Auftreten der Grausamkeit," which appears in *Bis hierher und nicht weiter: Ist die menschliche Aggression unbefreidbar?*, ed. Alexander Mitscherlich (Munich: Piper, 1969), 105–7.

21. Derrida, "Psychoanalysis Searches," 241. Translation modified.

22. "L'État freudien," issue of *Cahiers Confrontation*, no. 11 (Printemps 1984). Adami's capitalization is worth mentioning. In French titles that begin with a definite article, it is perfectly acceptable to capitalize only the "more significant" second word. Adami's use of "l'État" follows this convention but also plays with it. The open mouth of the scissors to the left resembles a capital "L," even though the

definite article in "l'État" is technically lowercase. A similar phenomenon occurs with the "missing" acute accent in the word "État" itself. The apostrophe in "l'Etat" does double duty, functioning both as a contraction and as the acute accent on the capital "E." Just as in the rest of the cover, Adami's visual choices help to blur the (seeming) distinction between "Freud" and "the state."

23. René Major, "Des conditions psychanalytiques d'une référence aux droits de l'homme," *Cahiers Confrontation*, no. 11 (Printemps 1984): 9.

24. Sigmund Freud, *Standard Edition of the Complete Psychological Works*, vol. 17, trans. James Strachey (London: Vintage, 2001), 37.

25. *The Wolf-Man by the Wolf-Man*, ed. and trans. Muriel Gardiner (New York: Basic Books, 1971), 89.

26. Nicholas Abraham and Maria Torok, *The Wolf Man's Magic Word: A Cryptonymy*, trans. Nicholas Rand (Minneapolis: University of Minnesota Press, 1986), 2.

27. Reprinted together in the *The Wolf-Man by the Wolf-Man*.

28. Derrida, "Psychoanalysis Searches," 241.

29. See Einstein and Freud, *Why War?*, 19–20. The League of Nations' sanctioned English translation departs from Freud's German in a number of important ways. "Menschliche Agressivität" becomes "aggressive instinct," and "die . . . unheilvollste, weil zügelloseste Form des Konfliktes unter menschlichen Gemeinschaften" is given as "the most typical, most cruel, and most extravagant form of conflict between man and man." The English adjective "extravagant" misses Einstein's reference to a force incapable of being controlled in the German, and the idea of a conflict between "man and man" potentially indicates aggression restricted to the level of individuals, as opposed to taking place on an interpersonal and international scale simultaneously.

30. Sigmund Freud, *Gesammelte Werke*, vol. 1 (Frankfurt am Main: Fischer Taschenbuch Verlag, 1999), 245, and Freud, *Gesammelte Werke*, vol. 17 (Frankfurt am Main: Fischer Taschenbuch Verlag, 1999), 197. Unless otherwise noted, all English translations of Freud that appear in the body of the text are from Strachey's *Standard Edition*.

31. Freud, *Gesammelte Werke*, vol. 9 (Frankfurt am Main: Fischer Taschenbuch Verlag, 1999), 47.

32. Freud, *Gesammelte Werke*, vol. 13 (Frankfurt am Main: Fischer Taschenbuch Verlag, 1999), 84.

33. Freud, *Gesammelte Werke*, vol. 14 (Frankfurt am Main: Fischer Taschenbuch Verlag, 1999), 471.

34. As part of an overall attempt to come to grips with the atrocities of World War II, Sade's understanding of cruelty was a major focus in postwar French critical theory. Whether cruelty in Sade is figured as a power of transformative self-negation (Blanchot); the expression of a cyclically self-destructive universe (Klossowski); an effort to forge emotional connection (Beauvoir); or the right to both completely forsake interpersonal responsibility and, simultaneously, become the victim of that

forsaking (Bataille), cruelty for French thinkers of the 1950s and 1960s was largely bloodless and embedded in an iterative process of instituting sovereignty. Klossowski and Beauvoir in particular take Sade's treatise as an argument that revolution merely pays lip service to an illusory freedom while nevertheless ensuring that everyone remain firmly in chains.

35. In the political treatise "Yet Another Effort, Frenchmen, If You Would Become Republicans" interpolated into *Philosophy of the Bedroom*, Sade defends the idea that murders of passion are less cruel than executions carried out by guillotine. Decrying the horrors of the death penalty and the hypocrisy of revolution, he envisions a republican future in which public institutions *support*, rather than check, libertine pleasure. The honesty and sincerity required to commit a murder of passion always make such a crime far less cruel in Sade's eyes than death by guillotine, imbricated in a twisted and spectacular logic of punishment and a mere theatrics of justice.

36. Quoted in Jacques Derrida, "Fors: The Anglish Words of Nicholas Abraham and Maria Torok," in Abraham and Torok, *The Wolf Man's Magic Word*, xxix.

37. Derrida, "Psychoanalysis Searches," 269.

38. Derrida, 280.

39. Sigmund Freud, *Standard Edition of the Complete Psychological Works*, vol. 21, trans. James Strachey (London: Hogarth, 1993), 113.

40. Lenin as cited in Clara Zetkin, *Erinnerungen an Lenin* (Berlin: Dietz, 1961).

41. Sylvère Lotringer, "Libido Unbound: The Politics of 'Schizophrenia,'" *Semiotext(e)* 2, no. 3 (1977): 8.

42. Jacques Donzelot, "An Antisociology," *Semiotext(e)* 2, no. 3 (1977): 34.

43. Martin A. Miller, *Freud and the Bolsheviks: Psychoanalysis in Imperial Russia and the Soviet Union* (New Haven, CT: Yale University Press, 1998), 64.

44. The two others were in Vienna and Berlin, respectively.

45. Miller, *Freud*, 68.

46. Miller, 53–68.

47. Vladimir Ilych Lenin, "What Is to Be Done?," in *Collected Works*, vol. 5 (Moscow: Progress, 1961), 422.

48. Lars Lih offers a superior and detailed historical analysis of how Lenin uses the terms *stikhinost'* and *soznatel'nost'* in *What Is to Be Done?* See *Lenin Rediscovered: What Is to Be Done? in Context* (Chicago: Haymarket Books, 2008).

49. L. Trotsky, *Literatura i revoliutsiya* (Moscow: Krasnaya nov', 1923), 189.

50. Trotsky, 123.

51. Trotsky, 189.

52. Quoted in Georgiy Malis, *Psikhoanaliz kommunizma* (Khar'kov: Kosmos, 1924).

53. Malis, 66.

54. Malis, 79.

55. Derrida, "Psychoanalysis Searches," 264.

56. Sigmund Freud, *Osnovyye psikhologicheskiye teorii v psikhoanalize: Sbornik statey* (Moscow: Gosizdat, 1923).

57. Ivan Dmitriyevich Ermakov, "Vvedenie," in Freud, *Osnovyye psikhologicheskiye*, 13.

58. Thomas Matza points out, citing the work of Raymond A. Bauer, that by the 1930s the idea of *soznanie* (consciousness) had been correlated with the materialist idea of "highly organized matter" and allotted a significant role "directing human affairs" on those terms. See Thomas Matza, *Shock Therapy: Psychology, Precarity, and Well-Being in Postsocialist Russia* (Durham, NC: Duke University Press, 2018), 42–43, and Raymond Bauer, *The New Man in Soviet Psychology* (Cambridge, MA: Harvard University Press, 1952).

59. Vera Schmidt, *Psychoanalytische Erziehung in Sowjetrussland* (Leipzig: Internationaler Psychoanalytischer Verlag, 1924).

60. N. S. Avtonomova in Laplanche and Pontalis, *Slovar'*, 15.

61. Avtonomova, 15.

62. See Franco "Bifo" Berardi, *The Soul at Work: From Alienation to Autonomy* (South Pasadena, CA: Semiotext(e), 2009); Bruno Bosteels, *Marx and Freud in Latin America: Politics, Psychoanalysis, and Religion in Times of Terror* (New York: Verso, 2012); Todd McGowan, *Capitalism and Desire: The Psychic Cost of Free Markets* (New York: Columbia University Press, 2016); Samo Tomšič, *The Capitalist Unconscious* (New York: Verso, 2015).

63. Khanna, *Dark Continents*, xii.

64. Anderson, Jenson, and Keller, *Unconscious Dominions*, 263.

65. Harriet Wolfe, "IPA in the World," International Psychoanalytic Association, accessed December 1, 2021, https://www.ipa.world/IPA/en/IPA1/our_mission_2021 .aspx. Current at the time I completed writing this essay.

Against Ion's Chain: Translatability in Antonio Gramsci's *Prison Notebooks*

Peter D. Thomas

Speaking during one of his rare appearances at the Fourth Congress of the Communist International on November 13, 1922, Lenin made the following remarks about the newly minted and much-contested politics of the United Front:

> At the Third Congress, in 1921, we adopted a resolution on the organisational structure of the Communist Parties and on the methods and content of their activities. The resolution is an excellent one, but it is almost entirely Russian, that is to say, everything in it is based on Russian conditions. This is its good point, but it is also its failing. It is its failing because I am sure that no foreigner can read it . . . because it is too Russian. Not because it is written in Russian—it has been excellently translated into all languages—but because . . . we have not learnt how to present our Russian experience to foreigners [in such a way that they might be able to] assimilate part of the Russian experience.[1]

The problem that Lenin posed for consideration by the assembled delegates of the self-characterized "party of world revolution" (unlike in earlier Congresses, now supported by the services of a professional translation bureau) was clearly not the problem of translation in a limited sense, as linguistically accurate "reproduction."[2] Rather, it was what has come to be known more recently as the broader problem of "cultural translation."[3] For Lenin, the translation of experiences from one cultural context to another could not be successfully undertaken mechanically or passively, with the simple re-presentation of meanings derived from the "source language" in the "target language," to use the classic binary opposition structuring so much reflection on translation, even today. In the debate over the United Front in which Lenin was intervening, such a conception of origins and transfers would simply mean the imposition of the policy by the Russian center on its "periphery" in the western European Communist Parties—precisely the position against which Lenin was arguing. Rather, the problem Lenin posed was one of understanding translation as an active process of communication, in which "meaning" is not univocal or constant, but plural and continually changing in context. It is not simply that the source language is transformed the moment it begins to enter into a relationship with the target language, because it is forced to reformulate itself in relation to its now unexpectedly intimate other; more radically, it is the fact that this relation has already begun, in the always given possibility of translation that is inscribed in their differential relation.

Appropriating a late-symbolist figure from T. S. Eliot, we might say that Lenin depicted the problem of cultural translation as one of finding the "objective correlative" that would permit the communication of the affective and gnoseological conditions of one cultural formation in the forms of another.[4] In Eliot's case, the objective correlative functions as that point of condensation in which what can only retrospectively be regarded as "pre-poetic experience" is transformed into a distinctively "poetic experience" (or as Eliot put it, emotion expressed "in the form of art"). For Lenin, the difficulty consisted in finding a way in which the complex relations of knowledge accumulated throughout the long Russian revolutionary process could be recapitulated and rapidly absorbed by and within the other "cultural worlds" of the non-Russian Communist Parties. In both cases, it is a "repetition" that is not a repetition at all, but rather, as the example of Eliot suggests, a distinct process of re-figuration. For Eliot, the objective correlative is constituted by an artistic or poetic "formula," or what he calls "a set of objects, a situation, a chain of events" capable of "re-evoking" a particular emotion; but as his key notion of a poetic or artistic emotion indicates, this is in fact not a "re-evoked" emotion at all. Rather, it is an entirely new emotion, that is, the emotional response proper to poetry, necessarily different from (and for the elitist Eliot, superior to) the "normal" emotional experiences of the "prose" of everyday life. For Lenin, on the other hand, it was a case of formulating the slogans, arguments, and strategic perspectives that would "correlate" the experiences of the Russian revolutionary process from the early twentieth century and the First World War with the very different conditions and challenges obtaining in western Europe in the early 1920s.[5] The presentation of the Russian experience needed to occur not as a claim to universal validity, but rather, precisely in terms of its specificity, allowing foreigners to "assimilate" its concrete particularity within their own different histories. The translation of the conditions of revolutionary organization thus needed to be accompanied by an ongoing process of self-critical reflection on the distinguishing features of the Russian experience, but also on the specific cultural and political traditions of non-Russian social formations and political traditions, in order to prepare both for their encounter. Translation, then, has always already begun, even and especially in its initial failures.

Translatio studii

Lenin's reflections on translation clearly made a strong impression upon a young Italian delegate at the Fourth Congress, who ten years later would repeatedly recall Lenin's intervention throughout the texts that would become his *Prison Notebooks*. Indeed, such was the impression on him that Antonio Gramsci's memory "translated" Lenin's remarks into the register of translation in a strong sense. Where Lenin had talked of the Russian Bolsheviks' not knowing how "to present" their experiences in a form comprehensible to foreigners, Gramsci made an explicit and immediate connection to the practice of translation as the concrete form of such a (re)presentation: *"Translatability of scientific and philosophical languages. In 1921: questions of organization. Vilici said and wrote: 'We have not known how to "translate" our language into the "European" languages.'"*[6]

Gramsci's life had been marked from the outset by an intense awareness of the difficulty and inevitability of translating between different languages and cultures. Growing up in a rural Sardinia integrated discordantly into the still relatively new Italian nation-state, caught between the Italian tongue that had colonized his father's distant Albanian origins and the Sardinian of his mother's family and the surrounding environment, it is not surprising that Gramsci remained particularly sensitive to the problem of translation in both narrow and broader senses throughout his life. At the University of Turin, as the country boy newly arrived in the big city not long before the outbreak of World War I, he had studied historical linguistics, with a particular emphasis upon how languages are historically transformed through contact with others, under conditions of dominance or subordination, in positions of prestige or subalternity.[7] *L'Ordine Nuovo*, the journal founded by Gramsci with others in the wake of World War I, had in part understood itself as an attempt to translate the still largely unknown perspectives informing the successful Bolshevik revolution into an Italian idiom. At the time of Lenin's speech in 1922, he had recently met his future wife, Julka Schucht, who on at least one occasion had acted as his translator while he delivered a political speech to Russian workers.[8] He would go on to court her with the proposal that they translate together some of the most recent Marx-Engels scholarship.[9] Later, upon his return to Italy as the head of the Italian Communist Party, he had overseen an intensive program of translation of classic and contemporary texts of the international workers' movement (particularly significant, in terms of the themes later explored in the *Prison Notebooks*, was the translation of Bukharin's *Theory of Historical Materialism*).[10] Indeed, much of Gramsci's energy during the mid-1920s, as the Fascist regime consolidated its grip on all forms of expression in Italian intellectual life, was dedicated to elaborating internationalist cultural institutions and practices, in which translation played a key pedagogical and political role.

After his imprisonment by the Fascist regime in 1926, it was only in early 1929 that Gramsci received permission to access writing materials. Remarkably, the first thing he did, even before beginning to write the notes and draft essays that would come to be known as his *Prison Notebooks*, was to spend much of the next year translating texts by Marx and Engels, Goethe, and the Grimm Brothers, among many others. These texts amount to over several hundred pages of translations in various states of completion and accomplishment, from naïve drafts overwhelmed by the literalisms of a neophyte's "translatese" to more polished compositions distinguished by the strategic and subtle choices of a maturing translator. These translations were not included in the original postwar publication of Gramsci's prison writings in a thematic edition, edited by Felice Platone under the guidance of Palmiro Togliatti. They were also largely excluded from the critical edition of 1975 edited by Valentino Gerratana, as they were thought to be merely preparatory literary exercises undertaken for personal-psychological reasons, and largely extraneous to Gramsci's "real" work; the only exceptions to this exclusion were some (though by no means all) of Gramsci's translations of Marx and Engels's texts.[11]

Although this omission was first and most forcefully highlighted by Lucia Borghese in 1981, it was only in 2007 that these translations were finally published in full in the new *Edizione nazionale*, in the first volumes of the section dedicated to Gramsci's carceral production under the editorship of Gianni Francioni.[12] We now know that Gramsci continued to work on these translations well beyond 1929, and that they were not "preparatory" to a later stage of more genuine and autonomous theoretical production. Rather, Gramsci continued to work on his translations for at least another two years, at the same time as and in parallel to the production of the notes that have been regarded as more properly his "own," as distinct from what were characterized as his mere "imitations" of lines ultimately "authorized" (in all senses of the word) by others. There instead seems to be a dialectical relationship between Gramsci's practice as a translator, his note-taking from a wide variety of sources, and his drafting of reflections, critiques, and tentative essay-style texts.[13] Translation, as a distinctively "fused" practice of writing and reading, here plays the role of a type of touchstone to which Gramsci returns time and again during the years of the composition of the *Prison Notebooks*.

Indeed, it is Gramsci's practice as a translator that often seems to provide the initial impetus for the elaboration of unexpected insights, themes, or distinct lines of research. The intermittent citation of or reference to some of Goethe's formulations throughout the *Prison Notebooks*, for instance, can at first sight seem a case of an arbitrary or odd eclecticism.[14] In particular, Gramsci's detailed objection to the aesthetic presuppositions of some of Bukharin's comments on Goethe's *Prometheus*, in the midst of an otherwise philosophically focused critique of the senior Bolshevik's manual on historical materialism, is a surprising departure from the main lines of his critique only for those unaware that Gramsci had been engaged in the close reading of Goethe's work in the preceding period.[15] Similarly, Gramsci often turns to translation in order to clarify, consolidate, or correct insights that emerged during the writing of his own draft essays or notes. His repeated meditation on Marx's 1859 "Preface," and increasing attention to the texture of its prose and the order of its arguments, is perhaps the most significant of these textual checks and balances.[16]

The development of his translations of the Grimm Brothers' fairy tales in particular reveals a remarkable exercise in both translation practice and theory: transposing those well-known tales from the Germanic terrain to rural Sardinia, Gramsci also progressively eliminated any reference to religion or themes of an otherworldly transcendence, producing what is either effectively a "new" secularized text, or a paradigmatic example of a thoroughgoing translation, transferring and transposing the source text into a radically different context, in the fullest sense.[17] This is not a case, to use Lawrence Venuti's terminology, of a "domesticating" translation that effaces the constitutive foreignness of the original text.[18] On the contrary, Gramsci's deliberately "unfaithful" translation of those iconic texts produces not a derivative "copy" of an original, but a conscious reflection, transformation, and rewriting of its limits. Translation here is practiced not simply as transposition. It is instead conceived, in an almost Wildean fashion, as the type of criticism that in a certain sense can be even more original and creative than its supposed artistic object.[19]

The *Prison Notebooks* "themselves" (that is, as traditionally conceived, the twenty-nine notebooks in which Gramsci compiled his "own" notes—a significant portion of which are, however, citations from or references to the writings of others) contain numerous theoretical reflections on translation in a strict (linguistic) and more expansive (cultural, or "paradigmatic") sense. Gramsci even dedicates a section of one of his most "organic" notebooks, Notebook 11, to "the translatability of scientific and philosophical languages."[20] Such is the prevalence and strategic significance of these reflections that it is remarkable (and perhaps symptomatically revealing of a certain previous leftist culture) that it is only relatively recently, in the last two decades, that the centrality of translation to Gramsci's theoretical and political proposals has been widely acknowledged.[21] Thanks to these works, we can now see that translation is not merely one among the many themes explored by Gramsci in the *Prison Notebooks*, but instead plays a crucial role in the general economy of their overall development. Indeed, in the form of the distinctive notion of a non-essentialist theory of the "translatability" of philosophical, scientific, and political discourses, or the dialectical relations of reciprocal translatability between history, politics, and philosophy, translation comes to figure as the central methodological innovation of Gramsci's proposed reformulation of Marxism as a "philosophy of praxis" and as a "living philology."[22]

The concepts of translation and translatability are developed in at least three significant directions in the *Prison Notebooks*, partially contemporaneously and partially in succession. The first line of research involves the question of the conditions of possibility for the translation of political strategies and techniques from one sociopolitical formation and historical conjuncture to another, ultimately leading to the translation of a particular political strategy—namely, "hegemony"—into a general framework for historico-political analysis. The second theme, which can be regarded as an attempted theorization and generalization of the first conjunctural focus, argues for a historicist theory of the potential for translation between different national and linguistic cultures, founded upon a fundamental "civilizational" similarity, if not equivalence. Finally, Gramsci's third development, both reinforcing and problematizing the first two, posits a non-essentialist theory of the translatability of different discourses, conceived not simply as systems of signification, but as conflicting or reinforcing forms of sociopolitical organization and action.

Translating Hegemony

The first line of research departs from Lenin's previously noted observations on the difficulty of translating the experiences informing the Russian revolution and its aftermath, particularly the politics of the United Front, into other cultural contexts. Gramsci paraphrases these comments several times at different stages during the writing of the *Prison Notebooks*, almost as if their repetition might serve to secure the underlying political coherence of his seemingly disparate research projects.[23] For Gramsci, the "objective correlative" (to use Eliot's term) by means of which the politics of the United Front could be translated into his own political reality was the concept that has sometimes been mistakenly regarded as his own invention, namely, that of hegemony.

Hegemony itself had a complicated history of translation before Gramsci encountered it in debates among the Bolsheviks in early 1920s Russia and sought to make it the cornerstone of his project of revolution in the West.[24] The semantic field at whose center stood ἡγεμονία [hegemonía] played a significant role in different forms of Greek historical, political, ethical, and even psychological discourses, from Homeric times through to the Hellenistic period.[25] Central to all of these usages was the notion of "leadership," variously conceived, from the assertion of predominance (above all in terms of relations between poleis) to the practice of guidance (particularly in metaphorical and philosophical contexts). Despite this prominence, however, the word later proved to be "untranslatable" into Latin, even in the limited form of translation that is the simple calque; as Bruno Bongiovanni has hypothesized, the absence of the signified at the geopolitical level in Roman imperial culture may have determined the neglect of the signifier. Thereafter the word "hegemony" (and insofar as indissolubly linked to it, also its "concept") vanished for centuries from the Western political and philosophical vocabulary. It is remarkable, for instance, that "hegemony" was not used by Machiavelli, or in the debates of the English Levellers. Even more notable is the fact that it did not occur to Hobbes, while translating Thucydides's History of the Peloponnesian War, that the Greek term might be communicated to his English audience by means of a literal translation or simple Anglicization. Indeed, Hobbes's need to render hegemonía and its derivatives in such various forms—the substantive oscillates between "governor," "leader," "command," "general," and even "ringleader," among other variants—indicates his instinctive sense that no exact equivalent for the Greek word existed in English, and that its meaning could thus only be conveyed in contextually specific forms.[26] It was precisely the "untranslatability" of the word that was the origin of his need to translate it and retranslate it again and again.

Hegemony reemerged in the western European political vocabulary only in the nineteenth century, as various modern nationalisms sought to imagine themselves in the translational mirror of classical inheritances. While an Italian line of reception focused in the work of Vincenzo Gioberti led to an expanded reading of hegemony as a process of ethical, moral, and pedagogical primacy (a sense also present in metaphorical usages by figures such as Hegel and Heine), in Prussia hegemony primarily came to be understood in the seemingly more "literal" terms of military competition and supremacy of one state over others (an emphasis also dominant in Marx and Engels's relatively rare uses of the word).[27] It seems that it was Georgi Plekhanov who first used the neologism *gegemoniya* in the Russian context, where it came to signify, especially but not exclusively with Lenin, a particular strategy in Russian social democracy that aimed to secure the leadership of a nascent and minoritarian working-class movement amidst a vast ocean of peasantry.[28] Hegemony here was understood as a concrete form of the translation of working-class politics into the multitudinous dialects of the peasantry.

By the time Gramsci encountered the term during his stay in Moscow in 1922–23, possibly thanks to celebrated public lectures in the period by the head of the Comintern, Dimitri Zinoviev, the term was therefore widely known to indicate a central element of the "Russian experience" alluded to by Lenin. It signified not a geopolitical metaphor transplanted crudely into domestic politics, but a distinctive focus on building the political capacities for self-government of the working-class movement and its allies among the other oppressed classes. This sense of the term as a distinctive method of political work remains central for Gramsci prior to his imprisonment, and throughout the *Prison Notebooks*, above all in those passages that invoke hegemony as an appropriate form of political struggle for the western European subaltern classes and social groups.

The decisively new element that Gramsci introduces in his translation of the term in the *Prison Notebooks*, however, is not simply a transposition from East to West, as has often been claimed. Much more, it is the introduction of historical, formal and methodological differences or 'deformations'.

Historically, Gramsci extends the range of the concept, from early twentieth century Russia back to eighteenth- and nineteenth-century western Europe, thus translating the term from one phase of political modernity to a previous one. This was an unashamedly "anachronistic" or "discordant" translation: a concept that had not been present in the political languages that had been deployed during the emergence, contestation, and consolidation of modern western European nation-states in the eighteenth and nineteenth centuries was proposed as a distinctively clarifying translation of their histories.

Formally, the concept of hegemony had functioned in the debates of Russian social democracy as the advocacy of the emergence of a qualitatively different form of political relationality, outside the institutional structures of an exclusionary absolutism (a new political relationality eventually consolidated in the distinctive form of the early Soviets). In Gramsci's historical translation, hegemony is instead used to analyze social formations (France, Italy, and so forth) in a nineteenth-century conjuncture defined by the consolidation of the principle of popular sovereignty and its simultaneous practical neutralization, by means of the passive inclusion of popular political forces in an established bourgeois hegemonic project. "Passive revolution" is the term that Gramsci gradually comes to propose for this translation of hegemony into the context of bourgeois politics, or his attempt to analyze the "hegemonic fabric" of the sovereignty of the modern representative political state.[29]

Methodologically, Gramsci translates hegemony from the register of the political program, where hegemony functions both strategically and prefiguratively, to that of historico-political analysis, in which the concept operates as description and critique. The particularity of "conjuncture" thereby "infected" the generic claims of "structure," or in other words, historical narrative was subordinated and reshaped by immersion in the temporality, rhythm, and horizon of the present.

This threefold translation strategy gives rise not to a simple re-presentation of the original concept of hegemony in foreign climes, as if translation were merely a case of transplantation, and thus expansion, of an originary meaning founded in an equally originary "intention," traveling unchanged along an equivalential chain from the beginning to an end that was already inscribed within it. Rather, hegemony has here become a qualitatively new and expanded concept, which now includes within the concept's semantic field dimensions that were not "there" at its origins, but which reconfigure our understanding of those origins. It has been enriched through the introduction of the difference that is the constitutive and enabling precondition and result of any translation.

Between Esperanto and *Ursprache*

The second line of Gramsci's research regards a historicist theory of the possibility of translation between different cultures, and is thus an attempted theorization and generalization of his "deformation" of the concept of hegemony. Here Gramsci's privileged reference was *The Holy Family*, where Marx, following upon a theme in Kant, Hegel, and Heine,[30] argues that the political language of the French revolution (particularly what Gramsci glosses as "Jacobin phraseology") "corresponds to" and "can be translated into'" the language of classical German philosophy.[31] In an early version of this argument, Gramsci argues, following Marx, that "the formulae of French politics of the revolution can be reduced [*si riducono*] to the principles of classical German philosophy," in a relationship of distillation.[32] In a later version, in a notable development already informed by his theory of translatability, he speaks instead, following Hegel, of the "parallel and reciprocally translatable juridical-political language of the Jacobins and the concepts of classical German philosophy."[33]

How could such a form of reciprocal translation, based upon two distinct linguistic registers being in "parallel," be possible? In a significant line of research, particularly in Notebooks 4 and 8 but also in Notebooks 11 and 15, Gramsci seems to argue that such translation can occur because different cultural and linguistic expressions are fundamentally only different ways of comprehending similar, if not the same, socio-political and cultural experiences, diversely expressed in different languages and genres due to different national traditions and institutions.[34] In other words, French politics and German philosophy— and, Gramsci soon adds, following Engels and Lenin, English political economy—would be reciprocally translatable because they represent particular forms of comprehension and expression of a more general if not universal experience, namely, the uneven emergence of political modernity in each of those social formations. Their linguistic or cultural diversity was grounded in the commonality or commensurability of a seemingly "pre-linguistic" experience.[35] Gramsci will even resort, in early 1932, to traditional metaphors of the Marxist tradition, arguing that "two structures have equivalent and reciprocally translatable superstructures."[36] He explains this position in more extended terms several months later, in the summer of 1932. He argues that

> translatability presupposes that a given phase of civilization has a "fundamentally" identical cultural expression, even if the language is historically different, determined by the particular tradition of each national culture and each philosophical system, by the predominance of an intellectual or practical activity, etc. Thus we should see if translatability is possible between expressions of different phases of civilization, insofar as these phases are moments of development from one to the other, and are thus mutually integrated, or if a given expression can be translated with terms of a previous phase of the same civilization, a previous phase, however, which is more comprehensible than the given language, etc.[37]

The possibility of translation in this version would thus seem to be determined by the existence of a fundamental identity or even "universalism" (within certain geopolitical limits) underlying and informing different cultures and languages, which are grasped as merely epiphenomenal, or superstructural elements that comprehend a phenomenal if not noumenal base. Translation in this perspective would appear to be premised on a detour via the generic, if not on a universal extralinguistic "grammar," that is, the grammar of a commonality of shared historical experience.

Even more intriguing are the claims that frame and supplement this argument. Gramsci had begun by asking "if the reciprocal translatability of various philosophical and scientific languages is a 'critical' element that belongs to every conception of the world, or only to the philosophy of praxis (in an organic way) and only partially able to be appropriated by other philosophies." He concludes by stating that "it thus seems that one can say that only in the philosophy of praxis is 'translation' organic and profound, while from other points of view it is often a simple game of generic 'schematisms.'"[38] Read on its own, it might seem that here Gramsci is suggesting, contrary to his insights elsewhere, that Marxism has a privileged access to an *Ursprache* or "grammar" of universal history.[39] It would be on the basis of activating this grammar, almost as a decoding machine, that translation between different particular languages or cultural paradigms would become possible. Marxism, that is, would be represented as a metanarrative, within which other narratives could be integrated and subsequently deciphered.

It is a well-known theme in the history of Marxism, from the formulations in the *German Ideology* that claim a privileged access to the real, to Frederic Jameson's arguments regarding the distinctive capacity of Marxism to narrativize other narratives (in this sense, Jameson seems at times to be a more "orthodox," or "classical" rather than "Western," Marxist than is sometimes thought).[40] In other words, confronted with the contingent and conjunctural particularity of other conceptions of the world, philosophies, discourses, languages, and so forth, the materialist conception of history would be called upon to play the role of universal storyteller, capable of integrating each particular history into its tale of a thousand and one nights, the universal narrative of human history in its entirety. It is, of course, a theme well known not only to Marxism, but to the main lines of modern Western historical consciousness as such.

While this formulation of the argument might be able to offer an explanation for the historical possibility of translation, each particular discourse being conceived as a "target text" that translates, in a relation of correspondence underwritten by a primordial identity, the "source text" of a nondiscursive historical reality, it is arguably unable to account coherently for the ways in which historical reality itself is always already "discursive" in a very specific sense: namely, in the sense that it is constitutively structured precisely by those diverse discourses as its active forms of organization and efficacy ("politics" in the broadest sense). This discursive organization is not simply a supplementary expression of historical reality, but inherent to its very mode of existence *as* historical, that is, as a narrativization and endowment with meaning of social-political action.[41] A purely historicist-foundationalist theory of the possibility of translation, on its own, it not yet able to provide an account of this inherently political status of historical reality itself, in which the successful or frustrated translation between different linguistic registers and cultural forms, their mutual comprehension or incomprehension, is already at work.

From the Untranslatable to Translatability

This tendency toward a certain type of foundationalism is modified and redimensioned, however, by Gramsci's contemporaneous development of a distinctive notion of reciprocal and therefore non-essentialist and non-foundationalist translatability. This third line of research is an attempt to explain why it is only within the philosophy of praxis that translation can be "organic and profound," without falling into a "schematism" of origins, primacy, or goals. This is particularly the case in Notebooks 10 and 11 (in which Gramsci's explicit reflections on translatability are most intensively developed), but it is a theme strongly present in often implicit ways throughout his later notebooks. Indeed, its presuppositions form the central preoccupation of the last notebook that Gramsci begins in prison, Notebook 29, which is dedicated to "Notes for an Introduction to the Study of Grammar," and in which he elaborates the crucial distinction between "normative" and "immanent" (or "spontaneous") grammars.[42]

As so often in the *Prison Notebooks*, Gramsci's engagement with Croce was decisive for the development of his thinking. Croce had famously theorized the untranslatability of artistic works in particular and of poetry specifically (as opposed to the equivalential translation that he eventually conceded may be possible within the other spheres of his theory of "distincts," the "practical"—economics and ethics—but also, within the "theoretical," the "logical" in its distinction from the "aesthetic").[43] True poetry for Croce—that is, what is genuinely poetic, and not merely "external" content or structure—is an immediate expression of pure, unified intuition, and is thus historically singular.[44] An attempted translation of such a unrepeatable moment could only "diminish" or "despoil" the original; even those translations that seem to be successful in fact don't translate at all, but instead produce what is in effect an entirely new poetic original, a new fusion of intuition and expression.[45] For all its sophistication, in its broad outlines Croce's theory is a variation on the Platonic theory of the primacy of origins, though now formulated in terms of a historicist theory of singularity.

Even before they stood opposed as authors of manifestos against and for the Fascist regime, Croce's erstwhile comrade in arms in the Italian neo-idealism movement, Giovanni Gentile, had decisively criticized the presuppositions of Croce's argument—though the way in which he did so arguably ended up affirming precisely the same conclusions regarding the nature of translation and the conditions of its possibility. For Gentile, rejecting Croce's distinction between the logical and the aesthetic, translation both never and always happens. On the one hand, nothing is ever translated from one language to another because all languages are merely expressions of a higher, "pure" language of spirit, which is always "actual" in the course of its historical development and only apparent variation. On the other hand, Gentile expands the notion of translation to the point that all linguistic practice (including within any given language) is conceived as translation, thereby effectively canceling out the term as a meaningful distinction. Translation here is understood as merely a form of interpretation, or the mode in which the historical process is interiorized in an always unified spirit from one temporal moment to the next.[46] Once again, translation is judged according to its capacity to guarantee the unity and continuity of origins, borne forth ceaselessly by the interpretative-translational activity of a unique historical subject.

Despite the post-Kantian terms in which they were formulated, Croce's and Gentile's different approaches are ultimately all too familiarly Platonic gestures that depict translation as yet another mimetic failure to recover origins (even if, in Gentile's case, a "successful failure" that redefines those origins in the actualist terms of the unity of omnipresent spirit). Gramsci's response to this line of reasoning is as brief as it is brutal: conceived in these identitarian terms, a "perfect" translation may not be possible, he admits, before asking: But "what language is exactly translatable into another language? What single word is exactly translatable into another language?"[47] Indeed, we might add, who but the most caricatured Platonist ever thought that such a re-production might be possible? Hardy's Jude the Obscure may have dreamt at the beginning of his studies that translation involved the discovery of a "secret cipher," "which, once known, would enable him, by merely applying it, to change at will all words of his own speech into those of the foreign one." The practice of translation itself, however, soon teaches any such budding neophyte that there is no alchemical "law of transmutation," as Jude had hoped.[48] The art of translation necessarily always involves provisional and contingent choices that are as much if not more dependent upon the supposed "imitation" than the so-called original itself.

As Gramsci suggests, the neo-idealist argument presupposes, first, that translation, strictly conceived, should involve the mimetic reproduction of an original.[49] It posits, that is, that the intensity or authenticity of an originary source could, at least in principle, be passed down along the famous chain that Socrates offers to Ion in an undiminished form, re-produced—or even more forcefully, literally "re-created"—in a relation of unmediated identity.[50] Second, particularly Croce's version of the thesis of untranslatability—and arguably also its "afterlife" in the contemporary notion of "the untranslatable"—posits the presupposition of the theoretical possibility of such identity, in order then to deny that such a theoretical possibility is ever realized in any particular act of translation.[51] Each empirical, particular act of translation is thereby measured against an absent universal possibility and found wanting. In other words, although there may regularly occur more or less "successful" acts of translation—success being determined differently in each case—translation as such, in its supposedly "pure" form, never happens. It is as if translation ideally should involve a complete and total transfer of both content and form, almost as if it would empty out the original but only in order for the original to "re-present" itself in the "copy" as its immutable self, in a journey that changes nothing.

It is precisely such a "pure" conception of translation, however, that Gramsci's pointed comments aim to put in question, because translation is always impure. When translation is thought in terms of maintaining the purity of origins, in a relation of identical, immediate and exhaustive re-presentation in the "copy," there is no need for translation in any sense at all (as Gentile had recognized), because such a perfect (equivalential) translation has always already occurred within the original itself. In a similar way, a detour via universality (for instance, in the form of grammar, conceived normatively as a universal language that enables the transposition of expressions from one particular language to another) also negates the possibility of translation. For if each particular language is already comprehended by a structure that precedes and thereby "explains" it, translation between it and any other language would again have already happened, in the purity of an equivalence that had been established before any relation between the terms in the equation. Any particular act of translation in this sense would merely tell us what could already have been known according to a formalistic universality, even if it were not yet realized in any particular textual performance.[52] A translation would simply be that dimension of any text that is latent, a potential waiting to be realized, or rather, one already realized in the form of a potentiality that is always "actual" (again, in Gentile's sense).

In reality, translation always and necessarily begins *in media res*, among the impure particularities that continually escape the imposition of any fictitious universality. It is governed not normatively, from above, but immanently, by the dynamic of the relations that the encounter that is translation sets in train. The concrete possibility of translation is never given, but is always overdetermined by broader existing relations of differential force between cultures, languages, genres, and so forth, which establish the need to translate in the first place. Rather than thinking translation in terms of the faithful reproduction of an original, or the establishment of an equivalence between terms, Gramsci instead attempts to think the problem in terms of the necessarily always incomplete model of communication, incomplete because reliant upon both speaker and receiver, or upon both "source" and "target" text. In this conception, translation is not called upon to produce and reproduce identity.

It is rather difference that is both its enabling precondition and its necessary result, which does not make it a "failure," but highlights instead precisely its status and specificity *as* a translation, as a form of relation between one cultural or linguistic community or paradigm and another (themselves dissolved from within by the relations of translation that constitute them in their provisional identities).

It is precisely in such an optic that Gramsci attempts to overturn Croce's distinction between the theoretical and the practical. Consistent with the conception of historical singularity that informed his thesis of the impossibility of translation, Croce had argued for a qualitative distinction between philosophy, as a universal theoretical discourse, and the particular discourses of political engagement or economic action, compromised by their mundanity. Between the two, reciprocal translation is literally impossible, for "translation" could only occur on the basis of the subsumption of the particularities of the practical within the universality of the theoretical, a universal that itself remains impervious to expression in anything but its native idiom.[53]

Gramsci, by way of his argument for the dialectical relationship between philosophy and *senso comune*, each "sedimented" within the other, instead argues for a quantitative rather than qualitative distinction between the two. The philosophical and ideological are conceived not in terms of the metaphysical distinction between universality and particularity, but in terms of their discursive specificities. Their always variable distinction is related to the different degrees of their organization and efficacy, and ultimately linked to the growth or decline of the political projects of the communities for which they constituted structuring discourses. In one particularly telling formulation, Gramsci even argues that "what is practice for the fundamental class becomes 'rationality' and speculation for its intellectuals."[54] He explains such a claim to universality "as the 'historical subjectivity of a social group,' as a real fact which presents itself as a phenomenon of philosophical 'speculation' while it is simply a practical act, the form assumed by a concrete social content."[55] "It is on the basis of these historical relations that all modern philosophical idealism," he concluded, "is to be explained."[56]

The reciprocal translation that Gramsci argues could be "organic and profound" only in the philosophy of praxis could occur not on the basis of Marxism aspiring to replace one universal with another (the notion of Marxism as a metanarrative of human history previously discussed). Rather, it would only become possible by annulling the claim to a qualitative distinction between supposedly universal and purportedly particular discourses, historically situating each as a decisive element of the sociopolitical realities that they do not express, but literally constitute. The relationship between theory and practice in this perspective is not to be conceived as application of the former to the latter, but as the mutual and ongoing translatability between discourses that depend upon each other to be that which they are, in a differential rather than identitarian relation. In other words, it is not a question of discovering, finally, the first authentic link in Ion's mythical chain, which would provide a measure by which to assess the success or failure of its successive imitations. It is rather a case of intervening in the practical reality of the relations of translatability between discourses that already constitutes the possibility of each and any discourse.

"Living Philology"

Translation in the *Prison Notebooks* is thus not merely imitative or derivative and not simply "creative" (thereby re-posing the problem of origins, "anew"). Rather, with the development of Gramsci's distinctive conception of translatability, it is conceived as a form of intervention, a modification of relations of force, and ultimately, as "transformation."[57] The problems confronted by this type of practice of translation are thus not only the problems that motivate any form or genre of writing, as integral elements in the production, remembrance, reworking of historical experience. They are also the problems that lie at the foundation of sociality in general, and of transformative politics in particular. It is in this expansive sense that translatability can finally be seen as the central methodological perspective in Gramsci's attempted reformulation of the Marxist tradition as a philosophy of praxis, or as he elsewhere characterizes it, as a dynamic practice of the "living philology" of the particular.[58]

Bibliography

Abrams, Meyer H. *The Mirror and the Lamp: Romantic Theory and the Critical Tradition.* Oxford: Oxford University Press, 1953.

Anderson, Perry. *The H-Word: The Peripeteia of Hegemony.* London: Verso, 2017.

Baratta, Giorgio. *Antonio Gramsci in contrappunto: Dialoghi col presente.* Rome: Carocci, 2007.

———. *Le rose e i quaderni: Saggio sul pensiero di Antonio Gramsci.* Rome: Gamberetti, 2000.

Bhabha, Homi. *The Location of Culture.* London: Routledge, 1994.

Bongiovanni, Bruno, and Luigi Bonanate. "Egemonia." In *Enciclopedia delle scienze sociali*, vol. 3, 470–77. Rome: Istituto della Enciclopedia Italiana, 1993.

Boothman, Derek. *Traducibilità e processi traduttivi: Un caso: A. Gramsci linguista.* Perugia: Guerra edizioni, 2004.

———. "Traduzione e traducibilità." In *Le parole di Gramsci: Per un lessico dei "Quaderni del carcere,"* edited by Fabio Frosini and Guido Liguori, 247–66. Rome: Carocci, 2004.

Borghese, Lucia. "Fra Goethe e i Grimm." In *Tornare a Gramsci: Una cultura per l'Italia,* edited by Gaspare Polizzi, 157–74. Grottaferrata: Avverbi, 2010.

———. "Lo scudo di Gramsci." In Antonio Gramsci, *I racconti dei fratelli Grimm,* edited by Nicola Caleffi and Guglielmo Leoni, 7–29. Modena: Incontri Editrice, 2011.

———. "Tia Alene in bicicletta: Gramsci traduttore dal tedesco e teorico della traduzione." *Belfagor* 36, no. 6 (November 1981): 635–65.

Brandist, Craig. *The Dimensions of Hegemony: Language, Culture and Politics in Revolutionary Russia.* Leiden: Brill, 2015.

Buci-Glucksmann, Christine. *Gramsci and the State.* Translated by David Fernbach. London: Lawrence and Wishart, 1980 (1975).

Budick, Sanford, and Wolfgang Iser, eds. *The Translatability of Cultures: Figurations of the Space Between.* Stanford, CA: Stanford University Press, 1996.

Butler, Judith. "Restaging the Universal: Hegemony and the Limits of Formalism." In Judith Butler, Ernesto Laclau, and Slavoj Žižek, *Contingency, Hegemony, Universality: Contemporary Dialogues on the Left,* 11–43. London: Verso, 2000.

Carlucci, Alessandro. *Gramsci and Languages: Unification, Diversity, Hegemony.* Leiden: Brill, 2013.

Carlucci, Alessandro, and Caterina Balistreri. "I primi mesi di Gramsci in Russia, giugno–agosto 1922." *Belfagor* 66, no. 6 (November 2011): 645–58.

Cassin, Barbara, ed. *Dictionary of Untranslatables: A Philosophical Lexicon.* Translation edited by Emily Apter, Jacques Lezra, and Michael Wood. Princeton, NJ: Princeton University Press, 2014.

Chernov, Sergei. "At the Dawn of Simultaneous Interpreting in the USSR: Filling Some Gaps in History." In *New Insights in the History of Interpreting,* edited by Kayoko Takeda and Jesús Baigorri-Jalón, 135–66. Amsterdam: John Benjamins, 2016.

Cortés, Martín. *Un nuevo marxismo para América Latina: José Aricó: Traductor, editor, intelectual.* Mexico City: Siglo Veintiuno, 2015.

Cospito, Giuseppe. "Egemonia/egemonico nei 'Quaderni del carcere' (e prima)." *International Gramsci Journal* 2, no. 1 (2016): 49–88.

———. "Traducibilità dei linguaggi scientifici e filosofia della praxis." *Filosofia italiana,* no. 2 (2017): 47–65.

———. "Verso l'edizione critica e integrale dei «Quaderni del carcere»." *Studi storici* 52, no. 4 (2011): 896–904.

Croce, Benedetto. *The Aesthetic as the Science of Expression and of the Linguistic in General.* Translated by Colin Lyas. Cambridge: Cambridge University Press, 1992 (1902).

———. *La poesia di Dante.* Bari: Laterza, 1921.

Derrida, Jacques. *The Ear of the Other: Otobiography, Transference, Translation.* Edited by Christine McDonald. Translated by Peggy Kamuf. Lincoln: University of Nebraska Press, 1985.

———. *Monolingualism of the Other; or, The Prosthesis of Origin.* Translated by Patrick Mensah. Stanford, CA: Stanford University Press, 1998.

———. *Positions.* Translated by Alan Bass. Chicago: University of Chicago Press, 1981.

Descendre, Romain, and Jean-Claude Zancarini. "De la traduction à la traductibilité: Un outil d'émancipation théorique." *Laboratoire italien: Politique et société*, no. 18 (2016).

D'Orsi, Angelo. *Gramsci: Una nuova biografia.* Milan: Feltrinelli, 2017.

Dryden, John. "On Translation." In *Theories of Translation: An Anthology of Essays from Dryden to Derrida*, edited by Rainer Schulte and John Biguenet, 17–31. Chicago: University of Chicago Press, 1992.

Eliot, T. S. "Hamlet and His Problems." In *The Sacred Wood: Essays on Poetry and Criticism.* New York: Alfred A. Knopf, 1921.

Francioni, Gianni. *L'officina gramsciana: Ipotesi sulla struttura dei "Quaderni del carcere."* Naples: Bibliopolis, 1984.

Frosini, Fabio. *Gramsci e la filosofia.* Rome: Carocci, 2003.

———. "Reformation, Renaissance and the State: The Hegemonic Fabric of Modern Sovereignty." *Journal of Romance Studies* 12, no. 3 (2010): 63–77.

———. *La religione dell'uomo moderno: Politica e verità nei "Quaderni del carcere" di Antonio Gramsci.* Rome: Carocci, 2010.

Gentile, Giovanni. "Torto e diritto delle traduzioni." In *Frammenti di estetica e di letteratura*, 372–73. Lanciano: Carabba editore, 1920.

Gerratana, Valentino. "Prefazione." In Antonio Gramsci, *Quaderni del carcere*, xi–xlii. Turin: Einaudi, 1975.

Gramsci, Antonio. *Edizione nazionale degli scritti di Antonio Gramsci: Quaderni del carcere.* Vol. 1, *Quaderni di traduzioni (1929–1932)*, edited by Giuseppe Cospito and Gianni Francioni. Rome: Istituto della Enciclopedia Italiana, 2007.

———. *A Great and Terrible World: The Pre-prison Letters, 1908–1926.* Edited and translated by Derek Boothman. London: Lawrence and Wishart, 2014.

———. *Quaderni del carcere.* Edited by Valentino Gerratana. Turin: Einaudi, 1975.

Guha, Ranajit. *Dominance without Hegemony: History and Power in Colonial India.* Oxford: Oxford University Press, 1998.

Guzzone, Giuliano. *Gramsci e la critica dell'economia politica: Dal dibattito sul liberismo al paradigma della "traducibilità."* Rome: Viella, 2018.

Hardy, Thomas. *Jude the Obscure.* Edited by Cedric Watts. Peterborough, ON: Broadview, 1999.

Haug, Wolfgang Fritz. "Hegemonie." In *Historisch-kritisches Wörterbuch des Marxismus* 6, I, 8–9. Hamburg: Argument, 2004.

Hrnjez, Saša. "Traducibilità, Dialettica, Contraddizione: Per una teoria-prassi della traduzione a partire da Gramsci." *International Gramsci Journal* 3, no. 3 (2019): 40–71.

Ives, Peter. *Gramsci's Politics of Language: Engaging the Bakhtin Circle and the Frankfurt School*. Toronto: University of Toronto Press, 2004.

Ives, Peter, and Rocco Lacorte, eds. *Gramsci, Language, and Translation*. Lanham, MD: Lexington Books, 2010.

Jameson, Fredric. *The Political Unconscious: Narrative as a Socially Symbolic Act*. Ithaca, NY: Cornell University Press, 1982.

Jervolino, Domenico. "Croce, Gentile and Gramsci on Translation." *International Gramsci Journal*, no. 2 (2010): 29–38.

Laclau, Ernesto, and Chantal Mouffe. *Hegemony and Socialist Strategy: Towards a Radical Democratic Politics*. London: Verso, 2014 (1985).

Lecercle, Jean-Jacques. "Lenin the Just, or Marxism Unrecycled." In *Lenin Reloaded: Toward a Politics of Truth*, edited by Sebastian Budgen, Stathis Kouvelakis, and Slavoj Žižek, 269–82. Durham, NC: Duke University Press, 2007.

Lenin, V. I. "Five Years of the Russian Revolution and the Prospects of the World Revolution: Report to the Fourth Congress of the Communist International, November 13, 1922." In *Lenin Collected Works*, vol. 33, 431–32. Moscow: Progress, 1965.

Lo Piparo, Franco. *Lingua, intellettuali, egemonia in Gramsci*. Rome-Bari: Laterza, 1979.

Moreiras, Alberto. *The Exhaustion of Difference: The Politics of Latin American Cultural Studies*. Durham, NC: Duke University Press, 2001.

Plato. *Selected Dialogues of Plato*. Translated by Benjamin Jowett. New York: Random House, 2001.

Schirru. Giancarlo. "Antonio Gramsci, studente di linguistica." *Studi storici* 52, no. 4 (2011): 925–73.

Shapiro, Stephen, and Neil Lazarus. "Translatability, Combined Unevenness, and World Literature in Antonio Gramsci." *Mediations* 32, no. 1 (Fall 2018): 1–36.

Spivak, Gayatri Chakravorty. "Translation as Culture." In *In Translation—Reflections, Refractions, Transformations*, edited by Paul St-Pierre and Prafulla C. Kar, 263–76. Amsterdam: John Benjamins, 2007.

Steiner, George. *After Babel: Aspects of Language and Translation*. 3rd ed. Oxford: Oxford University Press, 1998.

Thomas, Peter D. *The Gramscian Moment*. Chicago: Haymarket Books, 2010.

———. "Gramsci's Marxism: The 'Philosophy of Praxis.'" In *Antonio Gramsci*, edited by Mark McNally. London: Palgrave Macmillan, 2015.

———. "Gramsci's Revolutions: Passive and Permanent." *Modern Intellectual History* 17, no. 1 (2020): 117–46.

Tosel, André. "Philosophie marxiste et traductibilité des langages et des pratiques." In *Praxis: Vers une refondation en philosophie marxiste*, 115–35. Paris: Éditions Sociales, 1984.

Venuti, Lawrence. *The Translator's Invisibility: A History of Translation*. London: Routledge, 1995.

Wagner, Birgit. "Cultural Translation: A Value or a Tool? Let's Start with Gramsci!" In *Translation: Narration, Media and the Staging of Differences*, edited by Federico Italiano and Michael Rössner, 51–68. Bielefeld: transcript, 2012.

White, Hayden. "The Value of Narrativity in the Representation of Reality." In *The Content of the Form: Narrative Discourse and Historical Representation*, 1–25. Baltimore: Johns Hopkins University Press, 1987.

Wickersham, John. *Hegemony and Greek Historians*. Lanham, MD: Rowman and Littlefield, 1994.

Wilde, Oscar. "The Critic as Artist." In *The Complete Works of Oscar Wilde*, vol. 4, *Criticism*, edited by Josephine M. Guy, 123–206. Oxford: Oxford University Press, 2007.

Notes

1. V. I. Lenin, "Five Years of the Russian Revolution and the Prospects of the World Revolution: Report to the Fourth Congress of the Communist International, November 13, 1922," in *Lenin Collected Works*, vol. 33 (Moscow: Progress, 1965), 431–32.

2. On the development of the "relations of translation" and the shifting relations of linguistic prestige in the early years of the Third International, see Sergei Chernov, "At the Dawn of Simultaneous Interpreting in the USSR: Filling Some Gaps in History," in *New Insights in the History of Interpreting*, ed. Kayoko Takeda and Jesús Baigorri-Jalón (Amsterdam: John Benjamins, 2016), 135–66.

3. Homi Bhabha, *The Location of Culture* (London: Routledge, 1994); Gayatri Chakravorty Spivak, "Translation as Culture," in *In Translation—Reflections, Refractions, Transformations*, ed. Paul St-Pierre and Prafulla C. Kar (Amsterdam: John Benjamins, 2007), 263–76; Sanford Budick and Wolfgang Iser, eds., *The Translatability of Cultures: Figurations of the Space Between* (Stanford, CA: Stanford University Press, 1996).

4. T. S. Eliot, "Hamlet and His Problems," in *The Sacred Wood: Essays on Poetry and Criticism* (New York: Alfred A. Knopf, 1921), 92.

5. On the strategic significance of the "slogan" in Lenin's thought and practice, as a condensation of and intervention into the relations of force defining a conjuncture, see Jean-Jacques Lecercle, "Lenin the Just, or Marxism Unrecycled," in *Lenin Reloaded: Toward a Politics of Truth*, ed. Sebastian Budgen, Stathis Kouvelakis, and Slavoj Žižek (Durham, NC: Duke University Press, 2007), 269–82.

6. Q7, §2, p. 854, November 1930. As Peter Ives notes in *Gramsci's Politics of Language: Engaging the Bakhtin Circle and the Frankfurt School* (Toronto: University of Toronto Press, 2004), 100–101, Gramsci here confuses the date of Lenin's address to the Fourth Congress in 1922 (which Gramsci himself witnessed) with the Third Congress of 1921, to which Lenin refers in his remarks. References to Gramsci's *Prison Notebooks* are given according to the Italian critical edition of the *Quaderni del carcere*, ed. Valentino Gerratana (Turin: Einaudi, 1975), following the

internationally established standard of notebook number (*Q*), note number (§), and page number(s). Dates of individual notes are given according to the chronology established in Gianni Francioni, *L'officina gramsciana: Ipotesi sulla struttura dei "Quaderni del carcere"* (Naples: Bibliopolis, 1984) and the revisions contained in the appendix to Giuseppe Cospito, "Verso l'edizione critica e integrale dei «*Quaderni del carcere*»," *Studi storici* 52, no. 4 (2011): 896–904.

7. Among the first studies to emphasize the significance of Gramsci's university training in historical linguistics was Franco Lo Piparo, *Lingua, intellettuali, egemonia in Gramsci* (Rome-Bari: Laterza, 1979). More recent studies, alongside Peter Ives's previously cited study, include Giancarlo Schirru's exhaustive study of Gramsci's Turin years ("Antonio Gramsci, studente di linguistica," *Studi storici*, 52, no. 4 [2011]: 925–73) and the fundamental work of Alessandro Carlucci, *Gramsci and Languages: Unification, Diversity, Hegemony* (Leiden: Brill, 2013).

8. Angelo D'Orsi's *Gramsci: Una nuova biografia* (Milan: Feltrinelli, 2017) synthesizes the most important recent historical research on Gramsci's period in Moscow. See also Alessandro Carlucci and Caterina Balistreri's archival study, "I primi mesi di Gramsci in Russia, giugno–agosto 1922," *Belfagor* 66, no. 6 (November 2011): 645–58.

9. See Antonio Gramsci, *A Great and Terrible World: The Pre-prison Letters, 1908–1926*, ed. and trans. Derek Boothman (London: Lawrence and Wishart, 2014), 129, 196.

10. Christine Buci-Glucksmann, *Gramsci and the State*, trans. David Fernbach (London: Lawrence and Wishart, 1980 [1975]) highlights the significance of this translation for Gramsci's precarceral political activism.

11. For a discussion of the reasons for this exclusion, see Valentino Gerratana, "Prefazione," in Antonio Gramsci, *Quaderni del carcere* (Turin: Einaudi, 1975), xxxvii–xxxviii. The Marxian translations included by Gerratana were the *Theses on Feuerbach*, the 1859 *Preface*, and the programmatic conclusion to the *Communist Manifesto* (pp. 2355–62). Giuseppe Cospito (in "Verso l'edizione critica e integrale dei «*Quaderni del carcere*»") synthesizes and extends the scholarship that demonstrates why Gerratana's assessment of the relation between Gramsci's translations and his "own" texts now needs to be completely revised.

12. Lucia Borghese, "Tia Alene in bicicletta: Gramsci traduttore dal tedesco e teorico della traduzione," *Belfagor*, 36, no. 6 (November 1981): 635–65; Antonio Gramsci, *Edizione nazionale degli scritti di Antonio Gramsci: Quaderni del carcere*, vol. 1, *Quaderni di traduzioni (1929–1932)*, ed. Giuseppe Cospito and Gianni Francioni (Rome: Istituto della Enciclopedia Italiana, 2007).

13. See Giorgio Baratta, *Le rose e i quaderni: Saggio sul pensiero di Antonio Gramsci* (Rome: Gamberetti, 2000), for a compelling portrait of Gramsci's study habits in prison, between reading, writing, translating, perambulating, and cultivating roses.

14. See, for instance, Q4, §64, p. 508, November 1930; Q 7, §37, p. 887, February–November 1931; Q8, §239, p. 1090, May 1932. Gramsci translated some of Goethe's poems between April–June and December 1929, and selections from Eckermann's

Conversations with Goethe in early 1930. On this phase of his work, see Lucia Borghese, "Fra Goethe e i Grimm," in *Tornare a Gramsci: Una cultura per l'Italia*, ed. Gaspare Polizzi (Grottaferrata: Avverbi, 2010), 157–74.

15. Q8, §214, pp. 1071–75, March 1932.

16. See, for example, Q4, §38, pp. 455–65, October 1930; Q7, §4, p. 855, November 1930; Q7, §20, p. 869, November 1930–February 1931; Q8, §195, pp. 1057–58, February 1932; Q10II, §6, pp. 1244–45, May 1932; Q11, §22, pp. 1422–26, July–August 1932; Q13, §17, pp. 1578–89, May 1932–November 1933; Q13, §18, pp. 1589–97, May 1932–November 1933.

17. Lucia Borghese provides a detailed account of significant variations in "Lo scudo di Gramsci," introduction to Antonio Gramsci, *I racconti dei fratelli Grimm*, eds. Nicola Caleffi and Guglielmo Leoni (Modena: Incontri Editrice, 2011), 7–29.

18. Lawrence Venuti, *The Translator's Invisibility: A History of Translation* (London: Routledge, 1995).

19. Oscar Wilde, "The Critic as Artist," in *The Complete Works of Oscar Wilde*, vol. 4, *Criticism*, ed. Josephine M. Guy (Oxford: Oxford University Press, 2007), 123–206.

20. Q11, §46–49, pp. 1468–73, August–December 1932.

21. André Tosel's work, from the same period as Borghese's, constitutes an important early exception; see "Philosophie marxiste et traductibilité des langages et des pratiques," *La Pensée*, no. 223 (September–October 1981); reprinted in *Praxis: Vers une refondation en philosophie marxiste* (Paris: Éditions Sociales, 1984), 115–35. Significant early contributions on Gramsci's concept of translatability, alongside more recent studies, are collected in Peter Ives and Rocco Lacorte, eds., *Gramsci, Language, and Translation* (Lanham, MD: Lexington Books, 2010). The most extended studies of Gramsci's theory of translatability are those by Derek Boothman: *Traducibilità e processi traduttivi: Un caso: A. Gramsci linguista* (Perugia: Guerra edizioni, 2004); "Traduzione e traducibilità," in *Le parole di Gramsci: Per un lessico dei "Quaderni del carcere,"* ed. Fabio Frosini and Guido Liguori (Rome: Carocci, 2004), 247–66. The relevance of Gramsci to more recent theories of cultural translation was highlighted by both Giorgio Baratta in *Antonio Gramsci in contrappunto: Dialoghi col presente* (Rome: Carocci, 2007) and Birgit Wagner, "Cultural Translation: A Value or a Tool? Let's Start with Gramsci!," in *Translation: Narration, Media and the Staging of Differences*, ed. Federico Italiano and Michael Rössner (Bielefeld: transcript, 2012), 51–68. Fabio Frosini places the distinctive notion of translatability at the center of the reconstruction of Gramsci's philosophical thought in *La religione dell'uomo moderno: Politica e verità nei "Quaderni del carcere" di Antonio Gramsci* (Rome: Carocci, 2010), as well as in numerous other texts. More recently, among a burgeoning field, see the important contributions of Martín Cortés, *Un nuevo marxismo para América Latina: José Aricó: Traductor, editor, intelectual* (Mexico City: Siglo Veintiuno, 2015); Romain Descendre and Jean-Claude Zancarini, "De la traduction à la traductibilité: Un outil d'émancipation théorique," *Laboratoire italien: Politique et société*, no. 18

(2016); Giuseppe Cospito, "Traducibilità dei linguaggi scientifici e filosofia della praxis," *Filosofia italiana*, no. 2 (2017): 47–65; Giuliano Guzzone, *Gramsci e la critica dell'economia politica: Dal dibattito sul liberismo al paradigma della "traducibilità"*(Rome: Viella, 2018); Stephen Shapiro and Neil Lazarus, "Translatability, Combined Unevenness, and World Literature in Antonio Gramsci," *Mediations* 32, no. 1 (Fall 2018): 1–36; Saša Hrnjez, "Traducibilità, Dialettica, Contraddizione: Per una teoria-prassi della traduzione a partire da Gramsci," *International Gramsci Journal* 3, no. 3 (2019): 40–71.

22. On Gramsci's reconceptualization of Marxism as a "philosophy of praxis," see Fabio Frosini, *Gramsci e la filosofia* (Rome: Carocci, 2003), particularly 98–102; and Peter D. Thomas, "Gramsci's Marxism: The 'Philosophy of Praxis,'" in *Antonio Gramsci*, ed. Mark McNally (London: Palgrave Macmillan, 2015), 97–117.

23. Following their appearance in Q7, §2 in November 1930, Gramsci again recalls Lenin's remarks at the beginning of section V of Q11, §46, p. 1468, presumably penned in August 1932.

24. For the most comprehensive surveys of the conceptual history of hegemony, see Bruno Bongiovanni and Luigi Bonanate, "Egemonia," in *Enciclopedia delle scienze sociali*, vol. 3 (Rome: Istituto della Enciclopedia Italiana, 1993), 470–77; Giuseppe Cospito, "Egemonia/egemonico nei 'Quaderni del carcere' (e prima)," *International Gramsci Journal* 2, no. 1 (2016): 49–88. Perry Anderson, *The H-Word: The Peripeteia of Hegemony* (London: Verso, 2017) contains some useful insights on post–World War II usages in American political science, but provides a less accurate reconstruction of the concept's earlier history, particularly prior to the Italian Risorgimento and following the 1917 Russian Revolution.

25. On the development of hegemony among the classical Greek historians, see John Wickersham, *Hegemony and Greek Historians* (Lanham, MD: Rowman and Littlefield, 1994).

26. I.4; I.25; I.75; VII.15; VIII.89. Thucydides, *The Peloponnesian War*, trans. Thomas Hobbes (Chicago: University of Chicago Press, 1989).

27. On the distinctive understanding of hegemony produced in the dynamic of the Italian Risorgimento, see Cospito, "Egemonia/egemonico nei 'Quaderni del carcere' (e prima)." For Marx and Engels's use of the term, see Wolfgang Fritz Haug, "Hegemonie," in *Historisch-kritisches Wörterbuch des Marxismus* 6, I (Hamburg: Argument, 2004), 8–9.

28. The most comprehensive account of the dissemination of hegemony in Russian Social Democracy, both before 1917 and particularly in the early 1920s, is Craig Brandist's *The Dimensions of Hegemony: Language, Culture and Politics in Revolutionary Russia* (Leiden: Brill, 2015).

29. I have elsewhere analyzed the gradual emergence of the notion of "passive revolution" in the *Prison Notebooks* in relation to the concepts of hegemony and "the revolution in permanence." See Peter D. Thomas, "Gramsci's Revolutions: Passive and Permanent," *Modern Intellectual History* 17, no. 1 (2020): 117–46. I take the efficacious formulation of the "hegemonic fabric" of modern sovereignty from

Fabio Frosini, "Reformation, Renaissance and the State: The Hegemonic Fabric of Modern Sovereignty," *Journal of Romance Studies* 12, no. 3 (2010): 63–77. Focusing on this dimension of Gramsci's translation of hegemony alone (that is, considering it primarily as a theory of modern political power, rather than as a strategic perspective) has often led to his conceptualization of hegemony in general being regarded as a Marxist addition to a Weberian typology of domination, whether in the influential formulation of Laclau and Mouffe of hegemony as a process of (contingent, incomplete) universalization, Guha's notion of a metropolitan hegemonic normativity absent in the colonial peripheries, or the presuppositions of the theorists of post-hegemony (for most of whom hegemony is equivalent to and exhausted by sovereignty). See Ernesto Laclau and Chantal Mouffe, *Hegemony and Socialist Strategy: Towards a Radical Democratic Politics* (London: Verso, 2014 [1985]); Ranajit Guha, *Dominance without Hegemony: History and Power in Colonial India* (Oxford: Oxford University Press, 1998); Alberto Moreiras, *The Exhaustion of Difference: The Politics of Latin American Cultural Studies* (Durham, NC: Duke University Press, 2001).

30. Gramsci discusses the lineage at length in Q8, §208, pp. 1066–67, February–March 1932, adding to the traditional German line of inheritance the Italian Carducci.

31 The reference to the Jacobins occurs in Q1, §44, p. 51, February–March 1930; the reverberations of the historical experience of Jacobinism, both in France and internationally, remain a constant concern throughout the *Prison Notebooks*. The notion of a "correspondence" between languages is formulated both in Q1, §44 and, not for the last time, in Q4, §42, p. 467, October 1930.

32. Q3, §48, p. 331, June–July 1930.

33. Q19, §24, p. 2028, July–August 1934–February 1935. Q19, §24 is a revision of the previously cited Q1, §44.

34. See in particular Q15, §64, pp. 1828–29, June–July 1933, in which Gramsci uses the comparison of revolutionary France and philosophical Germany as a model for the relations between Greece and Rome.

35. Derek Boothman explores this interpretation of Gramsci's theory of translatability in relation to a broadly Kuhnian conception of paradigms. Fabio Frosini (*La religione dell'uomo moderno*) formulates Gramsci's notion of the linguistic diversity that underwrites the possibility of translation in similarly realist terms; "languages say the same thing in different ways; or better, they can say the same thing because they are different. There is thus a difference that not only does not impede, but rather is that which makes identity possible" (31); "the different national traditions need to be deciphered as different forms of response to historical problems . . . fundamentally identical" (176).

36. Q8, §208, pp. 1066–67, February–March 1932.

37. Q11, §47, p. 1468, August–December 1932.

38. Q11, §47, p. 1468, August–December 1932.

39. "Contrary to his insights elsewhere,", because Gramsci was a consistently fierce critic of the type of abstract universalism embodied in the enthusiasm for

Esperanto in his time, including in the socialist movement. See Q3, §76, p. 353, August 1930; Q11, §45, p. 1467, August–December 1932; Q23, §39, p. 2235, from July–August 1934.

40. Fredric Jameson, *The Political Unconscious: Narrative as a Socially Symbolic Act* (Ithaca, NY: Cornell University Press, 1981).

41. See Hayden White, "The Value of Narrativity in the Representation of Reality," in *The Content of the Form: Narrative Discourse and Historical Representation* (Baltimore: Johns Hopkins University Press, 1987), 1–25.

42. Q29, §1–9, pp. 2341–51, presumably April 1935. The aspiration to provide a new type of introduction to the study of this field (in terms of content, method, and order of arguments) mirrors the similarly innovative introductory approach to the study of philosophy that is attempted in Q11. Peter Ives's *Gramsci's Politics of Language* explores the significance of the notion of an immanent grammar not only for Gramsci's philosophy of language, but for his conception of philosophy as such.

43. On the debate between Croce and Gentile, considered in relation to Gramsci's notion of translatability, see the important contribution of Domenico Jervolino, "Croce, Gentile and Gramsci on Translation," *International Gramsci Journal*, no. 2 (2010): 29–38.

44. On the nexus of intuition-expression, see Benedetto Croce, *La poesia di Dante* (Bari: Laterza, 1921), 53–72, particularly 66. Gramsci directly criticizes Croce's separation of 'poetry' and 'structure' while elaborating his 'little discovery' in the field of Dante studies; see Q4, §78–§87, pp. 516–30, May 1930–August 1932.

45. Benedetto Croce, *The Aesthetic as the Science of Expression and of the Linguistic in General*, trans. Colin Lyas (Cambridge: Cambridge University Press, 1992 [1902]), 76.

46. Giovanni Gentile, "Torto e diritto delle traduzioni," in *Frammenti di estetica e di letteratura* (Lanciano: Carabba editore, 1920), 372–73.

47. Q11, §48, p. 1470, August–December 1932.

48. Thomas Hardy, *Jude the Obscure*, ed. Cedric Watts (Peterborough, ON: Broadview, 1999), 66–67.

49. There is a distinctive irony to the extent to which the notion of imitation as equivalence came to dominate discussions of translation during the nineteenth and twentieth centuries (and continue to overdetermine many theories of translation today). In the long period of Western literary history that Meyer H. Abrams characterized in his classic study *The Mirror and the Lamp* (Oxford: Oxford University Press, 1953) as being dominated by a "mimetic" paradigm (8), in which the relation of original to copy constituted one of the most powerful modes of literary judgment and classification, discussions of translation were surprisingly little concerned with questions of reproduction, repetition, or sometimes even accuracy. (Abrams's periodization effectively includes most theories of literary production that preceded anglophone and above all Coleridgean Romanticism, and in turn roughly corresponds to the first of George Steiner's four periods of translation theory; see *After Babel: Aspects of Language and Translation*, 3rd ed. (Oxford: Oxford University Press, 1998), 248). "Theorists" of translation in the earlier period (who were

invariably also practitioners, both of translation and "other" forms of writing) instead were more often interested in comprehending translation as a distinctive type of writing within a continuum of writerly practice, turning to figures that we would today characterize as more rhetorical rather than epistemological, and a more expansive notion of imitation as what today would be regarded as "inspiration" (consider, for instance, Dryden's reflections on a spectrum of translational practices; John Dryden, "On Translation," in *Theories of Translation: An Anthology of Essays from Dryden to Derrida*, ed. Rainer Schulte and John Biguenet (Chicago: University of Chicago Press, 1992), 17–31. However, with the shift to what Abrams calls the "expressivist" paradigm of Romanticism and its focus on the creative and not merely representative powers of the Imagination (21), suddenly translation seems to be subjected more intensely to Platonic criteria of equivalence, adequacy and reproduction, and invariably accused of constituting a "degeneration" of the force of the original. It is almost as if, defeated on the terrain of "original" literary and artistic production, the Platonic injunction took refuge in the neglected backwaters of the "lesser" genre of translation, sacrificed by its writerly siblings as the collateral damage necessary in order to secure the primacy of the new regime of the aesthetic autonomy of the privileged creator as origin of intention and meaning. The massive mimetic anxieties that define Western literary history were thereby projected onto translation, as if the relations between texts in different languages should now be required to provide the sense of certainty that had been denied to most other forms of writing by the loss of an objective link between word and sign promoted by Romanticism and its continuing aftermath.

50. Socrates provides this account of poetic inspiration as mimetic transmission of an original force to the rhapsode Ion: "there is a divinity moving you, like that contained in the stone which Euripides calls a magnet, but which is commonly known as the stone of Heraclea. This stone not only attracts iron rings, but also imparts to them a similar power of attracting other rings; and sometimes you may see a number of pieces of iron and rings suspended from one another so as to form quite a long chain: and all of them derive their power of suspension from the original stone." See Plato, *Selected Dialogues of Plato*, trans. Benjamin Jowett (New York: Random House, 2001), 10.

51. The notion of untranslatability in the work of Derrida, and influentially elaborated by such contemporary figures as Barbara Cassin and Emily Apter, clearly is based upon very different presuppositions from those that informed Croce's and Gentile's different arguments that translation never occurs. For this more recent debate, the untranslatable is precisely that which is most often translated, but in an always unsatisfactory form that prompts its retranslation; in Cassin's words, "the untranslatable is rather what one keeps on (not) translating" ("Introduction," in *Dictionary of Untranslatables. A Philosophical Lexicon*, translation ed. Emily Apter, Jacques Lezra, and Michael Wood [Princeton, NJ: Princeton University Press, 2014], xvii). Nevertheless, the decision to express this iterative relation in privative terms indicates a continuing indebtedness to the notion of "the singular event of the

original," which translation cannot but fail to restore, even and especially when the presuppositions of the very notion of an original are immediately problematized (Jacques Derrida, *Monolingualism of the Other; or, The Prosthesis of Origin*, trans. Patrick Mensah [Stanford, CA: Stanford University Press, 1998], 56). If, to use Derrida's phrase, "one always has to postulate an original," even in order to deny it, the untranslatable will always figure as an instance of lack, rather than as the surplus of the endlessly translated (Jacques Derrida, "Reply to Roundtable," in *The Ear of the Other: Otobiography, Transference, Translation*, ed. Christine McDonald, trans. Peggy Kamuf [Lincoln: University of Nebraska Press, 1985], 147).

52. In this sense, following Butler's reading of Hegel's critique of formalism, to found the possibility of translation in a universal grammar would be to transform it into the effect of a nihilistic "annihilating universality." See Judith Butler, "Restaging the Universal: Hegemony and the Limits of Formalism," in Judith Butler, Ernesto Laclau, and Slavoj Žižek, *Contingency, Hegemony, Universality: Contemporary Dialogues on the Left* (London: Verso, 2000), 22.

53. Herein, as Gramsci argued, lay the limits of Croce's claimed "historicism," which remained incapable of historicizing thought and thereby preserved an ahistorical realm that determined the possibility of historicization itself. I have explored this theme in greater detail in chapter 7 of Peter D. Thomas, *The Gramscian Moment* (Chicago: Haymarket Books, 2010), 243–306.

54. Q10ii, §61, p. 1359, February–May 1933.

55. Q10i, §8, p. 1226, April–May 1932.

56. Q10ii, §61, p. 1359, February–May 1933.

57. There are similarities here to Derrida's notion of translation as "a regulated transformation of one language by another, of one text by another," without deference either to origins or ends. See Jacques Derrida, *Positions*, trans. Alan Bass (Chicago: University of Chicago Press, 1981), 20.

58. Q11, §25, p. 1429, July–August 1932.

Universal Eco-homophony: Overtaking Translation

Naomi Waltham-Smith

In the mid-nineteenth century a circle of British music theorists, heterodox scientists, and missionaries engaged in an almost fanatical search for a universal musical instrument tuned to an Ur-scale of nature that would capture the rich variety of scales and tuning systems used around the world. This liberal quest sought in vain to subordinate the musical expression of racial difference to a global (read Western) measure of harmony. The fictional instrument was thus a kind of translation machine that hinged upon a European-expansionist notion of globalized exchange. The fantasy of a universal musical language that would escape the tyranny of a particular scale was, as James Q. Davies observes, to turn the British empire's network of telegraphic cables into "a vast intercontinental undersea musical instrument."[1] That musical instruments during the period of European imperialisms often bore close resemblance to other communications inventions often designed to translate from one code to another highlights the way in which such translation machines entailed an *attunement* of differences into an homophonous unison via a synchronization of different frequencies or speeds into an absolute speed that could outstrip all difference, whether spatial or cultural. The speed of such a globalizing economy will come in our "post-"imperialist times to underpin the empire of financial capitalism, suggesting the impossibility of outspeeding, of (sur)passing, getting past, such imperial fictions. And yet such fantasies of universalization also shatter on what in musical tuning are calls "beats"—not of the metrical kind but the periodic pulsation that results from the interference pattern between two slightly different frequencies.

At first blush, an appeal to the singular sounds of the musics that ethnomusicologists encountered in their imperialist adventures might appear to be the only—and unnegotiable—politico-ethico response to the appropriative violence of this leveling. And yet it was precisely as singularities that world musics were imported to the metropole and accrued values in cultural archives, as the gamelan found in Anglo-American music departments or as the recordings made by comparative musicologists (the forerunners of ethnomusicologists) and philologists precisely because the exact sounds of indigenous speech and music were deemed *untranslatable* into American or European idioms. The paradox is that it is precisely the shortfall between source and target—the falling short of translation, doomed to be *under*-translation and hence *no more* translation—that produces surplus value and that inflates the value of the colonialist's loot as a cultural commodity on the very global markets whose economy of translation it appears to obstruct. Indigeneity enters into circulation as singularity.

This commodification of untranslatability is thus not a limit to translatability. Rather, it shows that translation is always already *plus de la traduction*, no more and more than translation—a homographic *double entendre* that is itself not translatable, at least not with commensurable economy, into English. The opposition between translatability and untranslatability is thus an effect of what the later Derrida would call the autoimmunity of translation whereby it measures (itself) up to the untranslatable and no farther so as to stave off an absolute expansion of equivalence that would leave no scope for translation or measuring up and thus levels even itself. What is untranslatable, far from being the fictional outside of exchange or the survivor of its violence, just is this self-differentiating movement of translation.

The complexity of translation hinges on the syncopation of this no more or no longer. Derrida suggests: "Rien n'est intraduisible pour peu qu'on se donne le temps de la dépense ou l'expansion d'un discours compétent qui se mesure à la puissance de l'original [Nothing is untranslatable so long as one takes the time to spend or to expand a discourse that measures itself against—measures itself up to—the power of the original]."[2] What makes translation possible is the expenditure of this time of measurement. And yet the imperialist fantasies of subterranean telecommunications technologies and universal musical instruments are fantasies of *speed*—of an infinite speed, beyond measure, accelerated to the point where it arrives at once, instantly, and thus collapses the spatial extension of geography and of cultural difference. In "Negotiations," Derrida demystifies the "at once," showing that any purported indivisibility of an "at the same time" always already decomposes itself. Far from foreclosing the possibility of doing two or more contradictory things simultaneously—such as singular idioms and universal translatability—the explosion of the "at once" reveals the necessity of delegating what ostensibly falls under the power of an

"I can" or an "I must" to "a differentiated, diverse community with heterogeneous times and rhythms."³ In this way, Derrida, who takes the example of two
colleagues in women's studies, by analogy does not simply expose Eurocentrism
to its other but fragments the colonizer from within into the subject that legit-
imizes the institution and her ally whose "radical questions" threaten that
legitimacy.

The "at once" is decomposed into polyrhythm when a little later Derrida
argues that

> There is not an "at the same time," there is not, period . . . there are
> simply differences, multiplicities of rhythm. In the phenomenon, or in
> what has the appearance of "at the same time," there are already differ-
> ences of rhythm, differences of speed.⁴

To explain these multiplicities of speed and rhythm, Derrida reaches for
the figure of the knot—or of stricture, seriature, and interlacing, as developed
in *Glas* and *Cartouches*—but he also felicitously invokes the underwater telecommunications networks of empire as a metaphor for this entanglement,
thereby interlacing the themes of globalization and sonic transfer, passage of
information and differential, syncopated vibration. The knot is not simply a
subsumption of polyrhythm to the dictates of meter—that is, to measurement—
but is, moreover, a matter of another kind of rationalization, specifically that
of tuning, in which we might imagine the variously tensed strings of some
universal musical instrument cannot be harmonized within the ratios of the
overtone series.

> There is a word that keeps coming back to me, and the image of the
> knot. Negotiation as a knot, as the work of the *knot*. In the *knot* of ne-
> gotiation there are different rhythms, different forces, different differ-
> ential vibrations of time and rhythm. The word *knot* came to me, and
> the image of a rope. A rope with an entanglement, a rope made up of
> several strands knotted together. The rope exists. One imagines com-
> puters with little wires, wires where things pass very quickly, wires
> where things pass very slowly: negotiation is placed along all of these
> wires. And things pass, information passes, or it does not pass, as with
> the telephone. Also, cables that pass under the sea and thousands of
> voices with intonations, that is, with different and entangled tensions.
> Negotiation is like a rope and an interminable number of wires mov-
> ing or quivering with different speeds or intensities.⁵

Seriature is a way of *negotiating* the twin poles of this collection of essays:
translation and universality. It negotiates between the incommensurable

singularity of the idiom and the indifference that lubricates market exchange. But it does not negotiate dialectically. Rather the knot is tied more or less tightly. Stricture is more or less strict. The multiplicities are more or less loosely gathered together, neither a unified totality nor an atomized scattering but always differential forces of binding. Seriature or negotiation might therefore be other names for translation insofar as they consist in "the necessity of linking" singularities that resist being put into a series, whence the metaphors of ropes, chains, and telephone wires which demand a measure of binding.

> One has to link singularities, that is, put in a series things that do not let themselves be put into series. This can be a definition of negotia-tion. Why one must repeat and put into a series, in a kind of serial generality, things that do not let themselves be serialized, which are singular and nonnegotiable every time.[6]

One might imagine that such an imperative—to generalize the singular—comes up against the stubbornness of the idiom, whose value is thus rendered priceless. In "Du 'sans prix,' ou le 'juste prix' de la transaction," translated in *Negotiations*, Derrida expressly likens translatability to money as "l'équivalent général de tout échange et de toute transaction [the general equivalent of all exchange and all transaction]"[7] and hence to "ces trois prédicats de l'indiffé-rence (substitution, répétition, neutralisation) [the three predicates of indiffer-ence (substitution, repetition, neutralization)]" that are indissociable in money, thus linking translatability to "le mouvement d'universalisation [the movement of universalization]."[8] And yet Derrida's notion of seriature or negotiation cru-cially distinguishes itself from the economy of translation insofar as it recon-figures translation as a differential field of forces, speeds, rhythms, and intonations that are more or less translated—a self-dispersing field of under- and over-translation tending toward *no more* translation either because the substi-tution is so swift and easy as to disappear on the spot or so arduous as to be impossible. This differential translation thus holds itself back from absolute tightness (strict fidelity) or absolute looseness (to the point of mistranslation) for fear of its destruction. A bit of deflation, a bit of easing—that is the economy of translation.

But I'm getting ahead of myself. I've gone too quickly and gone past the question of speed. I've overtaken speed. I've sped past multiple differential speeds in a rush toward an absolute speed that economizes on speed. Or per-haps I haven't if money is time, or so Derrida conjectures, inverting the con-ventional formula into "le temps fait gagner de l'argent [money allows us to win time]."

En tant que substitut ou équivalent général, il économise d'abord le temps de l'échange des choses et des biens ; il accélère à l'infini la circulation : non seulement en fournissant des substituts, mais en substituant d'abord son principe au principe du troc. En ouvrant le règne de la répétition, de la substitution, c'est-à-dire de la neutralisation qui efface les caractéristiques individuelles des choses échangées et des sujets de l'échange, il fournit un élément de quantification ou de mathématisation de la valeur qui est d'abord une extraordinaire neutralisation du temps. C'est pourquoi, soit dit au passage, le gain de temps que la technologie de la communication assure au marché, à l'activité de la cotation boursière, aux mouvements de la spéculation chrématistique n'est pas un bénéfice secondaire ou accidentel ; c'est, pourrait-on dire, le déploiement même de l'essence de l'argent comme temps (l'argent, c'est du temps), comme accélération du temps social, comme quantification et économie du temps.

As substitute or equivalent in general, it begins by economizing on the time of exchange of things and goods; it accelerates circulation to infinity: not only by supplying substitutes but by first substituting its principle to the principle of barter. By opening the reign of repetition, of substitution, that is, of the neutralization that erases the individual characteristics of the things exchanged and the subjects of the exchange, it supplies an element of quantification or mathematization of value that is first an extraordinary neutralization of time. This is why, let it be said along the way, the saving of time that the technology of communication secures for the market, for the activity of the stock exchange, for the movements of chrematistic speculation, is not a secondary or accidental benefit; it is, one might say, the very deployment of the essence of money as time (money is time), as the acceleration of social time, as quantification and economy of time.[9]

Insofar as the telecommunications technologies that facilitate global finance depend upon the same logic of indifference, they allow not simply a time to measure (up) but, moreover, the measurement of time—an economy of time. Derrida therefore notes that the very medium of monetary exchange takes the form of money itself. What leads to the abstraction of chrematistic speculation, of a financialization that detaches economy from need and use, is a redoubling of money's mathematization or neutralization of difference. The economy economizes itself, money translates money, accelerating the collapse of time and space, and dissolving any hypothetical distinction between economy and chrematistics. This is the fantasy of the universal musical instrument capable of sounding the world in harmony all at once and the tuning of which would therefore have to be beyond measure—beyond the commensurability of ratios and hence the sonorous beyond the *logos*. The inassimilable other just is translatability.

What would it mean, then, to *translate* this passage from the sphere of economics into that of translation? In short, the hypothesis—taking up the second limb of the theme that motivates this book—is that hidden in this theory of universalization is a theory of translation. Or perhaps not so secretly, for Derrida already introduces their co-implication under the guise of a multilayered conventionality. First, it is *by convention* (and according to the context) that money (*argent*) is distinguished from currency (*monnaie*).[10] Furthermore, the conventional distinction operates on the basis of an apparent difference in conventionality, according to which there is a spectrum from the authenticity and reliability of gold and silver coinage through paper currency to the artificial fiduciary dimension of contemporary credit systems. Derrida observes that the narrative is often cast as a progressive degeneration or denaturation of credit that gives increasing credit to convention in order to free up circulation.[11] Finally, both the convention of distinguishing and the conventionalization that underpins that distinction rest upon "une conventionnalité plus générale [a more general conventionality]"[12] in which language and monetary geopolitics are co-implicated not only insofar as global communications technologies provide the medium for increasingly abstract economic instruments but, moreover, because "le marché est un langage [the market is a language]."[13] Market speculation is a kind of unformalizable writing or coding. If language acts as an accelerant unleashing an infinite form of accumulation as an end itself untethered from economic need, it is because economics is from the outset a semantic exchange or translatability.

Moreover, while the conventional distinction between money and currency implicates language in general, Derrida points out that this distinction is marked differently and to different degrees in different languages. Whereas English, like German, uses a series of linked terms—silver, money, currency, change—to express the spectrum, this series is untranslatable into French, which uses a single word for multiple senses.

> La série allemande (*Silber, Geld, Münze, Geldstück*) ou la série anglaise (*silver, money, currency, change*) ne peut se traduire immédiatement, sans de longues et laborieuses médiations dans l'idiome français qui n'a, par exemple, qu'un mot pour désigner l'argent comme métal naturel (*silver, Silber*), l'argent comme monnaie ou signe monétaire et l'argent comme monnaie investie, et investie, précisément à cause de

son homonymie avec la richesse naturelle, de toutes sortes de valeurs projetées selon les figures complexes et surdéterminées du désir ou de la haine, de la convoitise ou du dégoût, de la rétention dans l'avarice anale ou du rejet de l'excrément, etc. Ce que nous appelons l'argent en français (et qui n'est ni simplement le signe monétaire ni simplement la monnaie qu'on rend au cours d'une opération de vente—le « change » en anglais—ni simplement le métal qu'on trouve dans les mines ou dans des bijoux) ne peut pas se traduire d'un seul mot par *silver* ou *Silber*, mais pas davantage de façon stricte par *Geld* ou *money*.

The German series (*Silber, Geld, Münze, Geldstück*) or the English series (silver, money, currency, change) cannot be immediately translated, without long and laborious mediations in the French idiom that has, for example, only one word to designate *l'argent* as natural metal (*silver, Silber*), *l'argent* as money or monetary sign and *l'argent* as currency invested, and invested precisely because of its homonymy with natural wealth, with all sorts of values projected according to complex and overdetermined figures of desire or hatred, of covetousness or disgust, of retention in anal avarice or rejection of the excrement, etc. What we call *l'argent* in French (and which is not simply the monetary sign nor simply the *monnaie* that one gives back in the course of a sales operation—"change" in English—nor simply the metal one finds in mines or in jewelry) cannot be translated in one word by *silver* or *Silber*, no more than it can be translated strictly speaking by *Geld* or money.[14]

There are two elements that I want to focus on in this passage. The first is the incommensurability that is a part of the economy of translation. Because none of the English or German words available to translate *argent* have the same multiplicity of meaning, there is by necessity a loss of meaning, specifically the association of money in the abstract, as monetary sign, with a brilliant substance that is mined as a natural resource. This unnecessary undertranslation also affects common idiomatic phrases such as *"le temps, c'est de l'argent* [time is money]" insofar as there is an explicit association between money and precious metal.

This shortfall, as I have argued, only appears to contradict or escape the economy of translation, inflating the value of the singular idiom such that its untranslatability itself becomes a valuable commodity, like the exotic music that cannot be transcribed in Western notation but only recorded by ethnomusicologists *as sound*. In this way it resembles the logic that Derrida analyses in *Le toucher* where he credits Merleau-Ponty for thinking noncoincidence at one level only to think its coincidence with coincidence at a higher level, and something similar for Nancy at a higher level still insofar as Nancy ultimately privileges infinity over the finite. In a similar way, one can give credit for the idea that the untranslatable is not an exception but exemplary of the untouchable untranslatability that comprises all translation, while deconstructing the assimilation of this untranslatability into a system of exchange or more generalized translatability to produce as it were a *universal untranslatability*. In this case, it is not that there is no word in English or German for *l'argent*. Rather, there are too many words, which would mean that a translation could only capture the wealth of meaning by breaking the unwritten rule of word-for-word translation, that is by breaking with the principle of equivalence, or it would have to sacrifice one meaning for the benefit of the other. If this were taken as a general principle, then it could be said that all translation is necessarily—and not accidentally—*mis*translation. But this failure of translation is not a homogeneous category. All the kinds of untranslatability in their singularity cannot be gathered together under a single, universal concept. Rather, as stricture or negotiation, the untranslatable is differential, more or less tight, more or less over- or under-translated.

The type of over/under-translation at stake in this passage stems from homonymy—itself a kind of absolute homophony or sonic attunement. German, English, and French under- or over-translate one another because their internal distributions of meaning are incommensurable. Put otherwise, there is an intra-lingual translation in each language as a homonym is displaced and carried across different contexts. Homonymy is an extension of a language's capacity for use in multiple times and places, which is to say its conventionality. If homonymy is the movement of language, its metaphoricity and prostheticity, each language has a convention by which it distributes this substitutability, conventionality, iterability. Like amphibology, homonymy thus appears to point to an infinite translation which would expend the time to measure up *if only it had the time*. On this reading, untranslatability would be a premature stopping point on a teleological path, stopping short of absolute or universal translatability. Following this logic, Jacques Lezra distinguishes between two kinds of untranslatability: a contingent failure of translation potentially capable of correction with sufficient time and a structural impossibility of translation no matter how much time is expended.[15] Whereas the former is in some sense still a matter of (correctable) mistranslation, the example he gives of the latter is a much more complicated affair—a statement which is "always only mistranslatable" or perhaps "only accidentally translatable."[16]

A good definition of an 'untranslatable' phrase: what there is *there* that will always only be mistranslated; that, *there*, which we will always fail at translating; *that*, *there*, which, being mistranslated, cannot be corrected.[17]

Lezra's example of such untranslatability is a statement attributed to Marx that turns on an assertion of immediacy, a translation that takes no time at all: "Die Produktion ist unmittelbar auch Konsumtion." Over the pages that follow, Marx debunks this Hegelian fiction of coincidence, but the translator (unwittingly) gives the game away in advance, as it were. In the act of mistranslating *unmittelbar* as "simultaneously," she gives the lie to the purported immediacy of a statement and its translation. Insofar as the gap prefigures the philosophical gap that Marx will unfold over the course of his argument, the mistranslation inscribes this time lag ahead of and thus temporally out of step (and out of tune) with its philosophical exposition. Although Lezra does not make anything specifically of this antecedence, it will be important in what follows. Translation gains on, outspeeds, overtakes itself. And, to anticipate my argument, untranslatability just is this passing.

The self-differentiation of untranslatability, however, opens up another distinction. If Lezra in the end comes down on the side, if there is such a thing, of impossibility (untranslatable because always necessarily mistranslatable), the alternative that he poses earlier in the form of a question offers a different formulation: untranslatable to the extent it is translatable only by accident, never on purpose or predictably. Translation, then, would not be something of which a translator is capable but that which simply happens or arrives. Whereas Lezra in time—over time, given time—translates this accident into necessary *im*possibility (and thus performatively explodes the "at once" under deconstruction in his text), Derrida, in what Geoffrey Bennington presents as something that risks approaching a generalized theory, holds to the necessarily *possibly not*.[18] What is necessary is not mistranslation but the *contingency* of its translation: it will *perhaps* be translated, *perhaps not*.

This self-differentiation also echoes what Derrida argues in *Le toucher* about the multiplicity of deconstructions—deconstruction's self-differentiation, as it were—when he broaches the distinction between "his" deconstruction and Nancy's. Contrasting Nancy's formula "il n'y a pas 'le' [there is no 'the']" with his preferred syntagma, "s'il y en a [if there is any (such thing)]," he contends:

Chaque fois il fallait faire signe vers le possible (la condition de possibilité) *comme* vers l'impossible même. Et le "s'il y en a" ne dit pas "il n'y en a pas" mais il n'y a là rien qui puisse donner lieu à une preuve, à un savoir, à une détermination constative ou théorique, à un jugement, surtout pas à un jugement déterminant. C'est une autre manière de décliner le 'il n'y a pas 'le.'" Ce n'est pas la même, justement, et voilà deux gestes « déconstructifs » irréductiblement différents. Il reste que cette multiplicité s'annonce comme "déconstructive." Il faut rendre compte de cette analogie ou de cette affinité, dire encore la déconstruction au singulier pour la dire au pluriel, au "singulier pluriel"—et expliquer au mois pourquoi dans des deux syntagmes le "il y a" fait retour une fois *au conditionnel* ("s'il y en a") et l'autre fois sous *modalité négative* ("il n'y a pas . . . "). Le "en," s'il y *en* a, renvoie à ce que précisément, commandé par l'article définissant, il n'y a pas. Sûrement pas, pas sûrement.

Each time, it was necessary to point to the possible (the condition of possibility) *as* to the impossible itself. And "if there is any" doesn't say "there is none," but rather, there isn't anything that could make room for any proof, knowledge, constative or theoretical determination, judgment—especially not any determining judgment. It is another way of inflecting the "there is no 'the.'" It isn't the same precisely, for here are two irreducibly different "deconstructive" gestures. The fact remains to account for this analogy or affinity, to say deconstruction in the singular again, in order to say it in the plural, in the "singular plural"—and explain at least why in the two syntagmas, the "there is" turns *to a conditional* ("if there is any") in one instance and to a *negative modality* ("there is no . . . ") in the other. The "any [of something]" ("if there is any") precisely refers to what there is not, commanded by the defining article ("there is no 'the' . . ."). Surely not, not surely.[19]

To translate this economy of multiple, differential, slightly out-of-tune deconstructions: Each time, it was necessary to point to the translatable (the condition of translatability) *as* to the untranslatable itself. There is no scope for any determining judgment of whether there is translation or no translation. There is, on the one hand, no translation there where we will always fail at translating and, on the other hand, translation, if there is any: these two are irreducibly different untranslatables. They cannot be made to vibrate at the same frequency. Yet one must account for their affinity in order to say untranslatability in the singular again and in the plural—in the singular plural, in Nancy's formulation. Neither singular nor universal, translation is radically undecidable. If for Lezra there is no "the" untranslatable, only an untranslatable that is not one and thus surely no translation, Derrida is not so sure.

I've overshot again, so I'm going to swing back to the issue of speed. Instead of playing for or taking my time (as I appear to have done), it will be a question of going too quickly, more quickly even than speed itself. Describing Hélène Cixous's telegraphic address that passes down the telephone wires, Derrida weaves together the themes of speed, homonymy, and untranslatability:

> L'adresse prend la lettre de vitesse, mais la lettre, elle, prend le temps de vitesse, elle va plus vite que le temps, si on peut dire et si on peut faire arriver cette chose impossible : prendre le temps de vitesse, aller plus vite que la vitesse même, prendre la vitesse de vitesse, dépasser ainsi l'espace et le temps, doubler l'espace et le temps, comme on *double* un véhicule. Je préfère dire *doubler* pour deux raisons. Je préfère dire doubler, ici, parce que, comme toujours quand je préfère quoi que ce soit, c'est intraduisible—et ce qu'elle écrit est, selon moi, je m'en expliquerai encore, une expérience majeure et unique de l'intraduisible ; je préfère aussi doubler, ici, parce que ce qui gagne *de* vitesse et *sur la* vitesse, le temps et l'espace, cela gagne en doublant, selon la loi du double, de la substitution de l'unique à l'unique qui se vise en son spectre et en soi-même, se remplaçant lui-même à sa place, presque sans bouger. La lettre, donc, est gagnée et gagnante, gagnée en gagnant l'adresse, comme on gagne un lieu, en français, en y arrivant, par l'homonymie chanceuse, par la grâce de cette homonymie intraduisible des deux adresses en France.

> The address outspeeds the letter, but the letter outspeeds time, it goes faster than time, if one may say so and if one can make this impossible thing happen or arrive: to outspeed time, to go faster than speed itself, to outspeed speed, thus to overtake space and time, to pass or "double" space and time, as one says about passing a vehicle in French. I'd rather say *doubler* for two reasons. I'd rather say *doubler* here, because, as always when I prefer anything whatsoever, it is untranslatable—and what she writes is, according to me, as I will further explain, a major and unique experience of the untranslatable; I also prefer doubling, here, because what gains *in* speed and *on* speed, time and space, gains in passing or "doubling," according to the law of the double, of the substitution of the unique for the unique, which aims for its own specter and for itself, replacing itself at its place, almost without moving. The letter, therefore, is gained as much as it gains, gained as it reaches or gains the address, as one "gains" a place, in French, when one arrives there, through a felicitous homonymy, by the grace of the untranslatable homonymy of these two addresses in France.[20]

What happens here at great speed—such great speed that it outspeeds speed—is the displacement and replacement of one letter by another on the spot, with a deliberate ambiguity between the letter as alphabetic character and as a letter that one addresses and sends in the post, as well as between address as the destination of that postal letter and as directed speech. As Derrida elaborates a little later, homonymy is exemplary of instantaneous telephonic communications that cross the globe without delay—in other words, of a musical instrument that collapses the West and the rest. Homonymy's semantic inflation, like that of the imperialist's collectible instrument, is directly related to its gaining in and on speed.

> La vitesse absolue, la vitesse qui économise absolument la vitesse, c'est d'abord se rapport à soi comme rapport à l'autre d'une métonymie ou d'une homonymie qui *remplace* à l'instant, sur l'heure, sans attendre, un nom, une marque, l'adresse ou le sens d'un phonème, d'une syllabe ou d'un graphème, etc. Les remplace sur place, sur l'heure et sur-le-champ. Cette économie absolue de la vitesse est une *éco-homonymie* ou une *econométonymie* ou une *eccehomonymie*.

> Absolute speed, the speed that absolutely economizes on speed, is first of all the relation to oneself as the relation to the other of a metonymy or a homonymy that replaces a noun, a mark, the address, or the meaning of a phoneme, of a syllable, or of a grapheme, etc., instantly, at once, without delay. Replaces them on the spot, at once, and forthwith. This absolute economy of speed is an *eco-homonymy* or an *ecom-etonymy* or an *ecohomonymy*.[21]

Homonymy, as an economy of sonic substitution—"ce grand opus du remplacement [this great opus of substitution]"[22] so speedy as to be inaudible—is thus a paradigm for translation in general. It is, though, not a mark of generalization and indifference but the linking of singularities into a chain or braid, like a telephone or funambulist's wire, a prostheticity or substitutability that outstrips spatiality without violating difference. As such, insofar as it repeats and gains on itself on the spot, it articulates the "each time" of singularity. For Derrida, the question of homonymy is intimately linked to that of the untranslatable. Entwined they form the main thread of his reading of Cixous. Homonymy is "la croix de la traduction [the crux of translation]"[23] that signals and signs the untranslatable and as such is the cross borne by the translator who, unable to render the homonymy fully in the target language, is forced to return the letter to its address or, more precisely, to one of the two addresses between which she is forced to choose. What is untranslatable, what is singular, is not the particular meanings overtaken in the headlong rush to translate, to move instantly across the globe, but this homonymy itself, the very musical substitution of one tone or intonation for another.

This discussion of homonymy in *H. C. pour la vie*, though, introduces another dimension to an already self-differentiating untranslatability. Unlike the semantic multiplicity of *argent*, most of Cixous's "homonyms" entail a drift in orthography. They are typically *homophones* rather than homonyms, although Derrida prefers to subordinate them to the category of homonymy because, beyond their phonic or sounding quality, in their untranslatability they approach the proper name, in particular the homophone of Cixous's last initial C. with *c'est (pour la vie)*. I would only add the qualification that this affinity with the uniqueness of the name emerges not despite but because of the sonorous character of homophony. It is no accident that the suboceanic wires carry voices and intonations. What is untranslatable in this differential structure is the vibrational quality of its entanglements of different rhythms and speeds that beat against one another.

In an interview given on the occasion of her address as Distinguished Visiting Speaker at the University of Manitoba in 2008, Peggy Kamuf—a singular translator of Derrida and Cixous—offered the following advice:

> One has to look not just for what words and sentences are meaning; one can't go after simply meaning, although of course we are always dealing with meaning. But one has also, for example, to break down words and look for the repetition of phonemes and sounds, according to a poetic principle.[24]

Then, recalling the obsessive repetition of the strangled "gl" vocables in Derrida's *Glas*, Kamuf continues:

> There is something that another may make sense of, but it is not yet sense. It is something stuck in the body, in the glottis. Such pieces, fragments, or shards of not-yet-language remain available to readers everywhere. It's just that we have been taught to pay no attention to them, so as to get quickly to meaning. That is how you learn to read, you take the phonemes, the letters, the sounds, and combine them into words, and then you match the words to a picture, in order to arrive at the word-sense. That is how you are taught to read, that is how you *have* to be taught to read, otherwise you cannot read![25]

She laughs. It is also, no doubt, how you *have* to learn to translate, she concedes. Translation is *impossible* without what Derrida in "Qu'est-ce qu'une traduction 'relevante'?" describes as "l'unité indivisible d'une forme sonore incorporant ou signifiant l'unité indivisible d'un sens ou d'un concept" ["the indivisible unity of an acoustic form that incorporates or signifies the indivisible unity of a meaning or concept"].[26] The principle of equivalence, if not word-for-word, then "un mot *par* un mot" ["one word *by one* word"], is threatened by anything that undoes either of these unities—of sound or of sense—or the correspondence that binds them. Homophony is an exemplary category of the untranslatable. Forcing the translator to resign herself to clumsy glosses or parenthetical notes which confess the impotence of the translation, homophony and homonymy jeopardize not only the operation but also the very idea of translation, suggesting that ruin may in fact be its vocation and destiny.

> Chaque fois qu'il y a plusieurs mots en un ou dans la même forme so-nore ou graphique, chaque fois qu'il y a *effet d'homophonie* ou d'*homo-nymie*, la traduction, au sens strict, traditionnel et dominant de ce terme, rencontre une limite insurmontable—et le commencement de sa fin, la figure de sa ruine.

> This is why, whenever several words occur in one or the same acoustic or graphic form, whenever a *homophonic* or *homonymic effect* occurs, translation in the strict, traditional, and dominant sense of the term encounters an insurmountable limit—and the beginning of its end, the figure of its ruin.[27]

Why single out homophony (or homonymy) as the ruin of translation? At first glance it would seem that homophony is a particularly acute case of the multiplicity or plurality of meaning that tends to haunt all translation and as a result of which translation is always the transferential travail of mourning that Derrida seeks to indicate here by allowing us to hear the French translation of Hegel's *Aufhebung*, *relève*, in the English *relevant*. If translation negates as it preserves, if it loses as it elevates, or—now hearing in this lifting up the *art du vol* that Derrida praises in Cixous's writing—if translation's lifting up is at once a theft of meaning, it is because translation is also a plurality of analogical drives and transferential desires, what might also be described as an *art du volant et du voulant* following Cixous's quasi-homophonic effects in *Anankè*, a fictional re-treatment of psychoanalysis roughly contemporaneous with Der-rida's *La carte postale* and again focused on themes of journeying and destinnerance.[28]

Homophony, then, is an especially striking or searing example of this ana-logical wandering, an *intra*lingual drift that is not easily captured in the inter-lingual passage of translation and that thereby introduces a certain errancy into translation—or better, exposes it as constitutive and irreducible erring. I want, though, to begin to specify homophony's singular effects by distinguishing this drift not only from polysemy, or mere multiplicity of meaning, but also from various other practices of bilingual punning that destabilize or reconfigure the unity of sound and sense. Homophonic translation, for example, tends to invert the priority accorded to sense, preserving sound at the risk of producing a non-sensical text in the target language. Phono-semantic matching is more of a compromise, using semantically and phonetically similar components drawn from the target language, while calquing translates component-for-component or word-for-word by carrying over the semantic import or the loan words. But there is an element of calquing that is shared with homophony. Calquing is an example of itself. The word *calque* is borrowed from the French word meaning tracing or close imitation. Calquing thus re-marks itself, as Derrida would put it, or, thinking of tuning, beats rhythmically against itself. And it is because of this re-marking that calquing—like homophony, I shall argue—operates not only on a semantic level but, moreover, on a syntactical one, exposing another aspect of untranslatability's self-differentiation.

To grasp this, it is necessary to distinguish homophony from polysemy or mere multiplicity of meaning. In *Geschlecht III*, Derrida is at pains to separate out Heidegger's *Mehrdeutigkeit* (multiple-sidedness) from the more rigorous thought of *dissémination* set out in the book of that title.[29] While the former exacerbates semantic ambiguity and nonetheless submits to a certain gathering or univocity, *dissémination*, far from being a more radical semantic dispersal, is completely incommensurable, working on an entirely different level that Derrida calls syntactic or rhythmic. Derrida's attack surely extends to all unifying concepts in Heidegger's thought, but it is telling that in this text he is concerned with an expressly sonorous movement of totalization or indifference and one that hinges on *tuning* in that it harmonizes difference under a single, albeit silent, tonic or fundamental. This polysemia is "la plurivocité de la langue ou de la parole (*Mehrdeutigkeit der Sprache*) . . . cette bonne plurivocité qui doit être rassemblable dans la simplicité de *l'Einklang* et du *Grundton*, de l'unité harmonique et du ton fondamental [the plurivocity of language or speech (*Mehrdeutigkeit der Sprache*), of this good plurivocity that must be gatherable into the simplicity of *Einklang* and the *Grundton*, harmonic unity and the fundamental tone]."[30]

In the recently published seminar, *La vie la mort* (1975–76), Derrida articulates this incommensurability between generalizable multiplicity and *dissémination* by distinguishing textuality, insofar as it has the structure of the life of the living, from speech or verbal language. And in this context, we should recall how Derrida, prizing apart Benjamin's *fortleben* and *überleben*, thinks translation as *survivre*, living on, life-death. In *La vie la mort*, he argues that the genetic text is not dominated by either words or semantic meaning but instead operates on a another, syntactical level or, more precisely, that it renders undecidable the opposition between semantics and syntax. The sixth session of the seminar, which concludes Derrida's reading from earlier sessions of biologist François Jacob's *La logique du vivant*, begins with an analysis of a pair of statements in that text, the first of which concerns the self-referentiality of translation: "Le message génétique ne peut être traduit que par les produits de sa propre traduction [The genetic message can be translated only by the products of its own translation]."[31] To analyze the self-referentiality at stake here, Derrida turns to the first line of Ponge's *Fable*: "Par le mot *par* commence donc ce texte [With the word *with* thus begins this text]." In *Psyché* he will cite this line as an example of the undecidability between performative and constative, but here in the seminar, he poses this undecidability as that between translating and the translated.

Derrida demonstrates the quasi-transcendental structure of Ponge's fable: "il la dit à l'aide de (par) l'un de ses élements internes (par) [it says with the aid of (*par*) one of its own elements (*par*)]," which is thus inside and outside at once, both metalinguistic and borrowed within the message. "C'est en déchiffrant ce message, en le traduisant à l'aide de ce qu'il traduit, que je peux à la fois produire le message et le traduire. Sa traduction est sa production. [It is in deciphering this message, in translating it with the help of what it translates, that I can at once produce the message and translate it. Its translation is its production.]"[32] Note again the "at once" of text and translation and the similarity with the statement of Marx that Lezra analyzes. Moreover, the second iteration of *par* is only translational to the extent that it repeats the first, and the first is not a translation but already translated. The ordering of the words, which shows the logic of the *donc*, begins not with the translated but with *translating* as such. This event of translating which comes before any translated word or word to be translated—and which, I would venture, is named by Cixous's *puissance*—is what makes translation both possible and impossible, accounting for homophony's ruin of translation. Derrida goes on to explain this quasi-transcendental, self-destructive structure of the trace as a syntactical re-marking.

> Nous avons vu que le même contenu sémantique disposé dans un autre ordre . . . donnerait un énoncé qui certes pourrait décrire ou traduire ou reproduire le premier (énoncé B traduisant A), mais échouerait à se traduire ou reproduire lui-même. . . . C'est seulement à l'intérieur d'un système textuel plus grand, utilisant une partie ou un produit de lui-même pour se déchiffrer, qu'on pourra dire qui l'énoncé

"ce texte commence par le mot 'par'" se traduit and se reproduit. Mais le système le plus grand, le code général, a la structure de l'énoncé "Par le mot *par* commence donc ce texte" en tant qu'il ne peut être traduit que par les produits de sa traduction, que la structure, la syntaxe, l'ordre y précède et détermine les effets de sens ou de vouloir-dire, que cette structure syntaxique, par définition, n'est pas dominée ou déterminée pas les noms, c'est-à-dire des vocables référentiels, ayant une référence hors texte ou hors énoncé, mais par des articulations syntaxiques visant en dernière instance des éléments qui font partie du texte, remarquant le texte.

We have seen that the same semantic content arranged in a different order . . . can yield an utterance that might well describe or translate or reproduce the first (utterance B translating utterance A) but that would fail to translate or reproduce itself. . . . It is only within a larger textual system, using a part or a product of itself to decipher itself, that one will be able to say that the utterance "this text begins by the word by" can be translated and reproduced. But the largest system, the general code, has the structure of the utterance "by the word by begins thus this text" insofar as it can be translated only by the products of its translation, insofar as the structure, the syntax, or the order comes first and determines the effects of meaning or intention, insofar as this syntactical structure is, by definition, dominated or determined not by nouns, that is, by referential terms that have a reference outside the text or outside the utterance, but by syntactical articulations that are directed, in the final analysis, at elements that are a part of the text, that remark the text.[33]

Following this logic, the more rigorous thought of *dissémination*, unlike polysemy or mere multiplicity of meaning, involves this re-marking with appeal to an outside of translation. It is inside and outside, an example and performance of itself. Among the various undecidables in Derrida's writings—trace, *écriture*, autoimmunity, and so on—*dissémination* is perhaps not one singularity among others. It also re-marks the relation of each of them to one another—that is to say, the spacing between them that allows them to appear as non-identical in their semantic dispersion and allows their generalization into a series. It is what makes that unity both possible and impossible, which is why, unlike Heidegger's *Mehrdeutigkeit*, *dissémination* cannot be subordinated to a gathering or univocity. The case is similar with homophony. In "La double séance" Derrida argues that the richness and exuberance of the textual effects of re-marking come with "une pauvreté, je dirais presque une monotonie très singulière, très régulière aussi [a kind of poverty, I would even call it a very singular and very regular monotony]."[34] It is this monotony of *dissémination* that I believe is exposed in the practice of homophony and returns us to our scene of musical attunement.

To develop this idea further, I want to turn to a passage in "S'il y a lieu de traduire" in *Du droit à la philosophie* that connects the failure of translation exhibited by performatively self-referential statements with the question of the singularity of the idiom. In this essay, Derrida cites the example of untranslatability of an utterance such as "je parle français [I am speaking French]" into another language such as Latin (or, anticipating the text's translation right here, English). This kind of performative practice of the language in which the original is produced, similar to the self-referentiality of Ponge's fable or Jacob's claim about the genetic message, "prépare une sorte de *suicide à la traduction*, comme on dit suicide au gaz ou suicide par le feu [prepares a kind of *suicide by translation*, as one says suicide by gas or suicide by fire]."[35] Kamuf has a brilliant, if rather more terroristic metaphor: "idiom . . . is detonated by all the little bombs of [Cixous's] sentences."[36] There is in this autoimmunity of translation an erasure of the translating event that precedes any translation and that begins as soon as there is reading of a text. Translation, then, is a passage that erases the traces of its path. "La traduction passe son chemin, ici même [translation is passing its path, right here]," as Derrida puts it pithily.

Kamuf extends this metaphor of translation as burning through the fuel of language with a notion of "afterburn." Noting in playful imitation that Cixous's writing involves "complex patterns of many-voiced speech, dialogues external, internal, and maternal, telephonic, helenephonic, teleidiomatic, derridiomatic, telepathic, telegraphic" that demand to be heard as much as read, she observes that translation begins with a burning sensation "between ears and eyes, but also on the tongue and to the touch, the enveloping sensation of the untranslatable."[37] The untranslatable first of all burns down the walls within a language via homonymy or, as Kamuf illustrates, through quasi-homophonic effects that rely upon sonic affinities and show that Derrida and Cixous "have always shared an acute ear for the idiom's reserve stores of untranslatability"—a telephonic exchange expressly thematized by Cixous herself in the text under examination, "Le manuscript volant." Kamuf's afterburn is not simply a searing experience of the singular but is a temporal category, pointing to the time expended in trying to produce a translation that measures up. This smoldering, burning its way through from one language to another, is much slower and cooler than the spark of the "at once." Instead of getting ahead of itself, translation here appears as what refuses to be extinguished even after it burns itself out, that lingers on the retina. What kind of sonic or musical instrument harmonizes on this timeframe?

Cixous poses one answer. Igniting the singularly sonorous quality of this effect, she associates the metaphor of the flame's extinction and rekindling with what she dubs "le cri de la littérature" or "l'é-*cri*-ture." Writing about Derrida's "Le ver à soie," which also makes extensive use of homonymic and quasi-homophonic effects to play on Cixous's word "voiles," she writes:

> Il crie Vers, en vers, il crie comme un ver, cri inaudible, cri de soie, sachant . . . Il crie, et il m'envoie ce cri enveloppé dans du papier, depuis Buenos Aires en me recommandant de ne pas le recevoir avant qu'il se soit éteint, le cri. Je ne l'ai donc lu qu'éteint. Crihier. Pour dire la vérité: je ne le lus pas. Je ne le lus tellement pas que c'est en cet avril pluvieux que je le lis, "pour la première fois," que je l'écoute absolument, ce cri-ci, gardé vibrant, at parfaitement audible, car un cri repart comme une flamme, dès qu'il est couvé des yeux.

> He cries toward *Vers*, in verse, he cries vermiformally, like a worm, inaudible cry, the silky cry of a self . . . He cries, and he sends me this cry enveloped in some paper, from Buenos Aires advising me not to receive it before it/he has been extinguished, the cry. I read it therefore only extinguished. Cryore. To tell the truth: I read it not. I so much read it not that it is upon this rainy April that I read it, "for the first time," that I listen to it absolutely, this cry-sigh, kept vibrant, and perfectly audible, for a cry starts up again like a flame, as soon as it is kindled with a loving gaze.[38]

What Cixous describes here is not simply an address that can always go astray or fail to arrive but a cry that can arrive with its recipient only insofar as the cry has already been extinguished—a sonic instrument that cannot make itself audible in all places around the globe at once except as a kind of belated echo or syncopated harmony. Moreover, Kamuf's analysis reveals how, in playing on the presence or absence of gender agreement in French and English, that extinguishing is itself dispersed and cannot be contained within the cry. First, in French the *il* in "qu'il se soit éteint" toward the end of the second sentence need not refer to the subject of the sentence but could refer to the cry (*le cri*) or to Derrida, an undecidability that can only be over-translated in English. Then in the next sentence, translation into English yields a further scattering of meaning: "extinguished" can refer either to the cry or to Cixous as the subject of the sentence. Drift, then, is not a symptom of translation. Rather, translation as drift is a prosthetic articulationality that burns all the way through and across languages, syncopating European imperialist appropriation. The cry does not simply arrive at an intact recipient or target language but is the technicity by which language traverses, overtakes, displaces itself.

What is also fascinating in this passage is the treatment of the singular whose unprecedented emergence "for the first time" is also a rekindling of an extinguished yet inextinguishable flame. It is not merely that singularity calls (over the telephone) for iterability so as not to be extinguished but that it emerges as an intensification or tightening of generalizing technicity which for a moment becomes more incandescent, more searing, more alive. In *Le Monolinguisme*, Derrida similarly describes the singular as a more *à vif* universal.

> Que se passe-t-il quand quelqu'un en vient à décrire une "situation" prétendument singulière, la mienne par exemple, à la décrire en en témoignant dans des termes qui le dépassent, dans un langage dont la généralité prend une valeur en quelque sorte structurelle, universelle, transcendantale ou ontologique ? Quand le premier venu sous-entend: "Ce qui vaut pour moi, irremplaçablement, cela vaut pour tous. La substitution est en cours, elle a déjà opéré, chacun peut dire, pour soi et de soi, la même chose. Il suffit de m'entendre." . . . Comment déterminer ceci, un ceci singulier dont l'unicité justement tient au seul témoignage, au fait que certains individus, dans certaines situations, attestent les traits d'une structure néanmoins universelle, la révèlent, l'indiquent, la donnent à lire "plus à vif," plus à vif comme on le dit et parce qu'on le dit surtout d'une blessure, plus à vif et *mieux que d'autres*, et parfois seuls dans leur genre?

> What happens when someone comes to describe a supposedly singular "situation," mine for example, by testifying to it in terms which go beyond it, in a language whose generality takes on a value that is in some way structural, universal, transcendental, or ontological? When the firstcomer implies: "What goes for me, irreplaceably, goes for everybody. Substitution is in progress, it has already operated, everyone can say the same thing for and about themselves. It's enough to hear me." . . . How to determine this, a singular this whose uniqueness depends on witnessing alone, on the fact that certain individuals, in certain situations, attest to the features of a structure that is nonetheless universal, reveal it, indicate it, give it to be read more "*à vif*," as we say and because we say it especially of a wound, more *à vif* and *better than others*, and sometimes alone of their sort?[39]

It suffices to make the universal singular that it be heard. Cixous implies that translation is the attestation and witness of a loving gaze (or ear?) that ignites a smoldering generality into a brilliant spark.

The sonorous dimension is the accelerant in Cixous's "econohomonymy"— her word in *Anankè*, repeated and displaced by Derrida. Her writing reveals that amphiboly is at its most "recalcitrant" not simply when it draws upon the resources of homonymy, as Kamuf observes,[40] but specifically when it relies upon homophonic or quasi-homophonic effects, drifting into various phonemic slippages, as well as parapraxis and metathesis with transpositions of sounds within words. The univocity of homonymy is ruined from the outset here. In short, the homophonic effects of her writing are seemingly driven by accidental resonances, slips of the tongue, even brazen error, rather than analytical argumentation. Psychoanalysis, for instance, as Laurent Milesi has shown in an article teasingly entitled "Cixanalyses," is transformed through various Freudian slips (such as *vieux* for *dieux*, or *rêves* for *lièvres*).[41] Genders of French nouns are reversed, German neologisms forged, a *hapax legomenon* sprung on the reader, in a writing that is pluralizing certainly but more than that, betrays a broader intra- and inter-lingual drift or destinerrance. They reveal that the singularity of the idiom, if it is to survive, always already necessarily goes off course.

It is by way of these slippages that homophony has a syntactical structure of re-marking. In *Anankè*, where Cixous speaks of "la traduction des pulsions et pulsions de traduction [the translation of drives and the drives of translation],"[42] translation and untranslatability are themselves thematized through a series of quasi-homophonic displacements: *Übertragungswiderstand*, inverting to *Widerstandsübertragung*, translated to *résistances des transfrères* at the hour of *résistrance*! In this way, the passing of translation via sonorous contrails re-marks translation as semantic content, leaving its traces in the skids of homophony.

In various places, such as this one from the preface to the new 2010 French edition of *Le Rire de la Méduse* cited by Kamuf,[43] Cixous laments the loss involved in translating homonymy according to the traditional economy of under-translation, figured here as a one-winged bird. But she does not do so— and perhaps *cannot* do so—without introducing another homophonic effect:

> Le *Vol*, qui m'est si cher, et surtout grâce à l'homonymie dont il jouit en français, n'est qu'un demi-vol en anglais, où l'indécision s'éteint en traduction. C'est comme si ma Méduse ne volait que d'une aile, elle qui en a tant. Voilà qu'en traduction on nous aura volé un vol.

> The *Vol*, which is so dear to me, and especially because of the homonymy it enjoys in French, is but a half-*vol* in English, where the

indecision is extinguished in translation. It's as if my Medusa flew with just one wing, she who has so many. In translation they will have stolen from us one *vol*.[44]

Cixous can only explain the half-theft of the *vol* and as it were translate under-translation into words by metaphorizing herself as a one-winged bird and relying upon the even more radically untranslatable homophony *aile/elle* (wing/her). The shift from homonymy to homophony, with the deepening of the *résistrance*, thus re-marks the drift of displacement *within* re-marking itself. What I want to dub *transferrancy* might just be another name for the untranslatable as the dispersive drift that yields no universal concept but each time singular *untranslatable* untranslatabilities.

The chanciness of the untranslatable submits to no universal tuning system or fundamental tone but arrives at the ear without calculation or prediction. In Anne Dufourmantelle's words, the experience of hearing Derrida lecture is of thought being translated on the spot into sound and tearing in the process.

> La première impression retirée de l'écoute du séminaire est d'entendre se dérouler une partition musicale qui rendrait audible le mouvement même de la pensée. Tout se passe comme si on assistait à une pensée pensant au moment même de son énonciation. Celui qui philosophe ainsi à voix haute ne déroule pas une trame lisse et univoque, il en expose les déchirures. Il laisse place à l'étonnement.

> The first impression you draw from listening to the seminar is of hearing a musical score being played that makes the very movement of thinking audible. It is as if we were the audience for the thinking of a thought at the very moment of its utterance. Someone who philosophizes out loud in this way does not unwind a smooth, univocal thread; he shows the tears in it. He leaves room for astonishment.[45]

And that perhaps is another definition of translation: listening with as-*tone*-ishment.

Bibliography

Bennington, Geoffrey. "*Geschlecht pollachos legetai*: Translation, Polysemia, Dissemination." *Philosophy Today* 64, no. 2 (2020): 423–39.

———. "Hap." *Oxford Literary Review* 36, no. 2 (2014): 170–74.

Cixous, Hélène. *Anankè*. Paris: Des femmes, 1979.

———. "Un effet d'épine rose." In *Le Rire de la Méduse et autres ironies*, 22–33. Paris: Éditions Galilée, 2010.

————. *Insister: À Jacques Derrida*. Paris: Galilée, 2006. Translated as *Insister of Jacques Derrida* by Peggy Kamuf, with original drawings by Ernest Pignon-Ernest. Stanford, CA: Stanford University Press, 2007.

Davies, James Q. "Instruments of Empire." In *Sound Knowledge: Music and Science in London, 1789–1851*, edited by James Q. Davies and Ellen Lockhart, 145–74. Chicago: University of Chicago Press, 2017.

Derrida, Jacques. "Du 'sans prix,' ou le 'juste prix' de la transaction." In *Comment penser l'argent? Troisième Forum Le Monde Le Mans*, edited by Roger-Pol Droit, 386–401. Paris: Editions Le Monde, 1992. Translated as "On the 'Priceless,' or the 'Going Rate' of the Transaction." In *Negotiations: Interventions and Interviews*, edited and translated by Elizabeth Rottenberg, 315–28. Stanford, CA: Stanford University Press, 2002.

————. *Geschlecht III: Sexe, race, nation, humanité*. Edited by Geoffrey Bennington, Katie Chenoweth, and Rodrigo Therezo. Paris: Seuil, 2018. Translated as *Geschlecht III: Sex, Race, Nation, Humanity* by Katie Chenoweth and Rodrigo Therezo. Chicago: University of Chicago Press, 2020.

————. *H. C. pour la vie, c'est-à-dire . . . .* Paris: Galilée, 2002. Translated as *H. C. for Life, That Is to Say . . .* by Laurent Milesi and Stefan Herbrechter. Stanford, CA: Stanford University Press, 2006.

————. "La double séance." In *La dissémination*, 199–317. Paris: Seuil, 1972. Translated as "The Double Session" by Barbara Johnson. In *Dissemination*, 173–286. Chicago: University of Chicago Press, 1981.

————. *La vie la mort: Séminaire (1975–76)*. Edited by Pascale-Anne Brault and Peggy Kamuf. Paris: Seuil, 2019. Translated as *Life Death* by Pascale-Anne Brault and Michael Naas. Chicago: University of Chicago Press, 2020.

————. *Le Monolinguisme de l'autre, ou la prothèse d'origine*. Paris: Galilée, 1996. Translated as *Monolingualism of the Other; or, The Prosthesis of Origin* by Patrick Mensah. Stanford, CA: Stanford University Press, 1998.

————. *Le toucher, Jean-Luc Nancy*. Paris: Galilée, 2000. Translated as *On Touching—Jean-Luc Nancy* by Christine Irizarry. Stanford, CA: Stanford University Press, 2005.

————. *Negotiations: Interventions and Interviews*. Edited and translated by Elizabeth Rottenberg. Stanford, CA: Stanford University Press, 2002.

————. "Qu'est-ce qu'une traduction 'relevante'?" In *Quinzièmes Assises de la traduction littéraire*, 21–48. Arles: Actes Sud, 1998. Translated as "What Is a 'Relevant' Translation?" by Lawrence Venuti. *Critical Inquiry* 27, no. 2 (2001): 174–200.

————. "S'il y a lieu de traduire." In *Du droit à la philosophie*, 283–309. Paris: Galilée, 1990. Translated as "If There Is Cause to Translate I: Philosophy in Its National Language (Toward a 'licterature en françois')" by Sylvia Söderlind. In *Eyes of the University: Right to Philosophy 2*, 1–19. Stanford, CA: Stanford University Press, 2004.

Derrida, Jacques, and Anne Dufourmantelle. *De l'hospitalité: Anne Dufourmantelle invite Jacques Derrida à répondre*. Paris: Calmann-Lévy, 1997. Translated as *Of*

Hospitality: Anne Dufourmantelle Invites Jacques Derrida to Respond by Rachel Bowlby. Stanford, CA: Stanford University Press, 2000.

Kamuf, Peggy. "Afterburn: An Afterword to 'The Flying Manuscript.'" *New Literary History*, no. 37 (2006): 47–55.

———. "Hélène Cixous: Writing for Her Life." In *Literature and the Development of Feminist Theory*, edited by Robin Truth Goodman, 128–39. Cambridge: Cambridge University Press, 2015.

Kamuf, Peggy, with Dawne McCance. "Crossings: An Interview with Peggy Kamuf." *Mosaic: An Interdisciplinary Critical Journal* 42, no. 2 (2009): 227–43.

Lezra, Jacques. "The Untranslatability That Is Not One." *Paragraph* 38, no. 2 (2015): 174–88.

Milesi, Laurent. "Cixanalyses—Towards a Reading of *Anankè*." *Paragraph* 36, no. 2 (2013): 286–302.

Notes

1. James Q. Davies, "Instruments of Empire," in *Sound Knowledge: Music and Science in London, 1789–1851*, ed. James Q. Davies and Ellen Lockhart (Chicago: University of Chicago Press, 2017), 146.

2. Jacques Derrida, *Le Monolinguisme de l'autre, ou la prothèse d'origine* (Paris: Galilée, 1996), 100; *Monolingualism of the Other; or, The Prosthesis of Origin*, trans. Patrick Mensah (Stanford, CA: Stanford University Press, 1998), 56 (translation modified).

3. Jacques Derrida, *Negotiations: Interventions and Interviews*, ed. and trans. Elizabeth Rottenberg (Stanford, CA: Stanford University Press, 2002), 24.

4. Derrida, *Negotiations*, 28.

5. Derrida, *Negotiations*, 29–30.

6. Derrida, *Negotiations*, 30.

7. Jacques Derrida, "Du 'sans prix,' ou le 'juste prix' de la transaction," in *Comment penser l'argent? Troisième Forum Le Monde Le Mans*, ed. Roger-Pol Droit (Paris: Editions Le Monde, 1992), 392; "On the 'Priceless,' or the 'Going Rate' of the Transaction," in *Negotiations*, 320.

8. Derrida, "Du 'sans prix,'" 396; Derrida, "On the 'Priceless,'" 323.

9. Derrida, "Du 'sans prix,'" 395; Derrida, "On the 'Priceless,'" 322.

10. Derrida, "Du 'sans prix,'" 387; Derrida, "On the 'Priceless,'" 316.

11. Derrida, "Du 'sans prix,'" 388–89; Derrida, "On the 'Priceless,'" 316–17.

12. Derrida, "Du 'sans prix,'" 389; Derrida, "On the 'Priceless,'" 318.

13. Derrida, "Du 'sans prix,'" 391; Derrida, "On the 'Priceless,'" 319.

14. Derrida, "Du 'sans prix,'" 391; Derrida, "On the 'Priceless,'" 319.

15. Jacques Lezra, "The Untranslatability That Is Not One," *Paragraph* 38, no. 2 (2015): 174–88.

16. Lezra, 184, 180.

17. Lezra, 184.

18. Geoffrey Bennington, "Hap," *Oxford Literary Review* 36, no. 2 (2014): 170.

19. Jacques Derrida, *Le toucher, Jean-Luc Nancy* (Paris: Galilée, 2000), 323–24; Jacques Derrida, *On Touching—Jean-Luc Nancy*, trans. Christine Irizarry (Stanford, CA: Stanford University Press, 2005), 288.

20. Jacques Derrida, *H. C. pour la vie, c'est-à-dire . . .* (Paris: Galilée, 2002), 58–59; Jacques Derrida, *H. C. for Life, That Is to Say . . .*, trans. Laurent Milesi and Stefan Herbrechter (Stanford, CA: Stanford University Press, 2006), 63.

21. Derrida, *H. C. pour la vie*, 67; Derrida, *H. C. for Life*, 73–74.

22. Derrida, *H. C. pour la vie*, 65; Derrida, *H. C. for Life*, 60.

23. Derrida, *H. C. pour la vie*, 65; Derrida, *H. C. for Life*, 60.

24. Peggy Kamuf with Dawne McCance, "Crossings: An Interview with Peggy Kamuf," *Mosaic: An Interdisciplinary Critical Journal* 42, no. 2 (2009): 237.

25. Kamuf, "Crossings," 238.

26. Jacques Derrida, "Qu'est-ce qu'une traduction 'relevante'?" in *Quinzièmes Assises de la traduction littéraire* (Arles: Actes Sud, 1998), 28; Jacques Derrida, "What Is a 'Relevant' Translation?," trans. Lawrence Venuti, *Critical Inquiry* 27, no. 2 (2001): 181.

27. Derrida, "Qu'est-ce qu'une traduction," 28; Derrida, "What Is a 'Relevant' Translation?," 181.

28. Hélène Cixous, *Anankè* (Paris: Des femmes, 1979), 10. See also Laurent Milesi, "Cixanalyses—Towards a Reading of *Anankè*," *Paragraph* 36, no. 2 (2013): 286–302.

29. *Geschlecht III: Sexe, race, nation, humanité*, ed. Geoffrey Bennington, Katie Chenoweth, and Rodrigo Therezo (Paris: Seuil, 2018), 9ème séance. Jacques Derrida, *Geschlecht III: Sex, Race, Nation, Humanity*, ed. Geoffrey Bennington, Katie Chenoweth, and Rodrigo Therezo; trans. Katie Chenoweth and Rodrigo Therezo (Chicago: University of Chicago Press, 2020), 9th session. See also Geoffrey Bennington, "*Geschlecht pollachos legetai*: Translation, Polysemia, Dissemination," *Philosophy Today* 64, no. 2 (2020): 423–39.

30. Derrida, *Geschlecht III*, 107; Derrida, *Geschlecht III*, trans. Chenoweth and Therezo, 82.

31. Jacques Derrida, *La vie la mort: Séminaire (1975–76)*, ed. Pascale-Anne Brault and Peggy Kamuf (Paris: Seuil, 2019), 155; Jacques Derrida, *Life Death*, trans. Pascale-Anne Brault and Michael Naas (Chicago: University of Chicago Press, 2020), 115.

32. Derrida, *La vie la mort*, 156; Derrida, *Life Death*, 116.

33. Derrida, *La vie la mort*, 157–58; Derrida, *Life Death*, 117–18.

34. Jacques Derrida, "La double séance," in *La dissémination* (Paris: Seuil, 1972), 282. Jacques Derrida, "The Double Session," in *Dissemination*, trans. Barbara Johnson (Chicago: University of Chicago Press, 1981), 251.

35. Jacques Derrida, "S'il y a lieu de traduire," in *Du droit à la philosophie* (Paris: Galilée, 1990), 283–309. Jacques Derrida, "If There Is Cause to Translate I: Philosophy in Its National Language (Toward a 'licterature en françois')," trans. Sylvia Söderlind, in *Eyes of the University: Right to Philosophy 2* (Stanford, CA: Stanford University Press, 2004), 19.

36. Peggy Kamuf, "Hélène Cixous: Writing for Her Life," in *Literature and the Development of Feminist Theory*, ed. Robin Truth Goodman (Cambridge: Cambridge University Press, 2015), 129.

37. Peggy Kamuf, "Afterburn: An Afterword to 'The Flying Manuscript,'" *New Literary History*, no. 37 (2006): 47.

38. Hélène Cixous, *Insister: À Jacques Derrida* (Paris: Galilée, 2006), 73–74; Hélène Cixous, *Insister of Jacques Derrida*, trans. Peggy Kamuf, with original drawings by Ernest Pignon-Ernest (Stanford, CA: Stanford University Press, 2007), 102.

39. Derrida, *Le Monolinguisme de l'autre*, 40; Derrida, *Monolingualism of the Other*, 19–20 (translation modified and my emphasis).

40. Kamuf, "Hélène Cixous," 129.

41. Milesi, "Cixanalyses."

42. Cixous, *Anankè*, 121.

43. Kamuf, "Hélène Cixous," 129.

44. Hélène Cixous, "Un effet d'épine rose," in *Le Rire de la Méduse et autres ironies* (Paris: Éditions Galilée, 2010), 30; cited in Kamuf, "Hélène Cixous," 129, from which I lift the translation.

45. Jacques Derrida and Anne Dufourmantelle, *De l'hospitalité: Anne Dufourmantelle invite Jacques Derrida à répondre* (Paris: Calmann-Lévy, 1997), 26–28; Jacques Derrida and Anne Dufourmantelle, *Of Hospitality: Anne Dufourmantelle Invites Jacques Derrida to Respond*, trans. Rachel Bowlby (Stanford, CA: Stanford University Press, 2000), 22–24.

The Relapses of the Universal: Translation and the Language of the Political

Gavin Walker

Sometimes an expression has to be withdrawn from language and sent for cleaning—then it can be put back into circulation.

—LUDWIG WITTGENSTEIN

"Les non-dupes errent" dont je m'arme cette année.

—JACQUES LACAN[1]

Today, there are few concepts in the theoretical humanities employed in a more elastic sense than that of translation. From the now-canonical references to Benjamin, Derrida, and others, to contemporary critics like Emily Apter, Naoki Sakai, Gayatri Spivak, and many more,[2] translation is both widely theorized and—like the practice it names—the subject of an extraordinary range of popular and philosophical complications. The turn from the 1990s onward to the examination of "cultural translation," along with the newly examined question of translation in the discourses on world literature, is exemplary in this regard. It is difficult to imagine a concept or word more in need of deep cleaning than "translation," but "universality" gives it a good run for its money. Let us attempt to send, or maybe "take," these two concepts "to the cleaners" (that is, in the idiomatic sense, not only actually cleaning them, but possibly swindling them completely to induce bankruptcy), by exposing them to a broader concern about how we speak of the politics of translation, the possible relation this term can have with "universality," and what such a "political" relation to language might be in the end.

Translation and Its Discontents

When conceived of as a mere transfer or transmutation of knowledge from one putatively unitary register to another (languages, cultures, nationalities, and so on), translation comes to be merely a commonsensical stand-in for the endless articulations that occur within the inexhaustible proliferation of difference which constitutes a world and its historical becoming. Perhaps most importantly, if translation's horizon of signification as a concept serves no other function than to describe a supposedly existing and already given system of difference, it would be inseparable from what Alain Badiou would refer to as "the order of being," and what would be referred to more generally as simply "the status quo." In other words, if translation merely indicates the play of transpositions within an already historically constituted field of differentiation, it can serve no *critical* function as a perspective from which to consider the contemporary condition. It would be merely a form of description, rather than an emblematic break with the existing regime of difference. But translation as a concept and especially as a *practice* cannot be limited to such an understanding. Far from it, translation, despite or perhaps in addition to its frequent conflations, remains a general name for something absolutely central to the theoretical and political questions that animate our moment: How to consider, if such an encounter is even possible, the differing of difference—or to put it another way, *incommensurability beyond the regime of specific difference*—within the sphere of the social?[3] And further, how should we theorize the ways in which this differing is covered over or veiled by the communicative model of language and the seemingly smooth circuit process of economic exchange in the sphere of circulation, two forms of concealment of the historicity of difference?

Since the 1980s, the term "theory" has acquired a specific valence and unique set of attributes well beyond its generic meaning, and now constitutes an intellectual-historical field in itself deserving of rigorous historicization. At its best, theory's original impulse in the university provided a unique multidisciplinary language and conceptual set within which political and cultural inquiry could be undertaken beyond the typical disciplinary enclosure into national literatures and histories. At its worst, however, theory's institutionalization tended to "re-nationalize" itself in a recursive sense, resulting in a particularization of its own self-proclaimed universality: theory often came to be a set of canonical texts written in English, French, and German, and these languages came to be treated as quasi-universal containers of significations which would then be used in the study of specific literatures that remained hopelessly particular and national. In the historical gap between the pretense and actuality of theory, what arose was the dramatic change in political and institutional culture called "globalization" (a process we have yet to really *think* in terms of its effects on humanistic inquiry), which resulted in a naturalization of "theory" in supposedly "indigenous" conditions all over the globe. Today, Spanish (and it is important to mention the *differential* status of Spanish in Latin America, along with English in South Asia, as a decisively *non-European* phenomenon) and Italian, but also Arabic, Mandarin, Korean, Japanese, Hindi, Bengali, Russian, Serbo-Croatian, and other major world languages formerly treated as "peripheral" within the 1980s economy of representation, have been constituted as linguistic systems in which *theory proper* can be and is written. But what truly happens when the literary conditions of theory finally live up to their early billing of universality and begin to be expressed in other directions?

Stuart Hall famously argued that "theory is always closed, because theory can't match the infinite openness of the world. So you have to understand the arbitrary closure that is required to make sense of a thing theoretically."[4] The "arbitrary closure" that we are concerned with, then, is precisely that which goes under the name "culture," because it is precisely culture that is the most difficult particular closure (and enclosure) that conditions above all else our experience of the theoretical categories of universality and translation. We are ideologically conditioned to understand these quite abstract concepts, referential in essence to a wide swath of social phenomena, in specifically *cultural* terms. Universality thus often today becomes a stand-in for a certain unapologetic Eurocentrism, while translation becomes a kind of discourse of cultural hybridity in a simplistic and "official" multicultural orgy of "good" sentiment. But neither universality nor translation inherently refers to the field of culture exclusively, and certainly not if that field is implied to be the field of putatively *national* culture.

Today, in the theoretical field of the humanities, we are once again plunged into a discursive scenario in which a set of simple oppositions—culture vs. capital, economy vs. language, universal vs. particular, and so forth—is continuously posited. To be "universal" in such a schema is to privilege political struggle against narrow identitarianism, to support grand projects against the postmodern defeat, to emphasize the universality of theoretical inquiry (still often in its French, German, and English linguistic moments) against the provincialism of locality (no matter the analyses of scale or measure). But the fundamental danger of such contemporary universalisms lies in their misapprehension of the concept of the universal itself, which is always a *productive fiction* or "semblance" (after Hegel); that is, the *experience* of the universal, separate from its positing as an axiom of knowledge or politics "to come," always consists in falling short of itself.[5] There can be no universality that effectively attains its own full plenitude or realization and then proceeds to simply bask in it, both because universality as a conceptual division from its obverse would cease to experience the possibility of differentiation as such, but also because universality is never a fully achieved space of givenness or existing phenomena, but a space instead that must be *projected* in time and in knowledge. And such a fantasy of universality as a given has never prevented it from possessing an appreciative—although centered in an economy of separation—grasp of its "particularist" supplements. Any genuine universality, by contrast and as a projection, exists to compare itself not as an articulated alternative to the status quo, but rather as a regulative idea that orients our capacity to respond to the concrete circumstances in which we are already embedded. This emphasis on universality as an idea—a *rare* idea—recalls the typical misreading of Althusser's famous insistence on the concept of "determination in the last instance." Rather than show us the closed, positivist content of a system fully determined in accordance with some set of presuppositions attributed to the system's endpoint or zenith, for Althusser the "lonely hour of the last instance" never arrives, but is rather a kind of negative regulative idea, always deferring its own arrival, even perhaps actively preventing the ideal circumstance from fully coming "to pass," a kind of secular *katechon*.[6]

In the final analysis, what the category of translation shows us is no simple formula, such as "the universal is always specific" or "the universal is bifurcated into an oppressive dimension and an emancipatory dimension," or indeed "the universal does not exist, only the particular." Rather than all of these formulas—after all, the humanities today has long ceased to be able to genuinely appeal to the great universalities of the past (the national *Bildung*, the "expropriation of the expropriators," the category of "civilization"[7])—we would do better to assert a translational political optic, from which we can observe the "torsions" (Badiou) or "relapse" (*Rückfall*, Hegel) of the universal,[8] because it is precisely when the universal, in its forms of assertion, attempts to cover all possible ranges of meaning that it is most volatile and open as a concept. It is this point, what we might call the zone of volatility between the practice of translation (a point at which the subject's placement cannot be assured) and the regime of translation (in which a universal fiction of specific difference is enforced), that another concept of universality could be invested with different contents, transformed from its aspect of erasure to one of potentiality.

In thinking through the relation of the concepts "translation" and "universality," we require first a definition of the former (the definition of the latter is of a different theoretical character entirely, being in principle one side of a pairing). In fundamental terms, the many investigations of translation today often begin from the premise that translation occurs because a "we" located within one system of meaning seeks to understand content that is formally shrouded within another system of meaning belonging to a "they." In such a sense, translation merely means transposition, replacing one set of terms with another, for instance replacing "tree" with "arbre," and so forth, but not modifying some underlying structural arrangement generative of meaning in the text. From this basic premise, translation comes to be used as a way to understand how cultural practices, for instance, which ostensibly belong to one sphere (national, civilizational, linguistic, territorial), come to function in another sphere that is *presumed* to be different. Thus, no matter how this problem is explained away, the fundamental implication behind the concept of "cultural translation," for example, appears as the presupposition of culture as Substance, and *cultures* as pre-posited, holistic entities that come into "contact" with each other and then experience a "translation" between their terms.

Needless to say, this all stems from the first premise that translation merely names some interchange between already constituted systems of meaning. We imagine, for instance, that because I do not understand Mongolian, I must rely on someone to "translate" a text written in Mongolian into a language-system that I do understand. This would make me aware, for example, of the fact that the word "tree" in Mongolian is written in both a different script and with different orthographic and phonographic characteristics than "tree," "arbre," 木, and so forth. But what remains excluded in such an understanding is the fact that I am capable of learning, repeating, and utilizing a new word, whether or not we categorize this word within another linguistic system, usually given a fictive cultural-national substantiality. Language, when exposed to its historicity, is no more capable of being contained in civilizational or national barriers than it is able to cover the globality of meaning in a unitary system. Multilingualism is closer to the reality of the majority of the world's peoples than is the monolingualism of the core elites, for whom the genuinely "other" language is nearly always a mere emblem or antiquarian curio of the past and rarely a necessary modality of life. In this sense, the symbolic register of Derrida's important *Monolingualism of the Other* is perhaps more accurately understood as a reflection on the "Others of monolingualism," a reminder of the dissemination and dispersal of language as such out to and even past the borders of the thinkable, while it remains practical and ready-to-hand in the most basic sense. Translation, in the dominant optic, represents language as an absolute barrier, a world unto itself.

If it is not this, and such an idea is, of course, quite commonsensical in our world, then what is translation and why is it not merely a thing but a question? To answer that query is not easy, precisely because the commonsensical understanding of translation is so ubiquitous. In essence, the question cannot be answered without reflecting on the nature of language itself, its relation to the figure of the subject, its *political* constitution in the form of national language, and the distribution of meaning in language that comes to be policed as the most crucial site for the legitimating of the national people.

In other words, if we took the typical quotidian definition or common sense of the term "translation" as our guiding thread, how could we possibly even begin to consider the status of the universal from such a vantage point grounded in the putative fixity of particularity? Perhaps we could assert, somewhat whimsically, that "translation" itself is nothing other than the universal, with its concrete instances as forms of the particular, but this type of rhetorical reversal, in which the most vexatious and difficult concepts are evaded by simply raising them to the status of the ultimate perspectival point, is not very fruitful. After all, if we want to think a political universality, with concrete political goals, it would be ludicrous to hermetically assert the centrality of an unexplained concept of "translation" as if such an abstraction could immediately function in the realm of politics.

Thus, first and foremost we require a definition of translation from which to proceed. In my view, we ought to take up Sakai's attempt to rigorously define both the concept of translation, and also its polysemic function, in which translation is always bifurcated between translation as such and the representation of translation (especially in the model of communication), what he has long called "the regime of translation."[9] He writes:

> What is most problematic about the conventional conception of translation is that, due to its inherent metaphysics of communication, it presents translation as a process of homogenization and of establishing equivalence. But translation always inscribes itself in the social topos of incommensurability and difference, and what I specifically call *cultural difference*, to which translation is a *response*, is anterior to and fundamentally heterogeneous to the conceptual difference of species, the difference between particularities. Translation articulates one text to another, but it does not mean that translation merely establishes equivalence between two texts, two languages or two groups of people. On the contrary, it is in a specific *dispositif* or regime of translation that translation is represented according to the model of communication.[10]

This regime of translation, as an apparatus of bordering, shaping the heterogeneity of linguistic flux into communicative equivalences, is thus not a technique developed to allow us to understand another stratum of meaning, but the original division through which a situation is rendered into "two sides":

> The work of translation is a practice by which the initial discontinuity between the addresser and the addressee is made continuous and recognizable. In this respect, translation is just like other social practices that render the points of discontinuity in social formations continuous. . . . This is why we always have to remind ourselves that the untranslatable, or what can never be appropriated by the economy of translational communication, cannot exist prior to the enunciation of translation.[11]

When we speak of "translation," therefore, we are speaking essentially of *the forms of articulation* through which continuities are generated. National language is treated as a continuous system, an enclosed whole that constitutes an entire world unto itself, a mode of understanding and system of value. But like all such systems, it can only constitute an interiority insofar as something is outside of it. In this sense, prior to the articulational act of translation, two national languages are nothing but one general system of meaning expanded to accommodate all sorts of partial knowledges. Only when we demand translation do we in effect "create" these languages in a retrospective determination whose "origin" is erased by this determination itself, and once more "conjured up" as if it were a "meeting" or "contact" between two unities.

In 1981, Michel Pêcheux, already known for his works in the Althusserian frame around the question of language, wrote with the linguist Françoise Gadet a unique and unclassifiable book, *La langue introuvable*. Published in Althusser's *Collection "Théorie"* for Maspero, *La langue introuvable* attempts above all else to focus our attention on the status of language itself within an optic opened by Althusser on capitalist social relations, Lacan on the status of the subject within psychoanalysis, and Saussure on the differential systems of linguistics. "If the object of linguistics consists in the double fact that there is language and there are languages," write Gadet and Pêcheux in *La langue introuvable*, "what must be thought is the moment of their division."[12] How is it that we come to have languages, in the plural, when all such languages have polymorphous borders, fundamental volatility in orthographic terms, vocabularies that are built out of the substance of each other? How is it, in this sense, that we do not simply speak of language as a total system rather than in the terms of *national* languages? After all, what language on earth can be said to simply emerge fully formed into the historical flux?

The status of national language is at the core of the question of translation and universality. At first glance, the relation (and notably the political relation) between universality and translation appears fraught or even impossible from the outset. If the perspective of translation emphasizes partiality, incompletions, misunderstanding, division, splitting, and gaps, the rhetorical associations with the concept of universality tend to emphasize just the opposite: the whole, totality, the monumental and metatheoretical in opposition to the minor or local. But we ought to complicate or at least productively contaminate this apparent division, because it participates in a caricature of the concept of translation itself, tends to monumentalize the notion of the universal, and produces a serious political impasse, characteristic of the rhetorical foundations of our moment.

As an aside, but an aside that I would like to take up again elsewhere, the whole range of questions related to the theoretical explication of translation could be provocatively linked to and developed with Lacan, in a way that has not yet been done, to my knowledge. The point of connection here would be the Lacanian analysis of sexual difference, which culminates in the famous thesis that "there is no sexual relation."[13] As Alenka Zupančič, among others, has pointed out, this thesis is often misunderstood as meaning that there really are two actually existing positions of sexual difference but that they are incompatible, and can never relate to each other.[14] Lacan's point, however, is intended for precisely the opposite purpose. When he emphasizes that "there is no sexual relation," what he means is that the very relationality that would furnish the basis of *two* positions, of this side and that side, is itself a misrecognition, merely a semblance of a relation to an other, but rather a kind of solitary relation to oneself *by means* of the other. In other words, the sexual difference is never treated as *substantial*, but rather as an accumulation of effects according to which phenomena are parceled out into "masculine" and "feminine" traits (or other pairings), a series of effects that then exert a kind of force back onto their own putative origin, thereby forming "two positions." Lacan's point is that this apparent "difference" is merely an effect of an originary and untraceable difference that itself *produces* this effect of sexual difference—it is this structure that one might relate to the concept of translation, above all else because of the complex nature of the origin that is implied in it. Echoing this Lacanian formulation, Derrida once alerted us precisely to the mechanism of translation and its regime:

> Coupling is a mirror. The mirror is traversed of its own accord, which is to say that it is never traversed at all. This being-traversed is not something that happens by accident to the mirror—to the West—; it is inscribed within its structure. This is as much as to say that, forever producing itself, it never comes to be. Like the horizon.[15]

Translation in such a sense would be nothing more than the infinite traversal of a mirror: one national language is passed through in order to merely confirm, to mirror, the arrogated interiority of another national language. It is in this way that the relapses of translation—back onto the incompleteness of language as such, as in Pêcheux and Gadet—show us something about the relapses of the universal, constantly attempting to extend itself beyond its capabilities, constantly striving to achieve a wholeness that can only ever be partial.

To use the concept of translation as a mode of thinking the possibilities of another universality today is also to reflect on the status of knowledge in general, and its frequent (although certainly not exclusive) site of production: the university. "Translation" as a question has emerged most from those disciplinary places least obviously attempting to claim for themselves a universality: comparative literature and the field of study known broadly as "area studies," a topic that would be necessary to investigate extensively on its own.[16] Another way of posing this is to say that just as the regime of translation is ubiquitous but translation itself is rare, so too universality as a disavowed particularity is ubiquitous while universality itself is rare, almost absent. In the theoretical humanities, universalism and its discontents have long been under scrutiny.

Treating the universal *as* the particular is a position constantly reemphasized in knowledge production today but appears in our moment as a mere sophism politically, and as a naive fantasy theoretically. Even if we were to accept this "answer" to the conundrum, how would we describe this movement—in other words, through what conceptual physics could the particular be taken as the universal? The answer, in my view, lies much less in the two terms themselves than in the process of articulation between them, for which we have no better term than translation itself. But we also have a clear example of what this looks like, and it is not an affirmative project. If the notion of taking the universal as the particular is posed as a way out of the bind, we would do well to remember that the entire epistemological field of effects generated by the irreversible history of colonialism and imperialism functioned similarly, from the other side of the equation: the generation of a universal from out of a highly specific particular. But there is one "formal" social category that we can approach from this vantage point, and which may give us useful conceptual tools for the elucidation of this relation: the Marxian analysis of the circuit of capital's reproduction, and the centrality to it of the form of money.

Translation, Exchange, Citizen

> Concentrated within the idea of myth is perhaps the entire pretension
> on the part of the West to appropriate its own origin, or to take away

[*dérober*] its secret, so that it can at last identify itself, absolutely, around its own pronouncement [*profération*] and its own birth. The idea of myth alone perhaps presents to itself the very Idea of the West, in its representation and its permanent compulsion to return to its own sources in order to re-engender itself from them as the very destiny of humanity.[17]

We often inquire into the "forms" of the social world without any fundamental recourse to their basis. But capitalist society in particular can be said, after Hegel, to be easily divided between two registers: the sphere of the sovereign decision, that is, "political society"; and the sphere of exchange and circulation, what is normally referred to as "civil society." This social duality, close to what Tom Nairn understood as the two-sided function around the concept of the nation as "the modern Janus," or what Georges Dumézil theorized in terms of the split gods Mitra-Varuna (the law-giving and myth-making aspects of the social), remains the absolute basis on which we consider the idea of the social world in general terms.[18] When we consider the term "civil society," two lexical sequences are immediately opened up. These two lexical sequences are in turn related to two semiotic fields, two registers of signification: on the one hand, the existence of "civil society" expresses a "process without a subject" in which concrete individuals are merely shells, existing solely as the "bearers" (*Träger*) or "guardians" (*Hütern*) of the forms of commodities and money. On the other hand, precisely because "interest" and "need" are expected to appear at the basis of these social interactions, the individuals who engage in the social process of exchange are produced as subjects of these needs. This double structure itself returns back into the unstable core of the concept "civil society," where it exerts a specific set of forces, a specific theoretical physics that produces two fundamental limitations or boundaries within which the vast and aporetic question of the subject is located. For Marx, civil society (*bürgerliche Gesellschaft*) in the most general sense refers to "the total material intercourse [*Verkehr*] of individuals within a determinate stage of development of the productive forces."[19] He continues, "It embraces the whole commercial and industrial life of a given stage and, insofar as this, goes well beyond the state and the nation."[20] However, and in the following contrast I believe Marx gives us an absolutely decisive clue that we must pay close attention to, he critically reverses this claim, or better yet, adds to this claim a simultaneous paradox: "Yet, on the other hand again, civil society must assert itself externally [or "on the outside" (*nach Außen*)] as nationality [*Nationalität*], and internally ["on the inside" (*nach Innen*)] must organize itself as the State."[21] When Marx reminds us that "civil society" designates exactly the social level at which "exchange" [*Verkehr* and thus "intercourse" but also "échange" and therefore the later sense of *Austausch* for "exchange"] between "individuals" is made into the motor-force of social life, he draws our attention to the bizarre and paradoxical relation of the sphere of circulation and the sphere of production. That is, the productive capacity of society exerts a historical force on the way in which social relations can operate. But the image or schema of "civil society," which ought to be "rational" and based on the undivided unit, literally the In-dividual, is not derived from the production process, but from the circulation process, which itself must be presupposed. Therefore, there is always-already, at the core of civil society, some hard kernel of irrationality or impossibility, but an impossibility that has been made to operate as if it were not there.

In other words, it is this first order point—capitalism is a social system in which the fundamental human relation absolutely must circulate only as a thing that it simultaneously cannot be, which therefore presents itself as a kind of irrationality torsionally recoded as rationality—that we can call the "nihil of reason" characterizing the commodification of labor power, located at the "degree zero" of all social life. Sandro Mezzadra has reminded us of the importance of this question for our current moment, precisely because the entire question of what labor power is, how it is produced, and how it operates "signals the radical scission that marks the constitution of subjectivity in capitalism."[22] Capital cannot directly produce the labor power commodity, but through the formation of the relative surplus population in the accumulation process, it can indirectly produce it. Thereby capital gains a method of releasing the supply of labor power from the limitations of the given natural stratum: this is why the "historical and moral factors" contained in the determination of the value of labor power must be formed in such a way as to be commensurable with capitalist production.

Capital, as the fundamental concretization of social relations, and therefore as the apex of the social relation's violent verso, cannot rid itself of this fundamental "condition of violence" (*Gewaltverhältnis*), located in its logical alpha and omega, the labor power commodity, whose "indirect" production is located paradoxically outside commodity relations.[23] An excess of violence is haunting capital's interior by means of this constantly liminalizing/volatilizing forcible "production" of labor power. Precisely by this excessive violence, capital endangers itself and opens itself up to a whole continent of raw violence, showing us something important in terms of the question of how capital utilizes the "anthropological difference" to effect the "indirect" production of labor power.[24] The primal violence, sustained as a continuum or "status quo," appears as a smooth state, a cyclical reproduction cycle without edges. But this appearance or semblance of smooth continuity is in fact a product of the working of violence upon itself: violence must erase and recode itself as peace by means of violence. In other words, when we encounter the basic social scenario of capitalist society, the exchange of a product for money, we are already in a situation in which the raw violence of subjectivation, whereby some absent potentiality within the worker's body is exchanged as if it were a substance called labor power which can be commodified, is covered over by the form of money, which appears as a smooth container of significations that can serve as a measure of this potentiality. But in order for labor power to be measured and exchanged as money, there must be a repeated doubling of violence. What must remain on the outside of capital as a social relation is paradoxically what must also be simultaneously forced into its inside, perpetually torn between the forms of subjectivation that produce labor power as an inside, and the historical field of reproduction in which the worker's body is produced on the violent outside of capital. This internal exterior is the matrix of sociality in which violence's creative-formative aspect is brought out most prominently, exposing us to the pseudo-completeness of the exchange process, which is the very image of civil society: we might say that the principles of political economy, or the logic that inheres in capital, are only realized by traversing the wild exterior of the historical process, and particularly the transition to capitalism.

Here is where the inner topology of the logic and the outer cartography of history are linked, sealed, interlocked as gradients on the surface of the world of capital. This "world of capital," which presents itself as a total systematic expression of pure exchange, produces "civil society" in order to invert itself, and try to derive itself precisely from its own presupposition. Civil society in essence connotes the entire life of the sphere of circulation. In other words, it connotes a field in which is presupposed a "formal" equality between commodity-owners: one owner the seller of this strange thing called "labor power"; and the buyer, the owner of money. This exchange puts the form of money into the hands of the seller of labor power, who in turn uses it to purchase "means of subsistence" by which they can reproduce themselves. Thus, Marx importantly points out, the value of labor power as a commodity always "contains a historical and moral element," that is, this value always has a necessary reference to something outside the exchange process, outside the supposedly "smooth" sphere of circulation.

As Michael Hardt has pointed out in an important essay that resonates with the problem of the figure of "civil society" in capital and translation, the development of the concept—through Hegel's rereading and rewriting of early modern social thought—is fundamentally situated around the question of labor.[25] In other words, without the development of a conception of abstract labor, in which the basic elemental forms that characterize every concrete labor process are raised to the level of a principle, the equally abstract notion of a sphere of "needs and interest" situated between the "state of nature" and the sphere of the state could not be developed. But civil society is more than simply a correlate to the elemental form of labor abstracted from its concrete instances: "civil society consists of . . . all the institutions of capitalist society that organize abstract labor."[26] Therefore, civil society presupposes the form of the individual, endowed with these "needs" and socially engaged to pursue them. Civil society in this sense is a name for the field of effects in which the production of subjectivity is undertaken. Without this specific form of social life, characteristic of modernity and the world-scale of social relations, we cannot speak about the concept of the subject. On the other hand, in a disciplinary sense, we thus see that the production of subjectivity, in which the form of singularity must necessarily be violently re-produced as the form of individuality which belongs to a genus, is in no way separate from the logic of capital.

Civil society is a paradox: the relations that compose it can only be understood as adequately civil on the basis of an entire volatile historical sequence. The "pre-history" of capitalism's emergence into the world constitutes the genealogy of the concept: the bands of feudal retainers are broken up, the self-sufficient peasantry is transformed into the proto-proletarian small tenant on the one hand and the "beggars, robbers, and vagabonds" on the other; this movement of enclosure on the scale of the land is thus mirrored in the enclosure of bodies, sentiments, and so forth into the form of the "individual" or "property in his own person." In turn, it is this form of identification between the formation of the property-owner endowed with rights and the individual endowed with social rationality that forms the specific historical movement which would culminate in the figure of the "bourgeois" or indeed the "civilian" (*cives*). But the entire capacity of civil society to form the bond or articulation between social organization (state) and social legitimation (nation), which is presumed to be a rational, coherent, and necessary development from within its own logic, is therefore always reliant on its outside or reliant on what must be axiomatically excluded from its own process: the volatile space of historical time.

This returns us back once again to the broad question of translation. The belief in the communicative possibility of the universal, mirroring as it does the social relations of commodity exchange, remains based above all on what Althusser called the "naïve anthropology" of humanism haunting the world of capital.[27] Here the inner/outer split of social relations, in which the exchange process is doubly represented as the origin of both nation and state, must be transferred from the logical topology to the historical cartography, as if the cartography testified to an already-existing arrangement that would simply "prove" itself. Thus a split which characterizes the microphysics of the form of identification itself comes to characterize the gap or breach between "areas" or "national languages." This view, of course, consistently replaces Marx's emphasis on the constitution of real social relations through the objectification of labor with an empiricism and positivism that consistently misunderstands the abstraction of articulation between the empirical entities observed. Because all of these terms—"capital," "feudalism," and "democracy" (perhaps "modernity" also)—are consistently understood as "patterns," "models," "shapes," or "contours" of thought, the volatility expressed between them is treated as a kind of gap or leap between two unitary entities. Therefore, "feudalism" is positioned as the inverse of "capital," "capital" divested of "feudalism" is the "necessary" bridge or apparatus that would lead to "democracy," "democracy" is the necessary link to "normal" modernity, and so forth.

In turn, these concepts of the "normal" course of development and so forth presuppose a certain accomplished history, which would produce the individuals that would furnish the "needs" upon which such systems would emerge. But the very production of these individuals itself presupposes the unitary and eternal area or gradient which could legitimate those individuals as individuals by means of the form of belonging. Thus, the whole circuit constitutes a "vicious circle," one which never adequately returns to its starting point, because the whole sequence of presupposition forms an abyssal and regressive chain, in which something must always be given: "the homogeneous given space of economic phenomena is thus doubly given by the anthropology which grips it in the vice of origins and ends."[28] The field of "interest," which is supposed to represent therefore the pure or immediate expression of "need," separated from any extra-economic coercion, direct violence, and so forth, reveals itself as the ultimate expression of this "vice of origins and ends," insofar as it must always erase or cover over the production of interest, of need, itself.

The schema of civilizational difference, which requires the constant production of limits, but which then utilizes these limits as fields of intensity for its own deployment, is a mechanism through which social relations can be globally schematized through the field of "pure" economic phenomena: it introduces systematic difference, or commensurability, through the "measure" of "preassigned interest," which is always located in territorial, linguistic, ritual, or customary tropic structures. By situating the origin of interest within preexisting sequences or assemblages, the schema of civilizational difference can act as if it is simply the expression of an existing and substantive set of borders. Thereafter, what ought to function merely as an immense accumulation of heterogeneities and singular encounters instead comes to operate as a system of "exchange" between preassigned positions: this structure, which Marx referred to as the "deranged forms" of social phenomena, and Foucault referred to as the "empirico-transcendental doublet," is perhaps best described in the most general sense by what Sakai has long called the "schema of co-figuration."[29] Civil society, in effect, is a term by which the dangerous field of coexistence of the historical present is concealed, hiding the violent and hazardous life of history behind the veil of the co-figurative world schema, based on the presupposition of smooth exchange between owners.

Nationality, or the sentiment of nationality, covers over this paradox by means of the putative unity of the citizen: this citizen must be that which testifies to the inheritance or continuity of the presumed national subject, and yet, since the advent of this modern concept of the citizen, those who cannot be located in this continuity and are placed in a separate position of difference in one way or another must also be encompassed within the concept of the citizen. But strictly speaking, those placed in this position cannot be assumed to have inherited the nation in the expected manner. The figure of the citizen therefore expresses the paradox that everyone, regardless of position, can attain citizenship. Yet the very idea of citizenship is supposed to be something that expresses the continuity of the national subject on the level of the state. In this sense, this position of difference or minority (understood in a very broad manner, referring to any socially expressed divisions) is the quintessential position of the modern system of nation-states, because it expresses the irresolvable tension that it must be within the regime of citizenship, and yet simultaneously excluded from its most basic presupposition. When Marx discusses precisely the paradox that the "owners" of the labor power commodity must continuously reappear as if by magic, he refers to them specifically as "this *race* of peculiar commodity-owners" (*diese Race eigentümlicher Warenbesitzer*).[30] In other words, this "naïve anthropology" that is supposedly excluded from the circulation process or the total material exchange between "rational" individuals is in fact located at its very core. The form of the nation is already contained at the very origin of the supposedly "rational" and "universal" process of exchange, a process that acts as if it represents the smooth and perfect circle of pure rationality, but that is permanently suspended between its impossible origin, which it is compelled to cyclically repeat, and its end, which is equally impossible, because it would relativize the circuit of exchange and expose it to its outside, which it must constantly erase. Thus "civil society" itself must remain in its state of insanity or "derangement" forever pulled in two directions of the production of subjects. It cannot exit this "deranged form," but must try perpetually to prove its "universality" simply by oscillating between these two boundaries, two impossibilities: its underlying schema of the world, which "seems absent from the immediate reality of the phenomena themselves" because it is permanently located in "the interval between origins and ends," a short-circuit that incessantly reveals to us that "its universality is merely repetition," an endless process of relapses.[31]

Just like the representation of translation as pure exchange, the transition must always be represented as if it were a natural growth, a "simple and contentless" leap of inevitability from "one side" to "the other." But when we closely examine the transition, we find something truly disquieting: we discover not that the transition is an accomplished fact of history, or a necessary step in the evolution of social life, but rather that the transition is an endless loop of "falling short," never accomplishing its task, but always erasing or recoding its failure. In this sense, the paradox of civil society is not that it is "strong," "weak," "absent," "inverted," and so forth. It is rather that civil society is never fully established anywhere, precisely because the exchange process on which it is based must always "traverse" the historical outside, while pretending to be a pure interiority, a pure logical circle. What sustains this circle that is always not quite returning to itself is its repetition. But because this circular logic of civil society in the world of capital is compelled to repeat, it is also compelled to constantly re-remember its incompleteness, contingency, and relativity. Every repetition of transition and translation contains the potential for a new arrangement.

To think this question let us turn briefly to the work of Pierre Klossowski, and a text that is not widely known. Described memorably by Michel Foucault as "the most sublime book of our era," Pierre Klossowski's *La monnaie vivante* remains a peculiar and largely ignored theoretical text for complex reasons.[32] Klossowski's work has never found the reception given to his peers—Bataille, Foucault, Deleuze—and has remained relatively marginal. Best known outside France for his famed text on *Nietzsche and the Vicious Circle*, all of Klossowski's work, in this sense, is a vast meditation on the split of difference and its representation in the form of commensurable exchange.[33] *La monnaie vivante*, along with its related texts, might in fact teach us something about translation—and certainly its homology with the sphere of exchange when we read, "Between the fantasy and its market valuation, the numéraire, as sign of the unappraisable value of the fantasy, is an integral part of the representative mode of perversion."[34] Klossowski continues, "The perverted fantasy is in itself unintelligible and unexchangeable; this is why the numéraire, with its abstract character, serves as its universally intelligible equivalent. A distinction must be made here on the one hand between the fantasy function of money—i.e., the act of buying or selling—as a numeraire, externalizing and developing the perversity of the various partners; and on the other hand the *mediating function of money* between the closed world of anomalies and the world of institutional standards."[35]

Here there is what we might call a relation drawn between the *numéraire* and the "regime of translation," that mode by which translation *itself*—the genuine, nonpredicated Encounter with the absolute Stranger (a true fantasy of "unappraisable value")—comes to represented as a simple exchange, an encounter predetermined by a set of supposed predicates.

Before *La monnaie vivante*, Klossowski published a series of lesser-known and quite peculiar erotic novels (the "Roberte" series). The largest of them, *Roberte ce soir*, provides us with a remarkable insight into Klossowki's conception—or perhaps practice—of translation and the stranger, in which the host and hostess have an unusual custom.[36] When welcoming a guest, this guest is literally welcomed completely, all the way into their bed. From this primal scene, Klossowski derives a complete theory of hospitality, but also of the encounter with the stranger, the ownmost, and the foreign, and for which he literally gives the name *translation*:

> At the start the two are but isolated substances; between them there is none but accidental communication: you who believe yourself far from home in the home of someone you believe to be at home, you bring merely the accidents of your substance, such accidents as conspire to make a stranger of you, to him who bids you avail yourself of all that makes a merely accidental host of him. But because the master of this house herewith invites the stranger to penetrate to the source of all substances beyond the realm of all accident, this is how he inaugurates a substantial relationship between himself and the stranger, which will be not a relative relationship but an absolute one, as though, the master becoming one with the stranger, his relationship with you who have just set foot here were now but a relationship of one with oneself. To this end *the host translates himself into the actual guest.*[37]

There is here an important social consideration of what happens to the supposed "native speaker" when this process of translation takes place. Rather than one that simply allows the stranger to enter into the discourse of the native, the process by which this unfolds estranges the host as much as the guest, even if the host *believes him or herself to be at home.*

In the classical tradition of translation, one is situated in a conception of linguistic transfer between one's "own" (*le propre*) and what is "foreign" (*l'étranger*). It is Klossowski's device, in the *Roberte* texts and *Les lois de l'hospitalité*, to literally "personalize" this double structure in the *practice* of "hosting" the guest. It is crucial in this Klossowskian frame that the structure of this apparent doublet is in fact a recursion on the self—it is a formal presentation that "lets us understand the multiplicity of configurations of the relationship of the translator subject and his language to the foreign, from devouring to losing, but above all, and this is what interests us here in the first place, *the postulation of an identifiable nature and a limited essence of the proper, which is never acquired* but is the object of all the quests of translation."[38]

As Antoine Berman remarked, in a widely known formulation, "every culture resists translation, even if it has an essential need for it. The very aim of translation—to open up in writing a certain relation with the Other, to fertilize what is one's Own through the mediation of what is Foreign—is diametrically opposed to the ethnocentric structure of every culture, that species of narcissism by which every society wants to be a pure and unadultered Whole."[39] In a sense, however, it is exactly Klossowski who problematized this idea. If we are to say that translation is opposed to ethnocentrism, that it is solely about pollinating *le propre* with the mediating force of *l'étranger*, we would remain solely in a sort of communicative space, forever seeing the two sides of the ownmost and the foreign as the inevitable and even ontological categories of the world. But Klossowski's peculiar and even scandalous idea of the subjective destitution of the possession of the other reminds us of something much more fundamental: you yourself can be transformed, your whole being can become and absorb something else, what is "proper" to you is never fixed for eternity but always mutable, always capable of a development. At such a point, the boundary between what is "proper" and what is "foreign" itself shifts, reminding us that what is historically critical is not the two "sides" themselves but the *nomos*, the disavowed but structuring event, the act of division itself that created a space wherein two sides could compose themselves as interiorities.

Let me illustrate this point very simply. As one grows and acquires—whether through migration, necessity, or interest—new languages, the gap between what is one's "own" language and what is the "other" language becomes blurred. One does not develop a "theory" of the mutabililty of the ownmost and the foreign (and the line of division between them), one simply experiences that "tree" can also be orthographically represented as 木 and phonographically as *ki* or as "arbre." This becomes swiftly part of the mental architecture that forms the subject in relation to language. In other words, such lexical diversity—the presence of the supposedly "foreign" within the "proper"—is seamlessly integrated into one's function. If someone mutters to themselves in the private admixture of languages that characterizes them, they do not don alien garb, become "foreign," absolutely other, or even transform their practices of living in the world in accordance with those of another psychic or cultural universe, but simply express the phonetic-semantic lexicon within which they approach the world. One is born with one or more so-called mother tongues, but through the pure contingency of the social-historical world, other languages can become fundamental parts of one's discursive architecture, so much so that we could even say most people speak a language that is not national but personal, composed of phrasing, cadence, idioms that are distributed between multiple "national languages," a mixture in which what is "proper" to one is in fact not "proper" at all. This is a completely normal, everyday aspect of the "multilingualism" of the world. The point of such an excursus is not to say that any language is also mine, but to say precisely that it is not just societies that can never be a "pure and unadulterated Whole," but also subjects. There is no person anywhere on earth who can be a Whole subject of the ethnos, the language, the nation, the territory, the civilization.

What then do we do with the question of translation in our political climate of neoliberal austerity, resurgent fascisms, national chauvinism, and more? Following the powerful formulations of Sandro Mezzadra and others, we have to link closely the relation of translation to the structure of capital as such, to the deranged social system that is both ownmost to us, in the sense that we are its component parts, and most estranged from us, at the same time.[40]

The Subject in Translation

The theoretical analysis of translation as a concept tends to run up, in the final analysis, against the limits of what it can express in *affirmative* terms. This is not surprising in a sense, as the same can more or less be said for the forms of analysis of the category of the subject that it addresses. While we can say with no uncertainty that it is today nearly impossible to imagine some founding plenitude and originary substantiality of the subject, the political limits of this insight remain significant. What shall we do with this liminal, self-undermining, fragmented, and indeed *illusory* conception of subjectivity? How can such an understanding of the unstable realm of the subject assist in practical interventions wherein *there is a subject to be found* or in which we discover to our surprise and in the hazard of chance that we have been *called to be* subjects of a political process? In practical terms, subjects of political processes do in fact emerge. We can of course admit that they are retroactively convoked *as* subjects, in Badiou's terms, but nevertheless their emergence and function is neither impossible nor void: it functions in spite of this inherent slippage, which the theory of translation sees in its misidentification of the schema of substance, which the critique of political economy sees in the peculiar retroactive determination of the labor power commodity, or which psychoanalysis sees in the subject as an effect, not the origin, of the drive. But in all these circumstances, linked to the force of intervention around the advances of theoretical antihumanism, what possibility remains for politics, which is at base another term for the subjective intervention into or against the circumstances that gave rise to it? So we face in some sense a paradox, one in which we are torn between the negative identification of the subject as an *effect* that masquerades as an originary substance, and a positive identification of the subject as a necessary part of a process that *had to have happened*, and therefore must have been there from the start, always in this "future anterior" tense. It is not merely a confrontation between "humanism" and "antihumanism," but it is perhaps a question of forcing into existence another conception of the political consequences of antihumanism than simply its immediate applicability to the existing scenario. What we lack is a theory of *levels of analysis* that allows us to understand the logical, historical, and politically practical dimensions of the subject, this concept that seems to haunt us, returning with the force of necessity at exactly the conceptual point at which it appeared to have been exhausted.

A reflection on such levels of analysis of the figure of the subject—absent in one register, historically unstable in another, rare and impossible to access in yet a third—can be effectively understood as destabilizing the desire, practically constant in theoretical work in the humanities today, for *another* universality. If the "old" universality was thought to be exclusionary, linked to a simple class politics without reflection on the "new" social subjectivities coming to the fore, today there appears to be an equally insecure demand for slipperier conceptions of the universal, somehow capable of evading the old universality's hegemonic and homogenizing drive. The demand for "insurgent universalities," "competing universalities," and so forth is admirable, and an important corrective to the refusal of universality.[41] But perhaps the better logic is that we ought not to posit the full plenitude of universalities (whether insurgent, competing, minor, and so on), but rather the absolute political *rarity* of universalities. After all, the very order of being in the psychoanalytic sense is precisely an incompletion—of the subject, of language, of the Whole—that functions to paradoxically sustain the order of things, the *pas-tout* as "an objection to the universal."[42] If language is split and thereby "created" as national language by the very articulatory act of translation itself, it can only be conceived itself as a contradictory composite that is precisely "not all," as Pêcheux and Gadet emphasize in *La langue introuvable*.

Stanislaw Lem's famed science fiction novel *Solaris* describes an extraterrestrial world, covered entirely by a strange ocean, which generates peculiar hallucinations and communications in memory with the nearby scientists studying it.[43] They discover that in fact the ocean itself is a gigantic living organism, a sort of social brain whose function is unknown, and even unknowable. In turn engendering a series of speculations on what sort of relation could possibly be created with such an entity, Lem writes toward the end of the novel:

Besides, what do people expect, what can they want from "informatio-
nal communication" with the living ocean? A recording of experiences
of a being that endures through time, and is so old it probably cannot
remember its own beginning? A description of the desires, passions,
hopes and sufferings, that are released in the instantaneous birth of
living mountains, the transformation of mathematics into existence,
of loneliness and resignation into plenitude? Yet all this constitutes
incommunicable knowledge, and if one attempts to translate it into
any human language, all those sought-after values and meanings are
lost, they cannot be brought intact through the barrier.[44]

Because language enacts already a tremendous slippage with respect to the
gap between social practice and signifying practice, this can only be imagined
as an existential "barrier" through which nothing may pass. But to write in a
language at all is already *translational*. There is no signifying practice imaginable that does not involve the act of translation. To imagine translation solely
as an act that exists *between* national languages, as if these spaces themselves
consisted of given, stable, and natural substances bounded by clear and defined
borders, is precisely to imagine, in a classically theological or mystical manner,
the immediacy of the relation between social practice and signification. But
humanity, if there can even be such a universal placeholder in our world of
capital, racism, war, oppression, and division, is itself only imaginable as something mediational.

We might even say that this passage from Lem's *Solaris* expresses with respect to translation what Fredric Jameson's famous lines expressed with respect
to capital ("It seems to be easier for us today to imagine the thoroughgoing
deterioration of the earth and of nature than the breakdown of late capitalism;
perhaps that is due to some weakness in our imagination").[45] Fundamentally,
"we" cannot imagine an end to the social relation called "capital" because
"we" are its component parts. It is not a question of "attitude" or "position," or
in classical historiographical terms, "*mentalité*." It is a question of the degree
to which, in Althusser's words, objective positions speak through subjective
dispositions, and not the reverse. But to bring the question back to this volatile
term "translation," let's repurpose Jameson's famous point to say: it is perhaps
easier to imagine an end or absolute limit/barrier to signification—some great
barrier to other galaxies, or more prosaically, the belief that national languages
are fixed, proper, wholly different entities from each other—than it is to imagine
that signification itself is precisely an endless mediation without resolution.
The point in Jameson's famous statement is not that dystopian imaginings of
the end of the world are nonsense, ideological, and so on, while capitalism is

a system that, if only we had the eyes to see it, would be simple to overcome. Instead, the point is just the opposite: insofar as capitalism itself (the logical drive of capital) *coquets* as endless and produces the peculiar internal conditions for capital to *appear as* an eternal-natural relation, it is literally more realistic to think of the actual end of life on earth than the end of this perverse relation capable of encompassing its exteriorities into its own functioning. To imagine that we can be done with capital—as if *we ourselves were not its component parts*, as if it were some external substance—simply and easily is a mistake for emancipatory politics. The struggle against capital is an existential struggle to deliver an affirmative alternative, under conditions of extraordinary pressure to reverse course, that is also endless, just as the social practice of translation must always and endlessly struggle with its tendency to reify the very categories it puts into question.

In 1973, Jacques Lacan famously "armed himself" with the peculiar formulation "les non-dupes errent."[46] On the one hand a clever homonym for "le nom du père" (the name of the father), "le non du père" (the "no" of the father), and so on, this phrase has been variously explicated for decades. Perhaps in the context of the present argument, I would simply say that when we emphasize that it is the "non-dupes" who are "in error" or aimlessly "wandering about," we are also stating that it is those who imagine themselves to not be "duped," to be aware of ideology, aware of their enclosure, and so on who are most in error. The "non-dupes" are precisely those who believe most in the "regime of translation," who are most invested in the communicative model of the universal, whereby a "conversation," an "exchange" or "intercourse" (*Verkehr*) takes place between "sides" that we derive from an endlessly regressive set of presuppositions. Perhaps it is better for us, "armed this year with the formula 'les non-dupes errent,'" to say that if we ever discover a political universal, it will emerge *against* the regime of translation, not from it. It will emerge at a point when a subjective language is pulled from its encyclopedic-sociological determination and restored to a kind of nomadic sensibility, in which the hard borders of "culture" and "nation" are bypassed transversally. We are all the "dupes" of the regime of translation that structures our languages and their political function. We should take care not to pose as the "non-dupes" of a world in which the principal universal is that of the homology between commodity exchange and the regime of translation based on national language. Instead, insofar as we recognize how "duped" we are by language itself, how this "duping" is itself the irreversible constitution of our very modernity and indeed our quotidian partial subjectivity under capital, we will also see that diving further into our "being-duped" is the only possible way to imagine another *rare*, nearly impossible universality, that is, another possibility—fragile, remote, and volatile—of the political subject beyond the supposed "civilizational difference."

Bibliography

Althusser, Louis. *For Marx*. Translated by Ben Brewster. London: New Left Books, 1969.
———. "The Object of Political Economy." In *Reading Capital*. Translated by Ben Brewster. London: Verso, 2009.
Apter, Emily. *The Translation Zone: A New Comparative Literature*. Princeton, NJ: Princeton University Press, 2006.
Badiou, Alain. *Theory of the Subject*. Translated by Bruno Bosteels. London: Continuum, 2007.
Balibar, Étienne. "Reflections on *Gewalt*." *Historical Materialism* 17, no. 1 (2009): 99–125.
Benjamin, Walter. "The Task of the Translator." Translated by Harry Zohn. In *Selected Writings*, vol. 1, 1913–1926, edited by Marcus Bullock and Michael W. Jennings, 253–63. Cambridge, MA: Belknap, 2004.
Berman, Antoine. *The Experience of the Foreign: Culture and Translation in Romantic Germany*. Translated by S. Heyvaert. Albany: State University of New York Press, 1992.
Butler, Judith. "Competing Universalities." In Judith Butler, Ernesto Laclau, and Slavoj Žižek, *Contingency, Hegemony, Universality: Contemporary Dialogues on the Left*, 136–81. London: Verso, 2000.
Chauvin, Cédric. "Critique du sujet et traduction chez Pierre Klossowski." *Doletiana: Revista de traducció, literatura i arts* (Universitat Autònoma de Barcelona), no. 1 (2007): 1–16.
Derrida, Jacques. *Dissemination*. Translated by Barbara Johnson. Chicago: University of Chicago Press, 1981.
———. *Monolingualism of the Other; or, The Prosthesis of Origin*. Translated by Patrick Mensah. Stanford, CA: Stanford University Press, 1998.
Drew, Julie. "Cultural Composition: Stuart Hall on Ethnicity and the Discursive Turn." In *Race, Rhetoric, and the Postcolonial*, edited by Gary A. Olson and Lynn Worsham, 205–39. Albany: State University of New York Press, 1999.
Dumézil, Georges. *Mitra-Varuna*. Translated by Derek Coltman. New York: Zone Books, 1988.
Gadet, Françoise, and Michel Pêcheux. *La langue introuvable*. Collection "Théorie," edited by Louis Althusser. Paris: Maspero, 1981.
Hardt, Michael. "The Withering of Civil Society." *Social Text*, no. 45 (Winter 1995): 27–44.
Hegel, G. W. F. *Wissenschaft der Logik I*. In *Werke in zwanzig Bänden: Theorie Werkausgabe*, Bd. 5, edited by Eva Moldenhauer and Karl Markus Michel. Frankfurt am Main: Suhrkamp, 1969.

———. *Wissenschaft der Logik II*. In *Werke in zwanzig Bänden: Theorie Werkausgabe*, Bd. 6, edited by Eva Moldenhauer and Karl Markus Michel. Frankfurt am Main: Suhrkamp, 1969.

Jameson, Fredric. *The Seeds of Time*. New York: Columbia University Press, 1994.

Klossowski, Pierre. *Living Currency*. Edited by Vernon Cisney, Nicolae Morar, and Daniel W. Smith. London: Bloomsbury, 2017.

———. *Nietzsche and the Vicious Circle*. Translated by Daniel Smith. Chicago: University of Chicago Press, 1998.

———. *Roberte ce soir*. Paris: Éditions de Minuit, 1953.

Lacan, Jacques. *. . . or Worse: The Seminar of Jacques Lacan, Book XIX*. Edited by Jacques-Alain Miller. Cambridge, UK: Polity, 2018.

———. *The Seminar of Jacques Lacan, Book XX, Encore*. Edited by Jacques-Alain Miller. Translated by Bruce Fink. NewYork: W. W. Norton, 1998 [1972–73].

———. *Television*. New York: W. W. Norton, 1990.

Lem, Stanislas. *Solaris*. Translated by Joanna Kilmartin and Steve Cox. New York: Harcourt Brace, 1970.

Marx, Karl. *Capital*, vol. 1. In *Collected Works of Karl Marx and Frederick Engels*, vol. 35. New York: International, 1996.

———. *Die deutsche Ideologie*. In *Marx-Engels Werke*, Bd. 3. Berlin: Institut für Marxismus-Leninismus beim ZK der SED: Dietz Verlag, 1962.

———. *Das Kapital*, Bd. 1. In *Marx-Engels-Werke*, Bd. 23. Berlin: Institut für Marxismus-Leninismus beim ZK der SED: Dietz Verlag, 1962.

———. *The German Ideology*. In *Collected Works of Karl Marx and Frederick Engels*, vol. 5. New York: International, 1976.

McNulty, Tracy. "Hospitality after the Death of God." *Diacritics* 35, no. 1 (2005): 71–98.

Mezzadra, Sandro. "Forces and Forms: Governmentality and *Bios* in the Time of Global Capital." In "The End of Area: Biopolitics, Geopolitics, History," edited by Gavin Walker and Naoki Sakai. Special issue, *positions: asia critique* 27, no. 1 (2019): 145–58.

Nairn, Tom. "The Modern Janus." *New Left Review*, no. 94 (1975): 3–29.

Nancy, Jean-Luc. *La communauté désœuvrée*. Paris: Christian Bourgeois Editeur, 1986.

———. *The Inoperative Community*. Translated by Peter Connor, Lisa Garbus, Michael Holland, and Simona Sawhney. Minneapolis: University of Minnesota Press, 1991.

Sakai, Naoki. "Translation." *Theory, Culture and Society* 23, nos. 2–3 (2006): 71–86.

———. *Translation and Subjectivity: On "Japan" and Cultural Nationalism*. Minneapolis: University of Minnesota Press, 1997.

Sakai, Naoki, and Jon Solomon. "Introduction: Addressing the Multitude of Foreigners, Echoing Foucault." In *Translation, Biopolitics, Colonial Difference*, vol. 4 of Traces: A Multilingual Series of Cultural Theory and Translation, edited by Naoki Sakai and Jon Solomon, 1–35. Hong Kong: Hong Kong University Press, 2006.

Spivak, Gayatri Chakravorty. *Death of a Discipline*. New York: Columbia University Press, 2003.

Tomba, Massimiliano. *Insurgent Universality: An Alternative Legacy of Modernity*. Oxford: Oxford University Press, 2019.

Walker, Gavin. "Nationalism and the National Question." In *The SAGE Handbook of Marxism*. Edited by Beverley Skeggs, Sara R. Farris, Alberto Toscano, and Svenja Bromberg. London: Sage, 2021.

———. "What Comes after Area? The *Nomos* of the Modern in Times of Crisis." In *Epistemic Decolonization at the End of Pax Americana*, edited by Naoki Sakai and Jon Solomon. London: Routledge, forthcoming.

Walker, Gavin, and Naoki Sakai. "The End of Area." In "The End of Area: Biopolitics, Geopolitics, History." Special issue, *positions: asia critique* 27, no. 1 (2019): 1–31.

———, eds. "The End of Area: Biopolitics, Geopolitics, History". Special issue. *positions: asia critique* 27, no. 1 (2019).

Zupančič, Alenka. *What IS Sex?* Cambridge, MA: MIT Press, 2017.

Notes

1. The epigraphs are from Ludwig Wittgenstein, *Culture and Value*, trans. Peter Winch (Chicago: University of Chicago Press, 1989), 39e, and Jacques Lacan, *Television* (New York: W. W. Norton, 1990), 10.

2. Walter Benjamin, "The Task of the Translator," trans. Harry Zohn, in *Selected Writings*, vol. 1, *1913–1926*, ed. Marcus Bullock and Michael W. Jennings (Cambridge, MA: Belknap, 2004), 253–63; Jacques Derrida, *Monolingualism of the Other; or, The Prosthesis of Origin*, trans. Patrick Mensah (Stanford, CA: Stanford University Press, 1998); Emily Apter, *The Translation Zone: A New Comparative Literature* (Princeton, NJ: Princeton University Press, 2006); Naoki Sakai, *Translation and Subjectivity: On "Japan" and Cultural Nationalism* (Minneapolis: University of Minnesota Press, 1997); Gayatri Chakravorty Spivak, *Death of a Discipline* (New York: Columbia University Press, 2003).

3. For an entire archaeological investigation of this question see Gavin Walker and Naoki Sakai, eds., "The End of Area: Biopolitics, Geopolitics, History," special issue, *positions: asia critique* 27, no. 1 (2019).

4. Julie Drew, "Cultural Composition: Stuart Hall on Ethnicity and the Discursive Turn," in *Race, Rhetoric, and the Postcolonial*, ed. Gary A. Olson and Lynn Worsham (Albany: State University of New York Press, 1999), 225.

5. See the tension between the two foundational formulas for Hegel: "the truth of being is essence" (*Die Wahrheit des Seins ist das Wesen*) and yet, "being is semblance" (*Das Sein ist Schein*); G. W. F. Hegel, *Wissenschaft der Logik II*, in *Werke in zwanzig Bänden: Theorie Werkausgabe*, Bd. 6 (Frankfurt am Main: Suhrkamp, 1969), 13 and 19.

6. Louis Althusser, *For Marx*, trans. Ben Brewster (London: New Left Books, 1969), 113.

7. See for instance Antoine Berman, *The Experience of the Foreign: Culture and Translation in Romantic Germany*, trans. S. Heyvaert (Albany: State University of New York Press, 1992).

8. See Alain Badiou, *Theory of the Subject*, trans. Bruno Bosteels (London: Continuum, 2007), 148–57; G. W. F. Hegel, *Wissenschaft der Logik I*, in *Werke in zwanzig Bänden: Theorie Werkausgabe*, Bd. 5 (Frankfurt am Main: Suhrkamp, 1969), 154.

9. Naoki Sakai, "Translation," *Theory, Culture and Society* 23, nos. 2–3 (2006): 71–86.

10. Sakai, "Translation," 71.

11. Sakai, *Translation and Subjectivity*, 14.

12. Françoise Gadet and Michel Pêcheux, *La langue introuvable*, Collection "Théorie," ed. Louis Althusser (Paris: Maspero, 1981).

13. See for instance Jacques Lacan, . . . *or Worse: The Seminar of Jacques Lacan, Book XIX*, ed. Jacques-Alain Miller (Cambridge, UK: Polity, 2018), 5.

14. See Alenka Zupančič, *What IS Sex?* (Boston, MA: MIT Press, 2017), 23–24.

15. Jacques Derrida, *Dissemination*, trans. Barbara Johnson (Chicago: University of Chicago Press, 1981), 387.

16. For a reflection on this question, see Gavin Walker and Naoki Sakai, "The End of Area," in "The End of Area: Biopolitics, Geopolitics, History," ed. Gavin Walker and Naoki Sakai, special issue, *positions: asia critique* 27, no. 1 (2019): 1–31.

17. Jean-Luc Nancy, *La communauté désœuvrée* (Paris: Christian Bourgeois Editeur, 1986), 117–18; Jean-Luc Nancy, *The Inoperative Community*, trans. Peter Connor, Lisa Garbus, Michael Holland, and Simona Sawhney (Minneapolis: University of Minnesota Press, 1991), 46 (translation modified).

18. Tom Nairn, "The Modern Janus," *New Left Review*, no. 94 (1975): 3–29; Georges Dumézil, *Mitra-Varuna*, trans. Derek Coltman (New York: Zone Books, 1988). On these points, see the expanded remarks in Gavin Walker, "Nationalism and the National Question," in *The SAGE Handbook of Marxism*, ed. Beverley Skeggs, Sara R. Farris, Alberto Toscano, and Svenja Bromberg (London: Sage, 2021).

19. Karl Marx, *Die deutsche Ideologie*, in *Marx-Engels Werke*, Bd. 3 (Berlin: Institut für Marxismus-Leninismus beim ZK der SED: Dietz Verlag, 1962), 36; Karl Marx, *The German Ideology*, in *Collected Works of Karl Marx and Frederick Engels*, vol. 5 (New York: International, 1976), 89.

20. Marx, *Die deutsche Ideologie*, 36; Marx, *German Ideology*, 89.

21. Marx, *Die deutsche Ideologie*, 36; Marx, *German Ideology*, 89.

22. Sandro Mezzadra, "Forces and Forms: Governmentality and *Bios* in the Time of Global Capital," in "The End of Area: Biopolitics, Geopolitics, History," ed. Gavin Walker and Naoki Sakai, special issue, *positions: asia critique* 27, no. 1 (2019): 155.

23. Étienne Balibar, "Reflections on *Gewalt*," *Historical Materialism* 17, no. 1 (2009): 110.

24. See on this term Naoki Sakai and Jon Solomon, "Introduction: Addressing the Multitude of Foreigners, Echoing Foucault," in *Translation, Biopolitics, Colonial Difference*, vol. 4 of Traces: A Multilingual Series of Cultural Theory and Translation, ed. Naoki Sakai and Jon Solomon (Hong Kong: Hong Kong University Press, 2006), 1–35.

25. Michael Hardt, "The Withering of Civil Society," *Social Text*, no. 45 (Winter 1995): 27–44.

26. Hardt, 29.

27. Louis Althusser, "The Object of Political Economy," in *Reading Capital*, trans. Ben Brewster (London: Verso, 2009), 162.

28. Althusser, 163.

29. See Sakai, introduction to *Translation and Subjectivity*.

30. Karl Marx, *Das Kapital*, Bd. 1, in *Marx-Engels-Werke*, Bd. 23, 186; Karl Marx, *Capital*, vol. 1, in *Collected Works of Karl Marx and Frederick Engels*, vol. 35 (New York: International, 1996), 182.

31. Althusser, "Object of Political Economy," 163.

32. There are, in effect, three separate editions of *La monnaie vivante*: the first, published by Éric Losfeld (Paris, 1970) is accompanied by a series of black-and-white erotic photographs by Pierre Zucca of Klossowski's wife, and is the most "notorious" edition (I utilize primarily this rare first edition, which is *nonpaginated*). The text alone, without photographs, was republished as a paperback by Joëlle Losfeld (Paris, 1994), and subsequently reissued in 1997 by Rivages (Paris). There are no major changes in the text itself between these editions, but the absence of the photographs by Zucca significantly transforms *La monnaie vivante* as a textual object. See the recent English translation—*Living Currency*, ed. Vernon Cisney, Nicolae Morar, and Daniel W. Smith (London: Bloomsbury, 2017).

33. See Pierre Klossowski, *Nietzsche and the Vicious Circle*, trans. Daniel Smith (Chicago: University of Chicago Press, 1998).

34. Klossowski, *Living Currency*, 68–69 (translation modified).

35. Klossowski, 69 (translation modified).

36. For an important discussion of the theory of hospitality in Klossowski's *Roberte* novels, see Tracy McNulty, "Hospitality after the Death of God," *Diacritics* 35, no. 1 (2005): 71–98.

37. Pierre Klossowski, *Roberte ce soir* (Paris: Éditions de Minuit, 1953), 13.

38. Cédric Chauvin, "Critique du sujet et traduction chez Pierre Klossowski," *Doletiana: Revista de traducció, literatura i arts* (Universitat Autònoma de Barcelona), no. 1 (2007): 5.

39. Berman, *Experience of the Foreign*, 4.

40. See for a longer development of these points Gavin Walker, "What Comes after Area? The *Nomos* of the Modern in Times of Crisis," in *Epistemic Decolonization at the End of Pax Americana*, ed. Naoki Sakai and Jon Solomon (London: Routledge, forthcoming).

41. See for example Judith Butler, "Competing Universalities," in Judith Butler, Ernesto Laclau, and Slavoj Žižek, *Contingency, Hegemony, Universality: Contemporary Dialogues on the Left* (London: Verso, 2000), 136–81; Massimiliano Tomba, *Insurgent Universality* (Oxford: Oxford University Press, 2019).

42. Jacques Lacan, *The Seminar of Jacques Lacan, Book XX, Encore,* ed. Jaques-Alain Miller and trans. Bruce Fink (NewYork: W. W. Norton, 1998 [1972–73]), 102.

43. Stanislas Lem, *Solaris,* trans. Joanna Kilmartin and Steve Cox (New York: Harcourt Brace, 1970).

44. Lem, 172.

45. Fredric Jameson, *The Seeds of Time* (New York: Columbia University Press, 1994), xii.

46. Lacan, *Television,* 10.

Acknowledgments

The publication of this edited volume would not have been possible without the participation of friends and colleagues who generously agreed to share their writing and research. For believing in this project and for helping me realize it, I thank first and foremost the volume's contributors: Ben Baer, Barbara Cassin, Katie Chenoweth, Souleymane Bachir Diagne, Cate Reilly, Peter Thomas, Gavin Walker, Naomi Waltham-Smith, and Gary Wilder.

The idea of producing a book like this one emerged from a series of conversations that took place within and around Princeton University's Theory Reading Group, which I founded in 2012 as a graduate student with the financial and institutional sponsorship of Princeton's Interdisciplinary Doctoral Program in the Humanities. During the 2013–14 academic year, we read and discussed a series of contemporary theoretical texts on the topic of translation and universality. This is when I met Katie Chenoweth, who joined me in organizing the 2014 colloquium, "Theory, Translation, Universality." The colloquium featured presentations by Brent Hayes Edwards, Peggy Kamuf, Jacques Lezra, and Peter Thomas, as well as a roundtable discussion with Ben Baer, Sandra Bermann, and Lital Levy. After this event, Katie and I agreed to continue our collaborative efforts and to coedit this volume. We worked together to devise a list of potential contributors, to send out invitations to participate, and eventually to write the book proposal for Fordham University Press. At Fordham, we benefited immensely from Tom Lay's enthusiastic support of the project and from his patience as it slowly but surely took shape over the years. During that time, I joined the Department of Romance Languages and Literatures at the University of Michigan, Ann Arbor. My colleagues and students at Michigan—in both formal and informal settings—helped me clarify and refine my thinking about translation, universality, and their relationship. I also benefited from opportunities to present aspects of this project at Columbia University; Cornell University; Dartmouth College; Duke University; the Graduate Center of the City University of New York; the State University of New York at Buffalo; the University of California, Berkeley; the University of California, Riverside; and the University of Southern California.

I acknowledge and thank everyone from the previously mentioned events, groups, and institutions who supported my work and helped this project come together. Along with the individuals already named, I would like to express special gratitude to Arianna Afsari, Michael Arnall, Anthony Alessandrini, Michael Arnall, Étienne Balibar, Fadi Bardawil, Tani Barlow, Karen Benezra, Bruno Bosteels, Christopher Breu, Judith Butler, Óscar Ariel Cabezas, Eduardo Cadava, David Caron, Sarika Chandra, Zahid Chaudhary, Eric Cheyfitz, Youngkyun Choi, Rey Chow, Heather Cleary, Susana Draper, Nergis Ertürk, Anna Watkins Fisher, Alessandro Fornazzari, Moira Fradinger, Jackqueline Frost, Mary Gallagher, Enrique García Santo-Tomás, Erin Graff Zivin, Marvin Geller, Katerina Gonzalez Seligmann, Michael Hardt, Marta Hernández Salván, George Hoffmann, Jill Jarvis, Kate Jenckes, Michael Jennings, Adriana Johnson, David Johnson, Justin Joque, David Kazanjian, Robin D. G. Kelley, Ranjana Khanna, Anna Kornbluh, Victoria Langland, Horacio Legrás, Ross Lerner, Mukti Lakhi Mangharam, Barry Maxwell, Achille Mbembe, Peggy McCracken, Ramsey McGlazer, Natalie Melas, Ronald Mendoza-de Jesús, Sandro Mezzadra, Justin Mitchell, Cristina Moreiras, Dan Nemser, Nick Nesbitt, Gabriela Nouzeilles, Jaime Ortega Reyna, Donald Pease, Candela Potente, Rachel Price, Justin Read, Conor Tomás Reed, Eileen Reeves, Effie Rentzou, Giulia Riccò, Camille Robcis, Isis Sadek, Freya Schiwy, Bécquer Seguín, Ato Sekyi-Otu, Jeremy Siegman, Marcelo Starcenbaum, Alejo Stark, Horacio Tarcus, Antoine Traisnel, Massimiliano Tomba, Alberto Toscano, Gustavo Verdesio, Sergio Villalobos-Ruminott, Geoff Waite, Brian Whitener, Gareth Williams, Michael Wood, Robert J. C. Young, and Zahi Zalloua.

I dedicate this book to Ana Sabau and Moira Millie Arnall-Sabau. My most heartfelt thanks are reserved for you two.

Gavin Arnall
Ann Arbor, Michigan
October 2023

Contributors

Gavin Arnall is Associate Professor of Romance Languages and Literatures and Director of the Center for Latin American and Caribbean Studies at the University of Michigan, Ann Arbor. His research and teaching converge at the intersection of aesthetics, politics, and philosophy, with a special focus on Marxism and its (missed) encounters with Black and Indigenous radicalisms. He is the author of *Subterranean Fanon: An Underground Theory of Radical Change* (Columbia University Press, 2020), the translator of Emilio de Ípola's *Althusser, The Infinite Farewell* (Duke University Press, 2018), and the coeditor of *Between Revolution and Democracy: José Aricó, Marxism, and Latin America* (Brill's Historical Materialism Book Series, forthcoming).

Ben Conisbee Baer is Associate Professor of Comparative Literature and current Director of the Program in South Asian Studies at Princeton University. He is the author of *Indigenous Vanguards: Education, National Liberation, and the Limits of Modernism* (Columbia University Press, 2019) and the translator of Tarashankar Bandyopadhyay's *The Tale of Hansuli Turn* (Columbia University Press, 2011). Baer's most recent book, in collaboration with Smaran Dayal, is *Spider-Mother: The Fiction and Politics of Rokeya Sakhawat Hossain* (Warbler Press, 2024). His work in the fields of postcolonial theory, Marxism, deconstruction, and South Asian literature has appeared in journals such as *PMLA*, *boundary 2*, *Cultural Critique*, *Modernism/Modernity*, *Sikh Formations*, and many edited volumes.

Barbara Cassin has served as the Director of Research at the Centre National de la Recherche Scientifique and as the President of the Collège International de Philosophie. A recipient of the CNRS Gold Medal, she is a member of the Academie Française and an exhibit curator. Her recent books in English translation include *Jacques the Sophist: Lacan, Logos, and Psychoanalysis* (Fordham University Press, 2019), *Google Me: One-Click Democracy* (Fordham University Press, 2017), and *Nostalgia: When Are We Ever at Home?* (Fordham University Press, 2016). Her editorial work includes the seminal *Dictionary of Untranslatables: A Philosophical Lexicon* (Princeton University Press, 2014). A translator herself (notably of Hannah Arendt and Peter Szondi), she is the editor of several book series including L'Ordre philosophique.

Katie Chenoweth is Associate Professor of French at Princeton University. She is the author of *The Prosthetic Tongue: Printing Technology and the Rise of the French Language* (University of Pennsylvania Press, 2019). Her articles on Renaissance culture, media history, and deconstruction have appeared in venues such as *Discourse, Montaigne Studies, Symploke*, and *The Comparatist*. She is director of the Bibliothèque Derrida at Éditions du Seuil, a collection that includes Derrida's unpublished seminars and other posthumous works. At Princeton, she is the director of *Derrida's Margins*, an ongoing digital humanities project dedicated to Derrida's personal library.

Souleymane Bachir Diagne is Professor of French and Philosophy and Director of the Institute of African Studies at Columbia University. His areas of research and publication include history of philosophy, history of logic and mathematics, Islamic philosophy, and African philosophy and literature. His latest publications in English include *Open to Reason: Muslim Philosophers in Conversation with Western Tradition* (Columbia University Press, 2018); *Postcolonial Bergson* (Fordham University Press, 2019); *In Search of Africa(s): Universalism and Decolonial Thought* (with Jean-Loup Amselle, Polity, 2020); *African Art as Philosophy: Senghor, Bergson, and the Idea of Negritude* (Other Press, 2023).

Cate I. Reilly is Andrew W. Mellon Assistant Professor of Literature at Duke University. She is the author of *Psychic Empire: Literary Modernism and the Clinical State* (Columbia University Press, 2024). Her areas of specialty include Central and Eastern European modernism, biopolitics and translation, Marxism, psychoanalysis, and deconstruction. She has work published or forthcoming in *Ecokritike*, the *Slavic and Eastern European Journal, College Literature, Frontiers in Integrative Neuroscience*, and *The Journal of Literature and Medicine*. She currently sits on the advisory board for the Duke Institute for Brain Sciences. She is writing a new project on World Literature and the Left.

Peter D. Thomas is Professor and Head of Department in the History of Political Thought at Brunel University, London. He is the author of *The Gramscian Moment: Philosophy, Hegemony, and Marxism* (Brill, 2009) and coeditor of *Encountering Althusser: Politics and Materialism in Contemporary Radical Thought* (Bloomsbury, 2012) and *In Marx's Laboratory: Critical Interpretations of the* Grundrisse (Brill, 2013). Thomas also serves as a member of the editorial board of *Historical Materialism: Research in Critical Marxist Theory*. His translations include *Goodbye Mr Socialism* (Antonio Negri), *Philosophy in the Present* (Badiou/Žižek), *Marx's Temporalities* (Massimiliano Tomba), *Workers and Capital* (Mario Tronti), *Nietzsche, the Aristocratic Rebel* (Domenico Losurdo), and *A Failed Parricide* (Roberto Finelli).

Gavin Walker is Professor of Comparative Literature at Cornell University. His research and teaching focuses on contemporary theory in its intersections with global intellectual history, Continental philosophy and world literature, politics and aesthetics. He is the author of *The Sublime Perversion of Capital* (Duke University Press, 2016) and *Marx et* *la politique du dehors* (Lux Éditeur, 2022), the editor of *The End of Area: Biopolitics, Geopolitics, History* (Duke University Press, 2019, with Naoki Sakai), *The Red Years: Theory, Politics, and Aesthetics in the Japanese '68* (Verso, 2020), *Foucault's Late Politics*, a special issue of *South Atlantic Quarterly* (Duke University Press, Fall 2022), and *'Ronsō' no buntai* (Hōsei University Press, 2023, with Yutaka Nagahara). A member of the editorial board of the Historical Materialism Book Series (Brill/Haymarket) and *positions: asia critique* (Duke University Press), he is also the editor and translator of Kojin Karatani's *Marx: Towards the Centre of Possibility* (Verso, 2020). His new book, *The Rarity of Politics: Passages from Structure to Subject*, is forthcoming from Verso.

Naomi Waltham-Smith is Professor of Music at the University of Oxford and Douglas Algar Tutorial Fellow at Merton College. She works at the intersection of sound and music studies with deconstruction, decolonial theory, and Black radical thought, focusing on the politics of listening. She is the author of *Music and Belonging between Revolution and Restoration* (Oxford University Press, 2017), *Shattering Biopolitics: Militant Listening and the Sound of Life* (Fordham University Press, 2021), *Mapping (Post)colonial Paris by Ear* (Cambridge University Press, 2023), and *Free Listening* (Nebraska University Press, 2024).

Gary Wilder is Director of the Committee on Globalization and Social Change at the Graduate Center of the City University of New York, where he is Professor in the PhD Program of Anthropology, with cross-appointments in History and French. He is the author of *Concrete Utopianism: The Politics of Temporality and Solidarity* (Fordham University Press, 2022), *Freedom Time: Negritude, Decolonization, and the Future of the World* (Duke University Press, 2015), and *The French Imperial Nation-State: Negritude and Colonial Humanism between the World Wars* (University of Chicago Press, 2005). He is coauthor of *Theses on Theory and History* (special issue of *History of the Present: A Journal of Critical History*, 2020) and two edited volumes, *The Fernando Coronil Reader: The Struggle for Life Is the Matter* (Duke University Press, 2019) and *The Postcolonial Contemporary: Political Imaginaries for the Global Present* (Fordham University Press, 2018). He is currently writing a book on the political thought of C. L. R. James.

Index